The Priory of Sion

Published by Avalonia

BM Avalonia
London
WC1N 3XX
England, UK

www.avaloniabooks.co.uk

ISBN-10: 1-905297-41-6
ISBN-13: 978-1-905297-41-2

First Edition, September 2010
Design by Satori

Cover Art: Jean Luc Chaumeil (left) and Pierre Plantard (right)
Photograph © Jean-Luc Chaumeil

British Library Cataloguing in Publication Data. A catalogue record for this book is available from the British Library.

THE PRIORY OF SION

SHEDDING LIGHT ON THE TREASURE AND LEGACY OF RENNES-LE-CHÂTEAU AND THE PRIORY OF SION

BY JEAN-LUC CHAUMEIL

Translated from the French
by Chantal Low

Published by Avalonia
www.avaloniabooks.co.uk

To my father,
To my mother,
To my friend Michel.

OTHER BOOKS BY JEAN-LUC CHAUMEIL

1976 – *Le Sourire de Staline* (*Stalin's Smile*), co-written with Demou Dimitrios, published by Jean-Pierre Delarge

1979 – *Le Trésor du triangle d'Or* (*The Treasure of the Golden Triangle*), published by Alain Lefeuvre, Nice

1981 – *Apocalypse*, published by Institut Orphée, Paris

1984 – *Le Trésor des Templiers* (*The Templars' Treasure*), published by Henri Veyrier, Paris

1984 – *L'Alphabet solaire* (*The Solar Alphabet* – introduction to the universal language with previously unpublished texts from Father Boudet), co-written with Jacques Rivière, published by Du Borrégo, Paris; 1985 – republished by Guy Trédianel, Paris

1985 – *Du premier au dernier Templier* (*From the First to the Last of the Templars*), published by Henri Veyrier, Paris

1992 – *Le Temps et les OVNI* (*Time and the UFOs*), published by S.P.M.

1994 – *La Table d'Isis ou le secret de la Lumière* (*The Table of Isis or Secret of the Light*), published by Guy Trédianel, Paris

1994 – *Le Trésor des Templiers et son royal secret: l'Aether* (*The Templars' Treasure and its Royal Secret: the Aether*), published by Guy Trédianel, Paris

2006 – *Rennes-le-Château – Les Archives du Prieuré de Sion* (*Rennes-le-Château – The Archives of the Priory of Sion*) and *Rennes-le-Château – Gisors – Le Testament du Prieuré de Sion* (*Rennes-le-Château – Gisors – The Priory of Sion Legacy*), both published by Pégase, Villeneuve-de-la-Raho

Author's Biography

Jean-Luc Chaumeil

Jean-Luc Chaumeil was born in Lille, France, on 20th October 1944 and went into higher education after completing his secondary studies.

1964 – Journalist for the *Le Parisien Libéré*, *Le Monde* and *La Vie*, and *Tonus*

1968 – Director of a financial, economic and fiscal journal

1973 – Chief Editor of the journal *Pégase*

1974 – Chief Editor of the monthly *Europe Journal*

1975 – Editor at *L'Ere d'Aquarius*

Between 1973 and 1976 – Five thematic issues of the quarterly journal *Le Charivari*, namely:

"Les archives du Prieuré de Sion" (The Archives of the Priory of Sion)

"Les trésors Templiers" (Templars' Treasures)

"Magie et criminalité" (Magic and Criminality)

"De l'Orient à l'Occident, les sectes" (Sects from East to West)

"Histoire des sociétés secrètes" (History of Secret Societies)

1980 – Editorial writer for the weekly journal *L'Auvergne*

1989 – Editor at *L'Autre Monde*

Parallel activities:

1961 – Poetry prize, Melun

1978 - Shooting of a film *La Fée aux miettes, Petites annonces*, FR3 Toulouse

1979 - Shooting of a film *Le Templier*, FR3 Toulouse

Painting exhibitions in Paris at the Peintres du Marais, and in Carennac and Saint Céré in the Lot region (Midi Pyrénées)

TABLE OF CONTENTS

PREFACE

The charter of Henry VI of England, published in my work *Le Trésor des Templiers*, proves beyond doubt that the Templars had embraced the doctrinal corpus of a great tradition and establishes clearly the character and deep-rooted nature of the Templars' treasure; traditional corpus going back to the mists of time, as Saint Bernard had been initiated by the Druids, and colossal, inestimable treasure symbolizing the grandeur of the Templars' doctrine, whether concealed or unknown to history. These are the enigmas sought and researched by historians with greater or lesser success. However, new documents and the investigation of the myths and legends of the Order of the Temple transform a glimmer of light into an aurora borealis.

The places where the spirit blows keep the "egregore" - magical collective idea - of the Temple's causality intact. Gisors, Rennes-le-Château and the Krak des Chevaliers (the Fortress of the Knights Templar in Syria) of which an identical copy can be found at Château-Gaillard in Les Andelys, are, with Stenay, Valcroz and Saint Sulpice, so many pieces of a jigsaw, some of them faked, that can lead to the Holy of Holies; so many blank pages deserving our attention like the leaves of a large stone book written for Eternity. Each time the initiate designates a place where the treasure can be found, a piece of information reveals the way to the global corpus of the doctrine; gold is transmuted into light as a necessary step for seekers of the Grail.

The city of Gisors redirects us to Château-Gaillard in Les Andelys, birthplace of the painter Nicolas Poussin, who forces us by his stroke, golden number and colour subtlety, to discover the Arcadian society in the footsteps of the Templars. Château-Gaillard, the replica of the Knights' fortress built in a single year by Richard the Lion Heart, intrigues us to the highest degree by its prominent strategic position over the river Seine. The lost illusion of Rennes-le-Château leads us to seek the sunken capital of Reda and the variety of decoys employed fill us with great stupefaction. Only Father Boudet, parish priest of Rennes-les-Bains, developed the art of exploiting the Celtic legends to go back in time to the origins of primitive language.

In the second part of my book *Du premier au dernier Templier*, I have ascertained that the Aether or quintessence of the ancients summoned up the resurgence of an energy, or unknown and intelligent power, which unified the four fundamental forces. This concept was abandoned by the scholars of the Twentieth Century when, after the publication of the laws of Einstein, the latter had been accused of plagiarism by a famous magazine for reconsidering his former axioms and justifying his change of opinion at a conference in 1905. Contemporary researches, whether in the domains of cold fusion or biology, reintroduce the old concept of alchemy as that of the nature of Time for which the emblem is the Abraxas of the Secretum Templi with its letters I.A.O. whispered in the Turkish lodges of the temples in Istanbul as the master word symbolizing the Creator.

The secret doctrine of the Temple, evoked by Jules Loiseleur on several occasions, has been enhanced by the finding of new elements and suggests once more the idea of a gnosis followed by the secret Masters of the Temple; another controversy that fades away, discovery after discovery such as, for example, that made by Sir James Cochran Stevenson Runciman (better known as Sir Steven Runciman) or the allusion to the "Rubant" document mentioned by Benoist Rivière in his historical memoirs. The "Baphomet", or gold head, epitomizes in itself the supreme enigma of three elements: the Nature of Time, the alchemy of the Momentum - or the Instant - and the double movement of pure Light. These three notions are remarkably elucidated by the French scientist Louis Boutard as the I.A.O. letters surrounding the Cock and the Snake of the divine Abraxas or symbol of the big Whole.

Greek mythology places Arcadia in the Peloponnese; the area is majestic but the temples have disappeared. The Gods' residence expanded across Europe, first during the Renaissance in Italy, then in the Arcadian society, preserving in this manner the necessity to transmit tradition in the domain of the arts. Guercino, Poussin and George Sand were the contenders in the field, each with their own style. The Arcadian is by nature initiated into Death; he knows its primal cause and final outcome. He is free to choose between "Carpe Diem" or Rabelais' motto "Do as you please!", but he is warned that the wheel is turning with SATOR's magic square and that the work must, therefore, continue...

The association or connections between Rennes-le-Château and Valcroz evolve around Arcadia and the treasure of the Templars, the lost city of Reda, and the castle of the Grail in the Verdon region, an unknown gigantic door between two and possibly three worlds. The readership must, therefore, lend itself to an initiatory path based on historical, symbolical, and alchemical facts. In following this approach, or process of collective initiation, readers will perfect their quest in order to reach the Holy of Holies. However, they must guard against mixing up facts and must start from the beginning. That is, they must identify at the historical level all facts with a triple connotation, discern any symbol or portent, and right the helm of the Argo ship, as in the early days, without forgetting that we do not kill time. The reverse is true.

At the historical level, significant discoveries remain to be made. These include the exact location of the city of Reda, which is neither at Rennes-le-Château nor Rennes-les-Bains; the meaning of the two zodiacs - the first one in Rennes-les-Bains published by Father Boudet, the second one in Verdun uncovered by Alfred Weysen, author of *L'Ile des Veilleurs, Saint-Graal et fabuleux Trésor des Templiers dans une ville souterraine du Verdon* (*The Watchmen Island, Holy Grail and Fabulous Treasure of the Templars in a Verdon Underground City*); and the precise location of the chapel of Saint Catherine of Gisors, built in 1522 by the Lords of Fouilleuse de Flavacourt.

At the symbolic level, the architecture of the three places that form a golden triangle, demonstrates that the Arcadians transposed the celestial Jerusalem in a meticulous manner, as if it were a game, and this, maybe, is the biggest mystery.

At both the historical and alchemical levels, the affair of Rennes-le-Château begins in 1339 with a clerk from Rieux searching for an immense treasure on a hillside overlooking the town of Limoux. The key document in Appendix IV relates how, in a magical operation, this cleric and three other monks created a wax effigy which they placed on an altar dedicated to Saint Catherine; a real nod to Gisors! The adventure ended badly and resulted in a lawsuit.

But what is the nature of the gold guarded by the fairies? It is certainly not the Devil's gold, nor the gold extracted from mines near the spas of Blanchefort and Rennes-les-Bains "Bains de Règne", and even less that from the recently closed mine of Salsigne. Therein reside the pitfalls of this treasure, so difficult to find and yet so astonishingly wonderful at all levels.

An old adage stipulates that only the rich can borrow money. For those who do not know the story of the treasure near Rennes-le-Château, one must summarize, as for an episodic play, the extraordinary tale of a priest of modest origins in the last century to whom the literary soldiery has lent many intentions. Bérenger Saunière was born in Montazels, Aude, on 11th April 1852. His clothes looked more like the rags of a tramp from the Middle Ages than the refined accoutrements preferred by his Lord Bishop, Monseigneur de Beauséjour, who, it is said, resembled Talleyrand. Several descriptions and portraits of Father Saunière have been made in newspapers and in books, but the fact that they are all contradictory is of utmost importance.

Sometimes, he is presented as a royalist with wide influence and valuable relationships, for instance, with the Countess of Chambord and Father Hoffet, or upon the heels of the House of Hapsburg's archduke. At other times, he is portrayed as a mysterious being, stemming, as it were, from an Arsène Lupin detective novel, turning over tombstones, erasing epitaphs, building his own city worthy of science fiction writers such as Lovecraft and Ray Bradbury and leaving messages to the entire world for the future; our future of course.

The authors' cohesions shape him to ensure a logical thread, so much so that history is distorted to fill inconvenient gaps. The black hole widens when the "foreigner" interferes and drifts, in turn, in order to enrol the desiderata and hidden intentions of his readers. Nowadays, the full-timers, who are not as eternal as one might have thought, are facing the development of a booby trap that amalgamates the manipulations of extroverts to satisfy their secret desire, the end of the Church! This is why we are reaching the terminal phase, with polemics going rife on the Internet, especially amongst the anglophones. The tasteless conspiracy woven on several fronts is culminating now around extraterrestrial corpses found in the surprising site of the ruins of "Périllos" next to the tombs of Christ and Joseph of Arimathea! One knows that Rennes-le-Château and its surroundings have become the dumping ground of present-day mythologies hidden deep in the unconscious of the entire world. In this manner, this second Roswell, this Holy Sepulchre of a parallel world, supports secret circles and societies that lack imagination, foundation, and testimonial, which are, in short, devoid of "traditions". This Agartha - underground kingdom - of the black temples reveals the extent of the sidereal emptiness in contemporary human thought. How did we reach this point? Who are the actors and creators responsible for conjuring up a hill from obscurity and developing an idea that is warped and lacking in vision and simple common sense? Undoubtedly, we owe the launch and colossal emergence, the composts and other imaginative ingredients, the revoking of ideas, and the inversion of values such as the diabolic systematic strategy to make discoveries on one's own, to the writer Gérard de Sède, author of *Les Templiers sont parmi nous* (*The Templars are Amongst Us*). At the beginning of the 1960s, Robert Charroux grasped the subject quickly and refined the scenario that Gérard de Sède was going to develop. However, behind the writer, he discovered a mysterious man called Pierre Plantard and a similarly fortuitous marquis called Philippe de Cherisey. These three people formed an explosive trio that replaced Father Saunière, Marie Denarnaud and Noël Corbu.

The priest of Montazels was the solo player of the first waltz. Bérenger Saunière was a cold man with the eyes of Saint Teresa of Avila. He was a double-faceted man just like any other human being. His earthly awareness and heavenly elation blended with mystifying facility. It is perhaps this duality, unknown to many writers, which may have led them to conceive only part of the light in a fragment of truth. This fundamental error has arisen as the portrait of this individual has not been executed in real time. The priest was turning everything into cash, yet he believed in God and in his priesthood. The first mystery, therefore, lies in the real personality of Bérenger Saunière. Several documents assist in this exercise, particularly a letter confirming that he was the sole rapeseed oil sales representative for the region, together with estimates for various building works, self-published postcards, a sophisticated explanation regarding his Mass trafficking, details of loans against his property, etc.

Bérenger Saunière restored his church and built a tower dedicated to Mary Magdalene - the Magdala Tower. He installed the Devil in his church, Asmodeus, with a curious trident very promptly stolen by treasure hunters! This double-faceted living soul was undoubtedly enigmatic, but what was the real nature of the mystery surrounding him? Was it really the Devil with his trident? Was it the tower of Mary of Magdala that interested the Gallic secret services? Or was it the wealth of a businessman-cum-priest, to whom one attributes the discovery of a treasure, possibly of an historical nature when one combines the two facets of Saunière's life. This profound alchemy was accentuated by the introduction of the parchments. That is the heart of the one and only problem.

However, with the publication of *Pierre et Papier* (*Stone and Paper*) written by Philippe de Cherisey, today we are able to elucidate once and for all the story of Rennes-le-Château. The author proffered the handwritten version of his key document *Pierre et Papier* on the express condition that it would only be published twenty years after his death. The glorious Marquis died on 17th July 1985 and we made it a point of honour to keep our word, a done deed today. It is true that a great many will be very surprised to discover that Rennes-le-Château, Gisors and Stenay, have been fabricated exclusively for the benefit of an extremely dangerous contemporary myth. In compensation, a hidden intention takes shape during the reading under the ironic stare of Master Philippe de Cherisey. We leave you the opportunity to savour his intent fully, for our modern exegetes thought they detected it wrongly; in that, the marquis operated in an original manner as he wanted to settle accounts with the Vaudémont-Vaudressel family. His correspondence with Pierre Plantard, until their quarrel, is as revealing as the rest. We note, indeed, the skill and forgeries that, according to the anglophones, go beyond reality and imagination. But sometimes, one must ask oneself, who manipulated who? Nevertheless, these are the facts of the matter, and it is now up to the reader to decide.

The Gallic secret services, or guardians of the Reine du Midi (Midi Queen), have recorded, in less than a century, twelve apostles of the Messiah concerned with the story of Rennes-le-Château. Like the Wise Men, or magicians of old times, they all operated in threesomes in successive eras. The first trio is the product of a terrible imposture and prepares the preliminaries of the collective initiation. At that time, however, transmission of information would have been nearly impossible, particularly between Father Saunière and Noël Corbu, without the help and precious collaboration of Marie Denarnaud, the priest's servant, who, for all that, remained silent on the subject for the rest of her life. One thing leading to another, all that prevailed as truth and guarantee of the tradition were the papers from Father Saunière. Although these were highly suspect on several counts, they represented the earliest materials in a very complex affair. Amongst the documents were self-published postcards, letters and estimates, but not a single parchment. Only Noël Corbu, the last link in this ill-fated trinity, told Robert Charroux, the undisputed master of the treasure hunters, that Father Saunière had found various parchments wrapped in ferns within wooden tubes in a secret hiding-place inside a Visigothic pillar. Unfortunately, the pillar was neither hollow nor Visigothic, but just a replica made by the "Giscard House" in Toulouse.

Why on earth did Noël Corbu concoct this pivotal deception, this lost illusion? He was bored with the Corbières region and wanted to sell his castle-cum-hotel; a treasure story, therefore, could possibly attract a potential buyer. However, it is stipulated in the very first publications on the subject, including those from Pierre Jarnac, that there were some parchments of a chestnut colour and that Marie Denarnaud, the priest's maid, had shared the secret of Father Saunière without spelling it out! The authors of these works added that exact copies of the said parchments had been deposited at the mayor's office.

After that, Gérard de Sède received copies of these parchments in the post which, as clearly recounted by the Marquis Philippe de Cherisey, is not entirely true. From Pierre de France to Pierre Plantard de Saint-Clair, there is always a small thread that proves we are dealing with a strange individual. Sexton at the parish of Saint-Louis d'Antin, Pierre

Plantard very quickly acquired a taste for intrigues and mystery. On assignments for a while, notably during the war, he resembled Joan of Arc in a three-piece suit. Clairvoyant, prophet and astrologist, he conducted his consultations under the pseudonym "Great Chyren" which drew him closer to the Great Monarch. Draughtsman for the Chanovin establishments in Annemasse, he improved his sketching stroke, particularly for his blazon. It is while he was drifting in an attic room at No. 35, Avenue Victor Hugo, in Paris, and supervising his former employees from a distance, that he got wind of an article by Gérard de Sède concerning Gisors.

Subsequently, he developed his talents as secret master and the general public became aware of his existence through the publication of *Les Templiers sont parmi nous*, where the author Gérard de Sède portrays Pierre Plantard as a Hermetist. In fact, his interpretations of the magic square and the doors to the secret of Gisors were rather acrobatic. Mr. Plantard, Lost King of one night in his beautiful province of Redon, had been unfortunate indeed to meet an authentic nobleman in the person of Philippe de Cherisey. Since the latter was a Marquis, he believed he must be King. And he was King, until some outrageous anglophones bestowed upon him also the title of descendant of Christ. The Marquis was startled; the King-Messiah shook his head but did not disagree. Pierre Plantard moved to an elegant villa in Colombes. He took a second wife with whom he secured his descendants, Thomas and Irmine. Criticisms increased, and the Lost King exiled himself to Perpignan, making brief excursions to Spain. He died in his sleep, surrounded by followers who had flattered him. He had lost his true friends, those who had listened to him carefully and who had prevented him from going adrift on several occasions. He had forgotten that in the realm of fictitious heroes, professional manipulators could make use of a lie to develop an even bigger one. Fairy-tales included the "robbed thief" already, to which one should add "the rediscovered and biased Lost King". In passing away, Pierre Plantard left a dangerous vacuum that his admirers hastened to fill in their own way. Anonymous pamphlets were dispatched regularly to bookshops and their content was as deplorable as their authors.

The myth of the Priory of Sion subsided, together with that of the Lost King. However, the aberrations of the anglophones, such as their theory regarding the descendant of Christ, continued freely to become a settling of scores not just against the Church, but also against the Divinity. The Templars were no more amongst us, but Satan, the old Devil or Asmodeus, who reigns over this third millennium, with his roots and principal abode in Rennes-le-Château, with his false Priories of Sion, with his tombs of Christ, of Joseph of Arimathea or extraterrestrials on a binge... And there, it is probable that an expert hand was pulling the strings, just as in the past on Golgotha. The little men had better keep quiet, unless the skein of the aiguillette reconstituted, with the passing of time, the weft of these unpredictable gatherings. Here again, the hitherto unpublished text *Pierre et Papier* is clear and explicit.

The first part of the present book *Rennes-le-Château – The Archives of the Priory of Sion* is derived from the last 1973 quarterly periodical of *"Le Charivari"*, reprinted in its entirety by Pégase publishers in the first quarter of 2006. This was written at a time when few works existed on the subject and it gathers the bulk of the documentation to which most contemporary authors still refer in their approach to the enigma of Rennes-le-Château. At the time, one of the powerful contributions of Jean-Luc Chaumeil was, of course, his findings concerning the treasure found by Father Saunière.

The second part of this book *Rennes-le-Château – Gisors – the Priory of Sion Legacy* was published by Pégase in June 2006, over twenty years after the death of Philippe de Cherisey in 1985. This part revolves around the disclosures made by the Marquis in his handwritten manuscript *Pierre et Papier* (*Stone and Paper*), which shed light on the fantastic tales of the Priory of Sion, Gisors and Rennes-le-Château.

Part I

Rennes-le-Château

The Archives of the Priory of Sion

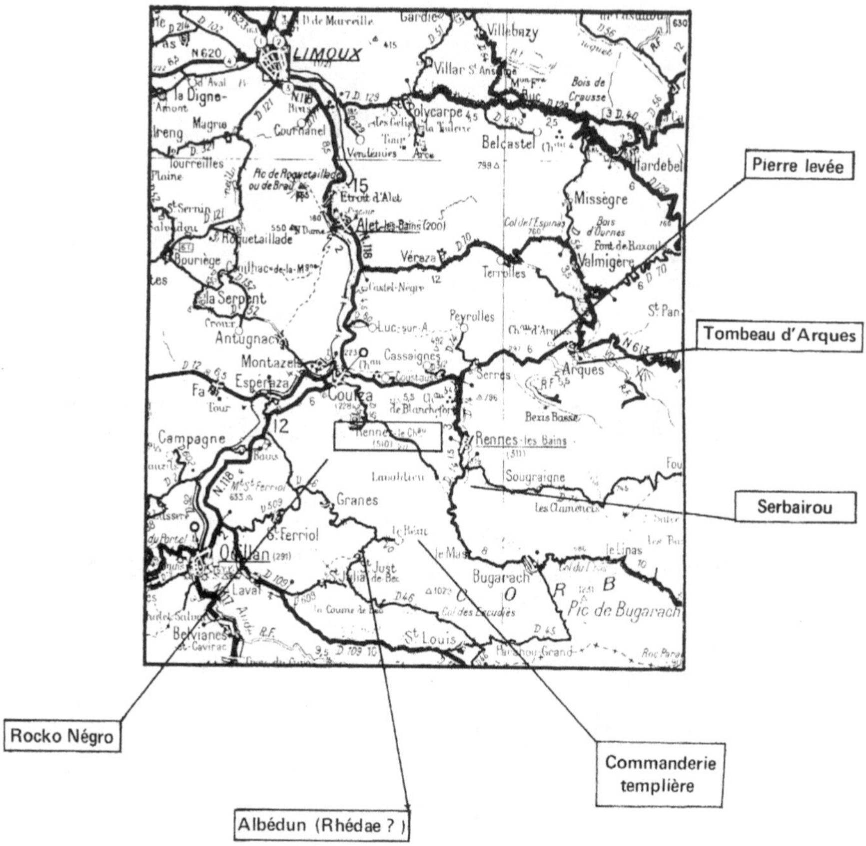

1 – Map of the area around Rennes-le-Château

From The Gold Of Rennes-Le-Château To The Descendants Of Merovaeus

Foreword By Claude Jacquemart

At the heart of one of France's oldest regions, scorched by the sun and shaded by the Pyrenees, rests an immense and fabulous treasure. Long ago, hordes of warriors such as Carthaginians, planning to destroy Rome by outflanking it over the Alps, Visigoths, Saracens, and Aragonese, crossed this land called the Razès - at times coming from the North and at other times from the South. The Razès was home to the large city of Reda with its defensive walls and towers. In the 6th Century CE, the kings of the Visigoths had made it one of their two capitals, the other one being Toledo, in Spain. Reda has disappeared, wiped out by Spanish troops led by Henri de Trastamare. In its place, there is now a small village called Rennes-le-Château. It is not an ordinary village and therein lies the clue to the treasure – both material and spiritual. Many have searched for the treasure of Rennes-le-Château; others are still looking for it. One person, a priest, who lived at the end of the 19th Century and beginning of 20th Century, found it, in part. His name was Bérenger Saunière, parish priest of Rennes-le-Château.

What Bérenger Saunière discovered is now safeguarded in a strongroom in the basement of a curious villa in Switzerland. But this material treasure is only one of the aspects of the dormant secret in the Razès Mountains. This secret, revealed little by little, is that of the descendants of Merovaeus, the first kings who reigned over France. History wiped them out with Childéric III, deposed in 752 CE. However, the dynasty of Merovaeus and Clovis did not perish. With its roots in the Razès region, it is still alive, as many claim their ancestry to the circle and fleur-de-lis represented on the coat of arms of the counts of Reda, heirs to the Merovingian blood. They appropriated Nostradamus' prediction "From a circle, from a lis, a great Prince will be born..." To serve them, a mysterious society was created and took the name of Priory of Sion. Its initiator was Godefroy de Bouillon, King of Jerusalem and descendant of Merovaeus.

This is the obscure and bloody story we have chosen to relate. We are not the only ones fascinated by the treasures buried away in the Razès region. Before and after Bérenger Saunière, many tenacious researchers have tried to unravel the mystery. Some lost their lives in their quest, others, only a little luckier, lost their minds. There is a wealth of literature surrounding this astonishing affair. Initially, there were chronicles left at a local level in the Languedoc libraries. Then, writers came along, like the Marquis Philippe de Cherisey with *Circuit* or Gérard de Sède with his book *Les Templiers sont parmi nous* (*The Templars are Amongst Us*), followed by *L'Or de Rennes* (*The Gold of Rennes*).

Two events fascinated us in this strange affair.

The first was an article published in the daily newspaper *La Dépêche du Midi* in December 1972 which related that researchers, believed to be Israeli, had started some excavations around Rennes-le-Château. In what way could the Razès region be of any interest to geologists from Israel? Let's think. In 70 CE, Titus and his legions took Jerusalem at the end of one of the most atrocious sieges in history. However, the treasure of Solomon and its main piece, the gold seven-branched candlestick so valuable to the Jews which Tradition says was created on the instructions of Yahweh Himself, was rescued from the blazing fire. The spoils of this pillage were taken to Rome. At the beginning of the 5th Century, the Visigoths of Alaric captured and ransacked Rome and the treasure of Jerusalem fell into their hands. When they settled in Spain and southern France, they hid their plunder in two capital cities, Toledo and Reda. Amongst the treasures was the self-same seven-branched candlestick from the Temple of Solomon. Jews are possibly the most mystical people on earth. During nineteen centuries, they dreamt of Palestine and could not rest until they were returned to it. Since 1967, when they reconquered Jerusalem, the Israelis have been proclaiming they would be prepared to negotiate everything to establish peace with their Arab neighbours; everything other than their authority over Jerusalem, the Holy City and historic capital of the Hebrew nation. Agents sent to Languedoc by the Israeli services to find the seven-branched candlestick will only appear as a foolish hypothesis to those unaware of the Jews' deeply held motivations.

The second event that aroused our interest was a file that Jean-Luc Chaumeil gave us at the end of 1972. He was young and passionate and, day after day, had roamed the tormented mountains of the Corbières region, interrogated the ruins and cemeteries, and met with the better-informed on the enigma of Rennes-le-Château. He told us, 'I know where the treasure items discovered by Father Saunière are kept. I have seen them. I was allowed to photograph them. I found out also that there is an occult society which knows the secret of Rennes-le-Château and preserves it in the shadows as well as being focused on the realisation of their mysterious objectives...'

The Israeli investigation in Languedoc and the case of Jean-Luc Chaumeil, supported by very convincing photographic evidence, were sufficient reasons for us also to take an interest in the Razès and its amazing past.

DÉPÊCHE du Midi — JOURNAL DE LA DÉMOCRATIE — MAGAZINE du Dimanche

25e année N. 8.893 DIMANCHE 10 DÉCEMBRE 1972 0,70 F Prix de vente en Espagne: 14 pesetas

TOULOUSE

LE CHANDELIER A SEPT BRANCHES DE RENNES-LE-CHATEAU INTÉRESSE LES SERVICES SECRETS ISRAÉLIENS

Nos lecteurs n'ignorent plus rien de la fabuleuse histoire du trésor de Rennes-le-Château où, depuis la « découverte » de l'abbé Saunière, chercheurs amateurs et professionnels ont déployé des trésors d'ingéniosité à la recherche, jusqu'ici vaine, des richesses des rois Wisigoths ou du Temple.

On sait notamment qu'il y a deux ans un ingénieur d'origine béarnaise, M. Léon Fontan avait confié en exclusivité à notre journal le fruit de ses déductions qui l'inclinaient à penser qu'il avait découvert la cachette du trésor. Depuis cette date, M. Fontan a poursuivi ses investigations, et escompte toujours mener à bon terme des travaux de fouille importants.

Mais que venaient donc faire, à l'automne dernier, ces quatre hommes installés dans une auberge de la route de Carcassonne à Limoux qui, partant en jeep tous les jours à l'aube ne rentraient qu'à la tombée de la nuit, fourbus et couverts de boue? Géologues, mentionnaient leurs fiches d'hôtel. Leurs relevés, leurs échantillons provenant du « carottage » des sols étaient destinés pourtant à une compagnie étrangère de pétrole.

Parlant un impeccable français ils utilisaient, lorsqu'ils se retrouvaient entre eux, un idiome difficile à retenir. Grâce à une personne ayant longtemps vécu à Tel-Aviv, et qui surprit un de leurs conciliabules il apparut qu'il s'agissait de chercheurs israéliens.

Le fait était d'autant plus bizarre qu'aucune concession pétrolière n'avait été accordée, dans la région, à une société étrangère. Alors, que faisaient-ils à Rennes-le-Château? Ne faudrait-il pas rapprocher leurs travaux de ceux menés à bien par le curé des lieux, car la nature des pièces rarissimes négociées à l'époque par l'abbé Saunière donne suffisamment de vraisemblance à l'hypothèse selon laquelle le trésor du Temple de Jérusalem soit resté dans la région.

Cela voudrait-il dire pour autant que les services secrets israéliens se remuent à présent autour de cette affaire, espérant ainsi récupérer le chandelier à sept branches dont nous parle l'Ancien Testament? L'avenir, peut-être, nous le dira.

2- "Dépêche du Midi"

3 - Léon Fontan

4 - Father Saunière

5 - Gérard de Sède

6 - Philippe de Cherisey

The Treasure Hunt

On 10th December 1972, the daily newspaper *La Dépêche du Midi* of Toulouse published the following lines "But what were the four men staying in an inn on the Carcassonne to Limoux road doing, last autumn; leaving in a jeep every morning at dawn and returning at nightfall exhausted and covered in mud? The hotel records mentioned that they were geologists. The samples and specimens from their core drilling of the lands were apparently destined for a foreign petroleum company. Although they spoke impeccable French, when they were amongst themselves they shared an idiom that was difficult to identify. Thanks to a person who had lived a long time in Tel-Aviv and had overheard one of their conversations, it appeared that they were Israeli researchers. The event was even more puzzling as no petroleum concession had been granted to a foreign company in the region. Therefore, what were they doing in Rennes-le-Château? What if they were secret Israeli agents?"

Everything that concerns the village of Rennes-le-Château is cloaked in mystery. A legend has been associated with it for centuries; that of a treasure, or several treasures, supposedly buried in or around the village. This legend is not without foundation as a local priest, Bérenger Saunière, revealed part of it at the end of the 19th Century. Rennes-le-Château, in the Cathars' territory of the upper Aude valley, is a little village of two hundred inhabitants perched on the top of a hill in front of the Black Mountain. Going up the river Aude towards the Pyrenees, the traveller crosses vast Dionysian valleys where vines stretch away as far as the eye can see. In the distance, one can see the crenellated walls of Carcassonne; the manifestation of a grandiose and dramatic Middle Ages. In the south, the Pyrenees dominate like imaginary castles. There, in the Razès, the fertile plains stop not far from the headspring of the river Aude where the countryside is nothing but red ochre against a pure sky, and it is in this rocky region that the grapes for Corbières wine ripen. Here and there, castles in ruins can be seen amongst the stones and bushes. They bear witness to the flamboyant past of the area which belonged, some fifteen hundred years ago, to the barbaric kingdom of the Visigoths. In the north, we have the towns of Limoux and Carcassonne, to the east Perpignan, and to the west Foix. This is the southern boundary of the old Albigensian territory. Forty kilometres to the south east of Foix as the crow flies, about eight centuries ago, the crusaders of Simon de Montfort, escorted by their inquisitors, went across that land wiping out in the blazing fire of Montségur the remaining witnesses of the Cathars' religion, strange men who were called "the Perfects". Going south from Limoux, past the towns of Alet-les-Bains and Montazels, a deep road with the peak of Cardou on its left and the rock of Blanchefort on its right, leads to Rennes-les-Bains, a small thermal town that is still surrounded by megalithic walls. South of Montazels, a sinuous road, dangerous and buzzing with cicadas, takes you to Rennes-le-Château. Positioned like a tiered cake on the plateau, the village is a belvedere over the two equally beautiful valleys of the Aude and the Sals. On one side, the eye embraces the country villages of Lavaldieu and Bezu where the Templars kept three commanderies; on the other side it envelops Arques and the ruins of Coustaussa which, as the name implies, is the custodian and vigilant guardian of these wild places. The origin of Rennes-le-Château is so ancient and so mysterious that historians and archaeologists dare not advance a date. Father Mazières, in his work on the *Venue et séjour des templiers à la fin du XIIIè siècle et au début du XIVè siècle dans la vallée du Bézu* (*Arrival and Sojourn of the Templars at the End of the 13th Century and Beginning of 14th Century in the Valley of Bézu*) merely notes that the region of the Razès became famous because of its legends, its traditions, its secrets, its enigmas and a great number of discoveries, some of which were sensational.

Rennes-le-Château, once upon a time called "Rhedae", derives its name from the Visigothic word "Rheda", meaning chariot. Very quickly, the area developed economically. The ferruginous springs and cold salt marshes of Rennes-les-Bains were exploited from ancient times for their therapeutic virtues. A Neolithic ossuary discovered in the last century indicates that the land was inhabited long before our era. Iberian tribes settled there, followed in the 4th Century B.C., by the Redone people from Belgium. In his work *Mémoires de l'Histoire du Languedoc* (*Memoirs on the History of Languedoc*), the historian Guillaume de Catel relates that the Romans also settled in this area, not because of its beauty as it is not blessed in that regard by nature, but for its profusion of diverse minerals. Indeed, besides the great mineralogical and hydrographical resources, the Razès has numerous deposits of amber, jet, iron, sulphur, silver and gold. The region owes its early development to the exploitation of these resources. The Roman road that crosses it to Spain was later used by pilgrims to Santiago de Compostela, and luxurious thermal baths for wealthy sick people were built in Rennes-les-Bains.

However, it is especially around the subject of its gold that the history of Rennes-le-Château becomes blurred. In 410 CE, Alaric the Ancient, King of the Visigoths, ransacked and pillaged Rome. Amidst the plunder was the treasure from the Temple of Jerusalem, stolen by Titus in 70 CE, with the famous gold seven-branched candlestick. In the 5th Century, the Visigoths conquered Languedoc and kept their plunder in two places. The Kings' personal items were secured in Toulouse, whilst the ancient treasure from the spoils of war was held in Carcassonne. In 507 CE, Clovis, King of the Franks, conquered and pillaged the city of Toulouse. The old treasure in Carcassonne was safeguarded thanks to the intervention of Theodoric the Great, King of the Ostrogoths in Italy. In the 7th Century, the Franks swept through the Languedoc region once more. The Frankish historian Fredeguaire relates that, after the capture of Narbonne, they found only 'sixty chalices, fifteen patens and twenty chains'. The Visigoths hid part of their ancient treasure near Toledo. From that moment, their power was restricted to the Razès region. Reda grew in importance and it became a diocesan capital. Today, only a village remains from the unassailable fortified city of Reda, which became one of the capitals of the kings of the Visigoths in the 6th Century, the other being Toledo, and which gave its name to Rhedesium, or the county of Razès. In 1361, Reda was completely destroyed by the Aragonese troops of Henri de Trastamare. This represents, therefore, the geographical setting and first historical context regarding Rennes-le-Château and the Razès. We will see later that many more well known and secret events in the history of France are linked to this village and region.

It is now time to mention the astonishing treasure hunt for which this region was the stage. Let's go back three centuries, to 1645 to be precise. In spring of that year, Ignace Pâris, a young shepherd from Rennes-le-Château, was looking for a stray sheep not far from the village. When he went close to the area where the sheep was bleating, he realised that the animal had fallen to the bottom of a crevice. He went down the hole and noticed a narrow fissure that was leading underground. He followed it and reached a cave. The spectacle on offer dazzled and scared him at the same time. There was a treasure, gold everywhere, so much of it that one would not know what to do with it all. Next to these riches lay the skeletons of macabre guardians. Pâris filled his pockets and left the cave as quickly as possible. Back in the village, he related his story. But, says Gérard de Sède in his book *L'Or de Rennes*, "as Pâris refused obstinately to reveal the location, nobody believed him. People accused him of theft and he was stoned to death." This is a true story, at least in part. The ruins of the house where the poor shepherd lived can still be seen not far from the village.

In inflaming the spirits, the treasure of Rennes-le-Château has given birth to stories that belong more to traditional tales than the historical truth. In his *Voyage à Rennes-les-Bains* written in 1832, Labouisse-Rochefort related the legend regarding the treasure of Satan, as follows, "One day, the Devil, guardian of an immense treasure, was counting his coins. A shepherdess, who was taking her flock to graze on the mountain, saw him spread his gold coins and promptly ran to the village to rally her neighbours. When they arrived on the mountain, the Devil had disappeared. Crestfallen, the villagers consulted a wizard who agreed to steal the Devil's treasure for a large reward; the promise of half the gold coins. 'As soon as I shout,' he told them, 'you must come to my rescue.' On the allotted day, the wizard went to measure his strength against that of the Devil. Soon, there was a dreadful racket and such horrible cries that the distraught villagers fled. Beside himself, the wizard came back and shouted 'Cowards! Because of you, we have lost everything. I was holding a string of his purse already, but you were not there to help me!' Labouisse-Rochefort added that the Marquis of Fleury, Lord of Rennes-le-Château and of Blanchefort and owner of the mountain that was the stage for this farcical tale, sued the villagers for trespassing on his property. Is this a myth or reality? It does not matter. There is now a strong belief in the region that there is a treasure in Rennes-le-Château. Tradition says it is distributed in forty hiding places. Two of them were discovered, by chance, in the 19th Century. In the first one, they found an ingot weighing twenty kilos made from an amalgam of Arab coins. In the second one, in 1860, an ingot of fifty kilos, enveloped in a bituminous material, was unearthed by a farmer.

But, the real treasure story only began in earnest at the end of the 19th Century with Father Saunière, parish priest of Rennes-le-Château. Of modest origins, François-Bérenger Saunière, born in Montazels on 11th April 1852, was a strange man. Being the eldest of seven children, his parents had great ambitions for him and decided that he should be priest. Ordained in 1875, he started as curate at Alès, then became parish priest of Clat. Three years later, he was appointed professor at the seminary of Narbonne. However, after occupying that post for only one month, he was disliked for his independent spirit and lack of respect towards the hierarchy; on 1st June 1885, he was transferred to Rennes-le-Château - more in exile than as a promotion. Tall and of strong build, Father Saunière had retained the appearance of a farmer. He had a determined chin, a broad nose, thick eyebrows, and a sensual mouth. The seeming brutality of his physiognomy was softened by a large high forehead and, more particularly, by a deep and gentle stare. Cut off and lost in his little village, the young priest had no other distractions than fishing, hunting and studying. He decided to learn Hebrew and Greek. Gérard de Sède related that, "to satisfy the desires of a man in his prime, an eighteen year old hatter, Marie Denarnaud, left her workshop to become his less than canonical servant". To her last day, she remained Bérenger's faithful companion who kept the secrets shared with him.

Poverty prevented him from renovating his run-down church. It was only in 1888, thanks to a legacy of six hundred francs from his predecessor Father Pons, that he began the most urgent repairs. At the same time, and although he did not know how he was going to reimburse the money, he obtained a loan of one thousand four hundred francs from the municipality. In 1891, he decided to renovate the most beautiful item in the church, the high altar with its two supporting pillars dating back to the Visigothic period. With the help of two builders, the priest removed the stone table which was extremely damaged and needed replacement. To their stupefaction, they found that the pillars were hollow. In this very old hiding place, they discovered three wooden tubes, sealed with wax and containing some parchments. These documents were coded and the priest could not decipher them. He suggested selling them so as to provide ample funds to repay the loan from the municipality. The mayor gave his agreement to this. However, before Saunière left for Paris to sell the parchments, the prudent mayor decided to keep a copy in the municipal archives of Rennes-le-Château. Meanwhile, the smart priest paid a visit to His Lordship Billard of Carcassonne, who gave him the address of Father Hoffet, an independent Parisian priest of the Trinity church, rue Blanche, who would be capable of decoding the documents. The Lord Bishop instructed Saunière not to sell the parchments and that his diocese would reimburse the entire loan to the municipality.

As soon as he arrived in Paris, Bérenger Saunière visited Father Bieil, the great-uncle of Father Hoffet and spiritual director of the Saint-Sulpice church. Gérard de Sède related that, "After reading the note of introduction from the Lord Bishop, Father Bieil welcomed our hero, examined the four hitherto illegible texts, and asked his visitor to leave them with him for a week so that they may be submitted to specialists." Alone in Paris, Saunière was offered full board by Friar Ané, editor and nephew of Father Bieil. For eight days, the modest country priest moved in artistic circles and kept company with the scholars of the capital. Thanks to young Father Emile Hoffet, he penetrated the intimate circle of Debussy's friends. The Debussy name is important as will be seen later in our story. At an evening reception, Saunière was introduced to Emma Calvé, a young opera singer famous across Europe, who started her soprano career a few years before in Gounod's *Faust*. With her, the priest forgot his amorous adventure with his servant in Rennes-le-Château. Bérenger was a womaniser. When one questioned the old female parishioners who knew him in their youth, they responded with a little mischievous spark in their eyes "Ah! He was a handsome man..." His affair with the opera singer lasted for years.

Paris was not just a place for misbehaviour for the debonair clergyman; he visited the great monuments of the capital, including the Louvre, and was particularly interested in the religious art of Saint-Sulpice which inspired him for the decoration of his own church a few years later. After eight days, Saunière went back to Father Bieil and was surprised to find that Father Hoffet did not want to return his documents. However, the latter explained that he had managed to decipher them and explained their content. Father Hoffet said that they were *Litanies to Our Lady* and *Gospels of Luke and John*. In fact, these texts, seemingly insignificant, concealed many more connotations.

From that time, everything changed for Father Saunière. On the way back to his village, he received two thousand francs from his Lord Bishop in Carcassonne and reimbursed the mayor to whom he did not breathe a word about the palaeographers' findings. He started to work feverishly on the restoration of his church. With a few youngsters, he moved the stone at the foot of the high altar and dug a pit in its place. They discovered two skeletons and a pot full of gold coins. In the calmest manner, Saunière pretended that they were valueless medals. After that, he excavated in his church on his own. For days on end, the priest, accompanied by his maid, roamed the countryside with a basket on his back. On his mysterious rambles, one could see him bend from time to time to pick up a stone. Most often, he would discard it absent-mindedly after closer examination. Occasionally, however, he would place it in his basket. Intrigued, the villagers would ask, 'Tell us, Father, what are you planning to do with all these stones?' And he would invariably reply, 'It is for the garden that borders the cemetery. I would like to build a nice grotto and, for that, not any old stones will do.' Indeed, the priest did build his own grotto by the cemetery. It is now in ruins after having been demolished by vandals. But the priest did not stop at roaming the countryside. At nightfall, he shut himself away in the cemetery, moved the gravestone slab of the Marchioness of Blanchefort, former lady of the manor of Rennes-le-Château, and applied himself to erasing the epitaph engraved upon it. Indignation brewed in the village. 'Leave the dead alone!' they would say. Decidedly, the priest's behaviour smacked of heresy. Why did he indulge in this scandalous nocturnal pursuit? Apparently, he got that idea after talking with Father Boudet, parish priest of the neighbouring town of Rennes-les-Bains, below Rennes-le-Château, whom he had befriended for some years.

Father Boudet, who was affable and well educated, had discovered many strange things about the region and, most interestingly, had studied the life of Father Bigou, squire of the Marchioness of Blanchefort. He confided in his friend Bérenger Saunière that Father Bigou, parish priest of Rennes-le-Château during the French Revolution, who knew of the treasure's existence, had engraved the few precise details in his possession in a coded manner amongst numerous inscriptions, notably on the stele of the marchioness. Hence, Saunière's relentless work at night in the cemetery...

Father Boudet related that, on her deathbed on 17th January 1781, Marie de Negri d'Ables, Marchioness of Hautpoul-Blanchefort, entrusted a parchment to her confessor Father Antoine Bigou, parish priest of Rennes-le-Château since 1774. Based on information provided by the Marchioness, Father Bigou visited the ruins of the old Saint Peter church located, if one believes the historians, on the south side of the village. Near the southern wall of the sacristy, a pivoting stone slab revealed a downward-leading passage and, along this pathway, a little hiding place containing two wooden rolls sealed with wax were discovered. The priest hurried back up the secret staircase strewn with bones and found four parchments in the wooden rolls transcribing the *Litanies to Our Lady* and two excerpts from the gospels of *Luke* (chapter VI) and *John* (chapter XII). Certain anomalies in the characters denoted that there was a coded message hidden in the excerpts. After decoding these documents, thanks to the parchment bequeathed by the deceased marchioness, Father Bigou decided that, as the political situation was becoming more and more uncertain, there would be no further transmission of the message either by hand or by word of mouth. He resolved, therefore, to engrave a coded message for the public on the stele of the Marchioness; thirteen lines of a text with a double meaning, the hidden message being the anagram of the visible text, which itself contained the clue to its decoding. The stele containing the famous words was engraved and erected in the cemetery. As the old Saint Peter church faced destruction, Father Bigou chose to hide the parchments in Saint Madeleine church. To that effect, he hollowed out the right pillar of the Visigothic altar, receptacle of the wooden rolls, and turned the tombstone that was in front of the altar over to face downwards. In accordance with the law of 26th August 1792, Father Bigou, the nonjuring priest, was deported the following September to Sabadel where he died on

26th March 1794. During the French Revolution, the secret of Rennes-le-Château was not totally overlooked by certain individuals such as Siéyès, Buhl, and, in particular, a mysterious Father Pichon, about whom we know very little except that he was a genealogist devoted to Siéyès and Bonaparte.

Bérenger Saunière found various signs left by Father Bigou. He often wandered alone in a land called "Le Pla del Coste" and a strange chess game started between the Roc Noir (Rokko Negro or Black Rock) and the Rocher Blanc (White Rock). The priest discovered the famous standing stone, known as Cheval de Dieu (Horse of God), and the thirty-five centimetre cross on a stone on the ridge mentioned by Father Boudet, located 681 "toises" (one toise equals 6 feet or 1.949 metres) from La Bergère de l'église de Rennes-les-Bains (the shepherdess of the church in Rennes-les-Bains). On the Serbairou slopes and in the steps of the shepherd Pâris, the busy and mysterious priest resembled a researcher with a precise mission. What was interesting was the speed at which he found the itinerary that many after him would try to retrace in vain. What was the exact role of Father Boudet in this treasure hunt? Very friendly with the parish priest of Rennes-le-Château, he was his confidant and offered him valuable assistance with his scholarship. Saunière, on the other hand, seemed to keep some of his discoveries to himself.

Some weeks later, Father Saunière started to travel frequently from Spain to Switzerland and from Germany to Belgium, sometimes for a whole week, with a heavy suitcase that was hard to carry. At that time, he corresponded with the Bank Petitjean, rue Montmartre in Paris, and Marie Denarnaud received foreign money orders in her name which she cashed in Couiza, a little town situated a few kilometres from Rennes-le-Château. Clearly, they had hit upon a fortune. In 1896, Bérenger Saunière started repairs to his church and almost rebuilt it at his own expense. At times, his architectural oddities confounded the builders, such as the priest's insistence on sixty four black and white tiles to be laid like a chessboard on the floor. He renewed the decoration and commissioned the sculpting of strange figures, all equally hideous and fascinating, and in the worst possible taste for Saint Sulpice. The Devil that supports the stoup has a flattened left flank or "pla costel" and is staring at a precise point on the chessboard. His left hand is clenched on his right knee. This deformed demon, who is limping and suffering from strabismus in one eye, is Asmodeus. Such was the wish of Father Saunière, who composed all the engravings, like Father Bigou. Seemingly following some pre-established plans, he had the windows moved and raised, and added a back-room to the sacristy with a secret door to a spiral staircase carved in the thickness of the wall leading to the pulpit. The building works were completed in time for the visit of Lord Bishop Billard from Carcassonne in 1897. On the tympanum of his church, the parish priest of Rennes-le-Château had engraved the words of Jacob to Bethel "Terribilis est locus iste" or "this place is terrible". His Lordship Billard appeared to understand the message since as soon as he entered the building he was overwhelmed by a muted anguish. The prelate curtailed his visit, blessed the Calvary in a hurry, cut short the niceties and left, never to return to Rennes-le-Château.

Three years later, Saunière started new building works. He commissioned the construction of a luxurious residence with a veranda, surrounded by a park, which he named "Villa Bethany". He assembled an outstanding library and accommodated a bookbinder in his home who worked solely for him for several months. Finally, he built an extraordinary edifice over several floors, with a covered way and battlements, which he named "Tower Magdala", in a neo-gothic style so popular in the 19th Century. That building was later used as an observatory. Saunière, who never left anything to chance, had chosen the symbolic name "Magdala", a Greek transposition of the Hebrew term "Migdol" used for many fortified towns of southern Syria and meaning tower or fortress. From the Magdala tower-cum-fortress, Father Saunière's telescope was permanently trained on the Castle of Albedun, presumed location of the ancient city of Reda, and on all key places in the region. Whilst giving free-rein to his megalomaniac whims, Bérenger Saunière executed his architectural work with care and precision, redoing some of the constructions if they were not to his satisfaction. Buildings and objects had to be orientated precisely, conveying accurately the true symbol and allegory intended by their creator. In his luxurious residence, the priest led a life of pleasure and enjoyed a sumptuous lifestyle. He kept an open house where a multitude of guests converged, artists like the composer Debussy and the opera singer Emma Calvé, real and fake aristocrats like the Archduke John of Hapsburg and the "Viscountess of Artois", scholars, writers, politicians, society and semi-society people. He even laid out a zoological park on his property where ducks from his farmyard had to be fed biscuits with a small spoon!

What did Lord Bishop Billard say about this? Nothing: he received one million gold francs. But in 1902, everything changed. His successor on the Episcopal throne, Lord Bishop of Beauséjour, looked unfavourably on the munificence and extravagances of Saunière and, in January 1908, decided to transfer him to another parish. The priest objected insolently, declaring with cynicism, 'My interests retain me here'. He was immediately summoned to Carcassonne, but turned a deaf ear and obtained medical certificates from his doctor and friend Paul Courrent which enabled him to shirk the summons.

However, after a year of tergiversations, Saunière was finally made accountable to his Lord Bishop. He explained to the prelate, 'My Lord, the considerable sums, that you seem to reproach me for possessing, are from generous donors whose names I cannot reveal without betraying the secret of confession. Furthermore, this money has been given to me personally and I am not accountable to you over it.' The Lord Bishop disapproved and publicly accused his vassal of making money from Mass trafficking. On 5th December 1910, Bérenger Saunière was declared "suspens a divinis" by the ecclesiastical judges and was deprived of his right to celebrate Mass and administer sacraments. Not admitting defeat, the priest appealed to Rome. The simony accusation was considered ridiculous since Father Saunière would have had to indulge in Mass trafficking for more than three centuries to raise the sums he had spent on his church. The case was dismissed. However, following a counter-appeal from the prelate in 1915, a definite interdict struck Bérenger Saunière and a new parish priest was appointed in Rennes-le-Château. Unperturbed, Bérenger built a chapel on his property to celebrate Mass and his unfortunate successor found himself alone in his empty church on Sundays. Furthermore, he had to lodge in Couiza as Marie Denarnaud, Saunière's companion and servant, had rented the presbytery from the municipality for ninety nine years in accordance with the separation law between the Church and the State. That same year, Father Boudet, Saunière's old friend, died. In 1916, after the Pontifical Court established a link between Father Saunière's Mass trafficking and the story of Father Bigou in 1890, they accused the priest of rebellion against the religious authority and insubordination towards his superiors.

In December 1916, discharged from his duties and responsibilities as a priest, Saunière decided to preach a new religion. He gathered eight million gold francs which he converted into notes. Panic reigned in the diocese, the Vatican became anxious, and several politicians judged this manoeuvre undesirable at a time of war. The priest received a number of warnings but, at the beginning of January 1917, decided nevertheless to build a road through the mountain in the direction of Couiza and to embark upon the construction of a chapel and a seventy-metre tower from which he could talk to his congregation. However, on 17th January, Saint Anthony the Hermit's day, Bérenger Saunière was hit by a stroke. Paul Courrent, his doctor, watched over him. In a last moment of consciousness, the priest requested the presence of a mysterious individual named Jean XXIII (John 23rd), who did not come. Saunière died on 22nd January at the age of sixty five. Between 1891 and 1917, he had spent between one and a half billion and two billion four hundred million old francs. His servant, Marie Denarnaud, outlived him for a long time and remained silent until the end regarding the origins of his astonishing fortune. Gérard de Sède related that, "When Bérenger felt the end was near, he summoned Father Rivière, parish priest of Esperaza, a neighbouring village. This jovial man had been a lifelong friend who had not broken up with him when he was interdicted. Broadminded, he knew that the flesh was weak and he believed in God's leniency... What happened between the two priests? Nobody will ever know. But when Rivière left his dying friend, he was deathly pale and deeply distressed. It was not a fleeting emotion. He became withdrawn, taciturn and silent, and never laughed again to his death. What was the terrible secret imparted to him in confidence? Or what spiritual abyss opened up in front of him? Had Bérenger's soul already turned to stone on which the divine mercy would break its wings? Did he think he was abandoning his friend on the doorway to hell? In any event, something happened that had never been seen before, as the one-time priest of Rennes-le-Château received the last sacraments only two days after his death. Thus, until the end and beyond the grave, Bérenger Saunière retained his aura of mystery."

Following the priest's death, more researchers became interested in the treasure of the Razès since the proof of its existence was nearly established. In 1938, a diviner asserted that there was some gold in one of the gorges near Rennes-le-Château. He started the research in the company of his engineer and dynamited the underground galleries. One morning, he refused the help of his colleague and went down the hole on his own, but never returned.

In December 1945, Henri Benderly, a researcher from Nice, disregarded the three cavities known to everybody and discovered a fourth one on the hillside, hidden by brambles and nettles and totally unexplored. Twice in a row, he went down the depths of the pit at the risk of his life. In May 1946, he made a third attempt with a few young men. A newspaper in Nice, *L'étoile du soir*, published the story of their odyssey on 12th May 1946 as related by those who accompanied Benderly, "Today, he (Henri Benderly) renews that perilous exploration. Before accessing the hole, we enter a cave. We go down a rope for about fifteen metres before reaching the first platform. The humidity and cold cut right through us. We must then crawl to reach the mouth of the pit. We prepare the ropes for the man's descent in the gaping opening, a deep chimney, narrow and smooth... The mystery is there, sixty metres underground. Big spiders run along the rocks worn by erosion. A bat, panicking in the light, twirls around our heads. The descent starts. Nobody has the courage to talk. He is the only one who commands the manoeuvre in a quiet voice. 'Let the rope slip... Stop... Continue... Stop... Can you hear me?' A few rocks break away and fall noisily into the depths, echoing gloomily after a few seconds. Big flies assail us. We are chilled to the bone, yet we must stay. We keep the life of a man at the end of a rope. I leave, exhausted. The air is too thin. The young Basques have remained. They hold onto the rope, but the lack of light scares them. 'Pull up... Pull up! It's over... Get away...' says the man in a hushed tone. But the peasants want to save the man despite the danger, in spite of himself. I am outside, worried and impatient. After an interminable wait, the four young men reappear, worn out, panting, haggard..."

At times, the treasure hunt brought about some strange discoveries. In April 1956, the librarian Descadeillas, author of a book on the last lords of Rennes-le-Château, together with Doctor Malacan and two other individuals, excavated in the church of Rennes-le-Château. In front of the high altar, where Saunière had dug up the ground previously, the researchers found a human skull with a gash in the crown of the head. This type of ritual wound was common during the Merovingian epoch. But was the skull from that era? In the priest's garden, one found the decaying corpses of three men in their mid-thirties, killed by bullets, a meter and a half underground, with pieces of flesh still stuck to the bones... In 1960, another researcher obtained the authorisation to dig up in the church. During the excavation works, a beam fell and nearly crushed him. It had been placed against the door so that it would fall on opening. The criminal intention was obvious...

Many people presumed to hold information about the treasure of Rennes-le-Château perished violently. The royalist Guillaume Servin was assassinated in 1340 during his quest. In 1897, Father Antoine Gélis, parish priest of Coustaussa and friend of Boudet and Saunière, was found lying in his own blood. He had fourteen head wounds above the nape of the neck. His skull was fractured in several places and his brain was exposed. The walls and ceiling of the presbytery were spattered with extensive blood stains. Everything was upside down. However, the full sum of five thousand five hundred francs was found. Father Gélis, it was said, possessed some papers...

In 1968, a Belgian aristocrat, the Marquis Philippe de Cherisey, Count of Vaudressel, curious about the secret history of France, became interested in turn in the treasure of Rennes-le-Château. His book entitled *Circuit* relates the tale of two heroes, Charlot and Marie-Madeleine, who appear to be on the trail of the famous treasure. Here is an excerpt.

"Amidst the thorns and rocks, they reach their final ordeal.

Marie-Madeleine - 'Well, what shall I do?'

Charlot - 'Nothing, just wait here, or rather, go over there, at the place I earmarked on this map. Have faith. Anyway, I will find you, and I will need you.'

Charlot undresses and gives his clothes to Marie-Madeleine. On all fours, in underpants and with two watertight electric torches, he climbs a very rough slope. One last time, he contemplates the countryside and mumbles to himself 'When you think that a group of barmy people believed they would find it in Montferrand or on the Cardou and that other idiots dug up the church and the cemetery of Rennes-le-Château!'

He crawls through one of the rocky cracks that our ancestors called 'catins', which one can pass a thousand times without noticing, and progresses slowly through the narrow bottleneck. At the end of a rather short leg that seems interminable, he reaches a junction. No matter what he chooses, it is the cesspit.

Charlot – 'Cellis or arcis? Right or left? Let's go left and long live the King,' he says, entering a whitish gunk face down.

After about thirty metres in the narrow passageway, Charlot finds himself in front of a smooth vertical wall. A few notches carved in the rock by his predecessors reassure him. A little rivulet oozes from the sixth notch and Charlot slips. He nearly looses his balance and hits the stone harshly with his left knee. Painfully, and with great effort, he reaches a solid platform at the top of the rock. Charlot, coated in white and with blood running down his leg, advances looking like a limping ghost. The platform leads to an elevated vaulted crossroads in the middle of which there is a tomb on a plinth with two inscriptions celebrating the great Roman Pompéïus Cartus, whose lead coffin is hermetically sealed. Quite moved, Charlot kisses the tomb, not out of admiration for the individual in it, but out of respect from a guest to his host.

There is no sign of a jewel, or any precious metal, other than significant copper veins on the inner walls of the vault. Several contiguous caves and a passage down the partially collapsed vault rejoin the right passageway he had disregarded earlier. He thanks Heaven for guiding him away from this deadly gallery and decides to inspect the knee-high flooded caves along which one can walk on all fours on a low narrow wall of piled up tiles. The ceiling is whitish and made of a slightly friable stone.

At some point, Charlot stops to get his breath back. His leg is hurting. He switches on his second torch and lifts a tile to see how tileries were working in the past. The tile of beaten metal is terribly heavy. When he scratches it, gold appears. With such a slab, and without extravagant spending, Charlot could live comfortably for at least two years, and there are kilometres of tiles, that is to say millennia of pleasure...

Charlot envisages going back with a tile. However, carrying fifteen kilos when one is naked and on all fours is exhausting. The cold atmosphere is getting to him. He recognises the return journey from his own blood. At the end of the cave, Charlot finds himself back behind the tombstone of the great Roman. He plans to follow his own footsteps, but the smooth vertical wall that was so difficult to climb seems so vertiginous on the way down that he chooses another path. After some distance, he sees sun rays through an opening. However, the passage is guarded by the sentries of the great Roman; corpses buried half way in a hole looking like legless cripples, seemingly of different ages ranging from the perfect skeletons to the wax figures of the Grévin Museum, as the air of the place prevents bodies from decaying.

Charlot infiltrates the dead, slips on a shinbone and falls, his head hitting a preserved skull which separates from its trunk with a sharp snap. 'Terribilis est locus iste' utters Charlot. His hand tries to find some support to help him back on his feet and touches a round object which he examines. The sun rays light up the cave. He looks around him and sees piles of diverse gold plates. So, there is the store of the multimillionaire priest!

Returning on his footsteps, Charlot notices a rather comfortable gallery on his right, which he descends slowly. He crawls more than he walks. His eyes are burning and his breathing is more and more laboured. Completely exhausted, he reaches a dead end. He screams, falls to the ground, screams again and faints. Marie-Madeleine hears his voice that seems to originate from under a large stone. She clears small stones, shrubs, and soil from the area. She finds an opening and, with great difficulty, extricates this poor old child, this modern Lazarus risen from the dead..."

In May 1971, Léon Fontan, another researcher of Béarn origin who lived in Strasbourg, pursued the hunt for the treasure. Sure of his findings, although he had not found anything yet, he lodged three certified reports with Mr. Gastoux, a lawyer in Limoux, Aude, to preserve his finder rights. He started his search in the Castle of Bézu, near Rennes-le-Château, where he dug a cesspit forty metres deep and performed the same at Campagne-sur-Aude and Luc-sur-Aude. In February 1972, Jean-Jacques Mourreau interviewed Léon Fontan and described him as a man of fifty-one who had come to the region as a simple tourist but left persuaded that he would be able to resolve the mysteries surrounding Rennes-le-Château. He related that Léon Fontan came back to the Razès time and time again and was seen by the locals wandering in the countryside, searching amongst the ruins where he proceeded with care, patience, and determination, studying the topography and carrying out drilling activities. Back home in Alsace, he read a lot and acquired an encyclopaedic knowledge of the Templars. Léon Fontan told Jean-Jacques Mourreau that the treasure discovered by Father Saunière did not belong to the Visigoths, but to the Bézu commandery of the Templars, and that it had probably been buried around 1307, the year of their arrest. He also stated that the treasure was not in Rennes-le-Château, but in a wild area in the countryside, buried some fifteen metres deep on the hillside, four kilometres from the village as the crow flies. *'In a few months time, you will know whether I am right or wrong'* said Léon Fontan. *'Anyway, my decoding pursuit indicates the existence of a crypt that was completely sealed. The documents I have come to examine suggest that the closure of this underground area built in the rock on the hillside was done before the end of the 13th Century, around 1292. Of course, the crypt might be empty. But the information provided on the stele and tombstone of the Marchioness of Blanchefort endorses that found on the steles of Arles-sur-Tech.'* For Léon Fontan, the crypt is a secret store, a "scella bello", an armoury, the safekeeping of which would have been entrusted to the Templars by Blanche of Castile. Saint Louis, Philippe III le Hardi (Philip the Hardy) and Philippe IV le Bel (Philip the Fair) knew of its existence but totally ignored its location. 'At the beginning of the 14th Century, aware of the forthcoming dangers,' said Léon Fontan 'the Templars ordered the destruction of the guard houses down to ground level. To thwart the searches, they returned the land to a natural appearance. The Blanchefort family, a member of which had been Grand Master of the Order of the Temple, were the guardians of the secret handed down through the centuries. At the time of the French Revolution, Antoine Bigou, squire of the Marchioness of Blanchefort, engraved the information on her stele. When they went into exile, the Blancheforts took the key to the secret with them and it was lost with the extinction of this renowned family. 'I am the first person to find it again.' Léon

Fontan added, 'I shall not give up, even though some people send me letters to try to intimidate me. What do you expect? The Templars have fed so many imaginations...' Léon Fontan believed that many discoveries were still to be made in the region of Rennes-le-Château. He explained 'I am not a professional treasure hunter. I am simply keen to resolve the enigma regarding the stele's inscriptions. I want to know if my conclusions are correct. My efforts at decoding have given me geographic information. All the investigations at surface level, in addition to the drilling explorations, confirm the existence of an underground passage. All that remains to be done now is to go and see for oneself'. Whilst trying to be discreet regarding future excavations, Léon Fontan admitted the difficulties of the operation. 'We will have to go through a thick layer of rock to reach the underground gallery. I cannot do this on my own and will need to appoint a specialised firm. The contractor can decide on the means of action that will succeed. I am only interested in the results.' He added, 'The discovery is interesting at archaeological and historical levels. It is not necessarily a treasure in the narrow sense of the word. The manuscripts mention some old relics and archives. It is not improbable that these are of crucial interest to humanity and that they may turn the religious history of faraway days upside down. Who knows? In that case, the unveiling of this treasure could be as far-reaching as the discovery of the famous *Dead Sea Scrolls.*'

7 - View of Limoux from Reda and View of Rennes-le-Château

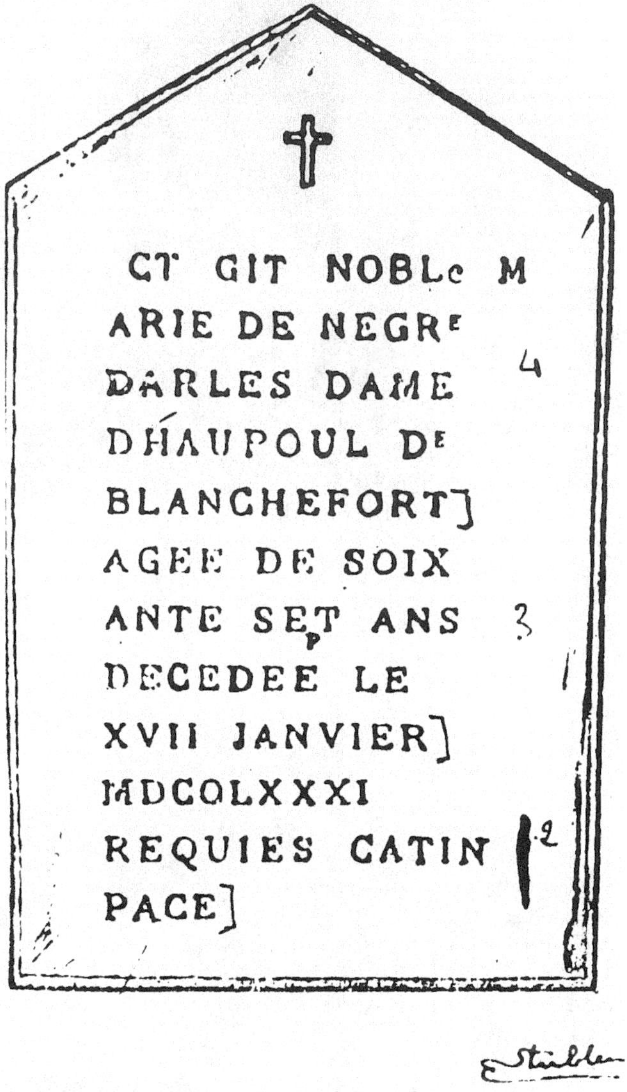

CT GIT NOBLe M
ARIE DE NEGRE
DARLES DAME
DHAUPOUL DE
BLANCHEFORT
AGEE DE SOIX
ANTE SET ANS
DECEDEE LE
XVII JANVIER
MDCOLXXXI
REQUIES CATIN
PACE

8 - The stele of the Marchioness of Blanchefort

9 - The Magdala Tower

10 - The Standing Stone called "Horse of God"

11 - Asmodeus

THE RAZÈS, A LAND OF ENCOUNTERS

To grasp the origin of the treasure, or treasures, buried around Rennes-le-Château, one must revisit the history of the Razès region and, more particularly, that of old Reda. The etymology of this word was mentioned in the previous section. The historian Louis Fédié advanced, rather naïvely, that Rennes-le-Château, formerly Reda, derived its name from the Visigothic word "Rheda" meaning "chariot", since the Visigoths possessed many chariots and the city location at the time was simply a camp. Other historians, however, favour the more Celtic etymology of "Aer Red", or Thunderbolt, Celtic God of Thunder. Others still derive the name from the Redone Belgian tribe that occupied the Razès in the 4th Century BCE. After the pre-Celtic populations, the Redone people occupied the existing encampment which became Reda. Expelled from Belgium by other barbarians, the majority of them went to Brittany where they founded the city of Rennes. The toponymic origin of Rennes-les-Bains is more certain. Formerly Bains-de-Règnes, this place derives its name from the Latin "Regnum" attached to the barbaric name "Is", designating either water or stone. Rennes-les-Bains, therefore, would mean Royal Water or Royal Stone.

After the sacking of Rome in 410 CE, the Visigoths infiltrated the Languedoc, halted some of their chariots near the Black Mountain, and conquered the fortified camp of Reda. The position of this oppidum was ideal. Laid out on the edge of a vast plateau that dominates the two valleys of the Aude in the north and La Sals in the south, it overlooked the two routes that link the Massif of the Corbières and the Pyrenees. Unassailable on three flanks, the entrenched camp was easily defended on the east side in front of the immense Lauzet plain where a large army could move. Louis Fédié explained, 'The Visigoths had learned the art of designing a camp from their Roman enemies and this style can be seen in Reda.' Thanks to its perfect strategic configuration, the town played an important role throughout history during numerous conflicts, first between the barbarians and then between the great lords in the Middle Ages. The fortified place survived the attacks under both Visigothic and Carolingian domination. 'It was the key route to Spain, invasion door for Muslim incursions. The presence of a large command there was increasingly necessary,' said René Descadeillas, librarian in Carcassonne, in a study on Rennes-le-Château and its last lords. In the 6th Century, the future land of the Cathars experienced its first religious war. The majority of the barbaric tribes practiced Aryanism, the schismatic doctrine originating from the East and stemming from Christianity. Around 323 CE, the heresiarch priest Arianus had contested the divinity of the Word. For him, the Son of God was a secondary and subordinate divinity. The Alexandrian priest was excommunicated for his beliefs but won many supporters to his preaching.

In a few years, the entire Orient was burning. During the 4th Century, the Goths embraced Christianity from their Aryan preachers. When they conquered the Occident, the schism seemed more alive than ever. Then there was the sudden conversion of Clovis. The King of the Franks found that he had the soul of a conqueror and, hiding his great thirst for power behind the pretext of a holy war, crushed the Visigoths at the battle of Vouillé in 507 CE. Clovis took Toulouse but Carcassonne was spared, thanks to the intervention of Theodoric, King of the Ostrogoths in Italy. As Alaric II, King of the Visigoths, had been killed at battle, Theodoric assumed the regency until the young Prince Amalaric, his grandson, was old enough to govern. The holy war only ended with the marriage of Amalaric to Princess Clothilde, Clovis' daughter.

The beaten Visigoths were driven back towards Spain. However, as well as Roussillon, they managed to retain a portion of the Gallia Narbonensis that included Narbonne, Carcassonne, and Reda, which during the 6th Century became the county town of the diocese to which it gave its name, the Rhedesium, or Razès. Traces of this camp and fortified place are still visible today. Fédié related that, in 1878, whilst digging a trench for the building of a wall, an inhabitant of Rennes-le-Château discovered a large slab under which there were human bones. He also exhumed, 'remains of substratum spread underground, hook bricks, shards of pottery, and fragments of weapons that left no doubt as to the existence of a Visigothic city.'

In the 7th Century, the Franks invaded Narbonne again and the Visigothic domination was reduced solely to the Razès region. Reda became even more important. With its thirty thousands inhabitants, its convent, its churches and fortifications, it played the role of a capital nearly on a par with Toledo, Spanish heart of the Visigothic kingdom. Under the rule of Charlemagne, Theodulphe, who had been sent as missus dominicus with Leydrade, recognised the dominance of the city and classified it as one of the great centres of the "Septimanie" region, equal in importance to Narbonne and Carcassonne. The ancient Visigothic estate had become an earldom. At that time, Limoux was just an ordinary town, 'Castrum limosum in territorio redensi' wrote Pierre de Vaux-Cernai.

The Razès was first administered by provosts, under the ruling of the Visigothic kings, and then by counts, who were military governors appointed by the sovereign residing in Toledo. 'The Count was reporting directly either to the Crown or to the Dukes of Septimanie who had superior command over the province,' explained Fédié. Charlemagne nominated the first Count in 781 CE. A century later, the Razès was handed over to the County of Carcassonne. In the 11th Century, it was bequeathed to Raymond Béranger I, Count of Barcelona, by way of inheritance. Not for long though, as twenty years later, owing to the upheavals that shook the House of Barcelona, the nobility of the region, hostile to the domination of a foreign prince, rallied round the Count of Carcassonne.

However, in the 12th Century, Alphonse II, King of Aragon, objected to this affiliation to the County of Carcassonne and, during a battle against Raymond V of Toulouse in 1170, razed the city and destroyed the citadel's surrounding walls, leaving only the towers. In the 13th Century, the repression stemming from the Albigensian crusade led by Simon de Montfort was bloody. After taking the possessions of Raymond VI of Toulouse and of his vassals, he went up the Aude valley, and Reda was once more ransacked. In 1209, the young Raymond Roger, Viscount of Béziers and Razès, died whilst he was held prisoner by Simon de Montfort in one of the palace towers in Carcassonne. The war lasted twenty years. Raymond Trencavel, who was only two when his brother Roger died, could only reconquer his domain against Amaury de Montfort, son of Simon, in 1228. Finally, in a treaty with the king of France, the county of Razès was attached to the Crown.

After the Albigensian war, the lords of Voisins rebuilt the battlefield to protect the land from attacks by rovers and bandits that swarmed the region. Then, in 1362, furious about the armed resistance, the Catalan and Spanish invaders led by the Count of Trastamare, future King of Castile, attacked the city. Pierre III de Voisins, Lord of Reda, had taken refuge in the citadel. The Spanish army, or rather the large corps of bandits, ravaged the entire region. Louis Fédié related the disappearance of the city as follows. "A large troop of Catalan bandits from the Corbières area arrived one day in front of Rennes-le-Château. They had taken the path from the hamlet "des Patiassés" between Rennes-les-Bains and Rennes-le-Château. They looted and burned down the big fortified convent on the outskirts of the city; the ruins of this convent were still visible in the 18th Century. The city put up a fierce resistance but succumbed in the face of an enemy with superior forces and artillery. The powder keg of Sallasse installed in one of the towers spared by Alphonse of Aragon was set on fire, leaving a huge gap in the walls of the city. This provided easy access to the assailants who became masters of the place. They razed the fortifications, destroyed the Saint Pierre church and turned Reda into a pile of ruins." Centuries later, in the plain at the bottom of the village, one would find remnants of this tragedy in the form of weapon fragments and small-calibre cannonballs.

This is how there was hardly anything left of the ravaged city of Reda, when it entered the estate of the Hautpoul in the 15th Century through the marriage of Pierre de Hautpoul to Blanche de Marquefave. Closely packed around its seigniorial castle and its small church dedicated to Saint Magdalene dating from the 8th or 9th Century, Rennes-le-Château is now just a little village of two hundred inhabitants that dominates and contemplates the Castle of Lauzet and its surroundings.

MANNA FROM MULTIPLE SOURCES

'There is no doubt about the existence of a treasure in the Razès,' wrote Madeleine Blancasall in *Les descendants mérovingiens ou l'énigme du Razès wisigoth* (*The Merovingian Descendants or Enigma of Visigothic Razès*). She added, 'We can even estimate its importance at nineteen million five hundred thousand gold francs and twenty five million of large objects and gold nuggets. Despite the few penitents who tasted the manna, we believe that a few millions remain.' Following the death of Father Saunière, a statuette in solid gold and partially melted was discovered in a derelict shack not far from Rennes-le-Château, and it appeared that Bérenger Saunière had offered a very old chalice to one of his colleagues, parish priest of Saint-Paul de Fenouillet. The turbulent story of the Razès can lead to umpteen suppositions on the origins of the treasure.

One possibility was advanced in 1734 by Lamoignon de Basville, a bursar in Languedoc. He said that, 'In the past, the Romans exploited gold mines in these mountains,' and added, 'Either the mines have been exhausted or the art of finding them has been lost, and if there are any treasures, they are now so well hidden that one forgets to look for them.' Indeed, there were gold and silver mines in the region, notably in Blanchefort near the fortress that defended the outskirts of the citadel of Reda.

Some historians, but mostly researchers, believe that part of the treasure of Solomon is in Rennes-le-Château. This treasure, brought by the Visigoths after their sacking of Rome in 410 CE, included spoils of war that the Romans had accumulated through the centuries, together with the objects from the Temple of Solomon taken by Titus in 70 CE After the conquest of Languedoc, the Visigoths split the treasure and placed the kings' tributes and personal jewels in Toulouse. The ancient treasure, the fruit of battles and pillages across the centuries, the magical and sacred symbol of Visigothic supremacy was kept in Carcassonne. It comprised jewels and gold plates of Roman origin as well as precious objects seized by Titus in Jerusalem. When Languedoc was invaded again by the Franks in the 7th Century, part of the ancient treasure was taken to Toledo which was itself ransacked by the Saracens in 711 CE. But what happened to the other part of the treasure that was not transported to Toledo and, therefore, not found by the Franks or the Arabs? Everything leads us to believe that it was stored in the mountains surrounding Reda.

The Merovingian presence could be felt in the Razès at the beginning of the 6th Century, when nearly all of Gaul fell under the domination of Clovis, heir to Pharamond and Merovaeus, and the Visigoths succumbed under the Franks' heavy javelins. In 674 CE, a century and half later, Dagobert II (The Young), grandson of Dagobert I (Good King Dagobert), was called back to the throne by the powerful lords in conflict with Ebroïn, the new Mayor of the Palace. Prior to this, he had experienced the uncertain fate of many Merovingian princes before him who had seen the crown vacillate on their head several times during their existence. Dethroned at the beginning of his reign by the Mayor of the Palace of Grimoald, he had escaped death by a hair's breadth by taking refuge in an Irish monastery. From 674 CE, Dagobert II reigned in the kingdom of Austrasia for five years, during which he contemplated strengthening the power of the Franks in Aquitaine. With this goal in view, he gathered large spoils of war which he stored in the citadel of Reda, fortified stronghold par excellence. But the King did not have time to implement his plans of conquest as, in 679 CE, in the forest of Wœvre not far from Stenay, he fell and died in an ambush organised by Pépin de Herstal who had become the Mayor of the Palace of Austrasia a few months before.

Was the treasure recovered? There is no evidence of this.

But, what if the Arabs had buried some of their riches in the region? Crossing the Pyrenees at the beginning of the 8th Century, they started to diligently plunder castles, villages, churches, and convents in the South of France. Nowhere was spared. Around Poitiers, in 732 CE, they confronted the Franks rallied round Charles Martel, Mayor of the Palace to the Merovingian King, whose empire was in the north of France. Beaten, decimated and pursued without quarter, they surged back towards Spain. Did they take all their loot with them? There is no certainty about this. They may have felt compelled to abandon some of it in various places, like Reda and its surroundings near the Pyrenees. One cannot exclude the idea that amidst these riches was the old Visigothic treasure from Toledo seized by the Moors during the conquest of Spain which accompanied them in their march to the north. The "missorium", a dish in solid gold weighing five hundred pounds that the Roman General Aetius had offered to King Thorismond, was one of the most beautiful pieces of this treasure.

In the 12th Century, the Templars established two commanderies in the Razès, one in Bézu and one in Campagne-sur-Aude. At that time, Lord Bertrand de Blanchefort had been elected Grand Master of the Temple. Once settled, the Templars sent for workers from Germany and forbade them from entering into contact with the local population. In his work regarding the arrival of the Templars in the Bézu valley, Father Mazières explained that these foreign workers had been charged with the exploitation of the mine of Blanchefort. However, in his observations concerning the ore mines of France, published in 1667, the engineer César d'Arcous remarked that this mine had been exhausted by the Romans and that the German workers employed by the Templars were not so much miners as casters. Did the Order, who had the safeguard of the Temple of Jerusalem, discover the treasure of Solomon in Languedoc? Otherwise, what interest could they have in implying that the mine of Blanchefort could still be exploited? 'Therefore,' reckons Gérard de Sède, 'one understands better the oldest legend concerning Rennes-le-Château, whereby the gold did not come from a mine. Rather, it came from a Visigothic hoard.'

The treasure seems to protect those who possess it. In 1307, Philippe le Bel ordered the arrest of all Templars, except those of the Bézu commandery. A possible explanation to this exception points in the direction of Clément V, reigning Pope at that time, Bertrand de Goth by birth, son of Ida de Blanchefort, and a great nephew of Bertrand de Blanchefort...

Thirty years later, a rather shady business brought back a whiff of gold around Rennes-le-Château. In 1340, Guilhem Catala, Lord of Bézu, and three associates were accused of minting false coins on several occasions in the Bézu. Catala was the son-in-law of Jacques de Voisins, Lord of Rennes-le-Château where the commandery of the Templars of Bézu was settled. He also had a powerful ally in his uncle, Pope Benoît XII. So, making false coins was one way to dispose of the gold without revealing the existence of the treasure.

The hypothesis of a Catharist treasure has not been dismissed by researchers either. In 1243, Montségur, the last surviving citadel of the Cathars, was still resisting the Catholic troops. After a siege that had lasted five months, Pierre-Roger de Mirepoix, who commanded the place, asked to negotiate with Blanche de Castile. No other solution seemed conceivable since the Count of Toulouse, sensing the lost cause, was attempting a reconciliation with the Pope. During the night of 13th March, on the eve of surrender, three heretics, Hugo, Aicard and Poitevin, left the citadel secretly by sliding down the ramparts of the castle on a rope. Arnaud-Roger de Mirepoix related that the heretic church did not want to loose their treasure in the forest and the fugitives knew of the hiding-place. The escape of these three men was endangering the lives of the defenders of Montségur following the pact they had made with their besiegers, through which Pierre-Roger de Mirepoix was committed to hand over the indomitable Cathars to the Church.

But what was the nature of this treasure that had to be rescued at all costs? For Professor Ferdinand Niel, author of a study on the Cathars and more particularly Montségur, 'the fugitives did not preserve a material treasure, but rather a spiritual one, possibly in the form of written parchments containing the secrets of a religion that prevented its followers from fearing death at the stake.'

Nonetheless, two months prior to the escape of the above three fugitives, other heretics had hidden "some gold, silver and a large quantity of coins" in a fortified grotto. It is worth remembering, however, that the citadel of Montségur is less than forty kilometres from Rennes-le-Château as the crow flies.

Is the treasure temporal and originating from the Temple of Solomon, the Romans, the Visigoths, the Merovingians, the Moors, and the Templars, or is it both material and spiritual from the Cathars? The mythology of Rennes-le-Château does not stop here. The configuration of the soil predisposed the region to become the sanctuary for mysterious riches. Precious stones and metals such as amber, jet, iron, gold, silver and nitre testify of the richness of the Razès. 'The veins of these mountains are often polar,' wrote Gérard de Sède, 'that is, they are positioned in relation to the magnetic meridian line.'

Thus, the location of Rennes-les-Bains, on the Parisian meridian line (red line), provoked some bold speculations wondering whether the treasure of the Razès could also be of alchemical origin. Sometimes, in Rennes-les-Bains, the springs secrete a little bitumen and, as Father Delmas related in a manuscript dating from 1707, 'From time to time, mercury is released from the bath waters from which one can derive the alkali mineral salt, the real nitre of the alchemists.'

Choosing from among all these hypotheses is not an easy task. However, we have every reason to believe that at least part of the treasure of Rennes-le-Château is of Visigothic origin. This is the source from which Bérenger Saunière drew his information. The proof of this exists in Switzerland...

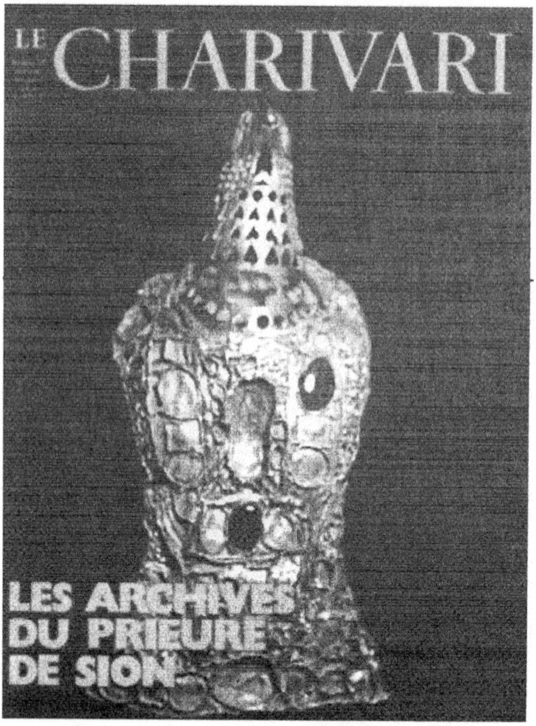

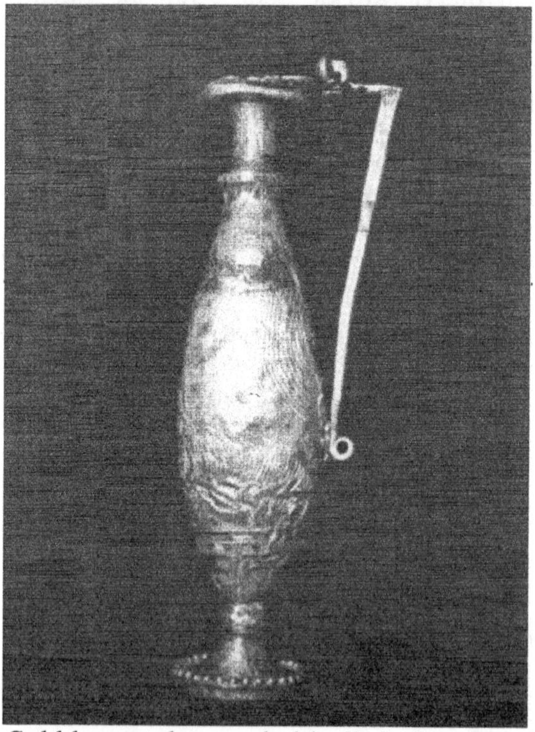
12 - Gold breastplate and chiselled silver amphora

13 - Shield-like silver plate and silver and gold goblet

14 - Gold necklace and solid gold “Catino Sacro”

The Treasure Exists

We Have Seen It, Says Jean-Luc Chaumeil

The car was moving at an average speed through the streets of Geneva. The two men, who had met my train from Paris, were staring at the road without a word. I was silent too, seized by the intense excitement that overwhelms one when approaching a long coveted goal. We were heading towards the treasure discovered by Father Saunière in Rennes-le-Château, sold by him, and now safeguarded in Switzerland in a place inaccessible to the public.

After leaving the Eaux-Vives area, the car went past the cathedral Saint-Pierre towards the Mont-Blanc Bridge, and arrived in front of the Notre-Dame church where it stopped. A third man, quite old, boarded the vehicle which set off again. Looking at the lake with the thin droplets of water falling from the immense fountain that covers it like a transparent bouquet, I suddenly felt we were going back in time.

Once more, the car stopped for a few moments in front of the Temple Saint-Gervais. Someone in the street waved at us; we set off again and left the city. I wanted to know where we were going. 'Dornach,' the man next to me replied laconically, in a slight German accent.

Dornach is a little town of some five thousand inhabitants not far from Basel. I knew that, in a verdant hilly setting four or five kilometres from the town, there was a philosophical, or rather theosophical, temple christened 'Goetheanum'. Founded in 1919 by Steiner, the temple had been built originally in wood for the followers of Goethe. Subsequently, various workshops appeared all around, literally encircling the temple. Shortly after its completion, the theosophists had coated it with a thin layer of beeswax which made it shine like the Sun. The Goetheanum became the meeting place of the "Companions and Sages of the Light". In 1927, the temple burnt down under mysterious circumstances. Not without reason, the members of an opposing society were accused of its destruction. In 1930, the Goetheanum was rebuilt in concrete. The influence of its philosophical circle spread across Europe. Since then, the Freemasons belonging to the Reformed Scottish Church meet each year at the Goetheanum festival where the Companions perform Goethe's *Faust*, in the new temple, in memory of Master Steiner.

We arrived in Dornach. Very soon after, the Goetheanum appeared in my line of vision. The monument struck me first by the oddity of its architecture where one could not see a single right angle. The building and surrounding villas were covered in sculptures representing various ancient figures, sometimes an ox, similar to the one in the Chartres cathedral, sometimes a goad, a "third eye", a head, a door, or the waves, symbolising both the water and superior Aether.

In Geneva, I had met an American archaeologist introduced to me as one of the people in charge of the Art School in the United States who was also on the trail of Father Saunière's jewels and gold plates. He was waiting for us at the door of the Goetheanum and came forward to greet us. The man was tall, with a pale complexion and refined smile. We entered the temple with him briefly as this was only a stop on our journey. Then, the American archaeologist joined us in the car and we set off back towards Geneva. I was at a loss and asked several questions. Someone replied with a quotation from Plato. 'The one who, through the mysteries of love, will have elevated himself or herself to the point we have now reached, having observed the beautiful at all levels and in the right order, will, at the end of the initiation, discover a stupendous beauty, that which was the aim of all his former efforts. Eternal, imperishable and uncreated beauty, exempt of expansion or reduction... Oh, dear Socrates, if something makes this life valuable, it is the contemplation of this absolute beauty.' After Plato, came a quotation from Goethe 'If in the flame of each lamp you recognise piously the reflection of a superior light, no misfortune will ever forbid you from celebrating the throne of God at dawn. There lies the imperial stamp of our life, the pure mirror of God for us and the angels. Anything that utters the praises of the Almighty is encompassed here in concentric circles...'

Quotation after quotation, and meditation after meditation, we had travelled some distance during which Switzerland had unfolded its panorama of mountains. We were now south of Cau, eighty kilometres from Geneva, on one of the Liboson slopes near the Roche de Noye. And, as in Dornach, a strange villa with no right angles appeared in front of our eyes. Visiting the building was not a simple affair. We had to wait a long time, show our credentials and answer many questions. It looked like some ritual elaborated by a society of initiates anxious to preserve their secrets during which I tried to remain silent, observing things in the background. However, my turn came and I had to participate in the game of questions and answers, displaying a patience that was more forced than real.

Eventually, we were authorised to enter the grounds. The gardens were strangely laid out with external spiralling stairs leading to the villa. The architecture of the building had been developed with great care and rigour. We were in another world. A little bell by a small door rang in the silence and a nonchalant man appeared. We watched him approach with measured steps. He uttered, 'Do visit', whilst opening another gate, and left. My four comrades let me go first. I saw a path to the right which I followed. We were walking in single file, one after another, without a word. An incredible labyrinth led to the actual entrance of the villa, an ingenious maze through which one had to find the way, and I suddenly thought about those at fun fairs and at the Zoological Gardens in Paris. Eventually, I found the exit. A door, with a large Greek tau cross that divided it into two equal parts, appeared in front of me. On the left side there was a carved ox with a goad at its feet. On the right, there was a strange head with a single eye. Its resemblance to that in the cemetery of Rennes-les-Bains struck me. I paused at the doorstep. What dream was I living? Behind me, my companions were watching in a wry manner. I finally pushed the door.

The villa was extremely beautiful. In the hearth was a sphinx with a gaze fixed forever on eternity. There were some old tools from an ancient forge in a recess with the sun illuminating the anvil through a loophole. A chessboard rested on black and white goat skins. At the back of the room, a wide picture window overlooked Lake Geneva. A certain peace impregnated the room thanks to the light reverberating from the water. I heard a noise. Blue velvet curtains were drawn back and the man who opened the gate to the gardens reappeared. He smiled, approached the chessboard and invited me to join him. We started to play... After a while, the American archaeologist intervened and asked to see "things". We headed towards a door which opened to a staircase spiralling downwards. I counted eighty four steps on the way down and estimated that the staircase went some fifteen metres underground. It led to a strongroom where gold and silver objects of extreme value were exhibited in small, well-lit niches. Jewels, plates and other items discovered by Father Saunière in Rennes-le-Château were amongst the pieces on display.

I stopped first in front of a small gold breastplate, embellished with polychrome inlays, and extended by a helmet resembling an eagle's head. It was probably an ornamental object. There seemed to be no doubt about its Visigothic origin, although our host explained that a similar piece was found in the treasure from the Goths excavated in 1857 in Petroassa, a village near Ploesti in Romania.

The second piece that drew my attention was a silver amphora, very finely chiselled, with a picture of a lis or an olive branch at its base.

Then, I contemplated the "catino sacro" or dish of the seven initiates. This solid gold object was about ninety centimetres in diameter. It displayed sixteen persons around a seated king holding a goblet, perhaps the one from the Eleusinian mysteries. At the king's feet, there were mythological animals and legendary fishes from left to right, and mystical individuals from right to left. The third circle exhibited vine branches evoking the eternal vine and Colchis grapes. The first character was a woman holding a sacred lyre. To her right, a man draped in a Roman toga seemed to listen to the musical notes. Another woman appeared to bless him with her hand and through this action confer on him the title of "Prince of Music". The other individuals of the "catino" were in various postures. One of them held a harp. Another contemplated the woman with the lyre whilst leaning slightly on his neighbour. Another admired the vase held by the woman next to him. The twelfth person resembled a warrior prince dressed in a coat of mail who was staring at the devilish-looking fourteenth character. We were in front of a Gallo-Roman object, probably seized by the Visigoths during one of their campaigns in Gaul.

Five-petal flowers were finely engraved at the base and top of a finely chiselled silver ewer of the same origin.

A shield-like silver plate constituted the fifth item in the collection. Also Gallo-Roman, it was ridged on its circumference which was partially broken and displayed several rings encircling a sun at its centre.

The sixth recess contained a gold necklace, probably from a Visigothic princess, embellished with rubies set in the polychrome style favoured by the Celts and Germans which I had noticed on the breastplate.

The seventh and eighth niches accommodated two silver and gold goblets, similar to those of the Visigothic treasure found in Petroassa. Each goblet was rather round in shape and fitted with handles representing legendary cheetahs stretching their necks towards the inside of the receptacle. The middle area was adorned in a polychrome style with eight-petal flowers that looked like circles interspersed by square alveoli, probably home to precious stones in the past.

So there was, at least in part. The treasure discovered by Father Saunière in Rennes-le-Château, sold by him to various intermediaries, notably the Parisian bank Petitjean, and now safeguarded in this villa full of mystery. The Razès enigma was somehow resolved, as it was indeed the Visigoths who had entrusted some of their personal treasures to the Languedoc area, together with those seized during their belligerent peregrinations throughout Europe, including Rome.

But I was not at the end of my surprises. I was on the point to leave, after having contemplated once more the gold objects and precious stones excavated by Bérenger Saunière, when my eye caught sight of a gold ingot amazingly protected. As well as the bars that prevented one from touching it, an alarm system linked to an electronic camera set off as soon as one came within fifty centimetres of the display window. Questioned about this, our host explained that it was an alchemical gold ingot.

Then, I remembered what the marquis Philippe de Cherisey had told me regarding Nicolas Flamel and his relationship with the Razès region... The marquis, Count of Vaudressel and descendant from a noble family in the Belgian Ardennes recounts, in one of his works entitled Circuit, the story of high esoteric places in France and talks about Gisors and Rennes-le-Château at great length. Cherisey explains, for instance, that Rennes-le-Château had not only been on the great migratory route of the first millennium, but also on the road that led the pilgrims to Santiago de Compostela. During one of my visits to his home, rue des Célestines in Liège, he told me that, "In the 14th Century, the pilgrimage to Santiago de Compostela, as well as the activities of Nicolas Flamel, were subsidised by Queen Blanche d'Evreux, who devoted her time to alchemy in the tower of Neaufles not far from Gisors. The widely-known route to Santiago de Compostela was the western road that crossed the Aquitaine and the Basque regions. But there was also an eastern road with stopovers in towns like Vézelay and Rennes-le-Château. I have good reason to believe that this route was the one followed by Nicolas Flamel for his pilgrimage, during which, after several years of fruitless research, the secret of the philosopher's stone was revealed to him."

Whilst contemplating the mysterious ingot that shone in its velvety niche, a phantasmagorical hypothesis crossed my mind whereby the sacred trust of Rennes-le-Château could have been increased through the centuries by a line of alchemists. In which case, the ingot in front of my eyes would belong to this stash.

Indeed, despite the discoveries made by Father Saunière, the enigma of the Razès is far from being resolved...

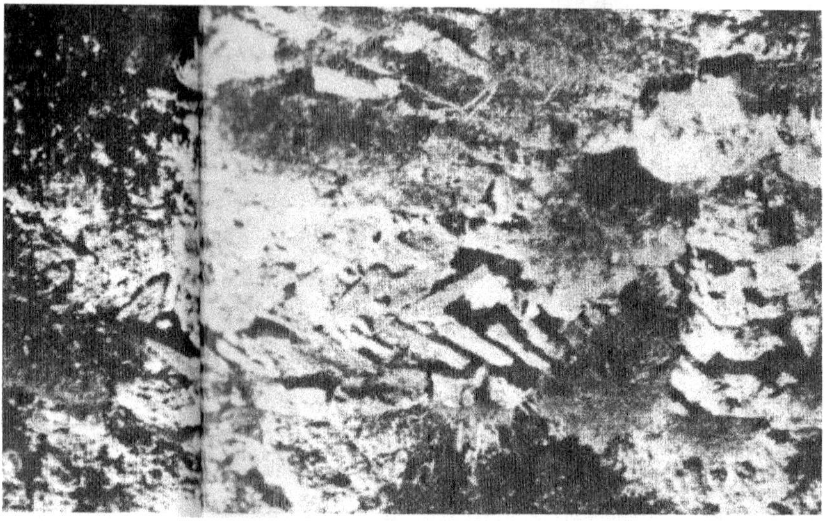
15 - Ruins of the Castle of Albedun

In Search Of Reda

Reda, the ancient capital of the Visigoths, was probably not on the site of Rennes-le-Château, but a few kilometres away in a locality known as "les Tipliès", or "Castle of the Templars", about two kilometres from Saint-Just-du-Bézu. This is the conviction of Professor. Ferdinand Niel, author of several essays on the Cathars and Montségur. Amongst the documents he consulted whilst climbing the Serbairou slopes and Cardou hillsides, was an ancient military map dating from 1830 with the inscription "ruins of Albedun" for a spot near Saint-Just-du-Bézu. This was described on a 1964 map as the "Castle of the Templars". For Mr. Niel, this is an erroneous interpretation as he believes the ancient ruins buried in the undergrowth are not those of the Templars' fortress, but rather those of Reda, the old and mysterious capital of the Visigoths. 'In Rennes-le-Château,' he says, 'it is difficult to discover anything that is reminiscent of the ancient capital. This is not the case for Albedun. During the study of the ground, I discovered vestiges of three concentric surrounding walls. In fact, several local historians had pointed out before me that the position of the ancient Reda was at the "Castle of Bézu" called "Castle of Albedun" in 1830. The ruins of Albedun carry the Visigothic imprint unquestionably.'

In 1950, Mr. Niel brought back four photographs taken by him at the presumed spot of the ancient Reda. Although vegetation has invaded the ruins, these photographic documents are sufficiently sharp for his theory to be convincing. One can discern blocks of cyclopean stone which, quite obviously, have nothing to do with the low walls local farmers usually erect to contain the cultivated grounds. 'At Albedun,' explains Mr. Niel, 'I have seen remnants of herringbone-patterned walls, very clear and very distinct. Whilst it is quite probable that Gallo-Roman engineers invented this type of architecture, it is also true that it was applied during the Visigothic era. With the help of a few hundred youngsters close to nature and not work-shy, it would be possible to clear the area. One would then see, emerging from the ground, a memento of old Reda, where some thirty thousand souls lived long ago. With regard to Rennes-le-Château, Mr. Niel says, 'I do not believe that the Visigoths possessed an exceptional treasure of their own but it is certain that they pillaged the treasure of Rome. Not far from Carcassonne, a few kilometres from Lusignan, there is a place called the "Mountain of Alaric". The locals, when they evoke the treasure found by Father Saunière, often utter in Occitan the saying, "Entre l'Alaric et l'Alaricou, hay la fortuna de tres reis", which means, "Between the Large Mount Alaric and the Little Mount Alaric, lies the fortune of three kings...". This tradition has not been maintained without reason in Languedoc, and it is probable that if Father Saunière did find a treasure, it was that of the Visigoths.'

The Archives Of The Priory Of Sion And The Genealogy Of The Merovingians

Amongst the parchments discovered by Father Saunière, later decoded by the abbots of Saint-Sulpice, there was an intriguing genealogy starting with the Tribe of Benjamin right up to the Merovingian kings. Henri Lobineau, or using his real name André Schidloff, completed this genealogy with information gathered from two folio volumes by Father Denyau dating from 1629 and various other documents written by Father Pichon in 1814, Doctor Hervé in 1843, G. Dubreuil in 1857 and the genealogist Hamberg in 1912.

The following were found amidst these works:

- the family tree of the counts of Bar from 850 to 1200 and from 1200 to 1500
- the family tree of the dukes of Bar and of Lorraine from 1500 to 1800
- the family trees of Merovaeus to Dagobert I from 400 to 600 and of Dagobert I to Bera V (from the Plant-Ard and counts of Razès) from 600 to 900
- the family tree of Bera V to Jean VI (the branches of Poher, Planta, Plant-Amor and Godefroy) from 900 to 1200 with proof of the Merovingian origin of Godefroy VI de Bouillon, King of Jerusalem
- the family tree of the counts of Boulogne and of Bouillon from 770 to 1100
- the family tree of Jean VI to Jean XV (the branches of Plant-Avit, Plant-Ade, and Plantard in Switzerland) from 1100 to 1600
- the family tree of the Gisors, Guitry, Mareuil, Saint-Clair, from 950 to 1600
- the origin of the lineage of Lusignan and Eix, including the famous kings of Cyprus
- the family tree of the Blancheforts

The first parchment that grasped our attention was one concerning the family tree from Merovaeus to Dagobert I. To follow tradition, according to Lobineau, one must go back to the beginning of Canaan and Benjamin. One day, some descendants of Benjamin left Palestine. Two thousand years later, one of these descendants, Godefroy VI became King of Jerusalem and founded the Order of Sion. By the return of the exiles' descendant to the Promised Land, the cycle was completed. A marvellous tale, the mystery of which is symbolised in Poussin's painting "The Shepherds of Arcadia".

Thus, some two thousand years before our Common Era, the Hebrews discovered the Promised Land and settled in the country of Canaan. In the Bible, *Deuteronomy 33*, it is said about Benjamin, twelfth son of Jacob, "The beloved of the Lord shall dwell in safety by him; and the Lord shall cover him always and he shall dwell between his shoulders". It is also said in *Joshua 18* that the territories given to the sons of Benjamin included, among others, Jebus (or Jerusalem) and three locations forming a triangle, namely Golgotha, Sion and Bethany. Finally, it is stated in *Judges 21* that, "None of us shall give his daughter in marriage to a Benjamin" and "O Lord, the God of Israel, why has this come to pass that there should be today one tribe lacking in Israel?"

From Merovaeus to Clovis, the kings of the Franks were pagans, worshiping Diana with her nine-flamed torch (Ardennes). Diana was the goddess who killed the female bear Callisto, daughter of Lycaon, King of Arcadia; this is why the kings of the Sicambrians were called the "Ursus". The Sicambrians, according to the secret tradition as related by Lobineau, arrived one day in Arcadia. After long migrations, the king of the Sicambrians decided to establish his kingdom in Germany. In the Middle Rhine, the Sicambrians faced the Roman General Claudius Nero Drusus, Augustus' son by adoption. Defeated, some of them were deported to the Belgo-Gallic region which later became Austrasia. The long-haired kings of the Sicambrian race were "enchanters", that is initiates. Their crimson banner with two bears tied to a gold elm demonstrated their origin and doctrine at the same time. Bishop Saint Remy's address to Clovis, 'Lower you head, proud Sicambrian,' before he poured the baptismal water over the head of the king of the Franks, is, therefore, very significant. It was not only the ruler of a powerful Germanic tribe that the Church of Gaul appointed as its secular arm, taking him therefore into the Christian family, but the king also priest, the wise man leader of nations, crowned with a divine "aura", like the Egyptian pharaohs before him and the Incas of Peru after him. In 378 CE, the Romans took advantage of the death of Marcomir V, thirty-ninth king of the Sicambrian dynasty, to abolish their monarchy. However, with the end of the Occidental Empire, the

Sicambrians were able to raise their head. Clovis conquered Gaul to his own benefit and imposed his law on all who, like the Roman Syagrius, tried to contest it. The Frankish monarchy lasted two centuries. In 656 CE, Dagobert II, grandson of the "Good King Dagobert", succeeded the throne; he was dethroned by Grimoald, the Mayor of the Palace, very soon after, to be reinstated on the throne in 674 CE. Five years later, he fell and died in an ambush in the forest of Stenay. Officially, his son Sigebert was killed with him. This is disputed by Lobineau who declares that Sigebert was saved from the massacre and taken, together with his sister Rathilde, to their grandfather Bera II, Count of Razès, in the county's capital Reda, where Dagobert II had already taken an important treasure for the future conquest of Aquitaine. In 877 CE, Sigebert VI, known as "Prince Ursus", lost his county in a conspiracy against Louis II "Le Bègue" (The Stutterer). Defeated at Poitiers in 881 CE, he fled to Brittany where he died in 884. Guillemon II, his son, buried his father in a monastery in Redon. Between 894 CE and 896 CE, he married his daughter to Arnauld, Count of Poher, under the reign of Alain le Grand, King of Brittany. In 914 CE, the family took refuge in England and a new branch started under the name of Planta. Their return to Brittany was celebrated in 939 CE. Bera VI had become an architect in England and his descendants continued the practice. In the 17th Century, only peasants remained from this sovereign family. The youngest brothers took the Plant-Ard title reserved until then to their eldest; Plant-Ard meaning "rejeton ardent" or ardent kid. The Plantard family originally from Reda are, therefore, the descendants and heirs of Sigebert. On 11th July 1659, on the orders of Mazarin, troops conquered the duchy of Nevers and set fire to the Castle of the Barbary in Nièvre, resulting in the Plantard family losing all their possessions.

Genealogy Of The Merovingians

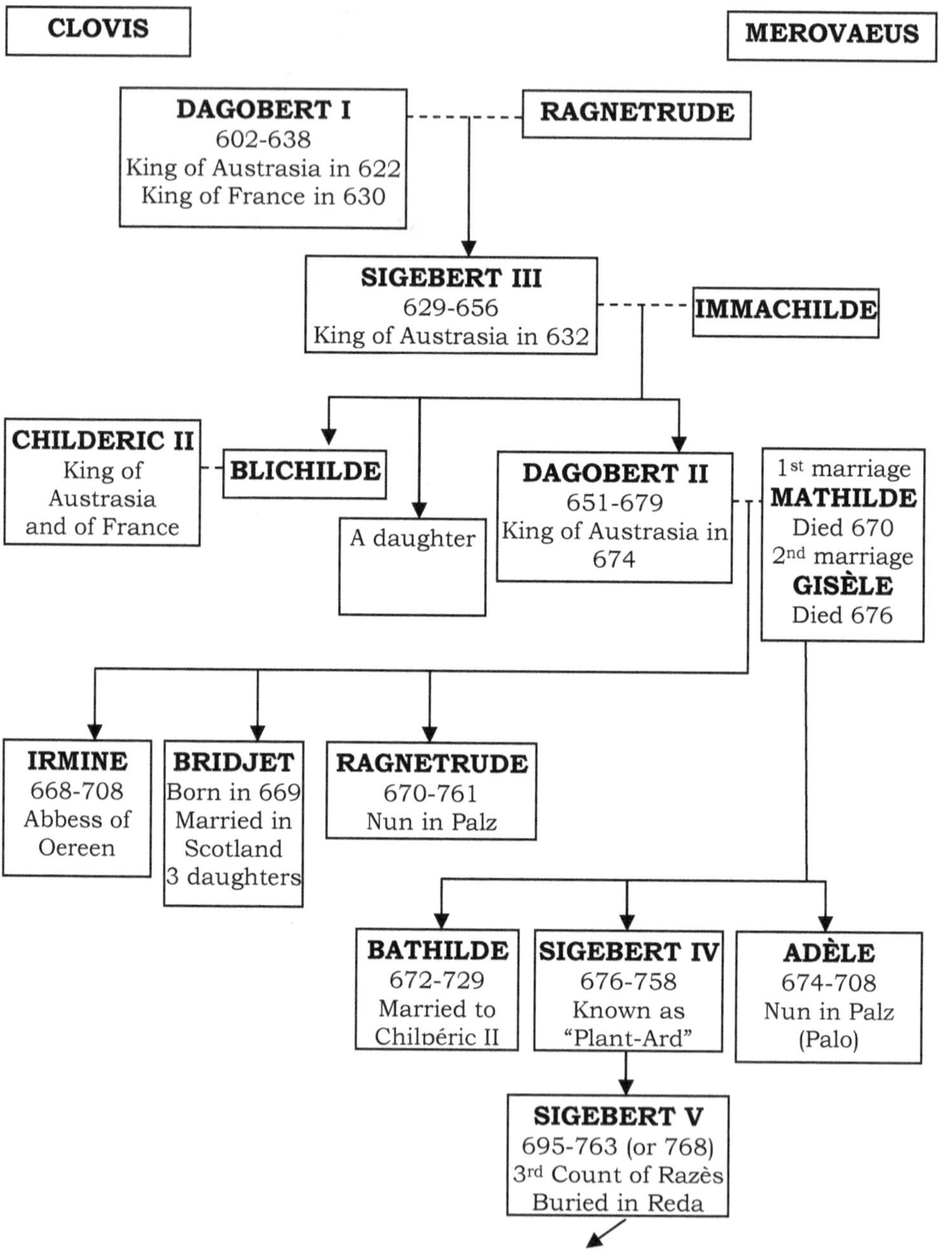
CLOVIS
MEROVAEUS
DAGOBERT I
602-638
King of Austrasia in 622
King of France in 630
RAGNETRUDE
SIGEBERT III
629-656
King of Austrasia in 632
IMMACHILDE
CHILDERIC II
King of Austrasia and of France
BLICHILDE
A daughter
DAGOBERT II
651-679
King of Austrasia in 674
1st marriage
MATHILDE
Died 670
2nd marriage
GISÈLE
Died 676
IRMINE
668-708
Abbess of Oereen
BRIDJET
Born in 669
Married in Scotland
3 daughters
RAGNETRUDE
670-761
Nun in Palz
BATHILDE
672-729
Married to Chilpéric II
SIGEBERT IV
676-758
Known as "Plant-Ard"
ADÈLE
674-708
Nun in Palz (Palo)
SIGEBERT V
695-763 (or 768)
3rd Count of Razès
Buried in Reda

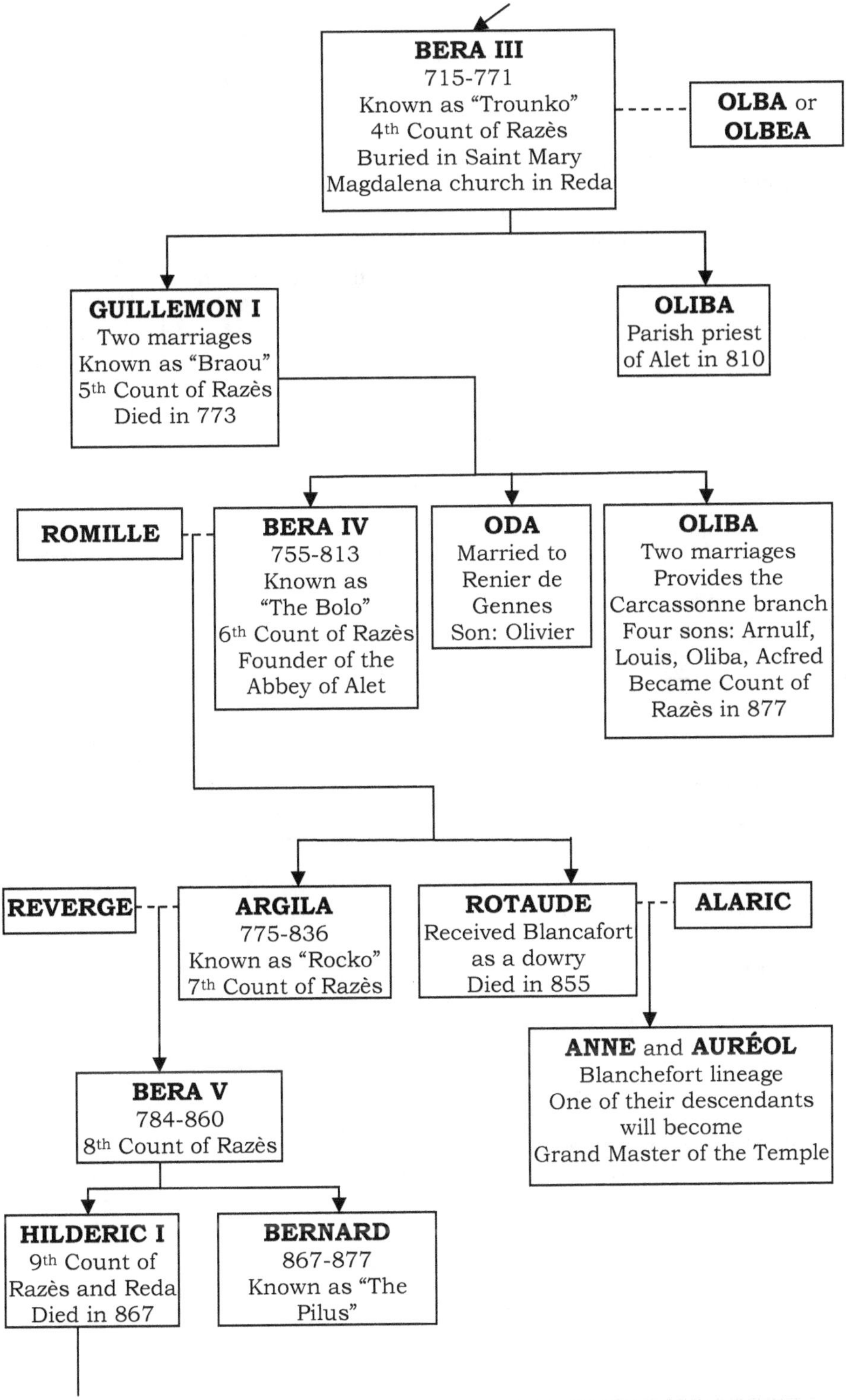
BERA III
715-771
Known as "Trounko"
4th Count of Razès
Buried in Saint Mary
Magdalena church in Reda
OLBA or
OLBEA
GUILLEMON I
Two marriages
Known as "Braou"
5th Count of Razès
Died in 773
OLIBA
Parish priest
of Alet in 810
ROMILLE
BERA IV
755-813
Known as
"The Bolo"
6th Count of Razès
Founder of the
Abbey of Alet
ODA
Married to
Renier de
Gennes
Son: Olivier
OLIBA
Two marriages
Provides the
Carcassonne branch
Four sons: Arnulf,
Louis, Oliba, Acfred
Became Count of
Razès in 877
REVERGE
ARGILA
775-836
Known as "Rocko"
7th Count of Razès
ROTAUDE
Received Blancafort
as a dowry
Died in 855
ALARIC
ANNE and AURÉOL
Blanchefort lineage
One of their descendants
will become
Grand Master of the Temple
BERA V
784-860
8th Count of Razès
HILDERIC I
9th Count of
Razès and Reda
Died in 867
BERNARD
867-877
Known as "The
Pilus"

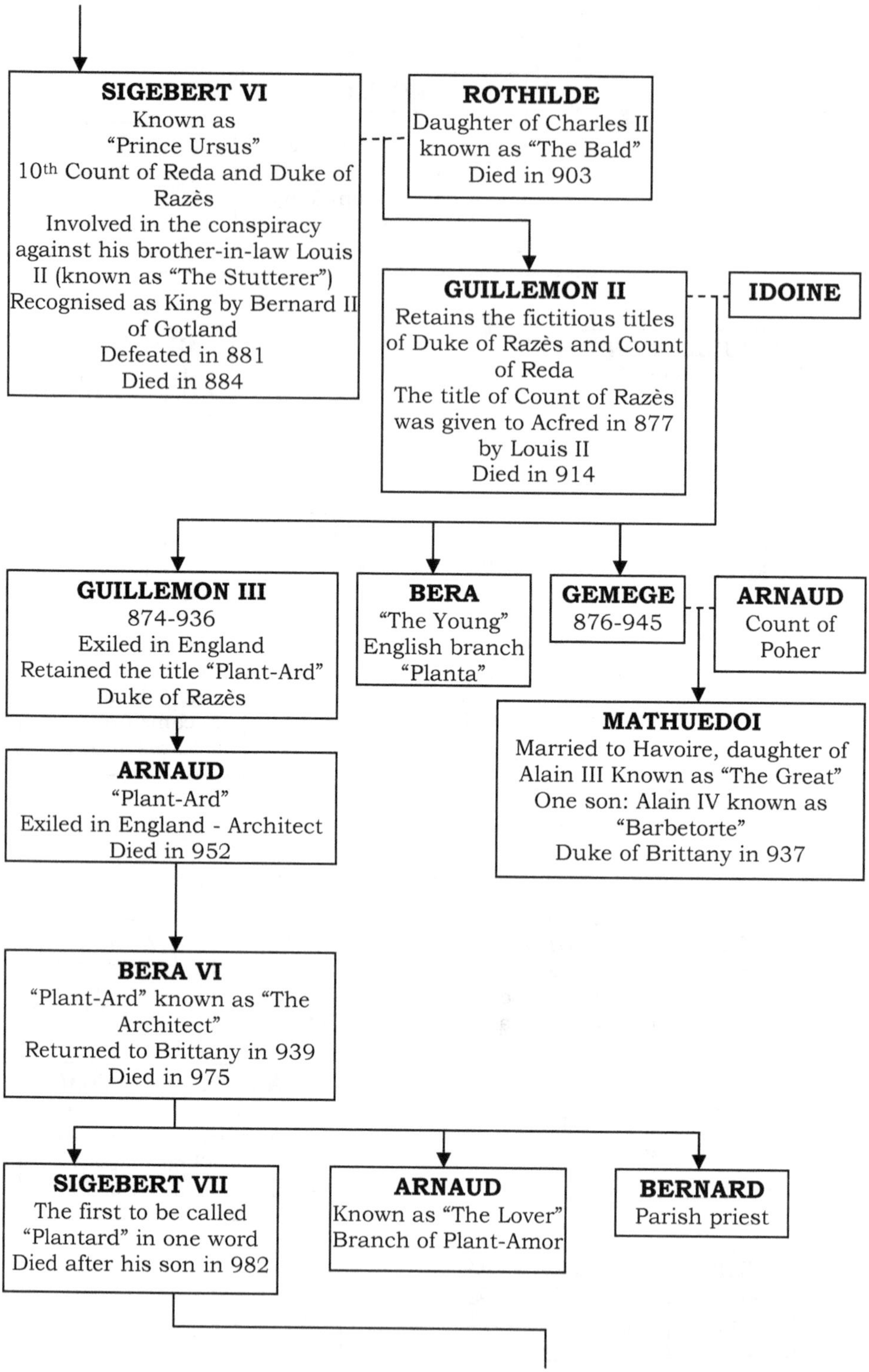
SIGEBERT VI
Known as
"Prince Ursus"
10th Count of Reda and Duke of Razès
Involved in the conspiracy against his brother-in-law Louis II (known as "The Stutterer")
Recognised as King by Bernard II of Gotland
Defeated in 881
Died in 884
ROTHILDE
Daughter of Charles II known as "The Bald"
Died in 903
GUILLEMON II
Retains the fictitious titles of Duke of Razès and Count of Reda
The title of Count of Razès was given to Acfred in 877 by Louis II
Died in 914
IDOINE
GUILLEMON III
874-936
Exiled in England
Retained the title "Plant-Ard"
Duke of Razès
BERA
"The Young"
English branch
"Planta"
GEMEGE
876-945
ARNAUD
Count of Poher
MATHUEDOI
Married to Havoire, daughter of Alain III Known as "The Great"
One son: Alain IV known as "Barbetorte"
Duke of Brittany in 937
ARNAUD
"Plant-Ard"
Exiled in England - Architect
Died in 952
BERA VI
"Plant-Ard" known as "The Architect"
Returned to Brittany in 939
Died in 975
SIGEBERT VII
The first to be called "Plantard" in one word
Died after his son in 982
ARNAUD
Known as "The Lover"
Branch of Plant-Amor
BERNARD
Parish priest

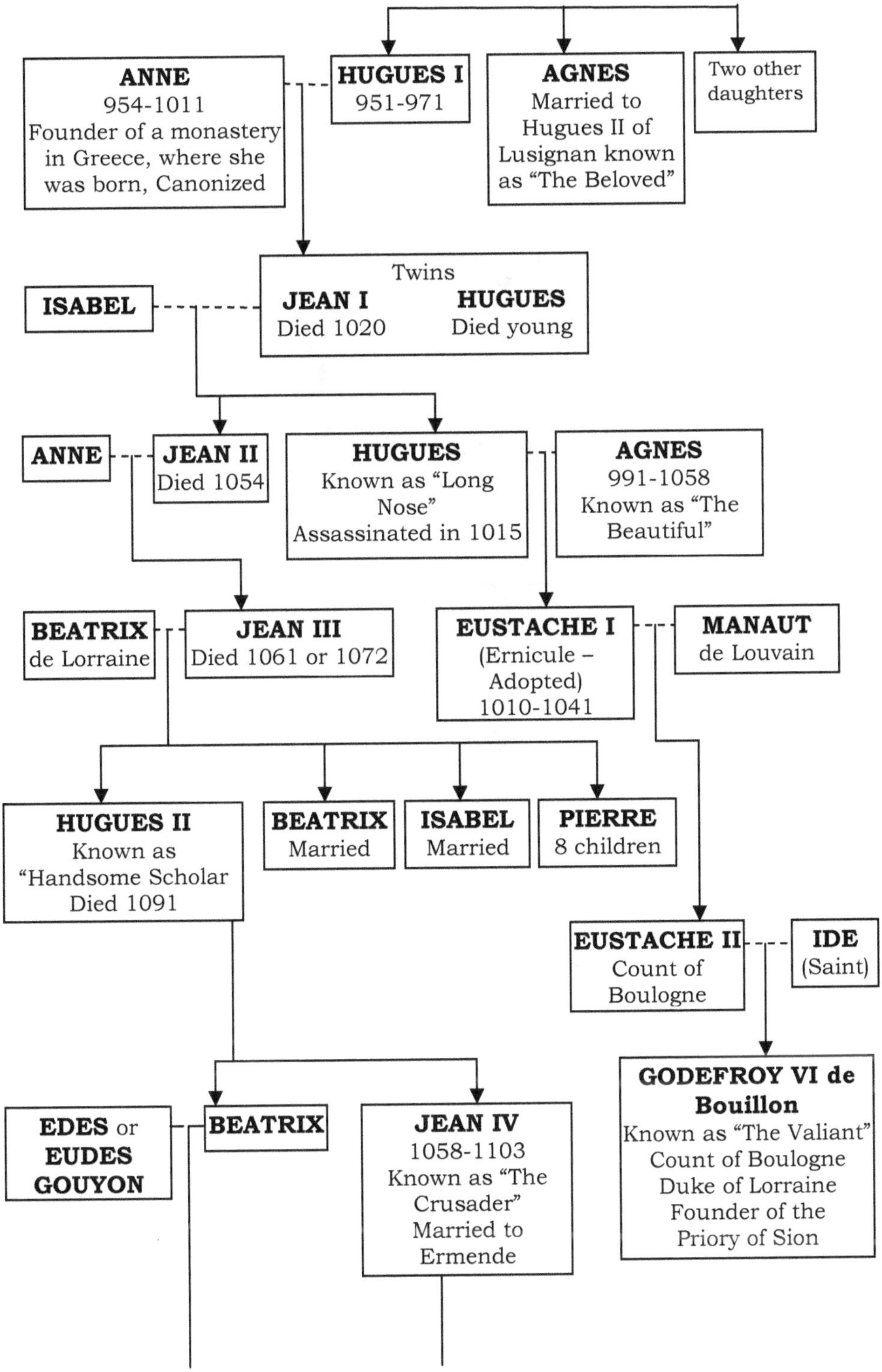
ANNE
954-1011
Founder of a monastery in Greece, where she was born, Canonized
HUGUES I
951-971
AGNES
Married to Hugues II of Lusignan known as "The Beloved"
Two other daughters
ISABEL
Twins
JEAN I
Died 1020
HUGUES
Died young
ANNE
JEAN II
Died 1054
HUGUES
Known as "Long Nose"
Assassinated in 1015
AGNES
991-1058
Known as "The Beautiful"
BEATRIX
de Lorraine
JEAN III
Died 1061 or 1072
EUSTACHE I
(Ernicule – Adopted)
1010-1041
MANAUT
de Louvain
HUGUES II
Known as "Handsome Scholar
Died 1091
BEATRIX
Married
ISABEL
Married
PIERRE
8 children
EUSTACHE II
Count of Boulogne
IDE
(Saint)
EDES or EUDES GOUYON
BEATRIX
JEAN IV
1058-1103
Known as "The Crusader"
Married to Ermende
GODEFROY VI de Bouillon
Known as "The Valiant"
Count of Boulogne
Duke of Lorraine
Founder of the Priory of Sion

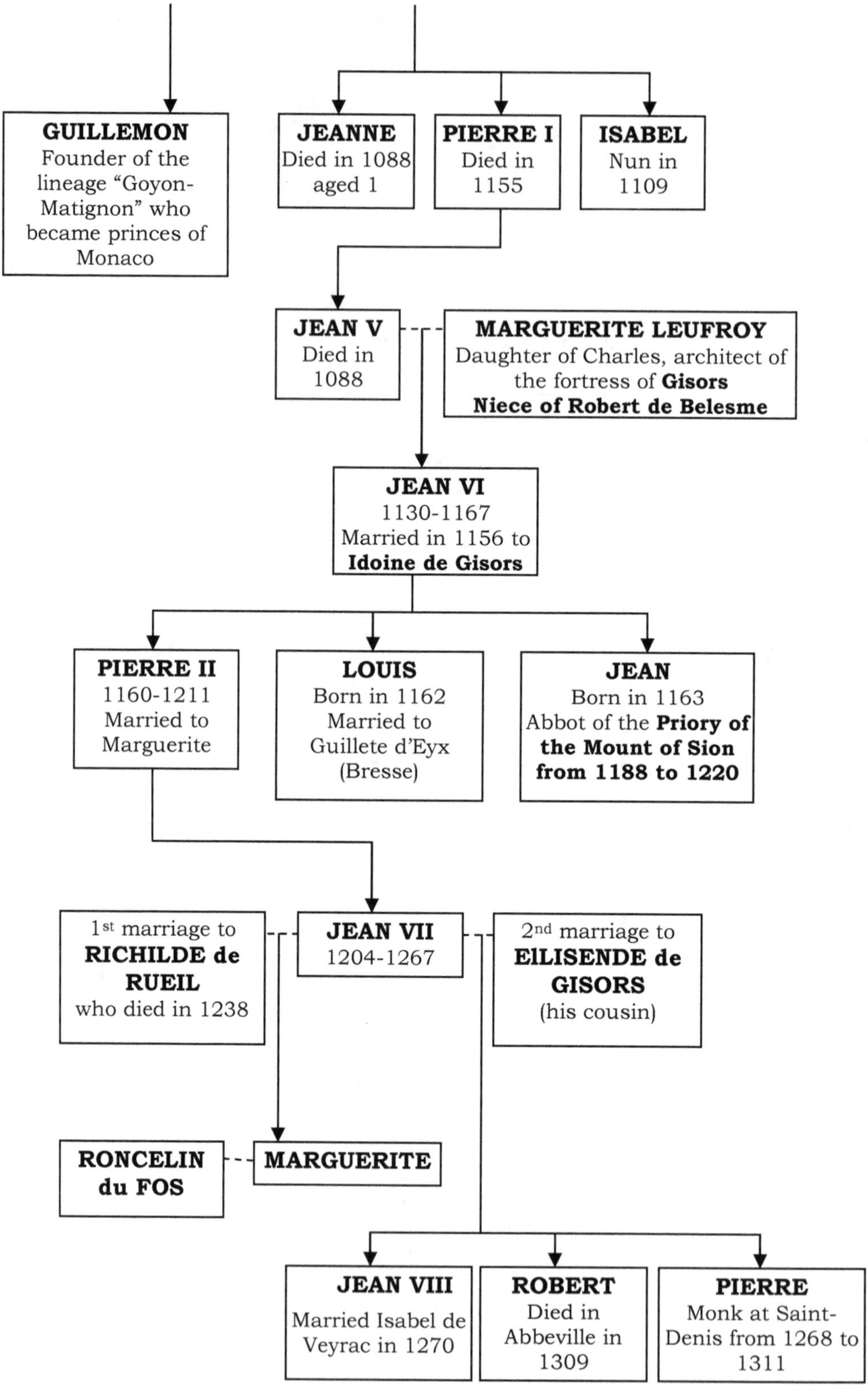
GUILLEMON
Founder of the lineage "Goyon-Matignon" who became princes of Monaco
JEANNE
Died in 1088 aged 1
PIERRE I
Died in 1155
ISABEL
Nun in 1109
JEAN V
Died in 1088
MARGUERITE LEUFROY
Daughter of Charles, architect of the fortress of Gisors
Niece of Robert de Belesme
JEAN VI
1130-1167
Married in 1156 to Idoine de Gisors
PIERRE II
1160-1211
Married to Marguerite
LOUIS
Born in 1162
Married to Guillete d'Eyx (Bresse)
JEAN
Born in 1163
Abbot of the Priory of the Mount of Sion from 1188 to 1220
1st marriage to RICHILDE de RUEIL who died in 1238
JEAN VII
1204-1267
2nd marriage to ElLISENDE de GISORS (his cousin)
RONCELIN du FOS
MARGUERITE
JEAN VIII
Married Isabel de Veyrac in 1270
ROBERT
Died in Abbeville in 1309
PIERRE
Monk at Saint-Denis from 1268 to 1311

In The Shadow Of Reda: An Amazing Tale

At the end of 1972, we were once again in Rennes-le-Château, interrogating the stones and contemplating the hills that had seen the grandeur and downfall of old Reda. One evening at the Hotel de la Tour, an astonishing dialogue took place between Mr. Buthion, the owner, and Mr. Arrache, one of his friends, regarding Reda, the Merovingians, and Father Saunière. Below is the essential content of their conversation.

749 years after the foundation of Rome, the long-awaited Jesus Christ was born in a manger in the province of Judea. At the age of thirty, he professed Moses' Law to the utmost perfection and proclaimed, 'Since my people do not recognize me, I shall choose another people and another nation.' At thirty-three, he died to save mankind from eternal death and shed his blood to revitalise the Earth eternally. His Holy Mother and his friends, Joseph of Arimathea, Lazarus of Bethany and Mary Magdala collected a few drops of his blood and became the sole sacred guardians of this relic.

Persecuted, they had to flee and were thrown by providence on the southern coast of Gaul which was under the Roman domination. Was that the new Promised Land chosen by the apostle risen from the dead and his sinful sister risen from the living?

Maybe. When Clovis embarked upon the invasion of the Visigothic Rhone valley, he was given the title of "Emperor of the Christians" prior to his victory in Vouillé. In 652 CE, his lineage produced the first King of the Franks to be honoured at the altar in the person of Dagobert II, son of Sigebert III and grandson of the "Good King Dagobert I".

Exiled to Ireland by the ambitious Grimoald, Saint Dagobert returned to Austrasia at the request of the lords of the country, but died five years later on 23rd December 679 CE in an ambush in the forest of Wœvre near Stenay.

A knight rescued his son Sigebert IV from the massacre and took him to Reda where he became Count of Razès on 17th January 681. His descendants would never ascend the throne again. In 771 CE, they erected the Carolingian part of the church in Rennes-le-Château to host the tomb of their ancestor.

The double external arcatures on the cemetery side and the sculpted font are vestiges from that time.

In 1153, Bertrand de Blanchefort, Count of Reda, who had become Grand Master of the Temple, resided in Jerusalem and introduced the Star of Solomon in his coat of arms. He died in 1170. Had the descendants discovered the precious relics of Saint Mary Magdalene in Reda?

Possibly, since in 1185 they dedicated the church to her, extended it by three bays with external buttresses, and named the city "Blessed Mary of Reda". Strangely, one can read the date 1646 "ISIS" in Greek on the 17th Century portal and, on the left pillar, Christ's symbol IHS, meaning in hermetic language "Iesus Hominorum Salvator", an allusion to the Holy Grail. To the left, above the portal, Mary Magdalene is portrayed with her crucifix.

On 17th January 1781, Marie de Negri d'Ables, last Countess of Hautpoul-Blanchefort and descendant of Merovaeus, was buried in the cemetery of Rennes-le-Château. She had probably bequeathed the treasure of the renowned lineage that had just died with her to the church.

Eight years later, the French revolution threatened the clergy. In 1791, Father Antoine Bigou, dean of the area and guardian of the secret, decided to go into exile. Prior to his departure, he engraved an astonishing inscription on the stele of the Countess destined to dissimulate her secret in those troubled times whilst offering the possibility for it to be revealed at a more peaceful and opportune moment in the future. A scholar could decipher the message without difficulty, as follows. "You position yourself at the place for the statues and follow the landmarks. These are in a cross format: bottom left, Arque in Greek; top right, Alpha, to be found underneath the altar; and finally Delta the Trinity and Iota Jesus, presently on the 8th Century pillar underneath Our Lady of Lourdes." In accordance with these instructions, Bérenger Saunière dismantled the pillar in 1891 and found a mysterious diagram amongst some parchments. On one of the tiles in the choir, he noticed a little cross drawn in the centre of a triangle; underneath the latter, a tomb. Saunière opened the tomb and discovered a treasure which he used afterwards.

In 1906, the church possessions were threatened. Saunière erased the inscription on the stele of the Countess of Blanchefort, bequeathed all he had acquired to his servant, and inverted the position of the statues of Saint Mary Magdalene and Saint Anthony the Hermit. In dismantling the Carolingian altar, Bérenger Saunière had unveiled a secret. He ignored the fact that, unwillingly, he was going to revive the most marvellous of mysteries.

The mystery is embodied in the amazing 8th Century tombstone which concealed the church's treasure. This engraved stone placed on the tomb of Sigebert IV in 771 CE is exhibited today in a little museum in the courtyard of the presbytery.

Is it not astonishing that it resurfaced in the area in 1971, exactly twelve centuries later?

Some of the parchments discovered in the church comprised the genealogy and descendants of Saint Dagobert. It confirmed that Sigebert IV had survived the deadly ambush against his father, the last King of the Franks and descendant of Clovis. Under the left arch of the building, there is a crowned individual on horseback, very likely Saint Dagobert, and on the right there is a rider with a child, most certainly Sigebert IV and his saviour. This child is the real "Lost King" and his lineage continues to date.

Mary Magdalene and her brother Lazarus collected the very precious blood of Jesus at the foot of his cross, under the gaze of Our Lady.

Christian chivalry roamed the world endlessly in search of this divine relic. Richard Wagner seemed convinced that the Cathars buried it in Montségur. Maybe it is to reignite the flame of this intangible Temple that Bérenger Saunière immortalised in stone the souvenir of Bethany and Magdala on the mount of the old Reda.

GODEFROY DE BOUILLON AND THE ORDER OF SION

There is an order, which originated in Jerusalem about a millennium ago and was christened The Order of Sion, and which has survived to the present day under the disguise of a secret society. Its founder was Godefroy de Bouillon, a descendant of the Sicambrians, and first King of Jerusalem. One of the aims of this society, later called the Priory of Sion, was to safeguard the destiny of the descendants of Merovaeus and to prepare for their eventual restoration to the throne of France from which they were divested in the past in an ignominious and unfair manner. The Mecca of this secret society is located in Rennes-le-Château where the three concentric surrounding walls of the imposing Reda were erected in bygone times. Indeed, it is in Reda that the heirs to the Sicambrian kings took refuge to flee their enemies; there that they founded a line and continued it across the centuries; there also that they buried an immense treasure, material, as well as spiritual - in the form of genealogical documents destined to prove the survival of their lineage.

To date still, the real Master of the Priory of Sion is a descendant of Merovaeus. Man amongst men, he does not distinguish himself from them through any glory or particular esteem. Except through his name - reminiscent of “Rejeton ardent” or “Ardent kid” given in the past to the son of Dagobert, and that his domain - exiguous remains of what was once the fief of the Counts of Razès - is still in Rennes-le-Château.

Father Saunière knew of the existence of the Priory of Sion. Whilst he was unveiling the secret previously entrusted by the Marchioness of Hautpoul-Blanchefort on her deathbed to his predecessor Father Bigou, messengers from the mysterious brotherhood came to Rennes-le-Château and enlightened him on their activity. It is thanks to the Priory of Sion that Bérenger Saunière, in complete support of their objectives, managed to dispose of part of the treasure from which both he and his servant Marie Denarnaud lived comfortably all their life. As official representative, he renovated the old church of Rennes-le-Château, which he covered with esoteric symbols, and built the impressive tower of Magdala from where he could permanently observe the ruins of the Castle of Albedun which he believed to be the site of the old Reda. He envisaged other grandiose projects when death unexpectedly caught up with him. The last word he uttered on his deathbed was, "Jean" (John), the name given to all the masters of the Priory of Sion throughout the centuries; unconditional vassals of the august Sicambrian descendants.

Such is the secret tradition. It comes to light through various works, like those produced by Madeleine Blancasall, Anne-Léa Hisler and Philippe Toscan du Plantier about the Merovingians and the dynasties that succeeded them on the throne of France. But, in this instance, tradition is History's daughter, and as they are both entwined, it is not always easy to determine right from wrong.

In 1099, following a fierce battle against the Arabs which the Christians turned into an absolute massacre, Godefroy de Bouillon, forty-one years old and the Duke of Lower-Lorraine, became the first Frankish King of the conquered city of Jerusalem in which he founded a knighthood called the Order of Sion. Godefroy, who was born in Brabant, resided in a fortress on a promontory along the river Semois in the heart of the Ardennes' wild countryside, long surrounded by mystery, where, centuries before, the Sicambrians had settled after being defeated and deported to the north of Europe by the Romans. He was aware of Sicambrian blood running in his ardent veins and derived strength and pride from it. He was guided by faith when he led his knights from the Meuse valley towards Palestine to reclaim the tomb of Christ from the Infidels. But he was also following the example of his ancestor Clovis. Like him, he felt endowed with a divine mission. Clovis had been entrusted by Remy and Clothilde with the task of imposing Christ's religion in Gaul. Godefroy's crusade was to win back the Holy Sepulchre. This is why he was amongst the first to respond to the calls for a crusade from Pope Urban II and the monk of Picardy, Peter the Hermit. This is also why he emerged naturally as the leader of the Crusaders and took the prestigious title of King of Jerusalem, for which nobody else had sufficient nobility. If he could not ignore the grandeur of his descent, neither could he disregard the felony that robbed the throne from his ancestors in the past. He knew that Dagobert II had been unscrupulously assassinated and that his son Sigebert had found refuge in the remote Razès beyond reach of the murderer Pépin de Herstal, whose ambition was to enable the advent of the Carolingian dynasty. He knew also that, after his victory against the Moors, Charles Martel, heir of Pépin de Herstal, had rushed to the Languedoc area, possibly to seize the descent of Dagobert II and destroy it forever. Godefroy was not the type of man to seek revenge from this four centuries' old felony. Besides, the

Carolingians, who had established their reign on a crime, had been replaced on the throne of France by the Capetians. At least the Duke of Bouillon, who had become the sovereign of the Frankish kingdom of Jerusalem, did not shy away from affirming the grandeur of his race when facing the ruling princes of Europe who, perhaps, had a tendency to consider him as a vassal and not as their equal.

That was when he met the Brothers of the Red Cross, or Brothers of Ormus. The Near East has always been the privileged point of contact for esoteric traditions where cults meet and sometimes intermingle. Egyptians, Jews, Arabs, and Persians have brought their contribution to it in turn. Magus and prophets appeared in numbers greater there than anywhere else. Amongst them there was a seraphic Alexandrian priest called Ormessius, or Ormus. Converted, with six fellow members, to Christianity by Saint Mark in 46 CE, he founded a society called the Sages of the Light to which he gave the emblem of a red cross. Around the same period, the Essenes, a mysterious Hebrew brotherhood to which Christ belonged prior to conveying His message to the world, had coalesced with other Jewish sects to found a Solomonic school of wisdom. Later, this school attached itself to the Ormus brotherhood to create a new society which, in turn, divided itself into various orders, the Conservatives, the Order of the Mosaic Secrets, the Order of the Hermetic Secrets, etc. After the conquest of Palestine, Godefroy learned more about these strange Christians who were following the initiatory traditions of both ancient Egypt and Judaism. Were they not representatives of the true Church, pure and noble in spirit, as conceived by its Founder and the apostle Jean (John), His favourite disciple? Were they not widely open to Knowledge, welcoming all men and, therefore, faithful to the teachings of Jesus of Nazareth?

Then, a great plan germinated in Godefroy's mind. In the past, his ancestor Clovis had become the sword and shield of Christ's Church, for which the keys had been given to the apostle Peter and which established its seat in Rome. In turn, Godefroy wanted to be the sword and shield of the Church of John, more connected to the Spirit. The Order of Sion was born, with its seat at Our Lady of Sion's Abbey in Jerusalem. Godefroy had little time to shape his plan as he died one year after the conquest of Jerusalem. But the Order of Sion survived. In 1118, a cardinal date, the Brothers of Ormus instigated the creation of the Order of the Temple, a military order to consolidate the power of the Order of Sion. Three of its founders belonged to the Order of Sion, namely Hugues de Payen, Bisol de Saint Homer and Hugues de Champagne. The first Grand Master of the Temple was indeed Hugues de Payen. Thus, the affiliation between the orders was immediately formed. It should be noted that Bertrand de Blancafort, or Blanchefort, was the fourth Grand Master who governed the Order of the Temple from 1153 to 1170. He belonged to the Blanchefort family that had founded a line in the Razès and whose ruined castle can still be seen on the outskirts of Rennes-le-Château. The Merovingian blood that ran in the veins of Godefroy also ran in the veins of Bertrand, a detail which was not overlooked by Father Bigou when, six centuries later, he recorded the last wishes of the Marchioness of Hautpoul-Blanchefort.

This is how, in the 12th Century, spiritual and temporal media were created to secure the outcome of Godefroy de Bouillon's ambitious dream. The Temple became the servant of the Church of John and that of the first and only legitimate dynasty. In the Orient, legions wearing the white mantle embossed with the red cross of Ormus upheld the authentic religion of Christ and the throne of Jerusalem. But soon History contradicted this great objective; the Frankish kingdom of Palestine was not destined to last centuries. In 1187, Jerusalem fell again into the hands of the Infidels and the knights, guardians of the Holy Sepulchre, had to retreat to Europe. The Brothers of Ormus fled with them. Some settled in the large priory of Saint-Samson of Orleans given by Louis VI to their Jerusalem house; others joined the Order of the Temple; others still preferred the small priory of the Mount of Sion, near Saint-Jean-le-Blanc, a village attached today to urban Orleans. Hence, the name of Priory of Sion frequently allocated to the order afterwards.

In 1187 or 1188, on returning from the Holy Land, an important event known as the "Rupture de l'Orme" (Schism at the Elm) occurred in Gisors, at the foot of the enormous fortress which defends the Île-de-France region on the north-west. By this severance, the Order of Sion and the Order of the Temple separated during a ceremony in a field called "Ormeteau ferré" near the actual station of Gisors. The members of the Order of Sion had a good reason for this rupture. At that time, the Order of the Temple, secular arm of the Order of Sion, was governed by the Grand Master François Gérard de Ridefort, whose disposition towards Saladin – one even talks of treason – was not alien to the fall of Jerusalem. So, in the eyes of the Order of Sion, the Grand Master of the Temple had possibly irremediably compromised the plan of Godefroy de Bouillon in Palestine. The "Schism at the Elm" between the two orders did not result in a war and they pursued their separate existences in an autonomous manner. Whilst Ridefort governed the Order of the Temple for a few more years, the Order of Sion elected Jean de Gisors as their Grand Master who held the post for more than thirty years until his death in 1220. At the time, the "Schism at the Elm" was undoubtedly devastating for the members of the Order of Sion, particularly since it happened straight after the heartbreak suffered by the loss of Palestine. For the Order of Sion, this rupture represented the deprivation of its temporal power; that of the Order of the Temple with its thousand knights spread over the Occident, with its commanderies and treasures... What appeared to be a mistake originally became justified later with the wiping out of the visible Temple by Philippe le Bel at the beginning of the 14th Century. United, the two orders would have given another reason for the King of France to take action since, originally, both the Order of Sion and the Order of the Temple were devoted to the Merovingians and looked upon the Capetians as usurpers. Although this reason was removed after the "Schism at the Elm", the Order of the Temple was destroyed nevertheless. The Order of Sion escaped the pursuit and massacre but was compelled afterwards to operate clandestinely and prudently.

In 1188, Jean de Gisors, first Grand Master of the Order of Sion, had received the symbolic title of Jean II (John II); Jean I (John I) being reserved for Christ Himself. Thereafter, all Grand Masters of the Order of Sion were crowned Jean (John), or Jeanne since, amongst the twenty-seven elected to the present day, four have been women, namely Marie de Saint-Clair from 1220 to 1226, Jeanne de Bar from 1336 to 1351, Blanche d'Evreux from 1366 to 1398, and Iolande de Bar from 1480 to 1483. For three centuries until the Renaissance, the Order of Sion was governed by men or women of the highest nobility, with the exception of Nicolas Flamel to whom tradition allocates the name of Jean VI and who would have presided between 1398 and 1418. What was the alchemist Nicolas Flamel doing in that organisation? It is worth remembering that Flamel was the protégé of Queen Blanche d'Evreux who was also interested in alchemy. Flamel succeeded as Grand Master to Blanche d'Evreux in 1398 and it is probable that the queen had personally encouraged his ascension within the order, possibly in exchange of some particular service. The Order of Sion needed money, and Flamel could fabricate gold...

Several princes, princesses and other people of noble lineage who became Grand Masters of the Order of Sion were of Merovingian descent. This was the case, for instance, of Jean and Guillaume de Gisors, and of Jeanne and Iolande de Bar, thus perpetrating the religious and dynastic ambition of Godefroy de Bouillon. From the 16th Century, the order became more "democratic". It still included great aristocratic names, such as the Constable de Bourbon, Louis de Nevers or Charles de Lorraine amongst its leaders, but the aristocracy of the blood was often substituted by the aristocracy of the mind, and artists, writers, and scholars succeeded each other as head of the order. It is in their company that the painter Nicolas Poussin, immigrant in Italy at the beginning of the 17th Century, had the revelation of certain secrets and realised, at Richelieu's request, a painting full of symbols which he entitled "The Shepherds of Arcadia".

From the 12th Century, the Order of Sion, or Priory of Sion, had lost all temporal power after its separation from the Order of the Temple. So, what means did it have to attain its objectives? Primarily, the order was the holder of "The Secret", the one about the survival of the first dynasty and its continuation in the Razès. It was a formidable secret in that the Capetians felt insecure on the throne since their position could be contested any time by the legitimate pretenders. In fact, throughout history, a conflict never ceased to oppose the descendants of Merovaeus to their "usurpers", sometimes in the open, but most often undercover. Godefroy de Bouillon thought that by edifying his kingdom in Palestine on a land that had been sanctified by Christ in the past, he would soon eclipse all others in prestige. For his followers, he surpassed them also in power, thanks to the Order of the Temple whose knighthood and militia became the most redoubtable military organisation of the time. Subsequently, the Dukes of Bouillon, who were established in their Ardennes principality, backed up by their fortress on the borders of the river Semois and their impressive citadel of Sedan along the river Meuse, defied the King of France on several occasions, where necessary by force, until the Capetian monarch became powerful enough to annex their principality to his domain and reduce those who considered themselves his equals into vassals. The other families with Merovingian blood were equally rebellious and were often implicated in the great conspiracies that shook the throne. Nicolas Fouquet was one of the ambassadors of the first dynasty in charge of reminding the Sun King (Louis XIV) of the existence of the "other" king. This explains the growing exasperation and anxiety of Louis XIV when Fouquet was increasing his power day by day, accumulating treasures, charges and benefits, affirming his authority through the control of troops and fortified towns, and gradually erecting a State within State. Hence, the King's brusque decision to arrest his overly-enterprising minister and incarcerate him in the fortress of Pignerol for the rest of his life.

The Priory of Sion claims to be the guardian of another secret, that which concerns the material wealth dormant in the soil of the Razès. Truthfully, their rights over these could be contested since they were from various sources and were Visigothic in part. Except for the treasure stored by Dagobert II in Reda when he planned to conquer Aquitaine, one finds it difficult to see how the Merovingian descendants could make a claim over riches that belonged to other families and other nations. To these arguments, the Priory of Sion gave two responses. Firstly, the kingdom of the Visigoths in the Languedoc had been crushed by the Merovingians in the past and the spoils of war they had stashed and hidden in Reda belonged to the latter by right of conquest. Also, the plunder included the treasure from the Temple of Jerusalem pillaged by Titus in 70 CE and Alaric three centuries and a half later, and the secret tradition stated that the Sicambrians, and later Merovingians, were descendants of the Tribe of Benjamin to whom Jerusalem had been given. Secondly, part of the Razès' wealth seems to come from the Templars' treasure that escaped the greed of Philippe le Bel in the 14th Century. Originally, the Order of the Temple was just the secular arm of the Order of Sion, the latter dedicated to the double task of spreading the Johannine religion and serving Merovaeus' dynasty. Therefore, the Templars' riches belonged to the Merovingians and the Priory of Sion by right. One can understand now why Father Saunière after finding the hiding-place, or one of the hiding-places, of the treasure of Rennes-le-Château, was approached by mysterious emissaries who enlightened him on the importance of his discovery and, in exchange for their assistance, charged him with a mission; also why the priest enlisted by the Priory of Sion and rejected by the Roman Catholic Church had the ambition to create a new religion, probably based on the Johannine Christianity that the founders of the Order of Sion had originally substituted for Peter's Christianity; and finally why Saunière on his deathbed requested the presence of a mysterious "Jean" (John) – the one who, through centuries, governed the clandestine destinies of the Priory of Sion. One should also remember that, in Paris, Saunière had met Claude Debussy, one of the highest dignitaries of the Priory.

How is it possible, therefore, that an organisation which is so old and powerful has not left any archives or documents enabling one to authenticate its history with certainty? The Priory of Sion seems to have traversed the centuries without leaving any visible trace. Documents relating to the Order of the Temple are plentiful. Those concerning the Order of Sion are practically non-existent. A likely explanation could be that documents regarding the Temple abound as a result of the Order's destruction. However, these consist mostly of minutes of Court proceedings. The secret history of the Temple has been built through confessions dragged out of the knights; a difficult reconstitution attempted by generations of researchers who have not been able to eliminate all question marks and controversies.

And whilst the Temple was clearly dying, the order of Sion was working behind the scenes, untouched by the persecutions that would have affected it too, had it remained associated to the Templars. The order of Sion probably benefited from the tragedy that struck the Templars. Its conviction that secrecy is preferable to openness must have been reinforced. The archives, if there were any, must have been carefully hidden.

Amongst the Grand Masters of the Priory of Sion were two members of the Gisors family, namely Jean and Guillaume. They appeared after the creation of the Order, which followed the "Schism at the Elm", under the titles of Jean II and Jean III respectively. In his book, *Les Templiers sont parmi nous*, Gérard de Sède relates, 'One can remember the strange object found in the Temple of Paris in the morning of the big raid which, in the eyes of the accusers, was the mysterious Baphomet represented by a woman's head in gold containing the skull of a little girl with the label "CAPUT LVIII m". After its discovery, this head was entrusted to an individual called Guillaume de Gisors.'

Strange coincidence! To whom did the investigators of Philippe le Bel hand over what they believed to be the Baphomet? They gave it to a man who, in the background, led the Priory of Sion from which the Temple was issued in the past. This proves at least that, at that time, the Order of Sion was already acting in a most clandestine manner. This can also be used to demonstrate that, to a certain degree, the Order of Sion wanted the disappearance of the Temple to punish it for Ridefort's former treason, and that it became briefly the ally of the Capetian to attain this goal. Later, at the end of the 14th Century, the role of Grand Master fell to Queen Blanche d'Evreux, Nicolas Flamel's protector, who retired readily to the tower of Neaufles, accessible from the citadel of Gisors through a tunnel, to indulge in her alchemic studies.

Schaebelé, in *Alchemy*, 1905, said the following about Nicolas Flamel.

'Nicolas Flamel, who was first a writer for the Charnel House of the Innocents, then for Saint-Jacques church, bought one day for two florins, a golden book "very old and very big", made of "loose parchments", in a cover engraved entirely with strange figures. The book contained three sets of seven sheets, the seventh one without any writing but showing paintings of a rod, serpents fighting each other, a crucified snake, deserts, and fountains. On the first sheet, there was an inscription in large characters "Abraham the Jew, prince, practically a Levite, astrologist and philosopher, of the Jewish race dispersed in Gaul under the ire of God. Hail to thee. D.I." The author taught metallic transmutation in plain words, enlightening about everything except the first agent which he had depicted in a figurative manner with ingenious artifices. Having this beautiful book at home, Flamel studied it day and night, understanding very well all the operations described in it, but not knowing where to start. When his wife Pernelle saw the book, she fell in love with it too, admiring the beautiful engraved images and portraits. He wanted a description of all the figures and showed them to several important scholars who could not understand any more than him. One of them, however, a Professor Anseaulme, told him that the first agent was mentioned in it, the quicksilver, which one had to stabilise through a long decoction in pure blood from young children. During the following twenty-one years, Flamel followed thousands of red herrings, not concerning the blood though, which would have been wicked and nasty. Having lost all faith in ever understanding the symbols, he made a vow to God and to Saint-Jacques of Galicia in exchange for their intervention. So, with Pernelle's agreement, carrying a keepsake of her, and having taken the pilgrim's habit and staff, he set off and reached Montjoye, then Santiago de Compostela in Spain where, with a great devotion, he fulfilled his vow. On his return after having done this, he met Léon, a Christian doctor, Jewish by birth, nicknamed Master Cauches, who was extremely learned in subliminal sciences. When Flamel showed him samples of the figures, he was filled with wonderment and joy and asked him straightaway if he knew anything about the book these came from, which the cabbalists thought had been lost for ever. When our pilgrim replied that he hoped to know more about it if someone could decipher the enigmas, Master Cauches started the decoding exercise at once, so much so, that with God's blessing and the intercession of the Blessed Virgin Mary and the Benedictines Saint-Jacques and John, Flamel obtained knowledge of what he had sought, that is, the first principles - not, however, their first preparation which is one of the most difficult things in the world. He found the latter after three and a half long years of trial and error, which he devoted entirely to his study and work. He finally discovered what he wanted. The first time he carried out the experiment, it was on mercury which he converted into half a pound of pure silver, better than that extracted from the mine. The event took place around lunchtime in his house, in the sole presence of his wife, on Monday 17th January 1382. Later, in addition to their lavish interventions in Boulogne, Flamel and his wife erected and let more than fourteen hospitals in Paris, built three new chapels, gave large donations and annuities to seven churches and effected several renovations in their cemeteries. On the fourth arch in the Cemetery of the Innocents, to the right of the large entrance, rue Saint-Denis, he represented in a hieroglyphic disguise two topics that were important to him, namely the mystery of our future resurrection on the day of Judgement by Jesus, and all the principal and necessary operations in natural philosophy's magistery.

The history of the castle of Gisors is closely linked to that of the Order of the Temple. Around 1090, Thibaud, Count of Gisors, also called Thibaud Payen and sole nephew of Hugues de Payen, one of the founders of the Order of the Temple, erected the first fortifications of the citadel. Later, and for a few years, the Templars had the safeguard of the castle of Gisors. These are just a few facts; one could cite others. Did the Templars and the Grand Masters of Sion know of the tunnels and hiding places around the castle and its vicinity? And did they use them to their own advantage? They probably did.

In *Les Templiers sont parmi nous*, Gérard de Sède talks at great length about the 1946 discovery made by Roger Lhomoy, warden of the castle of Gisors. Born in Gisors, the latter knew of the traditions surrounding the secrets that had been kept within the impressive walls of the citadel. He became warden of the castle in 1929 and, during the war when the castle was closed to the public, dug up a cesspit in the mound supporting the donjon. One day, his efforts paid of, as he told Gérard de Sède, 'What I saw then, I will never forget. It was an amazing spectacle. I was in a Roman chapel in stone from Louveciennes, thirty metres long, nine metres wide, and some four and a half metres high from the keystone. Directly to my left, near the gap through which I came, there was the altar and tabernacle, also in stone. Half way up the walls, supported by stone corbels, I could see life-size statues of Christ and his twelve apostles, and along the walls, on the ground, there were nineteen stone sarcophaguses, twenty metres long and sixty centimetres wide. What my torch was illuminating in the nave was incredible; thirty chests in precious metal aligned in rows of ten. And the word chest is probably inadequate, as they looked more like cupboards lying on their backs, each two metres long, one metre eighty high, and one metre sixty wide.'

What was the nature of the treasure discovered by Lhomoy? Could it be the riches of the Temple, sought in vain by Philippe le Bel? A more secret tradition, however, claims that it was the archives of the Priory of Sion, buried there at the beginning of the 16th Century; archives that Lhomoy could not have seen where he described, the myth of the underground chapel under the mound of the donjon being destined to mislead the curious and discourage researchers.

16 - Tower of Neaufles

17 - "The Shepherds of Arcadia" by Nicolas Poussin

The Shepherds Of Arcadia

The text below is surrounded in mystery. It was sent by post, unprompted and without notice, to the chief editorial section of the *Charivari* and was signed David Myriam, 135, avenue Mozart. Upon enquiry, it transpired that no such person lived at that address. The initials "D.M." were displayed in a strange script at the bottom of the article. We remembered then that the initials "D.M." were also those of the Latin motto "Diis manibus" or "in the hands of the gods" known by the initiates. The very tone of the article and its list of unusual precisions, emphasised by a relentless passion, convinced us that the text had been sent by a member of the Priory of Sion who wanted to reveal certain things whilst remaining anonymous. Here is this text.

'In the Louvre museum, "The Shepherds of Arcadia", a painting by Poussin, attracts the eye of the visitor. The matching piece to this first version was a painting of similar dimensions by the same artist, entitled "King Midas washing his face in the gold of the Pactolus". The association between Midas, coffer, and the two rivers Alpheus and Pactolus, can legitimately be taken as an allusion to a hidden secret. Certain aspects of Poussin's biography are not well known. Born in 1594, Nicolas Poussin was said to be of aristocratic descent, although this has never been proven. His apprenticeship years are ambiguous and one finds it hard to reconcile the astonishing classical culture behind his work with the banality of his writing. Poussin's career started in Italy where he settled with the firm intention never to leave. He only agreed to return to France in response to Cardinal Richelieu's persistent requests. As soon as he arrived in Paris, he was exposed to the cabal of his colleagues. Richelieu ordered the painting of a ceiling on the theme "Time exacts the truth from the attacks of Envy and Calumny". Having completed everything required of him, Poussin rushed back to Italy, never to leave again.

The definitive version of "The Shepherds of Arcadia" follows Poussin's return to Paris, although the exact creation date, around 1639, is being disputed. This painting was probably revisited many times over. It portrays three shepherds in affected positions who are interpreting an incomplete sentence under the stare of an unknown woman. But who is this woman? She represents a symbol, the allegory of the Priory of Sion - the former Lady of Sion - watching over the shepherds of Arcadia. In clear terms, one can understand that, "without the Merovingians, the Priory of Sion would not exist, and without the Priory of Sion, the Merovingian dynasty would be extinguished." Hence the epigraph "Et in Arcadia ego..." taken up in the painting.

It is in Rome that Poussin met members of the Priory of Sion, and it is there that he became the guardian of some secrets. It is there also that he made the acquaintance of Cardinal Rospigliosi, who was to become Pope under the name Alexander VII and who was also held in the secret of the gods, something the Bourbons were apparently very thankful for. Despite the differences of opinion that he faced constantly at the Court of France, it was at this very Court's request that he ascended the pontifical throne. At a time when the State coffers were empty, and regardless of the complaints made about him by his predecessor, His Holiness received each year a considerable gratuity levied on the royal treasure. Indeed, it seemed that on the eve of the Fronde, blackmail was being exercised on the French monarch and that the Arts were involved in it.

Allegoric works have this advantage that one word suffices to highlight associations that the general public does not grasp; offered to all but the meaning of which is only addressed to an elite. Above the masses, the sender and receiver understand one another. The baffling success of certain pieces comes from the intrinsic value of the allegory which, much more than a fashion, represents a form of esoteric expression. It is impossible for it to be otherwise for anyone who knows the spirit of the nascent 17th Century. What is bought from Cardinal Rospigliosi, Poussin's inspirer, is really nothing less than the silence of Asmodeus. There is a mysterious society somewhere that holds a genealogical secret more important than anything else. This society is the Priory of Sion for which the cardinal becomes an emissary. In these troubled times where kingdoms fight one another, it is not only the throne of France that is threatened, but every throne in Europe. Whilst blood is shed on the battlefields, there is one area where truce is not broken, namely the back-shop of the genealogists. There, kings help each other, peerage lists are rebuilt, and gaps where a Merovingian pretender could enter are sealed. To neutralise a cardinal, he is made Pope. Such an outlook on history may raise many objections to which only History can provide answers.

How come, one may say, this old Merovingian lineage never ascended the throne again? Has one ever heard of a Merovingian pretender? It is precisely because the real king cannot "pretend". He is, and therefore cannot "demand recognition" without demeaning himself. Far from being a sign of decline, the epoch of the so-called Rois fainéants (the last Merovingian Kings) denotes the apogee of the Merovingian dynasty. Before he exalts his sovereignty in the darkness, the king "fait néant", that is he "does nothing", since he is "all". Under his stare, the Sun King is exactly the opposite of a king by his stance in constantly trying to prove that he is "the Sun" or that he is "the State" for fear that he might be forgotten. Is not the throne the last place where the King can reign freely without wasting energy to prove it? In this instant, nothing prevents a little shepherd from governing us at the lift of a finger, without us even knowing that he is the King of France. He is Mr. Everyman, even though he is king. During times of unrest in history, the red colour of his banner, the true royal colour and the headdress that crowned Midas and the Kings of Arcadia resurface. The king is shepherd and guide. Sometimes, he sends some brilliant messenger to his serving vassal, his general handyman, whose felicity is predisposed to end. This includes René d'Anjou, the constable of Bourbon, Nicolas Fouquet, the cardinal of Retz, and many others, formidable and vulnerable at the same time, whose astonishing success is followed by inexplicable disgrace. As holders of the secret, one can only elevate them or destroy them. They are also Gilles de Rais, Leonardo da Vinci, and the Dukes of Nevers, Gonzague and Joseph Balsamo, whose wake leaves a scent of trickery where heresy mixes with flattery. If King Charles VII hid amongst his courtesans when Joan of Arc entered the large room of his castle in Chinon, it was not as a joke – where was the wit in such a move – but because he knew already who she represented and, in front of her, he was just another courtesan. The secret she delivered within the walls of the castle can be reduced to a few words, 'My Lord, I am here at the King's request.' Sometimes, the ambassador's career ended in a court case over witchcraft. The trial was fair and legal since the emissary was a heretic, disciple and follower of the god Pan of Arcadia, who died on the same cross as Christ and rose from the dead on the third day. The messenger did not take the judges seriously as he knew how the usurpers, deprived of their divine rights, forged their transcendence; how, in the early days, the Mayors of the Palace had elevated the Popes so that the Popes elevated them in turn; and how the Empire had to become a Holy Empire so that the Pope could have an army.

The Sicambrian kings, ancestors of Merovaeus, were the "shepherds of Arcadia". How come that this most desolate Mediterranean region is described as having experienced the golden age? Within living memory, one has not discovered anything in Arcadia. Polybius, its most famous offspring, talks about it fondly but does not conceal its hard life. From ancient times to the 18th Century, Arcadians are described as savages with only two qualities, the extreme antiquity of their race – they were born, it is said, "before the Moon" – and their love for music. Their proverbial stupidity has nothing to envy from the Boeotians. In *The Bucolics*, written upon the invocation of Theocritus about forty years before Christ, Virgil attests that the Sicambrians in northern Europe came from a barren land. One can find evidence of this in the tenth eclogue, the most enigmatic and beautiful of all, which one must read as a sort of farewell to Arcadia where the poet narrates how a young female dancer left for the North in the trail of a warrior called Antoine.

Tu procul a patria – nec sit mihi credere tantum
Alpinas, a, dura, nives et frigora Rheni
Me sine sola rides. A, te ne frigora leadant
A, tibi, ne tenera glacies secat aspera plantas.

Whilst thou – Ah! Might I but believe it not! –
Alone without me, and from home afar,
Look's upon Alpine snows and frozen Rhine.
Ah! May the frost not hurt thee, may the sharp
And jagged ice not wound thy tender feet!

The tenth eclogue does not allude to a migration in real terms. This would have been mentioned by the chroniclers. However, if one tries to establish who settled along the Rhine forty years before Christ, one finds the "proud Sicambrians", ancestors to the kings of the first dynasty. It is not without reticence that historians broach the subject of the Sicambrians. They do not understand how this below-strength tribe could dominate larger and stronger nations. This is because the Sicambrians were neither a nation nor a tribe, but a "race" in the narrowest sense of the term, that is a dynasty by Divine Right who could therefore reign over all the populations of the Occident.

The Sicambrians derive their name from the river Sieg, a tributary of the Rhine along which they first settled, having taken many other names before. This etymology is not without importance since from "Sieg-fried" to the Grail it provides the explanation to our occidental poetry. Another etymology mentions the race of Sun-Camara, those who sleep under the same roof, hence the term "kamarade" which came to us from the Greek through the German language. Why is it that until the 19th Century one believed that the city of Troy was in a place called Sigeum? Knowing that the first kingdom of the Sicambrians in Europe spread between the river Sieg and the river Semois across Bouillon, it was not in Sigeum that one had to look for the Homeric treasure, but between those two rivers, something Schliemann did with a "prodigious" intuition. Via this route, the themes of the *Iliad* and the *Odyssey* crept into our ancient folklore where Homer had never appeared before. Here, anterior to the Trojan War, arose the origins of Arcadia, since the large city was built on the tomb of Arcas, bear-prince and first Arcadian King. Reappearing and disappearing with Virgil, Arcadia came back to life in the Italy of the Renaissance at the incitement of Laurent de Medici, called Lorenzo the Magnificent. In his sumptuous villa, the Priory of Sion created a society of "shepherds", lovers of fine art. Then, France was governed by two generations of Medici who owed their supremacy to the custody of a fabulous secret until, Marie de Medici, mother of Louis XIII, fell into sudden disgrace and died in Brussels in near destitution, the key to the treasure having slipped from her hands into those of Cardinal Rospigliosi. The dazzling career of the Medici ended there.

Amongst the poets of late Renaissance, whose revelations are far more helpful than the texts of historians themselves, one must mention Le Tasse. His *Arcadia* and his *Liberated Jerusalem* cannot be separated. In Godefroy VI de Bouillon, Count of Boulogne, whom he exalted as an almost divine being, he glorifies one of the Merovingian descendants who went to the Holy Land to build a new Sicambrian kingdom and reconstruct Arcadia through the creation of the mysterious Priory of Sion, the Grand Master of which is still of Merovingian descent to date.

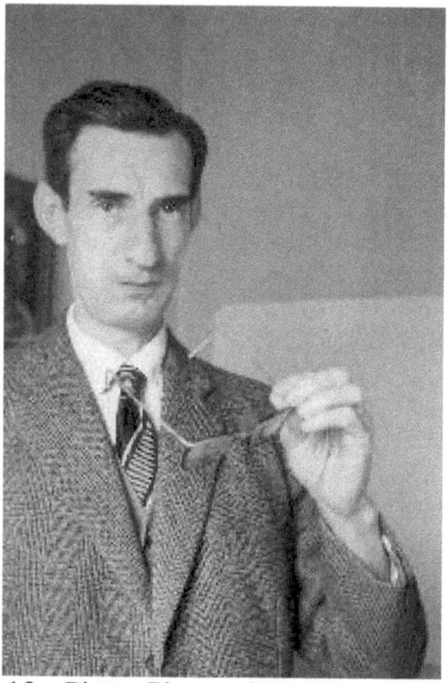

18 - Pierre Plantard de Saint Clair

In Search Of The Lost King

Discussion With Pierre Plantard in January 1971

During the 1960s, a strange magazine appeared in Paris under the title *Circuit*, with the sub-title Publication of social, cultural and philosophical studies. *Circuit* had its registered office in rue Pierre Jouhet, in Seine-et-Oise, Aulnay-sous-Bois. Its columns frequently included articles from a certain Chyren, as well as small display advertisements declaring that he was also a clairvoyant. His address was that of the magazine. In issue Number 8 of *Circuit*, published in March 1960, one could read the following portrait of Chyren, signed by Anne Hisler.

"Let us not forget that this psychologist was the friend of a variety of individuals such as the Count Israël Monti, one of the Saint Wehme brothers, Gabriel Trarieux d'Egmont, one of the thirteen members of the Rosicrucian brotherhood, Paul Lecour, philosopher of Atlantis, M. Lecomte Moncharville, delegate of the Agartha, Father Hoffet, from the documentation service of the Vatican, Th. Moreux, director of the observatory in Bourges, etc. Let us remember that, during the occupation, he was arrested, tortured by the Gestapo, and held political prisoner for several months. As a Bachelor of Science, he could appreciate the value of secret teachings. This probably justified the title "honoris causa" given to him by many hermetic societies. All that background has shaped this strange character, this mystic of Peace, this apostle of Freedom, this ascetic whose ideal is to serve the well-being of Humanity. How surprising, therefore, that this man has become one of the "éminences grises" whose advice is often sought by the great men of this world. Invited in 1947 by the Helvetic federal government, he has resided several years in Switzerland near Lake Geneva where a great number of official representatives and delegates from all over the world meet."

In a preceding issue of *Circuit*, in November 1959 - the launch year of the magazine, Chyren wrote the following about himself.

"We are not strategist and are beyond all denominational, political and financial formation. To those who come to us, we give the moral support and manna essential for the spirit. We are only messenger, addressing believers and non-believers with the sole purpose of transmitting grains of truth..."

Behind the pseudonym of Chyren hid, in fact, the managing director of *Circuit* in person. His name was Pierre Plantard and his wife was Anne-Léa Hisler, who died in 1971. *Circuit* does not exist any more. Plantard died in 2000. He was a strange individual; narrow in the face with visionary eyes. He held diverse posts such as industrial draughtsman, journalist and clairvoyant. Resistant during the war, he produced the monthly journal *Vaincre* (*Conquer*) in 1944. In 1961, he published *Gisors et son secret* (*Gisors and its Secret*). He was also the inspirer of a book by Anne-Léa Hisler *Rois et gouvernants de France jusqu'à nos jours* (*Kings and Rulers of France to the Present Day*). In 1972, he remarried an Anne-Marie Cavaille, a thirty year old woman of Montauban. Besides the fact that Pierre Plantard is not an ordinary person, three disturbing details attracted our attention.

Firstly, his name which, without being particularly original, is identical to the nickname given to Sigebert IV, son of Dagobert II, rescued from the deadly ambush organised for his father in the forest of Wœvre; "Plant-Ard", meaning "rejeton ardent" or ardent kid.

Secondly, Pierre Plantard was a landowner near Rennes-le-Château, where the lineage of Sigebert IV has been preserved. Did he inherit this land? If so, he extended his domain by acquiring three plots of land in the region in 1967 itemised 633, 634 and 635 in the cadastre of Rennes-le-Château and another three plots listed 616, 636 and 647 a few years later.

Thirdly, in 1956, Pierre Plantard was amongst the members of a society registered under the name Priory of Sion and regulated by the law of 1901, for which the Articles of Association are provided in the next chapter. This society was a reminder of the order founded by Godefroy de Bouillon in the Holy Land. The nature of the association, and the fact that Pierre Plantard was its secretary-general, indicated that the latter was its true inspirer.

Furthermore, Pierre Plantard seemed to move in a wide circle of acquaintances, not only those he knew through his first wife, Anne-Léa Hisler, but also people of great repute such as the Count de Bueil, who possessed an apartment in the avenue Victor Hugo where Plantard rented an attic room for a while, and the Count de Montpezat, father of the Danish prince consort. The Montpezat are amongst the families that can claim a Merovingian ancestry.

On the 6th January 1971, the day of the Epiphany (Twelfth Night), Jean-Luc Chaumeil (JLC) called Pierre Plantard (PP) to discuss the treasure of Rennes-le-Château and the Priory of Sion. This exchange was one of many telephone conversations, both before and after that date. The broad lines of their discussion are provided below.

JLC – 'You may be aware that, a while ago, Mr. Fontan, an engineer from Strasbourg, carried out some excavations in Rennes-le-Château, in Campagne-sur-Aude and in the Bézu. You may also know that, to protect his finder rights, he lodged three certified reports with Mr. Gastoux, lawyer in Limoux.'

PP – 'Yes, all that is very amusing since excavations are forbidden in Rennes-le-Château and Gisors. Besides, don't you think that we know very well where everything is? We know the precise position with absolute certainty. What we don't want is for people to search, that's all. They have no right to search, the land belongs to me. And without my authorisation, nobody is allowed to excavate. I will not give this authorisation. These plots of land belonged to one of my ancestors.'

JLC – 'Suppose these galleries, these gold mines, are very long and concern land that does not belong to you. What would happen then?'

PP – 'Listen, I own a big plot of land in Rennes-les-Bains and there is only one possible entrance. So, this can't be!'

JLC – 'Gérard de Sède wrote in black and white in his book *L'Or de Rennes* that Father Saunière had direct access to the mine some four or five kilometres away.'

PP – 'Yes, direct access. But you can pass that entrance a thousand times without noticing it. In any case, I maintain once more that I am opposed to all these searches and excavations on my land. People can search elsewhere. That does not bother us in the least.'

JLC – 'You keep telling me, people amuse "us",that does not bother "us"... Are you "the" landowner or are there many of you sharing the land?'

PP – 'I am the owner of the land. But there are a few of us looking after this business.'

JLC – 'What is your objective?'

PP – 'I can't tell you. The society to which I belong is very old. I succeed others, that is all there is to say. We safeguard certain things faithfully, without publicity.'

JLC – 'You mentioned once the publication of about fifty copies of a book in Belgium...'

PP – 'Yes, the book is entitled *Circuit*, by the Marquis de Cherisey. One has to read it carefully, and be capable of reading it. Cherisey has discovered many interesting things. To appreciate them, one must understand that *Circuit* conceals six different meanings. The same voluntary complexity can be found in the works from Madeleine de Blancasall and Henri Lobineau, where you will find the trail of the Blancheforts and the Hautpouls and you will know where they come from. You will also find the origins of the noble families of France and you will understand how a person called Henri de Montpezat could one day become king...'

JLC – 'The lost king...'

PP – 'You know, the king is not that lost. Let's say that he is forgotten. But he has never ceased to exist. And if you were fully informed about the secret history of France, you would understand why there was an affiliation of the Order of the Temple with the great families of Merovingian descent. As for our organisation, remember Cherisey's allusions to the initials P.S. You will often see them. They can open many doors. They are found in Rennes-le-Château and Gisors...'

This was the substance of the main exchanges between Jean-Luc Chaumeil and Pierre Plantard, alias Chyren. One cannot help but find them strange. Are we talking about mythomania, forgeries made by an individual taking advantage of homonymic and geographic coincidences, or the reflection of a reality with its roots in the farthest and most secret history of France? We have given our readers a number of elements for their appraisal. They can reject them altogether or attempt to reconstruct this strange puzzle for which a few pieces have been given to them.

ARTICLES OF ASSOCIATION OF THE "PRIORY OF SION"

In 1956, an association in the name of "Priory of Sion", regulated by the law of 1901, was created in Annemasse-sous-Cassan, Haute-Savoie. The four members responsible for its foundation were:

Pierre Bonhomme - President of the association. Born on 7th December 1934, secretary-accountant living No. 16, rue Emile-Millet, Château-Gaillard.

Jean Delaval - Vice-President of the association. Born on 7th March 1931 and living No. 28, rue du Commerce, Plein-Palais (his birth town), Switzerland.

Pierre Plantard – Secretary-general of the association. Born on 18th March 1920, draughtsman for the Chanovin establishments in Annemasse.

Pierre Defagot – Treasurer of the association. Born on 11th December 1928, watch-maker.

The Articles of Association of this strange society were as follows.

Article I

An association regulated by the law of 1901 and the decree of 16th August 1901 is created between the undersigned and any person who will adhere to these Articles of Association.

Article II

The association will be called "Priory of Sion", with the sub-title C.I.R.C.U.I.T. (Chevalerie d'Institutions et Règles Catholiques, d'Union Indépendante et Traditionaliste – Chivalry of Catholic Institutions and Rules, of Independent and Traditionalist Union). Its insignia is represented by a white lis, intertwined in a circuit called "Southern Cross". Its emblem is a white cockerel.

Article III

The purpose of the association is the creation of a Catholic order destined to restore, in a modern manner whilst retaining a traditionalist character, the old chivalry which, through its activity, was the promoter of a highly moralistic ideal and the medium for the constant improvement of humankind's rules of conduct.

With this in mind, and with the active participation of its members, the association will offer moral as well as material support and protection to all those in need, particularly the old, the infirm, etc.

With the help of its members, the association will develop a priory in a locality called "Montagne de Sion" in Haute-Savoie, which will become a centre for studies, meditation, relaxation and prayer.

In terms of propaganda, the association will publish a periodic bulletin under the name "Circuit" which will cover the subjects mentioned in the former paragraphs.

Article IV

The duration of the association is unlimited.

Article V

Provisionally, the association has its registered office at the domicile of the general secretary, namely Sous-Cassan, Annemasse, Haute-Savoie.

Article VI

The association welcomes all Catholics, aged twenty-one or more, who recognise its objectives and accept the obligations mentioned in these Articles of Association.

Admissions are only valid if performed legally by three members, in a province under the legitimate authority of the Board. All other so-called admissions are declared null and void. The candidate application is compulsory for a written admission request. After inquiry, the candidate will be notified to attend in writing.

Admissions are carried out within a closed Circuit of 9,841 members, without distinction of language, social origin or class, and independently of all political ideology.

For the passage to the first grade, the member must acquire a white linen gown at his own expense.

A member of the association against whom a sentence is pronounced through a Board's ruling, following a decision of the plenary assembly, can be suspended, provisionally or permanently, from the rights inherent to the position of a member of the association or those relating to its responsibilities. However, the member can appeal, justify himself, or request a review of the ruling.

Each member who is in line with the law of the association has the right to vote from the first grade.

Article VII

The candidate must forsake his own personality and devote himself to serve a highly elevating apostolate. In all circumstances of life, he must do good, assist the Church, teach the truth, and defend the feeble and the oppressed.

Article VIII

A joining fee is payable when requesting admission. The admission charge is set at 500 francs (in 1956). It will be refunded in its entirety should admission be denied, but will remain the property of the association from the moment admission is granted.

The monthly subscription, called "participation", is 100 francs (in 1956), payable in quarterly instalments of 300 francs. Subscriptions are payable in advance, either to the C.C.P. (Giro account) in Lyon or directly to the treasurer.

Article IX

On admission, the members of the association will receive a membership card and a distinctive insignia. The authorisation to carry and use the card must be validated quarterly. This validation is carried out at the meetings of the association, with a special stamp embossed with the initials A.P. "acquis de participation" (accepted participation).

Article X

Any member struck off from the association will be notified by registered letter. Any resignation will be dealt with in the same manner. In both cases, current subscriptions remain the property of the association.

Excommunication of any kind, and for whatever reason, whether enforced by the Church or by a sect to which the person is affiliated, prohibits admission. This person and any excommunicated member will be permanently excluded from the association.

Article XI

The plenary assembly includes all members of the association. It is constituted by 729 provinces, 27 commanderies, and one Arch called "Arche Kyria".

The Arch and each commandery must comprise forty members; and each province must have thirteen members. The members are divided into two strengths:

- the Legion, responsible for the Apostolate
- the Phalanx, guardian of the Tradition
- The members form a nine-grade hierarchy.

Article XII

The nine-grade hierarchy is as follows.

in the 729 provinces

- Novices (Novitiates): 6,561 members

- Croisés (Crusaders): 2,187 members

in the 27 commanderies

- Preux (Champions): 729 members

- Ecuyers (Squires): 243 members

- Chevaliers (Knights): 81 members

- Commandeurs (Commanders): 27 members

in the "Arche Kyria"

- Connétables (Constables): 9 members

- Sénéchaux (Seneschals): 3 members

- Nautonier (Pilot): 1 member

Article XIII

The Board comprises twenty members, elected by a majority of votes, acting as:

- President
- Vice-president
- Secretary-general
- Treasurer

- Sixteen members in charge of the documentation sections.

The Board is responsible for accepting the admission requests, for informing the candidates of the results and, in accordance with the resolutions of the plenary assembly, for contacting, on behalf of the association, the relevant persons within the association and official services.

The Board cannot enter into an important agreement without submitting the matter to the plenary assembly and obtaining full powers from the latter.

The Board or the committee meet upon notification from the president.

Article XIV

The resources of the association include subscriptions, grants, and revenue from its assets. The association may have financial commitments in the form of loans for the acquisition of movable and immovable assets considered essential for its activities by the plenary assembly.

In a winding-up situation, the plenary assembly must elect two receivers and must determine their powers and the terms of their operations.

The association is represented in Court by one or several legal practitioners, as the case may be, such as a lawyer, a solicitor, a bailiff, a barrister, nominated by one or several members of the committee appointed to that effect.

Article XV

In accordance with common law, the heritage of the association must be solely answerable for all financial commitments, movable and immovable, validly contracted in its name, without the possibility of any member of the association being held responsible.

All important decisions engaging the responsibility of the association must be mentioned in a special register, showing the page numbers, dates and signatures of the Board members. The minutes of the Board meetings must be recorded in the same register. The acquisitions and alienations of properties must be declared in accordance with Article V of the decree of 16th August 1901. A descriptive statement must accompany all acquisitions and, in all circumstances, the price of the acquisition or the alienation must be specified. This clause is also valid for the purchases or donations of land.

Article XVI

With the full consent of the Board, the treasurer must set up legal reserves for:

the payment of rents or purchases of premises that the association is authorised to acquire

the investment in movable and immovable assets, as well as the purchases of land and buildings required in the accomplishment of the association's objectives

Article XVII

All drafted resolutions and proposals must be ratified by the members in an absolute majority of the votes.

The decisions taken by the plenary assembly must be executed as deeds.

To operate lawfully and legitimately, all provinces and commanderies must obtain a proper authorisation duly accredited by the Board.

Article XVIII

The Articles of Association can only be altered on a proposal from the committee.

The Board assigned to modify them must obtain two thirds of the votes from the attendance. The project must be presented and ratified at a later date at a plenary assembly of the members.

Article XIX

Within the allotted time, the Board committee must notify the police headquarters or sub-prefecture of any alterations to the Articles of Association, registered office, or members of the committee.

These notifications must be recorded in the association's register after being stamped and countersigned by the police.

In this register, and in accordance with Article V of the law of 1st July 1901 and Articles V and VI of the decree of 16th August 1901, the committee must also state the receipt date of notification of alterations.

Article XX

The Board must establish a "charter" of the company's rules and regulations which will define the detailed provisos for the appropriate execution of the present Articles of Association and for the association's internal organisation relating to studies, ceremonies, miscellaneous meetings, etc.

Article XXI

The committee will fulfil all formalities required by law to obtain state-approval.

Annemasse, 7th May 1956

Pierre Bonhomme, alias Stanis Bellas

and Pierre Plantard, alias Chyren

PART II

RENNES-LE-CHÂTEAU

GISORS

THE PRIORY OF SION LEGACY

Operation Delta-Reda

'It is very difficult to exercise an original activity within a pre-defined operation and I would be surprised if the actors could take part in a well-established play'.

The man who uttered these words was sipping his coffee wondering if rain would be a blessing; he was looking westerly and opened his shirt in order to breathe better. He closed his eyes, remembered the instructions, imagined dancing figures and, leaning against the bar, settled his bill without flinching: €666. He stared at the owner and coughed in a rude manner to escape the smoky hypnotic atmosphere of the violet room.

A young woman with a mat complexion was watching him, as if intrigued by his behaviour and expression; she sensed that something important was happening. He felt her gaze and was annoyed by it, then turned away abruptly seemingly disconcerted and stormed into the lavatories to stare wide-eyed in the mirror. Reassured, he came back, played a grid of lotto, set his watch at 6:00 p.m. precisely and, nonchalantly, glanced in the direction of the troublemaker, to realise that she had disappeared. He gave a quick knowing look to the boss, whilst the latter stationed himself on the east side of the bar to resume his meditation.

The man looked south, his eyes blinking like shining strands of spaghetti; he was sinking in a piece of poetry from his childhood when the bells of the North Station started to chime... Operation Delta-Reda began this day in October, on the 20th to be more precise. He was aware he had a mission but he did not know its substance or manifestation. When he arrived in Lille, he took a taxi to No. 9, rue de Béthune, to meet Mr. Deuxaresvents, a former professor in history who was to give him a talk on the Celtic past of the lost city of Reda.

As he was early, he went to the Place de la Liberté to visit the Museum which he found closed that day. He took the boulevard of similar name, turned left rue de la Puebla, to finally reach rue Jacquemard-Giélée. This was the avenue of his childhood, the narrow door of his souvenirs, the sacred temple of his initiation, especially No. 87 where, long ago, he had been an expert in military strategy. The toy shop had disappeared and offices seemed to occupy the second floor. He leaned forward towards the golden door plate with apprehension to realise that the building had become a rehabilitation centre for maladjusted children; another premonitory portent or sign. Appalled, he looked for the corner bookshop on the circular place. It too had disappeared. So, the toyshop had been transformed into specialised commercial offices and the bookshop had changed name! Time had committed the ultimate outrage of "non remembrance". He stared at two motorcycle cops on the place and found the police very inadequate... He had a grudge against the Watchmen of Time and was wondering whether his high school existed still. He decided to retrace his steps and, whilst meditating on Alzheimer's disease, reached Boulevard Louis XIV. Cleaner, smarter, and taller, the building sat imposingly on the horizon against the old belfry. He did not dare ask for news about the former students for fear of learning things he guessed but did not want to hear. He left hurriedly, looking at his watch, since he knew that the professor was inflexible with regard to punctuality. With a heavy heart, he eyed greedily the stalls of mussels, piled up like pyramids, surrounded by packets of ginger-colour fried chips. He was hungry and thirsty, worn out by the coast roads of enchanting flexible Time, which is without mercy for lovers of stillness, of eternity rediscovered for the briefest instant.

Now, he felt ready to approach the professor in ancient sciences, who lived No. 9, rue de Béthune, and was looking forward to the encounter having just regained the memory's certitude of Kosirev, a Russian scientist in the 1960s, when the magazine *Planète* was widespread amongst the students. Also, he had just spotted a sign on the asphalt: two dice representing the number seven!

The edifice built by a successor of Vauban contained three houses in one: the Spanish tavern, the English shop of sailor jumpers, and the cottage or residence of the Dean of the Faculty of Lille, qualified high school teacher in history and philosophy, denigrator of both the ancient and modern world. Beams of a chestnut colour brightened up the yellow ochre of the artificial roughcast frontage where a griffin sign hung. Under the porch, set ablaze by grimacing chimaeras resembling those of the Rue Lebouteux in Paris, letterboxes adorned with gothic mushrooms rattled on each passage of a car or truck authorised to unload their merchandise in this pedestrianized street. The bark of a black dog was the only thing missing to transport oneself to the London of a century ago. The sound of the automatic gate screeched like a monotonous chant of the Incas. In the courtyard, embellished by wrought iron balconies, I found myself in Mexico, in a village of the Tepozland sacred valley. Unconsciously, somewhat dizzily, I climbed the stairs as if I was scaling the slopes of Tepozteco, home to the sacred temple. On the third floor, two Greek jars filled with ferns guarded flame-coloured birds of a strange family. My hand froze when pulling the silk cord of a different generation.

Professor Deuxaresvents had not aged, for which I was very glad. I could not imagine him in a wheelchair or with a sculpted stick from India. He still stood erect, true to his motto. People said he was a marquis, he claimed he was a republican. When people called him Don Quixote, he responded Armand, born in Wazem, a working-class neighbourhood of the northern city. Some people, who enjoyed Van Dyke's paintings, suspected him of having Flemish origins; in response, he would laugh and let mystery hang over it. But how old was this noble man? There could be no answer to this question as it was a secret and forbidden subject. His eyes, which were of a rather astounding sea blue colour, observed you avidly with liking and scrutinised you without any sense of shame. The student world nicknamed him the winged Sphinx, after the one in Delphi. He had met all the great scientists, even those unknown to us. He wore Scottish trousers, of a striking royal blue colour, and a sky blue shirt that scintillated, with the silk material clashing against a jet-black jacket which he tapped in a dandy manner. His attires won him the favourite nickname of Théophile. Théophile Gautier, of course!

'Good day, Mr. de Colomb. You are punctual. My secretary informed me in time, but, I must admit, I do not understand the meaning of your request. I thought this affair was closed since your meeting with Mr. de Vlaminck, at the Castle du Pré (*Le Trésor des Templiers et son royal secret l'Aether* p. 61).

Théophile's irony was well known at the University. Although he did not like to repeat himself, he still remembered my essay on Christopher Columbus with the illustrations that decorated my rather striking text. In those days, I was first in history... As to the Reverend Father Charles de Vlaminck, I had met him at the Manor du Pré concerning a tomb described in detail in a 1905 bulletin.

It concerned the famous story of Rennes-le-Château where a parish priest, Father Saunière, had found a treasure equivalent to several millions euros! Father Charles did not believe in the treasure. However, the story of the lost city of Reda fascinated him, like so many others, of course, who desperately dug up and are still digging the land of the Corbières, who sounded each grotto, who explored every mine, and who studied all the legends of the Pyrenees in order to find a key to the narrow gate of the lost city.

With the passing years, this lost capital had become the city of Troy, than Heliopolis, the lost paradise and City of Light par excellence, the key to both Paradise and Hell most certainly. The historical controversy and research needs converged on several new places from Rennes-le-Château to Opoul-Périllos, to terminate at Notre-Dame de Marceille. The entire land of the Corbières had been turned over within a radius of fifty kilometres; yet the city retained its secrets concerning the treasure. The latter had been exploited under every angle by the tourist professionals. The affair came to an abrupt end, very unfavourably for certain people, when, after an ultrasound of the substratum, excavations were carried out under the Magdala tower, in vain of course, and a similar analysis of the subsoil of the church dedicated to Mary Magdalene was about to be done. The DRAC, Direction des Affaires Culturelles (Department of Cultural Affairs), complained to the mayor and his team, refusing any intrusion in the crypt sheltering the tomb of the Lords. The affair terminated like the one in Gisors; a wall was erected to prevent the disinterment of the dead, especially since similar intruding visits had already taken place in the fifties. By continuously going round in circles, disaster struck as the DRAC, responsible for the preservation of the national heritage, considered that a greater catastrophe was about to happen.

I did not reply to the professor immediately, but greeted him with a faint smile. From the hall where we stood, he invited me in the living room whilst straightening a forelock of white hair, eager to know the reason for my visit. The room was immense, full of shelves filled with books, magazines and ancient objects. A smouldering fire animated the Persian masks hanging on the mantelpiece. Deer antlers watched this room where the wise man worked on the great ideas of his time.

Sunk in a huge leather chair, I inhaled the ambient atmosphere and recognised the smell of the master's favourite tobacco, a mixture of Amsterdamer blended with a touch of mint. It was in Greece, near Eleusis, that he took a liking for this mix of perfumed nicotine.

'You have not changed,' I said, 'and your interior is vibrating like the violin I see on this little pedestal table. I remember a poker game with the spirits in the past. Marcel wanted to understand spiritualism and, whilst talking him out of it, you chose to play with them to demonstrate that it was absurd...'

This is how I started the conversation somewhat lost in this awesome place where incantations were not acceptable.

'Well, my young friend, your books of investigations show that you are looking for something specific, ineffable and special, without really grasping its full scope, cognition, and remoteness in particular. At first sight, you are facing a wall higher than anticipated. By continuously living with the invisible, you do not see anything anymore! My secretary gave me a small synopsis of your investigations and I realise, in fact, that this lost city is a myth for you and, therefore, I cannot help you,' he proclaimed like someone who wanted to arbitrate, prune, and refine in a well determined direction.

'Have you been able to find historical vestiges of this ancient city,' I mumbled timidly.

'My dear Jean, I refer you to your first book *Le trésor du triangle d'or*, page 99 precisely,' he said in a mocking tone, observing me and picking the book on the table. He started to read slowly while scrutinising me as if he knew by heart the *Dictionnaire des lieux et des communes*, or, more precisely, *L'Histoire nationale ou Dictionnaire géographique de toutes les communes du département de l'Aude* by MM. Girault, de Saint-Fargeau, Berthomieu and Tournal Sons, from the Mazarine National Library of France.

'First quotation, page 122 – "Limoux is mentioned for the first time in 854 CE in a certificate from Charles le Chauve (Charles the Bald) in favour of Ana, parish priest of Saint-Hilaire in the diocese of Carcassonne. Certain authors, however, maintain that this city existed at the time of Julius Caesar and that it was defended by a castle called Rhedæ. The Razès, of which Limoux was the capital, was in the past the appanage of the cadets of Carcassonne. It derives its name from the old castle of Rhedæ, which does not exist any more. Charles le Chauve gave Carcassonne, together with the County of Razès which encompassed Capsir and Donazan, to Bernard, Count of Toulouse."'

'Second quotation, page 123 – "On the mountain side, where the ancient city of Rhedæ was built, Limoux offers the most charming and picturesque view."'

'Third quotation, also on page 123 – "The most vivid imagination would find it difficult to depict a more enchanting scene than the one discovered at a glance from the top of Rhedæ. It is from this scenery that we tried to reproduce the lovely view of Limoux which we owe to the deft hand of Mr. Roux."'

He closed the book very slowly whilst muttering, 'Following the Religious upheavals and wars of the Count of Toulouse, the town of Limoux, previously situated on a hill, was wiped out upon the instructions of the king of France and rebuilt in the valley. This concerns your page 101 which I have pondered over and studied at great length with Professor Niel who, in 1933, had mooched around on the hill of the Devil to discover Visigothic herringbone stone vestiges! For a long time, I thought that you had explored the region but realise that you have missed the point, obsessed by the story of Father Saunière. Now, today, it might be too late,' he said with a smug and sardonic smile.

A young woman came in to serve us some tea. At first, dumbfounded by the professor's demonstration, I hardly paid attention to her, but when asked if I wanted sugar I recognised the stranger from the bar at the North Station. The master of Reda had organised everything from the start and was definitely intent on entering the lists to enable me to go further, but his last remarks chilled me. Why too late? Did he know more? Since when was he interested in this affair? Professor Niel had died twenty years ago! What had he organised since?

He read my mind but did not utter a word, leaving me to deliberate in my thoughts. He was waiting for the right question in order to reply with the right answer, but I could not find it... I had known for a long time that Father Saunière's story was faked. I had demonstrated this in my book *La Table d'Isis*, but the myth had continued and amplified with old English theories that were marrying Jesus to Mary Magdalene, giving them little Merovingian children that were to start the lineage of the Holy Grail, in short, another fictitious story concerning a false treasure... He came to my rescue by saying, 'You located the city without discovering its secret, but if you had done the reverse, you would not have discovered the old city! As for me, I approached the secret without going in the city.'

I looked at him bemused whilst helping myself to a Moroccan cake from a copper dish.

Prieuré de Sion

C.V.E.N.I.T.

In Hoc Signo Vinces

O 0000 1118 N 0815

Paris, le 27 décembre 2002

Conformément à notre Livre des Constitutions,

Ce jour, à Saint-Denis, le Nautonnier a procédé à l'investiture des membres de l'Arche. La Tête de l'Ordre est rétablie par ses soins. Selon la Tradition, elle est formée d'un couple assisté de son gardien.

Au seuil de cette année 2003 fatidique, tout est ainsi disposé pour l'apogée de SION car la présence de la Femme est indispensable, c'est la condition sine qua non comme l'ont appris tous nos membres.

Les Commanderies de Saint-Denis, Millau, Genève et Barcelonne sont en fonction. Toujours selon la Tradition, c'est une femme qui dirige la 1ère Commanderie.

L'Assemblée des Provinces est convoquée le 17 janvier 2003. Elle se réunira en plein cœur de Paris. La cérémonie particulière pour la PAIX dans le monde sera célébrée. Des instructions seront données à ce sujet.

L'ensemble de l'Ordre du Prieuré de Sion est de <u>9841</u> membres constituant le CIRCUIT de la PAIX...

Un bureau sera prochainement constitué, destiné à servir de lien officiel entre le public et l'Ordre de Sion. Le Secrétaire Général est chargé de son administration et de la publication du bulletin intérieur CIRCUIT.

Le Nautonnier

Prieuré de Sion 1981

G. CHYREN

Le Secrétaire Général

Prieuré de Sion Secrétariat Général

Gino SANDRI

19 - Circular from the Priory of Sion dated 27th December 2002

THE GOLDEN TRIANGLE: TWENTY YEARS LATER

Gisors, Rennes-le-Château, and Stenay – the same story in three different places – a perfect trinity worthy of the greatest suspense in history.

On 23rd December 1978, I was at Saint-Sulpice in the company of a strange individual, who looked more like Arsène Lupin than a former sexton of the parish of Saint-Louis d'Antin where he had been a common parishioner in his youth.

Whilst I was writing *Le Trésor des Templiers*, Pierre Plantard explained to me the symbolism of the church of Saint-Sulpice, which was his own interpretation like a drop in the ocean of Rennes-le-Château...

On 27th December 2002 - is this a typing mistake or a nod to supervise another hoax? a circular was addressed to the principal actors in the myth of the golden triptych.

This is how we learn by the signal In Hoc Signo Vinces that, "In accordance with our Articles of Association, this day, in Saint-Denis, the Nautonier (Pilot) has proceeded to the appointment of the members of the Arche (Arch). The Head of the Order is reinstated by him. In line with Tradition, the Head of the Order is represented by a couple assisted by their guardian".

Let us pause for an instant to ponder about these affirmations. Besides the numerous capital letters decorating this first slice of the discourse, we do not know that the head of the Order was represented by a couple assisted by a guardian. This is sheer modern madness!

The rest of the circular is a list of affirmations that further enhance the author's mythomania, or indeed his indoctrination.

"On the eve of this fateful year 2003, everything is thus organised for the apogee of SION, since the presence of the Female is imperative; this is the sine qua non condition, as all our members have been told."

We can readily imagine the necessary ritual to achieve this and are reminded of five circulars addressed to some esoteric bookshops in 2001 and 2002. This leads us to scrutinise the signature of this presumptuous missive, so much in vogue indeed! The authors of these defamatory letters confirming the Order's existence through forgeries or filth in newspapers such as *La Camisole*, and God knows if the Priory of Sion made a habit of them in the past, continue to perfect and refine a genre that they have developed over some fifty years. In the past, they had a Master surrounded by opportunists of various backgrounds; today, they are left with a petty king manipulated by a number of mentors who do not have the same objectives. But, let us continue, so as to understand the finality of this unusual declaration...

"The Commanderies of Saint-Denis, Millau, Geneva and Barcelona are in office. Again, in line with Tradition, it is a woman who leads the 1st Commandery."

Once more, tradition has a broad back! If it is that of the Women's Liberation Movement of Sion, it is in contradiction with history, indeed nonexistent! In brief, a new attempt to attract a few Amazons, carried away by the thrills of a new Order of chivalry. This resembles very much certain Neo-Templar Orders in the sixties and opens the way to discovering the signature behind this ludicrous declaration!

Megalomania having free reins, the rest of the discourse borders on grandiloquent statements...

"The Assembly of the Provinces is convened on 17th January 2003 and will be held in the very heart of Paris. The special ceremony for PEACE in the world will be celebrated on that day. Instructions will be provided to that effect."

We are delighted to learn that the Order of Sion is peace-loving. But the banality of this affirmation leaves us a little flabbergasted as to the objectives of the said Order. The next sentence confirms our first impressions. "The entire Order of Sion comprises 9,841 members which constitute the CIRCUIT of PEACE."

We have already noticed that the importance of numbers is commensurate with the paranoia of the Grand Master, unless, of course, this is a code.

The last sentence is very commercial, even promotional. It takes us directly to a secretary-general whom, in our opinion and as we know him, could have done without that publicity. Otherwise, times have changed a great deal. Indeed, what do we read?

"A Board, destined to serve as the official link between the public and the Order of Sion, will be created in the near future. The Secretary-general is responsible for its administration and the publication of the internal newsletter CIRCUIT."

The circular is signed by the secretary-general Gino Sandri and the Nautonier Pierre Plantard, alias the Great Chyren. We have some reservations about Gino Sandri; regarding Pierre Plantard, however, we know that, on 3rd February 2000, he left us to be reunited with the Eternal Light, as confirmed by his death certificate.

In this circular, the myth of the Great Extraterrestrial Monarch is well preserved almost three years after his death!

But what did the intelligence service say when he appeared on the public stage?

S T A T U T S
de
L'ALPHA-GALATES

Grand Ordre de Chevalerie

27 Décembre 1937

(Déclaration à la Préfecture de Police)

Article Premier.- Il est formé entre adhérents aux présents statuts un " Grand Ordre de Chevalerie ", sous le nom de : ALPHA-GALATES.

Son siège social, dit Arche Centrale, est situé à Paris (17e), rue Lebouteux, n° 10. Il pourra être transféré partout ailleurs par décisions du Gouverneur Général.

Des Arches pourront être créées en province.

Sa durée est illimitée.

Article 2.- L'Ordre a pour but d'associer ses membres dans une oeuvre d'entr'aide mutuelle et nationale, de parfaire leurs connaissances, de diriger leurs aspirations dans un sens esthétique, de leur inculquer un idéal chevaleresque basé sur la volonté de se conformer à l'honneur et de servir pour la Patrie.

En conséquence, l'Ordre favorisera :

1° Les cercles d'études et conférences ;
2° Les séances récréatives, cinématographiques et musicales ;
3° Les institutions telles que : le camping, les séjours de repos, les dispensaires, ayant pour objet la santé de ses membres ;
4° Les oeuvres de charité, telles que la visite des malades, l'assistance aux nécessiteux, l'adoption d'enfants abandonnés ou orphelins ;
5° La création d'un Secrétariat Populaire.

Article 3.- Pour devenir membre de l'Ordre, il faut :

1° Avoir plus de 18 ans ;
2° Adhérer aux présents statuts ;
3° Etre présenté par deux membres de l'Ordre ;
4° Remplir une demande d'admission ;
5° Fournir un certificat de domicile et trois photographies d'identité ;
6° Etre agréé par le Gouverneur Général ;
7° Verser une cotisation annuelle variant suivant la générosité de chacun, avec minimum de cinquante francs.

20 - Statutes of the ALPHA-GALATES dated 27 December 1937

29 Novembre 1942

A.S. de l'Association "Alpha-Galates" qui a sollicité l'autorisation exceptionnelle de fonctionner.

L'association dite " Alpha Galates" n'a pas, jusqu'ici, souscrit de déclaration à la Préfecture de Police, bien que d'après les dires de ses dirigeants ell ait été fondée le 27 décembre 1937.

Se présentant comme un" Grand Ordre de Chevalerie", ce groupement a pour but " d'associer ses membres dans une oeuvre d'entr'aide mutuelle et national de parfaire leurs connaissances, de diriger leurs aspira tions dans un sens esthétique, de leur inculquer un idéa chevaleresque basé sur la volonté de se conformer à l'honneur et de servir la Patrie".

Les moyens d'actions envisagés sont:

- a) la création de cercles d'études et les conféré ces,
- b) les séances récréatives, cinématographiques et musicales,
- c) de favoriser le camping ,les séjours de repos en faveur des membres,
- d) l'institution d'oeuvres de charité, telles que la visite des malades, l'assistance aux nécessiteux, l'adoption d'enfants abandonnés ou orphelins, et enfin la création d'un Secrétariat populaire ayant pour but de renseigner les famil es sur toutes les questions pouvant les intéresser.

Les membres adhérents à ce groupement ont le choix d'opter entre:

la "Légion" chargée d'assurer la sécurité de l'Ordre et la " Phalange" chargée de l'instruction des membres.

Les différents grades peuvant être obtenus par un membre sont:

- Dans l'"Arche"(Section) Aspirant et Chevalier.
- Dans la " Cité" (centre d'instruction) Néophyte- Disciple- Apôtre,
- Enfin dans le " Temple" (Haute Cour de l'Ordre) Frère- Respectable Frère- Très Révérend Frère, Très Honorable Frère- Très Vénérable Frère- Son Excellence Druidique- Son Altesse Druidique, -Sa Majesté Druidique.

C'est au " Temple" qu'il appartient, en cas d'empêchement, de désigner le Gouverneur Général qui n'est pas obligatoirement " Sa Majesté Druidique".

Les ressources de l'association sont constitués

par les cotisations des membres fixées à 50 francs au m
mum.

L'"Alpha -Galatas" est administré par un comi
directeur composé comme suit:

-Gouverneur Général: Pierre Plantard,
-Secrétaire Général: M. Francis, Sadot,
-Trésorière, Melle Amélie Raulo.

M. PLANTARD Pierre, Athanase Marie, dit " Pier
France", dit Varran de Verestra né le 18 Mars 1920 à Pa
(7è) de Plantard, Pierre, et de Raulo Amélie est, céliba
re.

Depuis le Ier juillet 1942 il est domicilié 10
Lebouteux (17è). Auparavant, il demeurait 22, place Ma
harbes (8è).

Se disant journaliste conférencier, il est en
té, Sacristain de la Paroisse St Louis d'Antin depuis le
de l'année. Il était auparavant à la charge de sa mère q
jouit d'une petite pension, son mari étant décédé dans
un accident du travail.

M. Plantard a essayé, en 1937, de fonder un mo
ment politique anti-juif et anti-maçonnique ayant pour b
" l'épuration et la rénovation de la France", et il avai
sollicité de M. Daladier, alors Président du Conseil, l'
risation de faire paraître à l'intention des membres de
groupement un journal intitulé " La Rénovation Française

Cette autorisation lui ayant été refusée il a
fait alors paraître cette feuille sous forme de tract. C
diffusion a cessé en 1939.

En 1940, il a adressé une demande aux Autorit
d'occupation, aux fins de reprendre la publication de ce
feuille. Cette demande est restée sans résultat jusqu'à
présent.

D'autre part, il a dirigé le " Groupement cat
que de jeunesse", mouvement officieux destiné à la récr
des jeunes gens de diverses paroisses catholiques de la
capitale. Ce groupement organisait chaque année une col
de vacances à Plestin-les-Grèves (Côtes du Nord) et co
en 1939, 75 jeunes gens.

M. Plantard a pris la parole au cours de conf
destinées aux jeunes, organisées par le " Groupement Cat
que de la Jeunesse", notamment le 20 Juin 1939 à la Sall
Villiers.

Il a adressé le 16 décembre 1940 au Maréchal u
lettre qui, sous prétexte de dénoncer un complot juif e
maçonnique apparait plutôt comme un subterfuge destiné à
attirer l'attention sur lui.

Enfin il a fondé en mai 1941, une association
"Rénovation Nationale Française" restée d'ailleurs sans
fonctionner, l'autorisation lui ayant été refusée par l
Autorités Allemandes le 3 septembre 1941.

M. Plantard apparait comme l'un de ces jeunes
illuminés et prétentieux, chefs de groupements plus ou m
fictifs, qui veulent se donner de l'importance et profit
du mouvement actuel de la jeunesse, pour tenter de se
prendre en considération par les pouvoirs publi

Son nom n'est pas noté aux Sommiers

M. SADOT Francis, Joseph, Raymond, se disant " Jean Falloux" né le 8 avril 1920 à Bois Colombes, employé à la S.N.C.F., est célibataire.

Il a toujours habité 21, rue Mertens à Bois-Colombes.

Ancien Sacristain de l'église Saint Louis d'Antin il est employé depuis le 8 janvier dernier, comme auxiliaire au Service des Titres de la S.N.C.F. 23, rue de Londres (4è) .

M. Sadot n'a pas attiré l'attention au point de vue politique.

Il est représenté comme de bonne moralité, travailleur et bon camarade, mais faible de caractère.

Son nom n'est pas noté aux Sommiers Judiciaires.

Melle RAULO, Amélie, est née le 12 janvier 1884 à Doulon en Nantes (Loire Infre).

Elle est domiciliée 14 Grande Rue à Redon (Ille et Vilaine).

Son domicile étant situé hors du ressort de la Préfecture de Police, il n'a pas été possible d'obtenir de renseignements à son sujet. Il y a lieu cependant de remarquer que la mère de Plantard est née Raulo et serait âgée de 58 ans.

L'association " Alpha Galates" a fait l'objet en date du 18 Juillet 1942 d'une demande de renseignements de la part du Ministre de l'Intérieur, en raison de la diffusion dans la région bretonne de tracts circulaires signés " Varans Vincent" et situant le siège social de l'association 36 rue de l'Abbé Groult à Paris (15è). Or les recherches effectuées à l'époque n'avaient pas permis de trouver trace dans cette voie, d'un nommé " Varans Vincent", ou d'une association dite " Alpha-Galates". Il apparaît maintenant qu'il s'agissait en réalité d'un nommé Plantard qui on le sait adopte parfois le pseudonyme de " Varrans de Verestra ".

En résumé, on peut considérer que la création de l'association " Alpha Galates" ne constitue qu'une nouvelle tentative de Plantard , en vue de se faire prendre en considération par les pouvoirs publics. D'ailleurs le chiffre de 673 membres, indiqué par les dirigeants est bien loin de répondre à la réalité.

21 - A.S. of the Association "Alpha-Galates" 29th November 1942

On the 29th November 1942, Pierre Plantard is 22 years old. For the umpteenth time, he is trying to operate an Association that he created, supposedly, in 1937, at the age of 17!

Following an enquiry made by the Associations Committee at the Police Headquarters, a report is drafted on that date which is extremely eloquent on the subject and speaks for itself concerning the destiny of the future Great Monarch, as shown below.

Beginning of a report dated 29th November 1942.

A.S. of the Association Alpha-Galates, which has solicited a special authorisation to operate.

The association called "Alpha-Galates" has not, to date, made any declaration at the Police Headquarters, even though their directors claim it was created on 27th December 1937.

The group, which presents itself as a Grand Order of Chivalry, wishes "to affiliate its members in a charitable organisation that will offer mutual and national support, perfect their knowledge, fulfil their aspirations in an ethical manner, and instil a chivalrous ideal based on the determination to behave honourably and to serve the country."

The intended means of action are:

The creation of study groups and lectures.

The organisation of recreational, cinematographic and musical sessions.

The facilitation of camping and restful breaks for the members.

The implementation of charitable work such as visits to the sick, assistance to the infirm, the adoption of abandoned children and orphans, and, finally, the creation of a working-class Secretariat designed to inform families on all questions that may be of interest to them.

The members of this group have a choice between the "Legion", responsible for the security of the Order, and the "Phalanx", responsible for the education of its members.

The various grades that can be attained by a member are:

In the Arch (Division): Apprentice and Knight

In the City (Education Centre): Neophyte (novice)-Disciple-Apostle

In the Temple (High Court of the Order): Honourable Brother, Brother Most-Reverend-Brother, Very Honourable Brother, Very Venerable Brother (Worshipful Master), His Druidic Excellency, His Druidic Highness, His Druidic Majesty.

If there is an impediment, it is up to the Temple to designate the Governor-General, who is not automatically "His Druidic Majesty".

The financial resources of the Association are made of the members' subscriptions, set at a minimum of 50 francs.

The Alpha-Galates is administered by a committee of directors as follows:

Governor-General: Pierre Plantard

Secretary-General: Francis Sadot

Treasurer: Ms Amélie Raulo

Mr. Pierre Athanase Marie Plantard, known as "Pierre de France", known also as "Varrans de Verestra", born on 18th March 1920 in Paris, in the 7th district, son of Plantard, Pierre, and Raulo, Amélie, is unmarried.

Since 1st July 1942, he has been domiciled at No. 10, rue Lebouteux in the 17th district; previously, he lived at No. 22, place Malesherbes in the 8th district.

Claiming to be a journalist and a lecturer, he is, in reality, sexton at the Parish of Saint-Louis d'Antin since the beginning of 1942. In the past, he was dependent on his mother who benefited from a small pension after the death of her husband following an accident at work.

In 1937, Mr. Plantard tried to create an anti-Jew and anti-Masonic political movement with the objective of "cleansing and reforming France", and solicited from Mr. Daladier, Prime Minister at the time, the authorisation to publish, for the group members, a journal entitled *La Rénovation Française* (*French Reform*). When the authorisation was denied him, he distributed the newsletter in the form of a leaflet. The distribution ceased in 1939.

In 1940, he made a request to the Occupation authorities to resume the publication of this pamphlet. This request is without result to date.

Furthermore, he led the "Youth Catholic Group", an official movement for the recreation of young people from various Catholic parishes in the capital. This group organised a holiday camp in Plestin-les-Grèves, Côte-du-Nord, annually, and amounted to sixty five youngsters in 1939.

Mr. Plantard spoke during lectures for the young organised by the "Youth Catholic Group", notably on 20th June 1939 in the Villiers Conference Room.

On 16th December 1940, on the pretext of denouncing a Jewish and Masonic plot, he wrote a letter to the Marshal of France which appeared as a subterfuge to attract attention to himself.

Finally, in May 1941, he founded an association called "Rénovation" (Reform), which was left dormant, as the authorisation for him to operate was refused by the German Occupational Authorities on 3rd September 1941.

Mr. Plantard comes across as one of those visionary and pretentious young people, leaders of somewhat fictitious movements, who want to act important and take advantage of the current youth movement in order to be considered by the authorities.

His name does not appear in the police records.

Mr. Francis Joseph Raymond Sadot, who calls himself "Jean Falloux", born on 8th April 1920 at Bois-Colombes, employee of the S.N.C.F. (French National railway), is unmarried.

He has always been living at No. 21, rue Mertens, Bois-Colombes.

Former sexton at the Church of Saint-Louis d'Antin, he has been working, since 8th January this year, as casual employee for the Department of Stocks and Shares of the S.N.C.F., No. 23, rue de Londres, in the 4th district.

Mr. Sadot has not drawn attention in the political field. He is described as having high moral standards and of being hardworking and a good colleague but weak of character.

His name does not appear in the police records.

Ms Amélie Raulo, was born on 12th January 1884 in Doulon-en-Nantes, Loire-Inférieure.

She is domiciled No. 14, Grande Rue, in Redon, Ille-et-Vilaine.

Her domicile being outside the jurisdiction of the Police Headquarters, it has not been possible to obtain information about her. It is worth noting, however, that Plantard's mother's maiden name was Raulo and she would be 58 years old to date.

The Association "Alpha-Galates" has been the subject of an enquiry from the Minister of the Interior on 18th July 1942 following the distribution in the Breton area of leaflets signed "Varans Vincent", with their head office No. 36, rue de l'Abbé Groult, Paris 15th. However, investigations down that road at the time did not disclose the trail of the said "Varans Vincent" or an association called "Alpha-Galates". It now appears that the person concerned was, in fact, a certain Plantard who, as we know, sometimes uses the pseudonym "Varrans de Verestra".

In short, one can consider that the creation of the association "Alpha-Galates" is nothing less than another attempt by Plantard to be considered by the authorities. Besides, the figure of 673 members mentioned by the directors is far from matching reality.

End of the report dated 29th November 1942

This first report is a real gold mine for the investigator. In fact, everything was decided from the start at the Parish of Saint-Louis d'Antin by the two sextons Sadot and Plantard, sole founders of the association Alpha-Galates.

Three years later, on 13th February 1945, a new report confirms the preceding one in its entirety. However, the journal Vaincre, in Issue No. 3 dated 21st November 1942, stipulates that the first sexton has been struck off from the Order. Pierre Plantard is now free to impose his illusory authority and, there again, the conclusion of the second report speaks volumes on the subject...

Dramatic artists join the association in force; however, the comedians come and go, not always appreciating the role of their conductor. It is likely that the Marquis Philippe de Cherisey made his appearance at that time. Here is an excerpt of the second report which completes the first one.

Beginning of a report dated 13th February 1945.

A.S. of the Association Alpha-Galates.

The association called “Alpha-Galates”, with the caption “Grand Order for Social Support”, founded on 6th September 1944, was declared to the Police Headquarters on 12th September, pursuant to the law of 1st July 1901, and registered under number 79.501-6873. Its head office is located at No. 10, rue Lebouteux.

In accordance with the terms and conditions of its statutes, the motto of the association is “Honour and Country”, and its distinctive emblem is a Gallic cock and a lion.

The association’s objectives are:

The creation, maintenance, and development of one or more Help Centres for the young who suffered from the German oppression through labour camps, deportation and imprisonment.

The organisation of classes, study groups and conference circles, of cinematographic, theatrical and musical sessions, of centres for physical training, gymnastic and scouting activities, and, finally, each year, the organisation of trips and holiday breaks.

The publication of a special bulletin concerning the centres, the organisation’s propaganda and everything relating to it; in brief, the publication of everything that may contribute to the progress of the organisation.

The duration of the association is unlimited.

To become a member of the association, one must have:

- Completed a formal request for admission on which the Board gives its verdict in total sovereignty.
- Not belonged to a German or pro-German organisation, such as the Militia, the Legion of French Volunteers against Bolshevism, or other.
- Paid the admission fee of 5 francs and the annual subscription of 50 francs. This subscription can be bought back for the sum of 500 francs. The annual subscription for honourable members is 1000 francs.
- No document from the association is valid without the stamp and signature of the President.
- The resources of the association comprise grants, subscriptions, and income from its assets.
- In a winding-up situation, the Board designates one or more receivers and determines their powers and the terms of their operations.

Currently, the association is managed by a Board of the following members:

President:	Mr. Plantard, known as "Pierre de France"
Vice-president:	Mr. Theureau, known as "Vallauris"
Secretary:	Miss Libre, known as "Dartois Francine"
Treasurer:	Mr. Tillier

[Plantard's personal details are not repeated here since they are identical to those mentioned in the 1942 report, except for the following conclusion].

On 24th October 1942, Mr. Plantard was the object of an enquiry by our services at the request of the German Occupational Authorities, after having solicited their authorisation to found the association in question, which was in fact denied him.

Those various requests, and possibly his stance towards the German occupation, led to his incarceration for four months in the Prison of Fresnes.

Plantard comes across as a degenerate and visionary young man, who believes he is the only one capable of adequately leading French youth.

He does not attract attention in any other way, whether privately or politically, and an investigation report in his name was returned by the Criminal Records office with the mention "unknown".

Mr. Jacques Theureau, known as "Vallauris", born on 8th June 1921 in the 17th district of Paris, is unmarried. Since birth, he has been living with his parents, domiciled No. 12 rue Joffroy, in the 17th district, for a yearly rent of 3000 francs.

Dramatic performer by profession, M. Theureau is currently employed by the Ministry of Information and attached to radio station 45.

He is favourably portrayed privately and does not attract attention politically.

He is unknown in the Archives of the Police and his name does not appear in the Criminal Records.

Miss Suzanne Libre, known as "Francine Dartois", was born on 7th March 1922 in Arras, Pas-de-Calais. Since 1940, she has been living with her parents, domiciled at No. 127 boulevard Péreire, in the 17th district, for a yearly rent of 7000 francs. She is currently attending dramatic art classes.

Miss Libre enjoys favourable reports in conduct and morality. She does not seem to exhibit any political belief and has never attracted the attention of our services in this matter.

Miss Libre has no criminal records.

Mr. Jules Joseph Alfred Tillier, born on 26th April 1896 in Boulogne-sur-Mer, Pas-de-Calais, son of Alfred Philias and Marie, Joséphine Guyot, is divorced and without children.

Since 1914, he has been domiciled at No. 14, boulevard Ney, in the 18th district.

Mr. Tillier is Chief Accountant for the Compagnie des Forges et Aciéries de la Marine d'Homécourt, No. 12, rue de La Rochefoucauld, in the 9th district.

He has been working as a casual employee after some injuries during the 1914-1918 War and was placed in a reserved occupation in 1939. He is holder of the Military Cross with two mentions in dispatches.

He is favourably portrayed privately and does not attract attention politically.

Mr. Tillier is unknown to our services and is not mentioned in the Archives of the Police.

His name does not appear in the Criminal Records.

From the information gathered by our services, this association has never been operative. It comprises about fifty members, who resign in turn as soon as they appraise the President of the association and realise that the organisation is not of a reliable nature.

End of the report dated 13th February 1945.

In other words, the Order Alpha-Galates never existed except on paper! As for the Association, it was accepted in 1944 only with very limited aims, and was nothing more than a meeting of dramatic performers and comedians.

The idea of creating a Grand Order of Chivalry was soon replaced by more pragmatic interests. We will see later that the same causes produce the same effects; through other associations, all the way to the famous Priory of Sion...

From 1943, Pierre Plantard, under the pseudonym Pierre de France, embarks on the Secret Science of the Sages, and produces a digest of his thoughts concerning the esoteric doctrine of the Great Initiates' legendary kingdom. Once again, he uses intentions already attributed to the Law Professor Maurice Lecomte Moncharville in the journal *Vaincre*.

Apparently, the latter conferred upon him the Head of the Order just before his death. This time, he quotes excerpts from a book *Les Mystères de l'Inde* (*The Mysteries of India*) which, like many other documents, are just a product of the "Plantardian" imagination.

Indeed, on 19th April 1984, we received the biography and bibliography of this former Law Professor from the Faculty of Law in Strasbourg. The biography stipulates that Mr. Maurice Lecomte Moncharville was born in Bar-le-Duc on 6th April 1864. His diverse functions included:

Sub-director of the Journal on International Public Law (1897-1901)

Conference Lecturer at the Law Faculty of Paris (1898-1901)

Professor at the French College of Law in Cairo (1901-1915)

Legal Adviser for the Siamese government in Bangkok (1908-1912)

Assignments for the French National Bank in London and Switzerland (1916)

Legal Adviser for the Japanese Embassy in Paris (1917-1919)

Professor of Colonial Legislation and Economy at the Law Faculty of Strasbourg from 1st October 1919 to 31 July 1934

After studying his biography and bibliography, we examined the National Library records; no book was attributed to that author, no mission took place in Tibet. But it is true that, in that article, Plantard warns us, "That the initiates, wishing to confound the laymen's simple curiosity, designate a certain area of the planet with the word Inde (India), meaning "Sacred Land". Accompanied by the actor Philippe de Cherisey, Plantard seeks this Agartha everywhere, in Gisors, in Rennes-le-Château, and in Stenay, that is, in our golden triangle. He does this with unusual means such as the knowledge attributed to the Magi, and old and new scientific discoveries which could be read, at the time, in the journal *L'Ami de la Science* (*The Friend of Science*), supervised by Victor Meunier.

> *"I hold a discovery that frightens me... There are two types of electricity; one earthy and blind produced by contact between metals and acids; the other intelligent and clear-sighted. The electricity divided itself in the hands of Galvani, Nobioli and Mateuci. The crude current tagged along Jacobi, Bonelli and Moncel, whilst the other current followed Boirobert, Thirolier and Knight Duplanty... Thunder in a ball, or globular electricity, contains a mind that disobeys Newton and Mariotte, to do as it pleases. In the Annals of the Fourteen Academies, there are thousands of proofs concerning the intelligence of Lightning... But I realise I get carried away. I nearly gave you the clue that will uncover the universal principle that governs the two worlds."*

Thus, the programme and objectives of the "future King of France" take shape at that time. This article is too important not to continue with its analysis, as the young man, who is 26 years old at the time, discovers television, Atlantis and the underground kingdoms; in short, the two worlds of Plato with his timeless cavern, namely the World of Ideas, and the World of Men. Furthermore, he read with assiduity the works of Th. Moreux, notably *Le Ciel et l'Univers* (*Heaven and Universe*).

> *"The electricity of Agartha is similar to the one that governs mankind and the Universe; it comes from the disintegration of the atom. If an imprudent traveller entered the Agartha, what would be his behaviour? When one considers that everywhere, in every room... (one should write in every corner of the room), there are invisible screens, created from wavebands, on which, at will, the Masters can make monsters appear, wild cats, dangerous reptiles or televised individuals, which seem so real that nobody can fathom their unreality."*

The Great Chyren, or future clairvoyant, is making his debuts, but a few things are getting out of hand already; these will be on the increase with time. Indeed, behind these mystical-scientific visions, we can perceive a taste for power and the invention of a mission that form part of an inflated ego, as who are these hidden masters, apart from Moncharville already mentioned?

In fact, the person principally concerned realises this and warns us, "What would be the reaction of this imprudent traveller who would never know if a palpable being is talking to him or if it is its televised ghost; who would see light radiating around him without understanding its provenance; who could be put to a deep sleep, through waves, from a distance, without anaesthetic; who would have metallic automatons with human brains to guide and serve him, fulfilling his desires before he expresses them, and the most terrible thing for him would be, assuredly, that of not being able to think freely since the Sages, on a whim, could detect his most inner thoughts. Why, therefore, stress the legendary aspect only of this work, which inevitably diminishes its impact?"

We are reassured since he started from a symbolic tale only, but no explanation is given regarding the meaning of that legend; Plantard apologises to the reader as if something escaped him; he will tell us, "It is Moncharville's fault!"

Three months before the death of Maurice Lecomte Moncharville, Plantard wrote, in his own hand, as for a will, the tale of a trip that the professor undertook in 1904 and 1905, in Lhasa, and his visit to the Dalai Lama Ngawang-Lobsang, concluded by the story of his stay in 1907 in the sanctuaries of the Agartha.

If we examine the biography of this scholar, we realise that between 1901 and 1915 he was Professor at the French College of Law in Cairo. Unless Egypt belongs to Tibet, or other sacred land, we do not see how, and in which capacity, this Professor of Law could have met the Dalai Lama and visited the underground kingdom. This is, therefore, the final proof that Moncharville was not part of this Agartha saga and the Order Alpha-Galates! This does not prevent Plantard from continuing on the same theme.

According to him, Mr. Lecomte Moncharville did not wait for the arrival of Catholicism to know the secret of nature. Here is what Plantard make him say:

> *"In the course of my mission in Tibet, I was received in the Forbidden City in Lhasa, at the headquarters of the Buddha's Government represented by the Dalai Lama.*
>
> *During the many years of my mission in Lhasa, I won the trust and friendship of all. I probably learned what no other initiate from the West has ever known. As I was on the point to depart, the monks led me through never-ending staircases*

carved in the mountain to a real underground city located under the Temples. There, I was allowed to catch sight of the collection of objects rescued from Atlantis before the disaster. Then, I visited the Sanctuary of the Dragon where, for the first time, I attended a ceremony of superior rite in the East. Finally, in the last days, I could contemplate electrical machines brought from Atlantis, unknown today, capable of generating in the underground rooms a light and atmosphere exactly identical to that found in the open air, which had surprised me so greatly during my first visit to the mountain. These are machines that the Dalai Lama uses also for erecting magnetic walls around the Forbidden City and preventing access by unwanted visitors...

Very well for the East, you may say, but the West had the doctrine of Catholicism only to bring them civilisation. Glaring blunder, as France, via Brittany, also knew the Atlantean cult, of which the entire druidic faith is the preservation, with its sacrifice to the sun, mistletoe ceremony, menhir and dolmen, and institutions of chivalry.

Among other communities, the druids founded a monastery on the present location of Mont Saint-Michel (Mount Saint Michael). In those days, the monastery was called the Sanctuary of the Dragon. When Catholicism drove the druids out of Gaul, the monks acquired the Atlantean traditions and formed the Alpha of the Dragon, which divided itself into two sections: the Cistercians, who championed Christianity, and the Agartha, which preserved the Atlantean doctrine.

Of these two orders, only the Agartha is of interest to us for the moment, since our present-day "City" is nothing but a direct continuation of it. This is why I thought interesting to relate the following curious legend...

Less than a kilometre south of the eighty-metre rocky gable that dominates vertically the beach of Carolles and faces the promontory of Granville, the pebbles of the Chausey islands and the coastal cliffs of Brittany, one discovers an arid ravine and tortured shores covered with a mass of enormous fallen rocks. Better, between the Rock of Sâr and the Chain of the Devil which overlooks the total expanse with its amazing panorama of megaliths in ruins, it is a whole rampart that aligns its huge stones, so perfectly blended in the background on this ridge in front of the sea.

Without going back to the far-away days when the Earth convulsions tore Great Britain away from the Continent, let us say about a millennium ago, the waves had not submerged our land yet. The present Gulf of Saint-Malo and the Norman

Islands were attached to the mainland; Normandy and Armorica were simply separated by the Titus River, formed by the Breton rivers Sée, Salune, Rance, Arguenon, and others.

In those days, the forest of Jussy spread over the entire area between the Cho-Zech (now Chausey) Islands, the Mounts of the Dragon (now Mont Saint-Michel), and the Tom-Belen (now Tombelaine). The famous Val de Luth (now Lude) was the Knights' refuge which they turned into a fortified city where, for almost seven hundred years, the Catholics failed against their supremacy.

During that time, they exploited the But-Or (gold mines), finished the city of the Agartha underground, the largest in the world, and built a monastery called the Sanctuary of the Dragon on one of the mounts of the Dragon.

In 812 CE, they disappeared abruptly; a few days after, in a rumble of thunder, the sea covered the area where the last Atlantean people had lived.

Afterwards, dominating the waves, only one of the mounts of the Dragon remained; proof of the Knights' activity through its sanctuary.

Then, the Catholics decided to attack and destroy this monastery that seemed to defy them in an exasperating manner. With their leader called San Michael, they fought fiercely for three years. After victory, their leader having been swallowed by quicksand, they decided to name the island after their victor San Michael, nowadays Saint-Michel; this is where the phrase the Dragon beaten by Saint-Michael originated.

The Sanctuary of the Dragon was not abandoned but a new monastery was built on its site. Thus, underneath the crypt located under the Hall of the Galatian Knights, an older crypt from that period provides access to the ancient sanctuary. It is via the Sanctuary of the Dragon that the first Knights approached the underground tunnels that led them in the heart of the Breton crypts, three-hundred and seventy-nine metres down in the City of Agartha, where the Temple of Aga can be found. Is this the only entrance to the City of Agartha nowadays? No, but it is certainly the oldest."

Plantard has just sketched out a scenario that he will repeat in Gisors. Fundamentally and strategically, his discourse is derived from a simplistic anti-Catholic stance, since he is not sexton at the Parish of Saint-Louis d'Antin anymore, like his friend Jean Falloux. So, what happened? Has the sexton, son of a manservant, cousin of a priest in the 17th district, failed his minor, or even, major orders? We will find out in Saint-Sulpice, on 23rd December 1978. However, it is probable that he has already acquired a taste for crypts and underground kingdoms in the chapel of the old Capuchins' convent, and that he has retained a singular bitterness from it, like that of a blue apple, for example. From now on, the rebellious angel, the operetta's Lucifer, in short, the former sexton, will exploit priests as if the latter had hidden from him the secret of the Universe. For those reasons, he will become the great clairvoyant, the "saturnine Chyren with his kingdom and his church..."

Thus, he carries on and quotes, in turn, the legend of the town of Is, which he links, of course, to Isis, and tells us that it contains a very reliable truth regarding the Forbidden City of Agartha, which is partially underwater and from where sailors can hear chants and bells, those mysterious sounds that petrify them and from which he has been deprived.

He even includes a quotation from *Au Seuil du Mystère* (*On the Threshold of Mystery*) written in 1890 by Stanislas de Guaîta, "A vault, for which the key has been lost, opens somewhere in the Val. It is said that, across the centuries, rare audacious people were able to pierce the secret of the underground passage where umpteen galleries interlace; there is the seat of the inexorable minister of an ineluctable law."

Then, again, he (Mr. Lecomte Moncharville) discourses upon the science of the Magi and on the Plantardian trinity.

> *"It was possibly my penultimate trip when, in 1907, at the masters' constant pleas, I decided to go to Brittany. What I saw and learned reminded me exactly of Lhasa. There also, present-day science was outstripped, and the psychic culture of the Magi had nothing to envy from that of the Tibetan Sages. What I noticed primarily was an assembly of indecipherable signs covering most of the granite walls of the philosopher's stone; so, in front of my perplexity and in order to facilitate my comprehension, one of the masters of the secret explained promptly that only three symbols were underground and formed the oneness of all symbols...*
>
> *Then, he showed me the King's room, where engravings decorated the polished granite walls in several places; they were signed, in the main, by famous people who visited the heart of the Agartha in search of a fragment of the secret light; amongst others, a scene signed by Paracelse drew my attention. Finally, in the Circular Temple, my guide pointed towards something. As soon as I approached, I recognised the little circular altar of Lhasa; but here, voices seem to emanate from the mysterious altar, voices that I had heard before... somewhat muffled as if coming from the centre of the Earth. You see, said my guide, here you are very near Lhasa at the City of the Agartha; only terrestrial distance separates us."*

Here, we come to the end of the public revelations made by Mr. Lecomte Moncharville, deceased on 23rd January 1943, and those of his successor Pierre de France, who promised us a beautiful science-fiction programme which he implemented in a systematic manner...

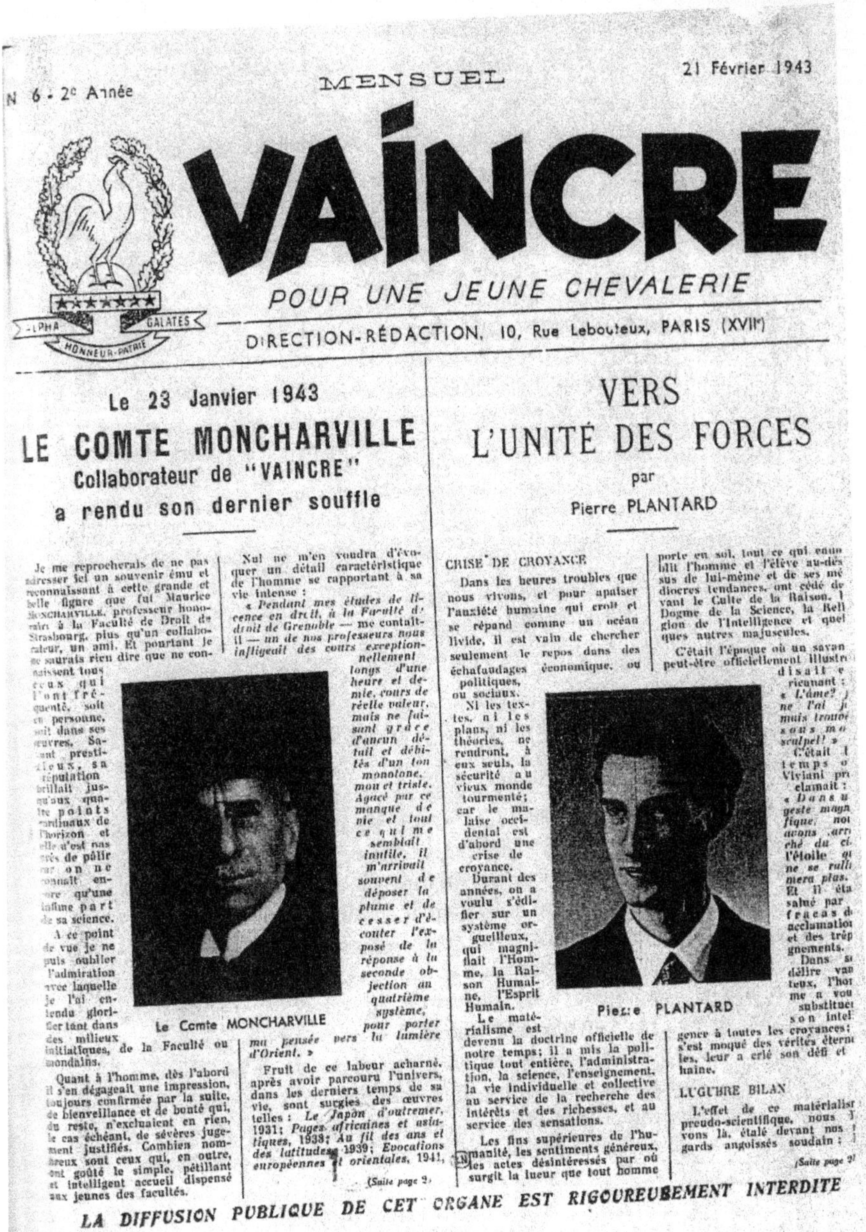

N 6 - 2e Année

MENSUEL

21 Février 1943

VAINCRE

POUR UNE JEUNE CHEVALERIE

DIRECTION-RÉDACTION, 10, Rue Lebouteux, PARIS (XVIIe)

Le 23 Janvier 1943
LE COMTE MONCHARVILLE
Collaborateur de "VAINCRE"
a rendu son dernier souffle

Je me reprocherais de ne pas adresser ici un souvenir ému et reconnaissant à cette grande et belle figure que fut Maurice MONCHARVILLE, professeur honoraire à la Faculté de Droit de Strasbourg, plus qu'un collaborateur, un ami. Et pourtant je ne saurais rien dire que ne connaissent tous ceux qui l'ont fréquenté, soit en personne, soit dans ses œuvres. Savant prestigieux, sa réputation brillait jusqu'aux quatre points cardinaux de l'horizon et elle n'est pas près de pâlir car on ne connaît encore qu'une infime part de sa science.

A ce point de vue je ne puis oublier l'admiration avec laquelle je l'ai entendu glorifier tant dans des milieux initiatiques, de la Faculté ou mondains.

Quant à l'homme, dès l'abord il s'en dégageait une impression, toujours confirmée par la suite, de bienveillance et de bonté qui, du reste, n'excluaient en rien, le cas échéant, de sévères jugements justifiés. Combien nombreux sont ceux qui, en outre, ont goûté le simple, pétillant et intelligent accueil dispensé aux jeunes des facultés.

Nul ne m'en voudra d'évoquer un détail caractéristique de l'homme se rapportant à sa vie intense :

« *Pendant mes études de licence en droit, à la Faculté de droit de Grenoble* — me contait-il — *un de nos professeurs nous infligeait des cours exceptionnellement longs d'une heure et demie, cours de réelle valeur, mais ne faisant grâce d'aucun détail et débités d'un ton monotone, mou et triste. Agacé par ce manque de vie et tout ce qui me semblait inutile, il m'arrivait souvent de déposer la plume et de cesser d'écouter l'exposé de la réponse à la seconde objection au quatrième système, pour porter ma pensée vers la lumière d'Orient.* »

Le Comte MONCHARVILLE

Fruit de ce labeur acharné, après avoir parcouru l'univers, dans les derniers temps de sa vie, sont surgies des œuvres telles : *Le Japon d'outremer*, 1931; *Pages africaines et asiatiques*, 1938; *Au fil des ans et des latitudes*, 1939; *Evocations européennes et orientales*, 1941,

(Suite page 2)

VERS
L'UNITÉ DES FORCES

par

Pierre PLANTARD

CRISE DE CROYANCE

Dans les heures troubles que nous vivons, et pour apaiser l'anxiété humaine qui croît et se répand comme un océan livide, il est vain de chercher seulement le repos dans des échafaudages économique, ou politiques, ou sociaux.

Ni les textes, ni les plans, ni les théories, ne rendront, à eux seuls, la sécurité au vieux monde tourmenté; car le malaise occidental est d'abord une crise de croyance.

Durant des années, on a voulu s'édifier sur un système orgueilleux, qui magnifiait l'Homme, la Raison Humaine, l'Esprit Humain.

Le matérialisme est devenu la doctrine officielle de notre temps; il a mis la politique tout entière, l'administration, la science, l'enseignement, la vie individuelle et collective au service de la recherche des intérêts et des richesses, et au service des sensations.

Les fins supérieures de l'humanité, les sentiments généreux, les actes désintéressés par où surgit la lueur que tout homme porte en soi, tout ce qui ennoblit l'homme et l'élève au-dessus de lui-même et de ses médiocres tendances, ont cédé devant le Culte de la Raison, le Dogme de la Science, la Religion de l'Intelligence et quelques autres majuscules.

C'était l'époque où un savan[t] peut-être officiellement illustr[e] disait e[n] ricanant : « *L'âme? j[e] ne l'ai ja[mais] trouvé[e] sous m[on] scalpel!* »

C'était l[e] temps o[ù] Viviani pr[o]clamait : « *Dans u[n] geste magn[i]fique, no[us] avons arr[a]ché du ci[el] l'étoile q[ui] ne se rall[u]mera plus.* » Et il éta[it] salué par [le] fracas d[es] acclamatio[ns] et des trép[i]gnements.

Dans s[on] délire van[i]teux, l'hom[me] a vou[lu] substitue[r] son intel[li]gence à toutes les croyances; s'est moqué des vérités étern[el]les, leur a crié son défi et [sa] haine.

LUGUBRE BILAN

L'effet de ce matérialism[e] pseudo-scientifique, nous [l'a]vons là, étalé devant nos [re]gards angoissés soudain ; [...]

Pierre PLANTARD

(Suite page 2)

LA DIFFUSION PUBLIQUE DE CET ORGANE EST RIGOUREUSEMENT INTERDITE

22 - Article regarding Moncharville in monthly journal Vaincre

EPIPHANY IN GISORS

On 6th January 2006, we celebrated the Epiphany (Twelfth Night) which became the kings' feast, ancient Roman Saturnalia.

Epiphany in Greek means "Apparition". It is the bygone Christmas day when the Heavenly King is presented to the three Magi: Caspar, Melchior and Balthazar.

Gisors, capital of the Norman Vexin region (Eure), eighty kilometres north-west of Paris, was also the capital of the apparitions since the building of its castle by Robert Bellême in 1097, on the orders of Guillaume Le Roux (William Rufus, more commonly called William II), King of England, until March 1946, when a certain Roger Lhomoy pretended to have discovered an underground chapel containing the treasure of the Templars.

Without going into detail concerning the rivalry between the Anglo-Norman and the French, let us present here the other "Epiphanies" or key "Apparitions" that impacted forever on the secret history of the Vexin capital.

About the first apparition: that of the luminous cross in 1188

This is related to us by Louis Régnier, in his book *Histoire de Gisors* (*History of Gisors*), 'At the bottom of the suburb of Capville, now Gisors' station, there was an old elm, which, according to tradition, covered three acres of land with its immense branches, witnesses to the most important revolutions. It sheltered sovereigns, warriors, popes and saints. Pierre de Tarentaise produced miracles there and the Archbishop of Tyr preached the Crusade. There also, unexpectedly, Philip II Augustus and Henry II of England, who were fierce enemies, embraced each other in tears and received the cross directly from the prelate. English and French knights, barons and prelates who were invited to this meeting were united by a similar impulse and desire, and shouted, 'The Cross, the Cross!' At that very moment, says the legend, a luminous cross appeared in the sky as if Heaven approved the enthusiasm of the Earth. It is in memory of this wonder that the coat of arms of Gisors was charged in gules with a cross engrailed in gold, to which Henry IV attached the azure chief of shield with three gold fleurs-de-lis. Above the coat of arms, the year 1188 commemorates the date of the heavenly apparition. The real elm has disappeared, but the grounds of the famous tree are still referred to as the sacred field. In compensation, and in memory of the celestial apparition, a four-hole stone cross was erected near Neaufles Saint-Martin; this cross was moved afterwards and can be seen nowadays on a secondary road, two kilometres from Gisors'.

About the second apparition: that of Christmas day 1848

Account from the mayor of Gisors to the Prefect of the Eure region, 'Tradition maintains that an immense treasure is hidden at the bottom of the underground passage linking the castle of Neaufles Saint-Martin to Gisors and that enormous iron gates guard its approach. It is only at a precise moment in the year, on a precise day, at a precise hour, that it is possible to enter this obscure dwelling under conditions that will make the most insatiable cupid shiver. On Christmas Day, when the officiating priest reads the genealogy of Christ, the obstacles that stand in the way of the desires and efforts of those who would like to penetrate this marvellous cavern, suddenly dissipate. The flames of hell die out, the diabolic guardian of the magic treasure falls asleep, and all the riches over which he keeps watch like another Argus can become the target of the first audacious individual who will dare the adventure. But, if this daring person takes the wrong measurements, woe betides him! When the genealogy is over, the gates close, the flames reignite, the devil wakes up, and the one who finds himself in the underground passage of Queen Blanche at that time will never see the heaven's light again.'

About Saint-Catherine chapel

Built by the Fouilleuse family, Lords of Flavacourt, the chapel is located south of the church Saint-Gervais/Saint-Protais, next to the southern gate that opens onto the alley of the Epousées, in Gisors. 'This chapel was dedicated to Catherine de Fouilleuse de Flavacourt on her birth date,' says Louis Régnier, in an article in the newspaper *Le Vexin*, on 20th November 1898.

About the discovery of an underground passage

Madame Dufour of Gisors, first witness in a long list, relates that after the 1941 bombings, an underground passage leading to a crypt was found under the rubble of the destroyed sections of the church Saint-Gervais/Saint-Protais. This subway was quickly filled in again by the neighbours A la Botte Bleue, a property belonging at that time to the informant's sister.

About thirty chests in precious metal aligned in rows of ten, found in a chapel, under the donjon of the castle of Gisors

Warden at the castle of Gisors since 1929, Roger Lhomoy declared the following in March 1946, 'I was in a Roman chapel in stone from Louveciennes, thirty metres long, nine metres wide, and some four and a half metres high from the keystone. There was the altar and tabernacle, also in stone. Half way up the walls, supported by stone corbels, I could see life-size statues of Christ and his twelve apostles; along the walls, on the ground, there were nineteen stone sarcophaguses, twenty metres long and sixty centimetres wide; in the nave, thirty chests in precious metal aligned in rows of ten. It was an amazing spectacle.'

A modern myth about Gisors and its secret; this could be the last Epiphany in Gisors, or how to concoct a contra-history, creating an "egregore", or collective animated idea, to lead the seeker towards a well orchestrated propaganda.

First of all, find the adequate individual in Roger Lhomoy, a treasure hunter, former seminarist who, in March 1946, announced that he had found a chapel. Then, give a name to this chapel, namely Saint-Catherine, and fabricate or invent false documents from real archives, such as the manuscript from Alexandre Bourdet with ten missing pages found, of course, in a private collection. Rely on the allegations of Pierre Plantard, a specialist in hermeticism. Write a book whilst filling the gaps, and start a polemic in newspapers such as *L'Express* and *La Tour de Feu*, so that a minister, in the name of André Malraux, instructs the Military Engineers, in the person of Colonel Lefebvre, to dispatch men in the field. With the outcome known in advance, proclaim the following evidence, as did Plantard during an interview, 'As you may have guessed, because of this hullabaloo, the chests have been moved!' This is how, for the first time, the Priory of Sion appeared on the scene. Dan Brown had not yet been born...

Nonetheless, three accomplices in search of fame sign contracts with the mayor of Gisors. Just in case...

The first one, Roger Lhomoy, was, according to the mayor of Bézu Saint-Eloi, a neighbouring village of Gisors, an average diviner and an imperfect clairvoyant, endlessly roaming the countryside in search of lost treasures, in search, with his pendulum, of old coins, fibulae and shards of pottery. He was particularly equipped with big ears and a ready tongue. Initiated to the minor orders, he nurtured a taste for the secret, listening behind the pillars of the church Saint-Gervais/Saint-Protais to legends regarding Gisors and its surroundings related by the parish priests. One talked about an altar's stone covered in gold, mentioned in a 1629 poem by the ostiary Antoine Dorival. One made allegations that underground passages connected the castle of Gisors to Neaufles, a village situated three kilometres away. There were reckonings that the passages linked the castle to the church under the donjon... One related the odyssey of the "Prisoner" of Gisors and extrapolated his last wishes from mysterious graffiti and strange inscriptions found in the said Tower of Gisors where the initials N.P. had been carved in the stone; N.P. deluded one into believing that the initials were those of a certain Nicolas Poulain, whose identity, of course, was not established and could open the way to many interpretations. It went from François II, Lost King condemned by Catherine de Medici, to the illegitimate son of a cardinal from Rouen, without forgetting Elie de Beaumont, the loving spouse of Catherine de Basian. Finally, in the bars of Gisors, from the Grand Monarque tavern to the Taverne des Templiers, public rumours substantiated one or other legend following the Second World War bombing by the English, which did not spare the church of Saint-Gervais/Saint-Protais and revealed one or other archaeological piece. Roger Lhomoy listened and polished his 1946 epiphany until, one day, the man of letters came on the scene.

This second accomplice was a pragmatic character. He realised that one had to organise legends that were running in all directions. To establish some coherence, it was necessary to find a logical thread. The perforated cross of Neaufles Saint-Martin, in the shape of the Templars cross pattée, came in handy. One had to crystallise the legends around a myth with a strong point, namely the treasure of the Templars, with a complementary idea, thanks to Pierre Plantard, derived from the theory that the Templars are still amongst us, seven centuries later, and that their big secret is contained in thirty iron chests...

At the time, this man, Géraud de Liéou de Sède of his real name, better known as Gérard de Sède, was unemployed and lodged at a friend's farm, where one of the employees was Roger Lhomoy; and not the reverse, as claimed by Gérard de Sède in his book *Les Templiers sont parmi nous* (*The Templars are amongst us*), which thus began with a lie...

An agreement was clinched; an article was written by the journalist in Paris-Normandie, which resulted in the intervention of the third villain, a certain Pierre Plantard, christened Le Sphinx from the start, who knew, of course, all the ins and outs of this secret story. As proof, he had filed a copy of his 1961 opuscule entitled *Gisors et son secret* (*Gisors and its Secret*) at the National Library.

This time, the capital of the Norman Vexin region became the centre of interest in the History of France by being promulgated to the role of Agartha of the Temple through a network of proofs wittingly superimposed and, with the luxury of false parchments, elaborated, depending on the circumstances, in the style of an Arsène Lupin or a Charles Nodier. What was just a highly symbolic legend, related by the author of *La Fée aux Miettes* in the manner that Gérard de Nerval described the Master's rituals under the guise of legends in his *Voyage en Orient*, became a hotchpotch in the 1960s genre, where one saw neo-Templar Grand Masters claim their heritage in order to attract some cheap publicity. In fact, Charles Nodier had understood the extraordinary message of the prisoner in the Tower of Gisors, deprived of real and symbolic light. He had grasped that the graffiti, reminiscent of the church décor, notably the stele of the Perfect Master, could touch not only the imaginary world of mankind, but also its subconscious. He knew that the prisoner, likened to the initiate, would, in his dark cell or meditation closet, be able to reflect on his death by carving a recumbent figure from a tomb that he had vaguely spotted in the church, and which, consequently, gained a most particular significance. This prisoner, lover of Queen Blanche d'Evreux, relying on his symbol as he was a lover of pure light, could only die in the tale so as to reach the ineffable. He was killed by the arrow of a soldier who, by pure coincidence, looked like Longinus with his crossbow; the writer's favourite word since he talks about coincidence three times.

This formula will be taken up, naturally, by Pierre Plantard, albeit in another context of course. Let us retain simply that the Epiphany of Gisors, as well as the symbolism of Queen Blanche's treasure, mingled with the reading of Christ's genealogy on Christmas Day, the setting for the legend, is very well adapted by Charles Nodier; whilst the trio Gérard de Sède, Pierre Plantard and Roger Lhomoy, wanders by sacrificing the idea for the benefit of a materiality that is shrouded in the myth and treasure of the Templars. This inversion will continue in Stenay and Rennes-le-Château. I believe you know the rest.

Besides the Epiphanies that I related to you, the history of Gisors, which illustrated the rivalry between France and England well before The Hundred Years War, is marked by the presence of the Templars who played the role of arbiter between the two Nations for three years. But, it is worth noting that they had a preference for the English; of course, in those days, the Grand Master shared the same aspirations.

Open Discussions With Pierre Plantard And Philippe De Cherisey

Jean-Luc Chaumeil was in contact with the two main protagonists of the Priory of Sion, namely Pierre Plantard and Philippe de Cherisey, for a long time. He had numerous conversations with them, some more formal than others. We find it relevant to put the following two interviews, which were published separately, at the reader's disposal.

Exchange Between Jean-Luc Chaumeil (JLC) And Pierre Plantard (PP) On 13th January 1972

[Excerpt from *Pégase*, Issue no. 6, November 1973]

The discussion begins straightaway with Gisors...

PP – 'I have told Gérard de Sède, time and time again, why look for that here? In Gisors we had to conceal the crypt for exactly the same reason. Since, at the end, what would have happened? Let me point out to you that regarding Gisors I have never believed in a material treasure. There was no gold and there has never been any treasure!'

JLC – 'I hear what you are saying; even though, for instance, there is a passage at Mr. Rouët...'

PP – 'There was a passage indeed, but it was not the passage at Mr. Rouët, through which...'

JLC – 'In any event, it was an important passage, since people...'

PP – 'Yes, quite; there was a passage at Rouët, this is absolutely true; but it is not that passage, as there was yet another access underneath that of Rouët, at a lower level, which one can visit.'

JLC – 'In fact, the well of Miss Breton, next door, is significant. It is a well that is not a well; it is a ventilation shaft that proves the superposition of a third underground passage.'

PP – 'Yes, that's right. There is indeed a passage between the northern portal of the church and the rue de Vienne, as in front of the northern portal there was the extremely old cemetery of

Gisors and a tomb called Les trois frères de Saint-Clair (The three brothers of Saint-Clair). This tomb was completely destroyed during the 1940 bombings. So, for a while one could see the tomb, the entrances, and the galleries; then these were purely and simply filled in again and the affair was closed. Not only was it over, but there was no access between the church of Gisors and the underground passage that led to the crypt of the chapel. Now, I just want to say, like I said so many times to Gérard de Sède, the chapel is not under the mound supporting the donjon.'

JLC – 'Ah, I agree entirely, since I have been told, amongst other things, that within the surrounding walls of the castle, on the extensively tiled area on the east side of the donjon where theatrical performances take place nowadays, there was a workshop for the repair of tanks on the very spot of a petrol depot. Thus, at any moment, a catastrophe could have happened from the stroke of a matchstick or a pick. How is it possible, therefore, that an esoteric group as old and structured as you claim, would have left an important heritage in such a proximity, at the risk of seeing it wiped out overnight...'

PP – 'Well, wait! On the northern side, I see the portal of the church; the theatre is not on the east side; oh, you are right. Correct! The theatre is on the side of the underground chapel...'

JLC – 'Mr. Plantard, in these circumstances, I would like to ask you the following. We have interviewed several persons who know the location of the crypt very well [You should note that my interlocutor made a distinction, at the beginning, between the crypt and the chapel Saint-Catherine; then, through a diversion, he amalgamated the two by locating both under the tiled area on the east side, which is wrong]. We have received a totally unprecedented testimony from Commandant Delie de Louviers, who belonged to the Alliance Network.'

PP – 'And you still believe that the thirty chests are full of archives?'

JLC – 'In my view, no...'

PP – 'Well, you are right! Because of the hullabaloo surrounding these chests, you may have guessed that they were moved.'

JLC – 'That's what I thought.'

PP – 'You would not want them to be found, and if they are found, it is very unlikely that they will be full. It goes without saying.'

JLC – 'Yes, it goes without saying.'

PP – 'Indeed, the more noise one makes around an affair, the more likely nobody will touch it. Therefore, it is more or less certain that nobody went near the chests; prevention, however, is better than cure. The best thing to do was to move the contents. In all evidence, there is a large entrance, but one cannot go through it any more; nothing proves that there is not a second entrance, less important, possibly as practical, or at least as viable and working, which does not require any particular investigation, deterioration of the ground or digging. Let me point out to you that Lhomoy, whom I know very well, never found anything.'

JLC – 'I don't agree with you entirely, since a report from the gendarmerie mentions that the old warden found a gold Virgin in an oak, in a field next to Gisors.'

PP – 'No, Lhomoy never found anything. I know him very well. He is a tramp and has often needed me. Besides, he trusts me and I got him out of a mess on several occasions. I just wanted to tell you one thing: he never found anything. He simply heard that there were thirty chests in Gisors; that is all. He is not the only one who knew about this... In any event, there are some proofs that the thirty chests did exist. So, it is only because of this knowledge that he dug up the ground and declared afterwards that he had found the chests, so as to bring his search to a successful conclusion. But, in fact, he never found anything. However, he did excavate... that is undisputable. In 1914, the Count de Bueil of Gisors hid a casket belonging to his family in one of the underground passages of the city of Gisors. This small chest has never been found and it is possible that it is still there, or that it has been stolen; but this is another story, like the one of the gold Virgin and the Alliance Network you mentioned.'

JLC – 'This being said, one thing strikes me; you often say, "We have done this, we have done that"... I hope the group to which you belong, and of which you seem to be a representative, applies itself to the structure of the restoration of the Order of the Temple.'

PP – 'Maybe...'

JLC – 'Can you tell us more about this revival?'

PP – 'No, sorry; on that subject, we cannot say anything. However, do not expect the present Order of the Temple to resemble the former one.'

JLC – 'No?'

PP – 'This is not conceivable, out of the question! Besides, the society to which I belong has not been in existence for very long, although it is very old. I succeed others, that is all there is to say. We safeguard certain things faithfully, without publicity.'

JLC – 'Are you, by any chance, at the origin of the destruction of the neo-Templar orders, such as the Order of Jerusalem to which the Marquis de Vaulx belongs; and are you also behind the scandals that are hitting some members of the Government today?'

PP – 'Maybe. Don't you think these people are getting in the way? They use esoteric orders to extort money and all the rest. Don't you think these people are better somewhere else?'

JLC – 'I agree with you entirely.'

PP – 'You see, one must be able to give a room a sweep. Do you know that the Marquis de Vaulx won fame a few years back through the affair of Gisors? He wanted to see me at all costs. At the time, he worked in plumbing and central heating. So, he came to see me. I welcomed him simply. Afterwards, he lodged his claims with Mr. Pellisson, my friend and former mayor of Gisors before Mr. Beyne and Mr. Larmanoux. He was a kind man with whom I was on excellent terms. We were not always in agreement, which is quite normal. But, regarding Gisors, he has always been extremely amiable. However, the Marquis de Vaulx went to see him, dressed in a white coat under which he had hidden a tape recorder...!'

JLC – 'A strange book entitled *Circuit* by Philippe de Cherisey was published in Belgium. Do you know this author?'

PP – 'Yes, I do. He is a trustworthy character who developed his novel on the twenty-two verses of King Dagobert's song.'

JLC – 'By the way, regarding King Dagobert, two books have been published in Switzerland, under the aegis of a society which you must have heard of, in principle, since it concerns the Great Alpina Lodge. The authors of these works are Madeleine Blancasall, who wrote *L'énigme du Razès* (*The Enigma of the Razès*), and Henri Lobineau, who wrote *La généalogie des rois mérovingiens* (*Genealogy of the Merovingian Kings*).' [Note: At Pierre Jarnac's initiative, all texts from the so-called Priory of Sion have been combined in one volume and published by Pégase in 2006, under the title *Les dossiers secrets du Prieuré de Sion* (*The Secret Files of the Priory of Sion*)]

PP – 'If you manage to read these books in their entirety, you will find the trails of the Blanchefort and the Hautpoul, and you will know where they come from. Not only will you find the origins of the French noble families, but you will understand how an individual in the name of Montpezat can one day become king.'

JLC – 'Are you talking about the myth of the Lost King?'

PP – 'No, not just him, but the other one. You know, the king is not that lost...'

JLC – 'Let's just say that he is forgotten.'

PP – 'That's it. Let's just say that this famous descendant has always existed, not very far from the King of France; the ruling king next to the king on the throne, if you see what I mean. Furthermore, many things are unknown to the public at large. How do you explain, for instance, that the Merovingians never disappeared? How do you explain the certainty that, in the past, people were looking for them in the Razès and that Intendant Fouquet was the ambassador of the Merovingians to the kings of Naples and France? It is worth remembering that the sole aim of Charles Martel's offensive was to destroy the descendants of that lineage, hence the fire of Rennes-les-Bains in 737 CE. Thus, one can ask oneself: who were the Merovingians? Were they Francs? No. Were they Sicambrians? Yes. And who were the Sicambrians? They were Jews! And what did France produce? Merovingians! If you know the secret history of France well, you will understand why there was a bringing together of the Temple and the families of Merovingian descent, and why history follows one direction only, the one we know and which has been identified by some materialist thinkers!'

JLC – 'Tell me; let me ask you one more question. I went to Nice to make a report and I met an extraordinary character with the name of Henri Benderly. Do you know that individual?'

PP – 'Benderly; he is a rather strange character.'

JLC – 'Aside from his "Messiah mania", it looks as though he belongs to the Rose-Croix d'Or (Golden Rosicrucian brotherhood) of Pau, in a word, that he is their spokesman; or, in short, that he is being manipulated!'

PP – 'But who is not being manipulated when wanting to attain something?'

JLC – 'Maybe...'

PP – 'In any event, I can tell you one thing, and that is that you are more or less right regarding the Great Alpina Lodge.'

JLC – 'You know, I have in my possession a coded letter between the representative of the Great Italian Lodge and the Chancellor of the Great Alpina Lodge. There is no doubt about that!'

PP – 'I can tell you that the documents concerning the Merovingians are authentic and that, one day, these documents must be revealed, will be revealed, but this is not yet the right time.'

JLC – 'However, Mr. Benderly gave us two documents that address that problem.'

PP – 'Really, I didn't know! Fundamentally, you see, I don't know everything and I know very little regarding the Temple.'

JLC – 'Mr. Benderly does not stand out by a particular charisma; he knows many things and possesses many document folders. He is the informant of many known authors. However, his Master is called Almega; that is AL meaning LE (The) in Arabic, and MEGA in Greek, meaning Great, Whole, Divine. In short the Pan god. So, there again we revert to a certain system of symbols easy to interpret and to extrapolate from. But, basically, one could ask oneself whether ALMEGA is not the primary cause of everything that passes and lives; the first Monad, as Leibnitz said. He is all at once an individual, a symbol, a link between all secret societies, and a force, marching towards a definite goal in accordance with the law of transformations issued from a reversible process between the Psyche, the Soma (Heredity) and the Fatum (Fate)...'

PP – 'No!'

JLC – 'This is odd, since we find this again on the subject concerning the "Moors' treasure", near Oloron-Sainte-Marie, in Rennes-le-Château, in Gisors, and in Etretat, where, on each occasion, the descendants of noble families won fame through...'

PP – 'Did you read a book by Maurice Leblanc entitled *La Comtesse de Cagliostro*? And did you find out to what the Abbey of Caux, of Saint-Wandrille and the Aiguille Creuse corresponded? Did you notice that it was to the Meridian 0?'

JLC – 'Yes, I don't think it concerns the Aiguille Creuse of Etretat or the sea race, nor the story of the South of France.'

PP – 'Yes, of course, there is something else.'

JLC – 'Indeed, we always come across the same type of story, and, at the end, amongst all the stories, we realise that there is one and only one story.'

PP – 'Precisely. Philippe de Cherisey knows that story very well.'

JLC – 'In fact, I have talked about this with Pierre Carnac, pseudonym of the Romanian scholar Doru Théodoriciu, who mentions the book of Prophecies from Christopher Columbus and a mysterious map resembling a large chessboard in the style of Philippe de Cherisey.' [Pierre Carnac has devoted a few pages on this subject, starting from page 281, in his book *Prophéties et prophètes de tous les temps*, published by Pygmalion in 1991.]

PP – 'This is very interesting. The same holds true for Philippe de Cherisey's book and its addenda in particular. Indeed, at the end, when Charlot enters the cave, the place is completely unravelled and everything becomes clear. [See Appendix III]. You know, I have the references to all the books, even those who are not available to the public. You see, you won't have any difficulty in finding them; all you have to do is to knock at the right door. It is a mistake to believe that there is a secret. The secret exists only in the internal organisation of our Society and everything that concerns it.'

JLC – 'But, why is there a secret?'

PP – 'You know, everything pertains to a greater or lesser extent to the political field. This, in turn, forces us to respect diplomatic secrecy. This is why the documents are coded, notably in the affair of Rennes-le-Château and Gisors. But, tell me, while we are on the subject, what is, in your opinion, the role of the Great Alpina Lodge in this affair?'

JLC – 'I believe this organisation is owned by another group which I do not know. But it could well be a very important group.'

PP – 'You are very well informed. Did you know that I lived in Switzerland for ten years? And what name do you give to this organisation?'

JLC – 'Le Serpent Vert (The Green Snake).'

PP – 'No, this is not correct. Try to remember Philippe de Cherisey and the letters P.S. You often come across these two letters. They can open many doors to you. Philippe de Cherisey talks about these letters in his book. Furthermore, one can find these initials in Rennes-le-Château.'

JLC – 'In Gisors too.'

PP – 'Are you sure? One only needs to know how to handle them well. Indeed, that hat suits many organisations; this is almost certain. You should read the work of Lobineau. At the penultimate page, you will find a nice lineage. Do you know Jean Marais?'

JLC – 'No, I don't'

PP – 'Call him. He is a very good friend of Lobineau.'

In 1973, Jean-Luc Chaumeil (JLC) Met Philippe De Cherisey (Pdc) In Liège, In Belgium.

[Excerpt from *Pégase*, Issue no. 5, October 1973]

Talks about this and that concerning the Temple, Gisors and Rennes-le-Château.

JLC – 'The Order of the Temple: an anonymous society or a sterile Order?'

PdC – 'When I was in Brussels during the investigations about Gisors and Rennes-le-Château, I remember questioning an historian who specialised in the Templars about this. He replied, "Don't talk to me about this commercial enterprise. What they produced best was the anonymous society and the letter of credit; for the rest, can you cite any architectural achievement, painting, or literary work, anything that could be attributed to someone from the Temple? This order is absolutely sterile; the only thing worthwhile about them comes from the Cistercians, through Saint Bernard and his whole ethic. Yes, for him, we can speak. But as far as the Templars are concerned, apart from the design of the octagon copied, in fact, from the architecture found in Jerusalem, there is nothing." We can say a lot of bad things about the Templars, but not about the Temple, as this is another matter. There was a trial of the Templars and their defence was more or less nonexistent. Of course, torture provoked many reactions; but when one is under the pressure of the wheel, well, one shouts and one says many stupidities; and they certainly did, unable to defend themselves in an intelligent manner. Yet, this could be done; for instance, spit on the crucifix which simply means that no image of the divinity is susceptible of adoration. The head of the Baphomet is a mediaeval technique, known to the architects, that enables them to draw up the proportions of a given building, for example, a large nave or the height of a church tower, without drafting plans on paper. This is why the Head of the Heads (Baphomet) is merely the plan of a cathedral. But there you go, they are furious when the pope accuses them of sodomy. No, I don't agree and I must say that those who died in 1314 were not very intelligent and did not assume an important function in the Temple...'

JLC – 'What do you think about the role played by the fortified town of Gisors?'

PdC – 'Gisors is very significant insofar that the Temple genuinely occupied a prominent position. It was important too after the fall of Jerusalem, since in 1187 or 1188, the division of the Temple took place in Gisors.'

JLC – 'But what was the nature of that rupture?'

PdC – 'It happened in a field called "Ormeteau ferré", near the present station of Gisors, between the Order of Sion, a small order founded by Godefroy de Bouillon in 1100 after the capture of Jerusalem, and its military secular arm, the Order of the Temple, founded in 1118; each went its own way whilst remaining united. Of course, the two orders stayed in contact, but these were more like distant courteous relations. One thing led to another, notably the creation of the Templars' Constitutions by Roncelin de Fos who did not belong to the

Order of the Temple, but to the External Chapel. Basically, the Temple had only one function; that of assuming a relay system, invented in fact by Saint-Bernard, to protect the pilgrims. The Templars were settled individuals in a mobile Crusade. That is, they had the onus of building a series of fortified castles, from Castel Blanc to Château-Rouge; sort of stopovers on the road to the Holy Land. But these combatants, these servicemen, these pioneers, guardians of the way, aroused suspicion one day as they were as much the authors of the spread of Christianity in Islam as the ambassadors of Islam in the Occident.'

JLC – 'You mentioned earlier the creation of the Order of Sion by Godefroy de Bouillon in 1100. Yet, for instance, one has never been able to determine the exact date of the Temple of Paris, in the New City. An historian, amongst many others, places it in 1100, precisely.'

PdC – 'That would be great in one sense. However, there is one area in which I have no sympathy for the Templars. It is the following. In 1100, an admirable building is erected by Godefroy de Bouillon. It is located on the hill of the Temple, on the ruins of the Great Synagogue, where the Mosque of Omar (Muslim mosque of Haram esh Sherif), then second Mecca of Islam, is finally erected. This mosque communicates partially with the Basilica of Our Lady, of which there are no vestiges. In other words, we have three religions which inaugurate by themselves the first ecumenicalism. The corresponding example is in Toledo, where what is called a cathedral is a surrounding wall which encloses the University of Toledo. Of course, there is no link between cause and effect. But, it transpires that in 1118, the Crescent on the Mosque of Omar is replaced by the Cross. This is the true beginning of the Holy War. That very same year, the Order of the Temple is created. Therein lays an unmistakable proof, which is why I have no sympathy for the Templars.

I know that, at the time, there is no connection between the red cross and the red crescent, and yet... There is some link however in the imperial emblem of the Hapsburg family represented by the Globe and the Cross, or what would appear to be the Earth and the Cross. As for the relationship between the Moon Crescent and the Cross, one can think about Jupiter, the god of the gods; therefore, about a certain alliance between opposites. But it is difficult and too complicated to establish all the connections between civilisations that are seemingly opposed, but for which the ultimate goal is Unity and the secret "Work" of Anonymous (Secret) Societies.'

JLC – 'With regard to Gisors and Rennes-le-Château, how do you link the two events?'

PdC – 'In 1153, when Gisors was occupied by a small group of Templars, Bertrand de Blancafort, from the Blanchefort family of Rennes-le-Château according to some sources, was nominated Head of the Temple. In 1188, the Order of Sion and the Order of the Temple separated.'

JLC – 'Apparently, there is a descendant of the Blancaforts today in Mr. Olivier de Fleury.'

PdC – 'Correct! In any event, genealogies are subtle. This is how, nowadays, we have, in principle, a Merovingian sovereign in Europe, who appears to be Mr. de Montpezat, prince consort of Denmark. In fact, he is only a descendant on the female side, which would take you back to his grandfather. He is one under his real name of Vaudressel. We have, for instance, two troubling burial places; one in Cherisy, the other one on the Meuse borders, where one of the vaults is linked to the Armoises family. Namely, to those who claimed that Joan of Arc was an Armoises damsel and that she did not die at the stake! Apparently, we are of the same family. Maybe, at some point in time, there was an alliance with the Armoises family. I don't know really; but why are we in the same vault?'

JLC – 'After that diversion regarding the genealogies, may I return to my first question about the link between Gisors and Rennes-le-Château, besides the Grand Master of Blancafort?'

PdC – 'It involves Queen Blanche and the discovery of the philosopher's stone by Nicolas Flamel on the road to Santiago de Compostela. Nicolas Flamel's pursuits were subsidised by Queen Blanche d'Evreux who devoted time to alchemy in the tower of Neaufles, near Gisors; this tower was connected to the citadel of the city of Gisors through an underground passage that might never be found. The passage was three and a half kilometres long and marked out with the famous Templars Cross, which was unfortunately moved during the construction of the railway. As a result, one does not know its exact location any more; the fact remains that Queen Blanche was, if I may say, the finance manager of Nicolas Flamel, who brought his experiments to a successful conclusion in the tower of Neaufles.

In my mind, regarding the pilgrimage to Santiago de Compostela, one should not search too much on the road along the West coast, but rather on another road, less known. Raymond Ourcel mentions the latter in fact in a work on the subject matter. He goes from Vézelay to the coast, I do not mean the Galilean road; he says that this pilgrimage was so important that there were many deviations to the East. Even when one follows the longest way round, these deviations grow to a considerable size, notably when reaching Spain, so much so that one is forced to retrace the return trip in the original triangle between Vézelay, Bayonne and Marseille.

In other words, there was a road to Santiago de Compostela which went through Rennes-le-Château and was dismantled at the epoch of Blanche de Castile. It is this road that skirts the Pyrenees and where Nicolas Flamel appears on the scene.'

JLC – 'Do you think Nicolas Flamel went through Rennes-le-Château?'

PdC – 'Yes, because during the Catharian conflicts, that section of the road became extremely important. The figure of Mary Magdalene is the explanation for this as she is the link between Marseille, where she died, or is supposed to have died, and Vézelay, where her relics are kept. Moreover, she is evoked five times in the church of Rennes-le-Château, which demonstrates people's devotion to her and is significant for the decoding of the tomb of the Marchioness of Hautpoul-Blanchefort.'

JLC – 'Do you believe in the treasure of Rennes-le-Château?'

PdC – 'It depends how you look at it. It is as if you were asking me whether I believe in the Grail. In fact, what matters is the approach much more than the discovery in itself.'

JLC – 'Did Father Saunière genuinely discover some parchments in his church in 1891?'

PdC – 'Yes, he did. But these documents are in London; they have been kept in the private safe of a bank for the last twenty years! They are genealogies, which one must not mix up with the parchments of the Gospel according to Saint Luke fabricated by me and for which I pinched the uncial text from the work *L'archéologie chrétienne* (*Christian Archaeology*) by Dom Cabol at the National Library, section C25. To realise my encoding, I utilised the text from the stele and the moves of the knight on a chessboard.'

JLC – 'Indeed! In your manuscript Circuit, you do mention the letters engraved on the tomb and give them a particular significance.'

PdC – 'Not enough, unfortunately; when I completed that book, I already had a second manuscript in mind devoted to the decryption and manner of decoding the stele. It has to be said that it is a superb anagram of one hundred and twenty eight letters and that there isn't a more splendid one in any of the other alphabetic languages. What is fantastic too is the manner in which this anagram decodes itself; namely, that the clue to the anagram is provided by the anagram itself. It is a brilliant logical piece, although at the time I thought it would take at least one hundred twenty pages to explain its mechanism. It must be said that the Cipher Office failed, but I can explain how it works. It is very simple and anybody could decipher it in two hours.'

JLC – 'Well, is there a primary method with the letters P.S.?'

PdC – 'Yes, that's right. But this is something else still. In fact, you must take what appears in second place and move it to the first place. It is a bit like a Japanese moneybox where the key is inside. The entire beauty of the decryption resides in a Chapter of the Gospel according to Saint Luke which starts with In Sabbato Secundo Primo. This phrase has given headaches to the anonymous (secret) societies. It has to be said that "A day of Sabbath, second first" is really not translatable. No one has ever heard of that. So, as the disciples walk through a corn field and, being hungry, eat the corn there and then, it must mean "Second Sabbath following the first day of the showbread". This is the only interpretation we could find. In fact, the passage of the gospel, which is superb, continues with "The Son of man is also Lord of the Sabbath." For that, you must go to the beginning of Saint Luke which is very surprising and which says "Excellent Theophilus (we don't know who Theophilus is) I will relate to you the things that happened among us according to the reliable testimonies of those who told us." So what! Did he or did he not see it? He calls upon external witnesses and says that things happened among us. But this becomes clear if we take one of Saint Paul's teachings "I have known a man who is Holy; did I or did I not know him? I do not know. Only God knows." What does that mean? Effectively, that what Luke saw as a pagan, prior to his conversion, is valid for information only and can be contested at any time. Therefore, this means that when Luke was following Christ, he was not converted and not a Christian yet. He was not amongst the apostles, although one must go back to Tradition when Luke was patron saint of artists and physicians. Some people claim that he made the first portrait of the Blessed Virgin and Christ himself. Indeed, there is a portrait of Christ painted by Saint Luke in Genoa. It is a Byzantine painting which has been released recently. It is supposedly the oldest painting of that time.

Another legend pretends that Abgar, King of Hedes, sent his Phrygian servant on a mandate to find and bring back Christ, so that the latter could heal his leprosy. This servant is none other than Saint Luke. He meets Christ who cannot free himself in view of the mission he had undertaken at the time. Luke decides to make his portrait, although the result is not very good. While Saint Luke's name is not mentioned in the story, it can only be him. Saint Luke feels quite piqued at the sight of his abortive chef-d'oeuvre. He returns with his portrait to King Abgar who, on admiring it, is healed instantly. This is why, although his name is not mentioned in the legend, Saint Luke is the patron saint of painters and doctors.

In conclusion, In Sabbato Secundo Primo does not mean “A day of Sabbath, second first” but rather “As second in command, Sabbasius became first”. What is interesting is that the witches’ meetings are called “Sabbaths”, not because of the Jewish celebrations, but because of Sabbasius, god of the Phrygians. In fact, the witches’ Sabbath worships a god who, through the Eucharist, has the quality of being cut in morsels and eaten, as it represents the primal bread. There was a leap to be made in the vocabulary that Luke mastered very well already; the theory of a Eucharistic God closely connected to Dionysus, that is cut in morsels and which everybody shares, so that everyone has a piece of the “whole”. This concept belongs to a cycle and Luke, if he was a good “Sabbasian”, would not have found difficult to understand Christ’s parables and start a revolution with principles, that were, in fact, familiar to him. The meaning of that sentence is “what is in second place comes first”.

I wanted to expand on the decryption, but Plantard told me, “No, we are not going to explain everything; we can come back to that later!” This is why I do not talk about the subject matter in my book and only provide the result.

Therefore, the text on the stele of the Marchioness de Blanchefort which reads as follows:

CI GIT NOBLE MARIE DE NEGRE DARLES

DAME D’HAUTPOUL DE BLANCHEFORT

AGEE DE SOIXANTE-SEPT ANS DECEDEE

LE XVII JANVIER MDCOLXXXI REQUIES

CATIN PACE

Becomes:

BERGERE PAS DE TENTATION, QUE POUSSIN,

TENIERS GARDENT LA CLEF, PAX DCLXXXI,

PAR LA CROIX ET CE CHEVAL DE DIEU,

J’ACHEVE CE DAEMON DE GARDIEN A MIDI,

POMMES BLEUES.

A first remark is imperative, namely that this text must date from after 1861...’

JLC – ‘After?’

PdC – 'Yes, because of Delacroix, "QUE POUSSIN, TENIERS GARDENT LA CLEF". There is a key attached to Poussin and it is Arcadia; and another clue with Teniers because his religious theme is Saint-Anthony.

"PAR LA CROIX ET CE CHEVAL DE DIEU"; it must be said that we found many "horses of God". The first one on the Serbairou, a small hill around Rennes-les-Bains; the second one at the entrance of the road from Bugarach towards the Roko-Negro (Black Rock), another hill opposite the ancient Visigothic capital of Rheda. But all this did not mean very much, since one had to think about the painter Delacroix and one of his works entitled Cheval de Dieu (Horse of God), which can be found in the Chapel of the Angels in the church Saint-Sulpice in Paris. This work is from 1861, like the text on the stele of the Marchioness of Blanchefort.'

JLC – 'Why was Father Saunière desperate to erase it?'

PdC – 'Father Saunière understood the importance of that stele immediately. So, he proceeded to scrape the stone. What he overlooked is that the entire authentic text can be found in the *Bulletin de la Société d'Etudes Scientifiques du Département de l'Aude* (*Bulletin of the Society of Scientific Studies of the Aude Department*) volume XVII of 1906, under the precise reference Excursion du 25 juin 1905 à Rennes-le-Château, by Tyssère Elie. It relates the reporting of an excursionist who visited Rennes-le-Château many years before and who took down the text on the stele due to its strangeness. Now, this text can only be decoded through Eugène Delacroix. Therefore, the inscription engraved on the stele of the Marchioness of Blanchefort, who died in 1781, was made between 1860 and 1910, and not, as alleged, by Father Bigou. I do not know who wrote the text, but one must admit that in those days there were people with real genius.

Firstly, one must distinguish between the letter "e" and the letter "é".

Secondly, one must know that "Marie de Négri d'Ablès" was not called "Marie de Negre Darles", as inscribed on the stele. There are, therefore, two spelling mistakes which must be taken into account.

Thirdly, there are five steps to follow (there are five representations of Mary Magdalene in the church of Rennes-le-Château).

Fourthly, there are one hundred twenty eight letters, or two chessboards of sixty four squares. Now, the first coded letters were the work of Vigenère, secretary of the inventor of Arcadia, namely Laurent de Medici. It is the latter who founded Arcadia or first academy of the Arcades. Assuming a chessboard of sixty four squares, the first coded message consists in writing a text of eight letters and performing the Knight's Tour around the board. Indeed, there is only one perfect circuit; you leave the squares blank [after the knight's passage] and take the letters down in the order that the knight decodes them.

Fifthly, and this will be our last point, there is a double transposition to be made since one must take the two evangelical excerpts into account. One is more important than the other; it is the one about IN SABBATO SECUNDO PRIMO (Sabbath, second first) which we talked about earlier. Now, this text is dense; I mean there are no gaps between the letters. We must, therefore, remove some characters in order to obtain our eight significant letters. After that, it becomes easy. You must then perform two transfers and one exercise with the knight. This is the decryption of the stele of the Marchioness of Blanchefort.'

Cher Monsieur

Votre lettre à l'instant

Il m'est à peu près impossible de vous donner
la reference exacte à Dom Cabrol, mais elle ne
doit pas être tout à fait irrationnelle. Je me
rappelle qu'il s'agisse d'un systeme anterieur
à l'usage des Synoptiques. Au lieu d'exposer
sur quatre colonnes les versions d'un meme evenement
le clergé fabriquant une version moyenne.
D'où vient en particulier le texte hybride qui
debute par "In Sabbato secundo primo". Je
suis tombé là-dessus à peu près par hasard ensuite

Le plus interessant reside dans ce "Sabbat
Second Premier", chiendent des exegetes qui n'y
trouvent aucune reference biblique, mais qui
commente joliment le sigle (PS) addition fort
tardive à la dalle et commentaire à la formule
PRAE-CUM. S'agit-il du premier sabbat qui suit
le second jour des pains sans levain, ou du second
sabbat qui suit le premier jour; on n'en sait rien.
Aussi est-ce que l'actuelle bible de Jerusalem
se contente purement et simplement de censurer
la formule.

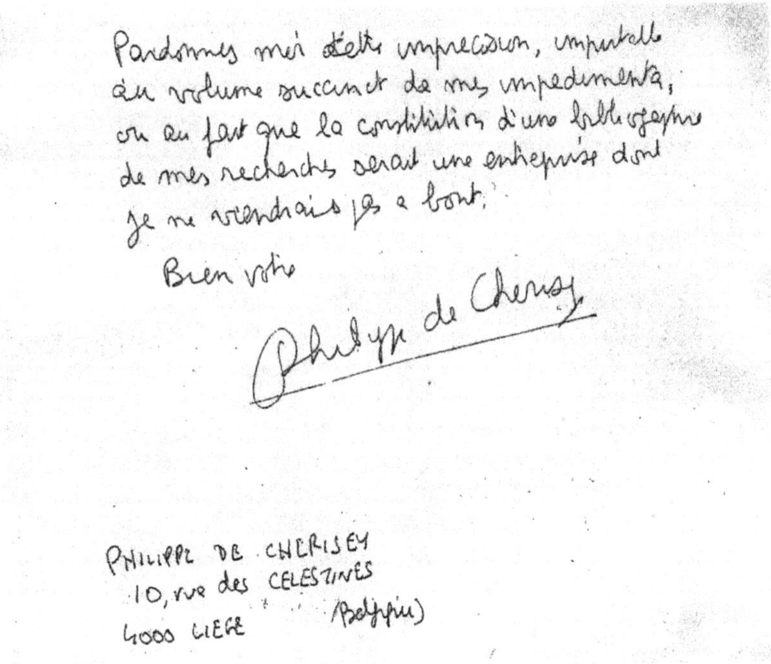

Pardonnez moi d'être imprécision, imputable au volume succinct de mes impedimenta, ou au fait que la constitution d'une bibliographie de mes recherches serait une entreprise dont je ne viendrais pas à bout.

Bien vôtre

Philippe de Cherisey

PHILIPPE DE CHERISEY
10, rue des CELESTINES
4000 LIEGE (Belgique)

23 - Letter from Philippe de Cherisey to Jean-Luc Chaumeil

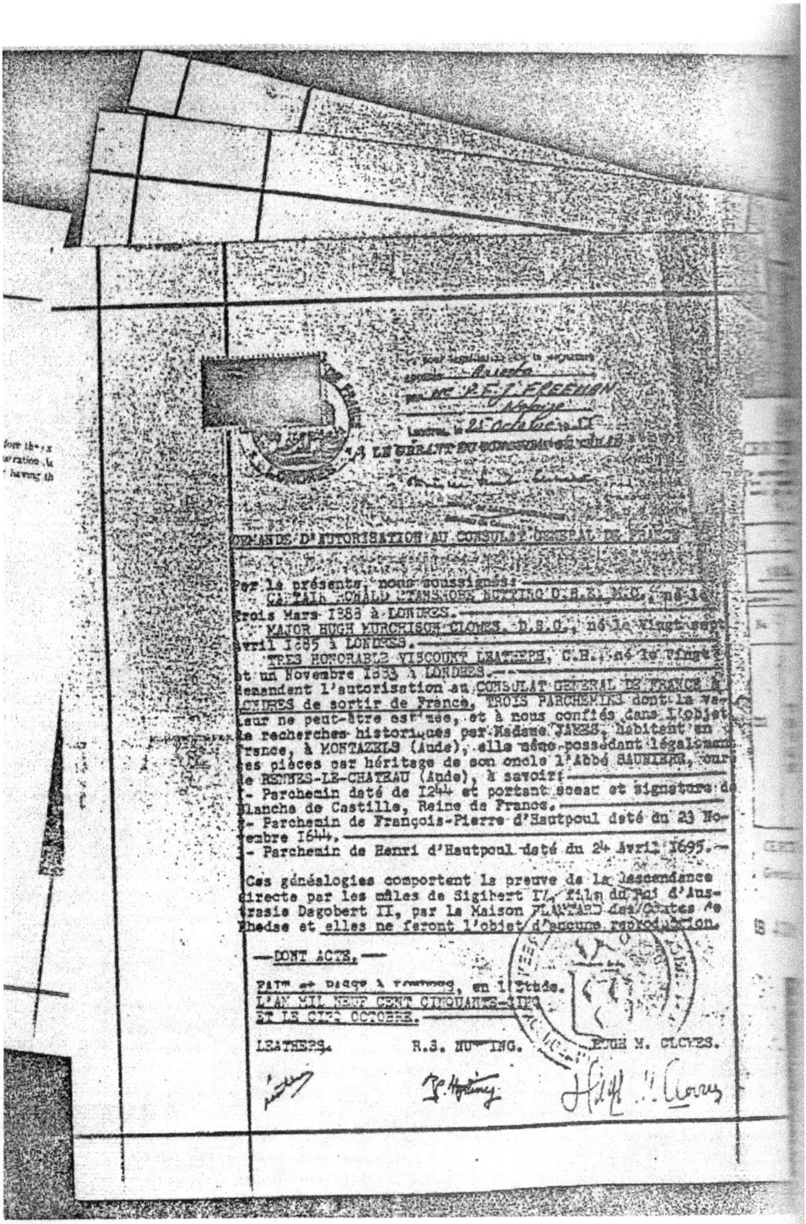

DEMANDE D'AUTORISATION AU CONSULAT GENERAL DE FRANCE

Par la présente, nous soussignés:
CAPTAIN RONALD STANSMORE NUTTING D.S.O., M.C., né le Trois Mars 1388 à LONDRES.
MAJOR HUGH MURCHISON CLOWES, D.S.O., né le Vingt-sept Avril 1385 à LONDRES.
TRES HONORABLE VISCOUNT LEATHERS, C.H., né le Vingt et un Novembre 1333 à LONDRES.
demandent l'autorisation au CONSULAT GENERAL DE FRANCE à LONDRES de sortir de France, TROIS PARCHEMINS dont la valeur ne peut-être est'mée, et à nous confiés dans l'objet de recherches historiques par Madame JAMES, habitant en France, à MONTAZELS (Aude), elle [illegible] possédant légalement ces pièces par héritage de son oncle l'Abbé SAUNIERE, curé de RENNES-LE-CHATEAU (Aude), à savoir:
1- Parchemin daté de 1244 et portant sceau et signature de Blanche de Castille, Reine de France.
2- Parchemin de François-Pierre d'Hautpoul daté du 23 Novembre 1644.
3- Parchemin de Henri d'Hautpoul daté du 24 Avril 1695.

Ces généalogies comportent la preuve de la descendance directe par les mâles de Sigibert I., fils du Roi d'Austrasie Dagobert II, par la Maison PLANTARD des Comtes de Rhedae et elles ne feront l'objet d'aucune reproduction.

—DONT ACTE.—

FAIT et PASSE à LONDRES, en l'Etude.
L'AN MIL NEUF CENT CINQUANTE-CINQ
ET LE CINQ OCTOBRE.

LEATHERS. R.S. NUTTING. HUGH M. CLOWES.

24 - Formal request dated 5th October 1955 to the French Consulate in London to take three historical parchments from Father Saunière out of France for investigation purposes in London.

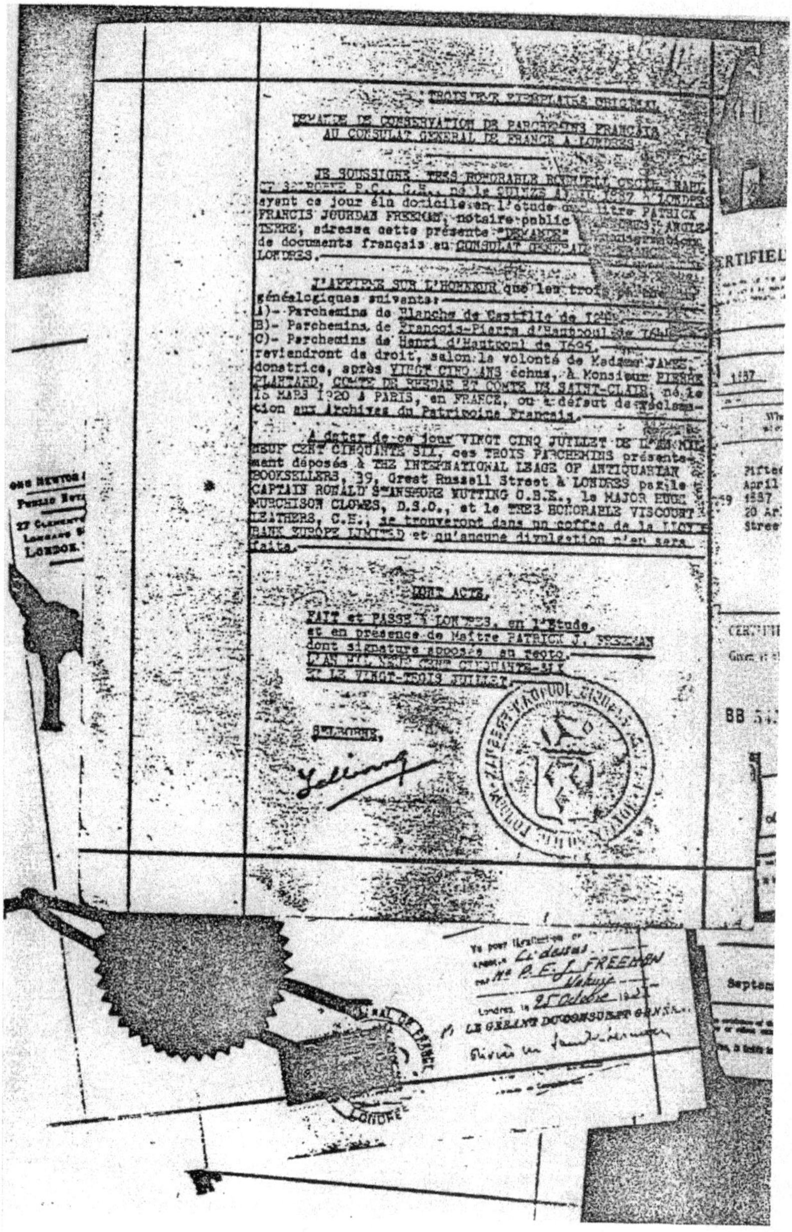

TROISIEME EXEMPLAIRE ORIGINAL

DEMANDE DE CONSERVATION DE PARCHEMINS FRANÇAIS AU CONSULAT GENERAL DE FRANCE A LONDRES

JE SOUSSIGNE TRES HONORABLE [illegible] P.C., C.H., né le QUINZE AVRIL 1887 A LONDRES ayant ce jour élu domicile en l'étude de Maître PATRICK FRANCIS JOURDAN FREEMAN, notaire public [illegible] ANGLETERRE, adresse cette présente "DEMANDE" [illegible] de documents français au CONSULAT GENERAL [illegible] LONDRES.

J'AFFIRME SUR L'HONNEUR que les trois [illegible] généalogiques suivants:

A)- Parchemins de Blanche de Castille de 12[illegible]
B)- Parchemins de François-Pierre d'Hautpoul de 164[illegible]
C)- Parchemins de Henri d'Hautpoul de 1695,

reviendront de droit, selon la volonté de Madame JAMES donatrice, après VINGT CINQ ANS échus, à Monsieur PIERRE PLANTARD, COMTE DE RHEDAE ET COMTE DE SAINT-CLAIR, né le 18 MARS 1920 à PARIS, en FRANCE, ou à défaut de réclamation aux Archives du Patrimoine Français.

A dater de ce jour VINGT CINQ JUILLET DE L'AN MIL NEUF CENT CINQUANTE SIX, ces TROIS PARCHEMINS présentement déposés à THE INTERNATIONAL LEAGE OF ANTIQUARIAN BOOKSELLERS, 39, Great Russell Street à LONDRES par le CAPTAIN RONALD STANSMORE NUTTING O.B.E., le MAJOR HUGH MURCHISON CLOWES, D.S.O., et le TRES HONORABLE VISCOUNT LEATHERS, C.H., se trouveront dans un coffre de la LLOYDS BANK EUROPE LIMITED et qu'aucune divulgation n'en sera faite.

DONT ACTE,

FAIT et PASSE à LONDRES, en l'Etude, et en présence de Maître PATRICK J. FREEMAN dont signature apposée au recto. L'AN MIL NEUF CENT CINQUANTE-SIX ET LE VINGT-TROIS JUILLET.

SELBORNE,

Vu pour légalisation de la signature ci-dessus apposée de Me P.F.J. FREEMAN notaire

Londres, le 25 Octobre 195[illegible]

LE GERANT DU CONSULAT GENERAL

25 - Notarial Deed dated 23rd July 1956 registered at the French Consulate in London confirming that three historical documents from Father Saunière will be kept at Lloyds' Bank Europe Limited in London for 25 years before being handed over to Pierre Plantard

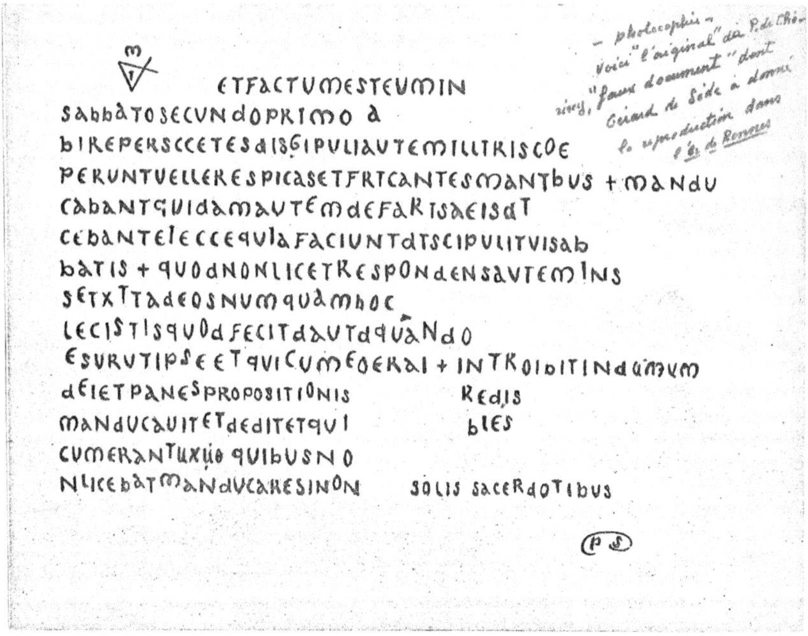

ETFACTUMESTEUMIN
SABBATOSECUNDOPRIMOA
BIREPERSCCETESDISCIPULIAUTEMILLIRISCOE
PERUNTUELLERESPICASETFRICANTESMANIBUS + MANDU
CABANTQUIDAMAUTEMDEFARISAEISDT
CEBANTEIECCEQUIAFACIUNTDISCIPULITUISAB
BATIS + QUODNONLICETRESPONDENSAUTEMINS
SETXTTADEOSNUMQUAMHOC
LEGISTISQUODFECITDAUTDQUANDO
ESURUTIPSEETQUICUMEOERAT + INTROIBITINDOMUM
DEIETPANESPROPOSITIONIS REDIS
MANDUCAVITETDEDITETQUI BLES
CUMERANTUXIO QUIBUSNO
NLICEBATMANDUCARESINON SOLIS SACERDOTIBUS

– photocopie – Voici "l'original" du P. de Chérisey, "faux document" dont Gérard de Sède a donné la reproduction dans l'Or de Rennes

26 - "Document I – Small Parchment"

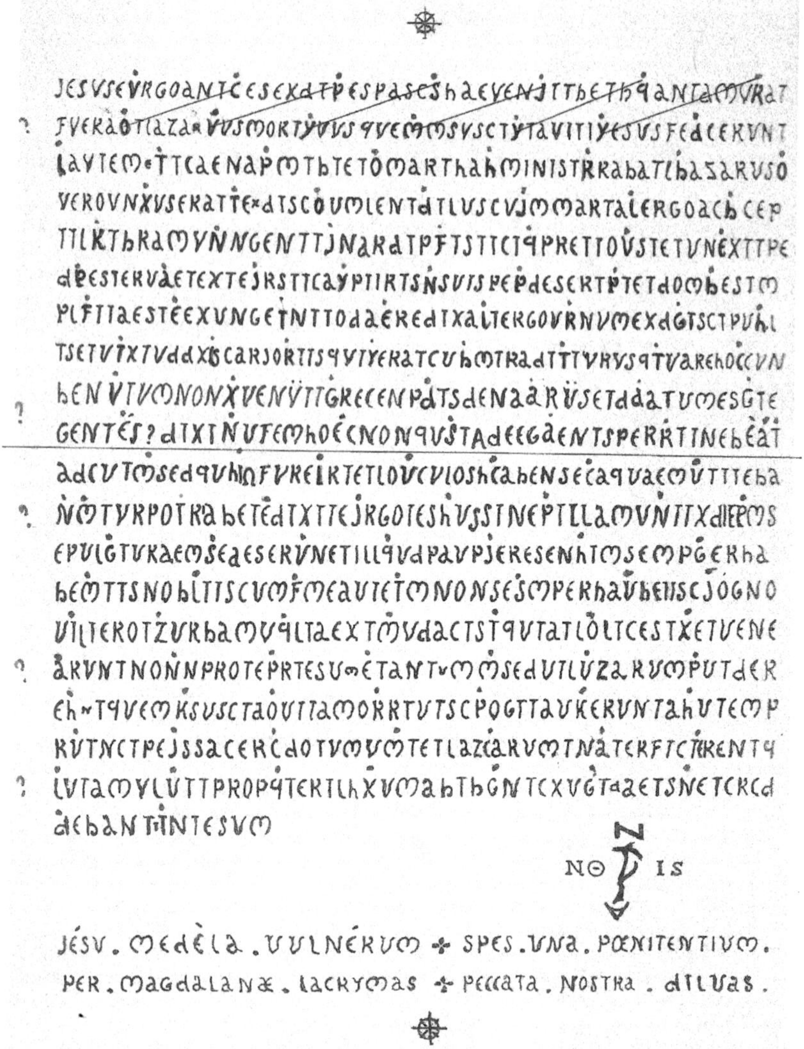

27 - "Document II – Large Parchment"

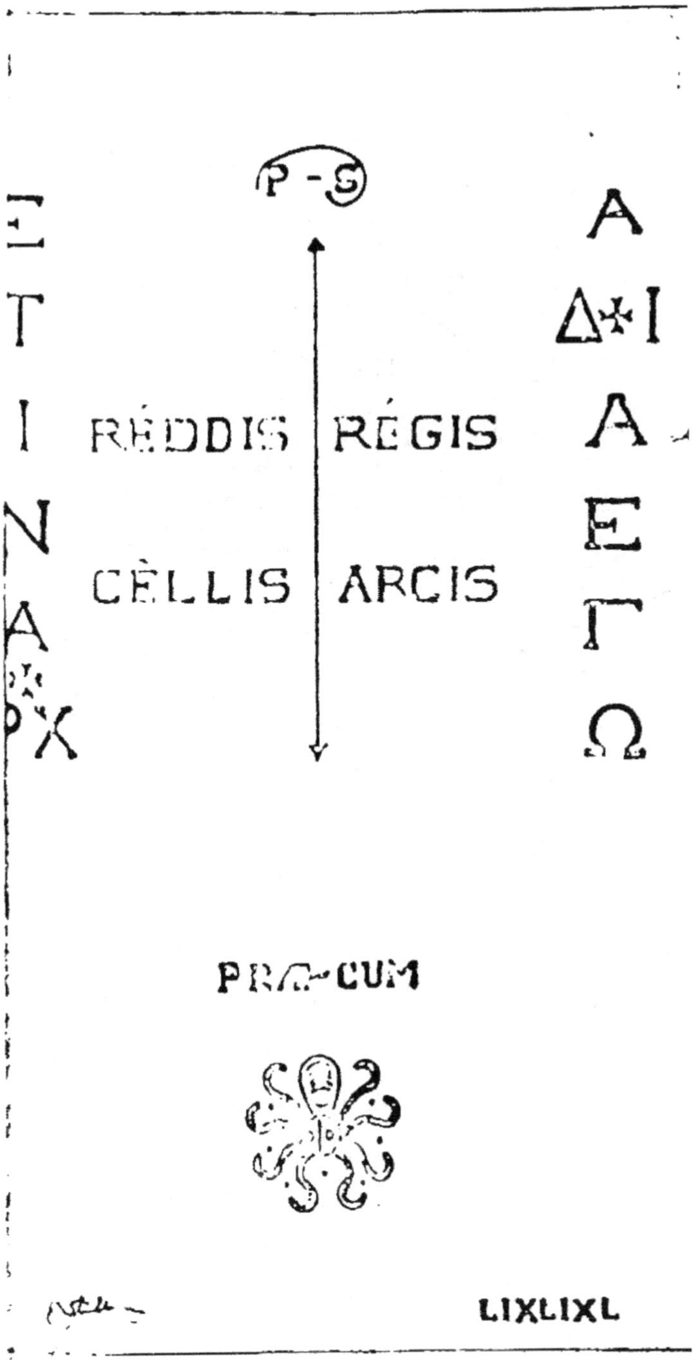

28 - Tombstone of the Marchioness of Blanchefort

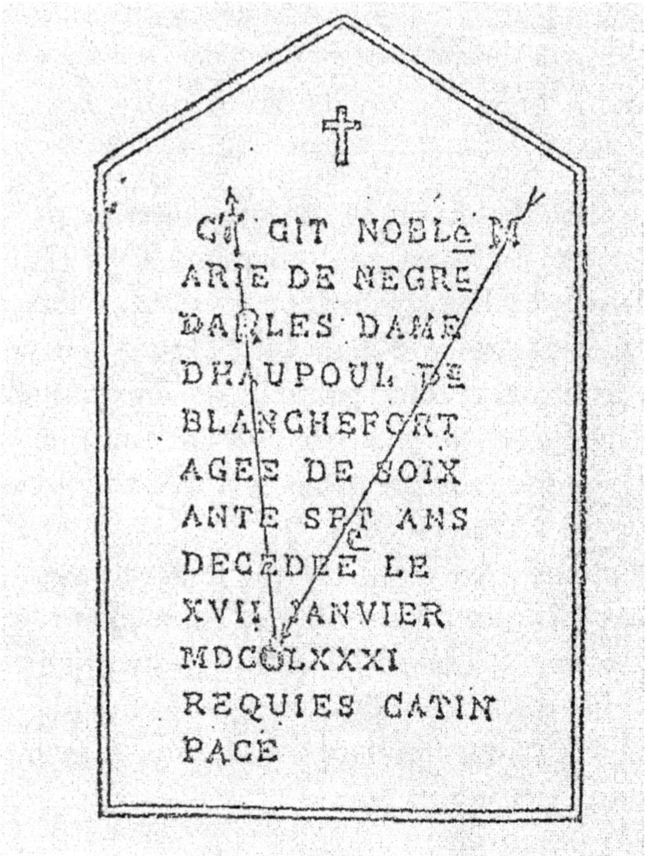
CT GIT NOBLe M
ARIE DE NEGRE
DARLES DAME
DHAUPOUL DE
BLANCHEFORT
AGEE DE SOIX
ANTE SEPT ANS
DECEDEE LE
XVII JANVIER
MDCOLXXXI
REQUIES CATIN
PACE

29 - Stele of the Marchioness of Blanchefort
(photocopy)

Stone And Paper

A short while before his death, our friend Amadeus or Asmodeus – you have recognised Philippe de Cherisey, on bad terms with the Great Extraterrestrial Monarch Pierre Plantard, made me swear to publish *Pierre et Papier* (*Stone and Paper*) twenty years after the disappearance of its author.

It is a choice piece which opens fantastic horizons. There are several approaches and a double strategy. It looks as though the Dead Sea scrolls are the clue to the history displacement. We are told about the gold in Rennes-le-Château when, in fact, it is the gold of King Solomon! Gérard de Sède was not mistaken when he noticed this voluntary or involuntary transposition.

But there is more. The Small Parchment is made of three quotations, enriched with several letters, referring to three excerpts from the Gospel, and, more importantly, an inscription from the altar in Rennes-le-Château.

Below is Philippe de Cherisey's explanation translated from his manuscript *Pierre et Papier*; the French original handwritten version of this document can be found in Appendix II.

Pierre et Papier (*Stone and Paper*) by Philippe de Cherisey

While investigating the treasure of Rennes-le-Château (Aude), and after umpteen tergiversations, Gérard de Sède received two important documents which he was allowed to publish providing he did not disclose their origin.

Two years later, the Editions Julliard published *L'Or de Rennes* (*The Gold of Rennes*) in which Gérard de Sède stresses the importance of these two documents for which he provides a photocopy. This work was sufficiently successful to be republished at a more modest price in 1970, by the Editions J'ai Lu, under the eye-catching title *Le Trésor Maudit de Rennes-le-Château* (*Accursed Treasure of Rennes-le-Château*).

These two documents are introduced below for the third and, probably, last time, with the way to interpret them and criticise the critics who take an interest in them; in short, to disassemble the mechanism of a rather good hoax.

Document I, or Small Parchment, is an assembly of three synoptic Gospels relating the same event, namely *Saint Luke*

(VI,1-5), *Saint Matthew* (XII, 1-8), and *Saint Mark* (II, 23-28). The first sentence in these Gospel readings contains enigmas which exegetes have renounced to elucidate. Jesus in sabbato secundo primo reads "Jesus on a day of Sabbath, second first", which could either be the second Sabbath after the first day of the showbread, or the first Sabbath after the second day. Unfortunately, there is no reference of this "Sabbath, second first" in the biblical literature. The truth is much simpler and one must remember that, prior to his conversion, Saint Luke was a Phrygian, therefore a worshiper of the sun god Sabbasius. Jesus IN SABBATO SECUNDO PRIMO signifies that Luke worshiped Jesus as a second Sabbasius who became First. The clever transcriber did think about isolating the mention SOLIS SACERDOTIBUS at the bottom of the page, which could mean "For priests only" as well as "For priests of the Sun". Needless to say that the same Luke never heard of the rest of the reading not stated in the parchment, namely that "the Son of man is Master of the Sabbath", as this does not mean anything, but rather that he is the "Master of Sabbasius". Similarly, we can say that the witches' Sabbath has little to do with a given day of the week, but with the "Sabbasies", feast days dedicated to the fallen god who had taken a diabolical appearance.

Document II, or Large Parchment, relates an evangelical text from *Saint John* (XII, 1-12). It concerns the famous story of Mary Magdalene the Sinner pouring a jar of very expensive balm over Jesus' feet one week before the Passion. This generous gesture annoyed the apostles who estimated that a perfume worth 300 pieces of silver could have been sold and the proceeds distributed to the poor. In his position of treasurer who received 10% of the revenue, Judas felt particularly frustrated, but recouped his loss of earnings by selling Christ for 30 pieces of silver. Through this parable, John the Evangelist sent a warning, which the Church historians do not seem to have grasped very well; the body of Christ to his perfume is in the proportion of 10%, his story belonging to its legend in the ratio of 30 to 300.

With regard to the treasure, this text has two further meanings. It is a warning to the eventual discoverer that, when finding himself in Judas' position, he will not be entitled to glean more than a tenth from it. Father Saunière learned at his own expense the cost of exceeding the bad apostle' honorarium, since he died on 22nd January 1917, a few days after an excessive tapping of the lungs. It is also about accustoming the seeker to the perspective of pillaging a necropolis where, for centuries, the dead remain naturally mummified and in a rather good state of preservation. From this angle, one is asked to consider the sinner Mary Magdalene as patron saint of the embalmers, something Christ did very well when he declared that she had poured the balm for his inhumation.

The disposition of the characters in Document I, or Small Parchment, illustrates the section of a mountain where the cave of the treasure is represented by an almost inaccessible opening. Yet, the sinkhole above the cave's entrance provides INTROIBIT IN DOMUM meaning "he enters the house". The treasure is, therefore, both accessible and inaccessible. This is also what Father Saunière intended with his double-sacristy, a very well-laid-out and obvious dummy through which one could just walk in the back sacristy. This indicates simply that the cave is sufficiently humid for a wall of mud to re-form as soon as it is pierced. The one who enters the cave without being forewarned believes he has reached a dead-end and does not realise that all he has to do is clear the mud.

This scenario was exploited in *The Count of Monte Cristo*, when the hero, on entering a cavern with an alleged treasure, is disappointed to find it empty, until he discovers that one of the walls is made of carton-pierre that can be taken down without difficulty. The famous novel of Alexandre Dumas offers one of the best trails to the treasure of Rennes-le-Château. One would gain a lot from reading the postscript where the author denies having plagiarised a former work; there is a real challenge for the reader in the last paragraph.

The evangelical text dissimulates a message in French which, for some unknown reason, has never been discovered by any critic or reader even though it is extremely easy to find. First, one must realise that the characters are not well aligned. Then, by placing the side of a sheet of paper on a level with the top edge of the bulk of characters in every sentence, one will identify a total of forty five letters that are sticking out, as follows:

2nd line	ADA
3rd line	GO
4th line	B
5th line	ERT
6th line	II
7th line	ROI
8th line	ETA
9th line	SION
10th line	ESTCETR

11th line	ESOR
12th line	ETILES
13th line	T
14th line	LA MORT

Namely, A DAGOBERT II ROI ET A SION EST CE TRESOR ET IL EST LA MORT, where the name of SION is provided by the letters that form the breast wall of the cavern. The sentence means "The treasure belongs to King Dagobert II and to Sion and it is death".

After examining the two documents, Commandant Lerville, president of the A.R.C. "Association des Réservistes du Chiffre" (Association of Cipher Reservists) and Colonel Arnaud, well-known decipherer, told Gérard de Sède that they were indeed coded "via a double-key substitution followed by a transposition on a chessboard", and that mistakes had been introduced deliberately to thwart the decoding attempts and send searchers on the wrong tracks.

Their first conclusion is more or less correct and we will use that approach, having for tools the text of document II (Large Parchment), the texts of the stele and tombstone of the Marchioness of Hautpoul-Blanchefort, a transposition grid and a chessboard. Document I (Small Parchment) does not apply. This exercise, which is somewhat laborious but very simple, will place the most ordinary reader in a position of superiority over the most sophisticated computer.

The second conclusion of Commandant Lerville and Colonel Arnaud is totally wrong since the mistakes, far from having been inserted to baffle searchers, were there, in fact, to give them a clue.

Let us, therefore, use the approach advocated by the military men, that of a double-key substitution and the transference over a chessboard game.

The first exercise consists in eliminating from Document II all parasitic letters introduced by the author in Saint John's evangelical text, which make it difficult to read.

VCPSJQROVYMYYDLTPOHRBOXTODJLBKNJ
\+ FQUEPAJYNPPBFEIELRGHIIRYBTTCVXGD
LUCCVMTEJHPNPGSVQJHGMLFTSVJLZQMT
OXANPEMUPHKORPKHVJCMCQTLVQXGGNDT

Thus, 128 letters, which impart to the cryptologist the idea of two chessboards of 64 squares each.

Indeed, the text of the vulgate starts with JESUS ERGO ANTE SEX DIES PASCHAE VENIT and not, as shown in Document II, JESUS EVRGO ANTCE SEX DIPES PASCSHAE VENJIT.

The second exercise consists in looking for a total of 128 letters on the stele and tombstone which will enable the substitution, or the encoding of one set of characters through the other. By eliminating the fourteen Greek letters which border the tombstone vertically, we arrive at a total of 150 letters, 22 of which are superfluous. These extraneous letters are, of course, those of the reference:

REDDIS REGIS

CELLIS ARCIS

This leaves a total of 128 characters made of all the letters on the stele plus those of the reference P S PRAECUM on the tombstone. To intensify the difficulty, the funeral text reads backwards, starting with the last letter of the mention P S PRAECUM on the tombstone, followed by the text on stele, as follows:

MUCEARPSPECAPNITACSEIUQERIXXXLOC
● DMREIVNAJIIVXELEEDECEDSNATPESETN
AXIOSEDEEGATROFEHCNALBEDLUOPUAHD
EMADSELRADERGENEDEIRAMELBONTIGTC

The third operation consists in a substitution which is made from a keyword designated by the multiple mistakes on the stele.

1st line	Should be C I instead of C T	T
	Should be NOBLE instead of NOBLe	e
	M should be on the next line	M
2nd line	Double mistake in the spelling and character case	e
	Should be NEGRI instead of NEGRe	
3rd line	Should be DABLES instead of DARLES	R
4th line	Should be DE instead of De	e
7th line	Should be SEPT instead of SEPt	P
10th line	Should be MDCCLXXXI instead of MDCOLXXXI	O

To place the letters TeMeRePO in the right order, one must remember that one is in front of a stele with a cross at the top and, therefore, it is appropriate to cross oneself. The right hand is taken to the forehead (In the name of the Father) corresponding to M, the highest and most obvious mistake. It then reaches the lowest mistake which is O (and of the Son), and returns to the left shoulder, arriving in T having encountered the letter R on the way.

The keyword begins, therefore, with MORT (dead), which one expects for a deceased person. We are left with the letters "eeeP" which can only be read as "épée" (sword). The double mistake in the spelling and character case on the second line serves as a junction between Mort and épée to produce MORTEPEE (Dead Sword). The small e is a reminder that the people of Languedoc have a tendency to sound silent letters, pronouncing Noblé for Noble, but cannot do so when the word is épée [as it would sound like épéé].

△ MORTEPEE

The fourth operation consists in applying the keyword △ [MORTEPEE] on the set of characters ✚, using the simplest grid of all, the one that places the alphabet in y-axes and x-axes. When the eight letters of MORTEPEE have been applied [to the first eight characters in the set], you utilise them again and again until you have gone through the entire text [namely, all the characters in set ✚]. When the axis from the letter V meets the axis of the key letter M, it produces the letter I; however, to spice up things, you take the next letter to the right or below, in this instance J. Using this technique, C to key O gives R, P to key R gives I, S to key T produces N, and so on. This is how I obtain the set of characters ▣ of the first substitution:

▣

JRINOHXTJNFSDTQZDEAMGFCZCSCGGBSO
SGNZVQODBFIVKUNJZHZCNZXDOJMXBNLI
ZKUXBDZJXXIIUXYBEZABRCKZGLZCGEHRZ
CMSIUURADDDJXGPMJZUHHQZQJGPBLEIZ

The fifth operation consists in applying the set of characters ● as keys over series ▣, using once more the same alphabetic grid and technique, where J to key M gives X, R to key U gives N, I to key C gives L, N to key E gives S, and so on.

The second substitution produces the following set of characters:

XNLSPANNASITTIATEXRRPBTEUCAEENIR
✱ XTGEENDELORSIAAOELEFSDQRPEDCUPGX
AIEMUIDOCEJDNMEGMCOCEEPDSHRXAIAD
HATMOAESEBICELERNEEAIEEDLVEVULDC

Before going to the next step and in order to wake up the readers a little, who like me may feel overcome by nausea, I would like to point out a prodigious phenomenon, which no logistician has been able to work out. Having compared text ✚ with text △ to obtain text ▣, and compared the latter with text ● to obtain text ✱, text ✱ is the exact anagram of text ● and contains an identical set of 128 letters, as follows:

A 12	B 2	C 7	D 9	E 24	F 1	G 3	H 2	I 9	J 1	L 6
M 4	N 7	O 5	P 5	Q 1	R 7	S 6	T 6	U 4	V 2	X 5

Knowing that the substitution game is completed and that we must now use a chessboard to place these 128 letters in the right order, it would be amazing if at the end of this exercise we could reconstitute the funeral text; fantastic and completely ridiculous. But I wish to reassure the readers that we will uncover another text, which is an anagram of the gravestone's text.

The last operation, which is carried out on a chessboard, is well known to the cryptologists, under the heading "Vigenère cipher", as one of the oldest form of secret alphabet. It is described in *La Cryptographie* by René Cerlier, published by "Que sais-je?". It saw the light in Jerusalem, in the stables of King Solomon's Temple, at a time when those famous Temple's grottoes sheltered a society of knights, who were also chess players. However, it was only disclosed during the Renaissance by Blaise de Vigenère, secretary to the Duke of Nevers. It consists of successfully leaping with the knight over the sixty four squares of a chessboard without ever passing twice over the same square. This patience game has left a marvellous mark in mediaeval novels where a knight enters a deserted castle to confront an invisible adversary at chess and, most of the time, is angry to have lost; where one should understand the particular dissatisfaction of patience adepts when they fail and feel, therefore, beaten by themselves.

The passage from one chessboard to the other is done without interruption, as if we are not leaving the first chessboard but simply refilling it with the second contingent of sixty four letters. The second tour around the board will be done, of course, on the same circuit, but twice symmetrical, placing to the right what was on the left, and to the top what was at the bottom, in the manner that the branches ⌊ ⌉ of the Suavastika 卍 are symmetrical which result in +. In other words, the passage from one chessboard to the other is analogous to going through a mirror and explains, therefore, the degree of dissatisfaction encountered by anyone who, failing a patience game, is unable to beat or be beaten, since he/she could not meet himself/herself.

Let us, therefore, fill up the two chessboards with the 128 letters of the character set ✱ which we dispose in the normal order of reading, and break down the two symmetrical circuits into three laps each, so that the readership can better savour the charm of this operation. At the end of one lap, we mark the start of the next lap by a dotted line.

The result of this exercise is:

BERGEREPASDETENTATIONQUEPOUSSINT
ENIERSGARDENTLACLEFPAXDCLXXXIPAR
LACROIXETCECHEVALDEDIEUJACHEVECE
DAEMONDEGARDIENAMIDIPOMMESBLEUES

Which reads as follows:

BERGERE, PAS DE TENTATION
QUE POUSSIN, TENIERS GARDENT LA CLEF
PAX DCLXXXI
PAR LA CROIX ET CE CHEVAL DE DIEU
J'ACHEVE CE DAEMON DE GARDIEN
A MIDI
POMMES BLEUES

The art of the anagram is a mathematical one where the perfection of a given anagram is proportionate to the number of letters used in its composition. To create TUB with BUT, is easy, LEGER with GRELE, more difficult, SABRES with BRASSE even more complicated, and so forth. The anagram of Gisors introduced by Gérard de Sède, which comprises nineteen letters, is an amazing feat when one finds AMO DEMETER ET TIMEO behind O MATER DEI MEMENTO MEI; the many critics who objected to such an interpretation would have found difficult to provide another version.

Two anagrams, believed to be exceptional, can be found in the dictionaries.

The first one made of the first twenty eight letters of the "Ave Maria", or:

AVE MARIA GRATIA PLENA DOMINUS TECUM

Provides:

VIRGO SERENA PIA MUNDA ET IMMACULATA

The second, comprising thirty eight letters, is an Italian homage to the bel canto, where:

RIME DI AMORE CHE TENNE LA LUCIA DI LAMMERMOOR

Gives:

UDRAI NEL MAR CHE MORMORA L'ECO DEI MIEI LAMENTI

The anagram championship seems to be detained by a ballet of thirteen dancers rallied in honour of Stanislas Leczinski. Each of the dancers carried a letter of the words DOMUS LESCINIA, from which five figures were derived, as follows:

1st figure:	ADES INCOLUMIS
2nd figure:	OMNIS ES LUCIDA
3rd figure:	MANE SIDUS LOCI
4th figure:	SIS COLUMNA DEI
5th figure:	I SCANDE SOLIUM

Compared to these anagrams, the one we have revealed, which comprises one hundred twenty eight letters, exceeds by far anything that has been done in the genre, not only in France, but in all the spoken languages of the world. The author enters the geniuses' category at once, more particularly so since, contrary to his fellows, his anagram is decoded by itself. A prevailing opinion believes that Father Bigou, parish priest of Rennes-le-Château in 1781 and writer of the text on the stele, is the author of this diversion. We do not share this opinion; the anagram was conceived in this day and age and even bears a signature that we discover through the analysis of the coded text.

Shepherdess, No Temptation

The nosy people around the treasure of Rennes-le-Château know this anecdote very well. Gérard de Sède mentions it in one of his works. A shepherdess of Rennes-le-Château wakes up early and sees the Devil spread his treasure in the sun. "Toute la bonne colline en était illuminée" (The entire beautiful hill was lit by it). The area is known to the local literature and the still alive popular tradition understands that "bonne colline" (beautiful hill) means Mont Serbairou, located south of Rennes-les-Bains and separating the valleys of la Blanque and la Sals which converge at its foot. There we find an artificial labyrinth formed by the tunnels of an old jet mine which was closed shortly before the French Revolution, that is around the time of the death of the late Marchioness of Hautpoul-Blanchefort. The area appears even more attractive due to the oozing of a Magdalene's headspring, referring to the evangelical text of Document II and the dedication in the church of Rennes-le-Château.

How many trips did we make, my friend Basil and me, in these nauseating passages until, one day, whilst musing better over the words BERGÈRE PAS DE TENTATION, the search seemed as fruitless to us as trying to grab the reflection of a treasure and take the shadow for prey. There was a temptation to which one should not succumb. If, at sunrise, the shepherdess was dazzled by the reflection of the gold, and not by the gold itself, it was because the sun was behind her and, therefore, she was looking west. Thus, it was more important to know where the shepherdess was than where she was looking. Asmodeus, the Devil who guards the church of Rennes-le-Château, confirmed this, "Anyone claiming to have seen the treasure of Asmodeus will never reach it since it is under one's feet". This is one of the reasons why, as keen as you are to find the treasure, you will find it reasonable that I stop at that. Not having the presumptuousness of considering myself more intelligent than the readers, I invite them to pursue the meditation about the mirror, and to envisage with me how the stare and reflection are less important than going through the mirror and the anti-symmetrical phenomenon that opposes ⌊ ⌉. As long as one is not trained to this gymnastic, it is no use going to Rennes-le-Château or even looking at the map; it is better to look at oneself in the mirror, with courage.

That Poussin, Teniers Holds The Key

Poussin and Teniers have no connection other than having illustrated the art of painting in the seventeenth Century. They go on the treasure trail via two different routes.

Nicolas Poussin was born between Les Andelys and Gisors, in a little village that we have been unable to identify. Apart from a stormy interval in Paris, where Richelieu had commissioned some painting from him, the entire career of the painter took place in Italy. It is thought that his parents belonged to a small noble lineage around Soissons, but he always refused the ennoblement offered to him. Many reviews have been devoted to Poussin, leaving only the Poulains (Protégés) in the dark, a society of French freethinkers living in Italy, so fond of their country of origin that they swore not to return to it until it came closer to their ideal image of it. Poussin kept company with the Poulains even before his departure for Italy. It is very likely that the graffiti signed "Nicolas Poulain" in the Prisoner's tower in Gisors were in fact from Nicolas Poussin and not from a mysterious captive from the fourteenth or fifteenth Century.

The insertion of Poussin's name on the tomb in the cemetery of Rennes-le-Château makes us ponder whether there is a play on words with hautes poules (noble hen chickens) which are the emblem of the Hautpoul family, facilitating therefore the transition between Poulain and Poussin. Besides, one should note that if three cocks are the emblem of the Hautpoul, the tombstone on the male side of the Hautpoul-Blanchefort under the church's altar, which represents a two-rider horse, enabled to place the pun "Poulain-Poussin" prior to the seventeenth Century.

Furthermore, an even more obvious connection between Poussin and Rennes-le-Château is apparent in the motto ET IN ARCADIA EGO of the Shepherds of Arcadia's painting by Nicolas Poussin, which appears also in Greek lettering ET IN APXADIA ΕΓΩ on the tombstone, thus referring to the injunction bergère, pas de tentation. This small association is sufficiently appealing to suggest Nicolas Poussin legitimately or illegitimately belonging to the Hautpoul-Blanchefort family.

If Poussin is a reference to the shepherdess, Teniers is a reference to the temptation. Profane painter, Teniers exploited one religious theme only, namely the "Temptation of Saint Anthony", which he did time and time again. The death of the late Marchioness of Hautpoul-Blanchefort, which occurred on 17th January MDCOLXXXI, could be the trademark of Teniers, since:

17th January is Saint Anthony the Hermit's day, the day of the famous temptations.

MDCOLXXXI is a graphic mistake since there is no O among Roman numerals. When reading 16081 instead of 1781, or correct date of the death, we find a reference to the most famous

"Temptation of Saint Anthony" dating from 1681 and exhibited in the Louvre museum.

The principal temptress of Saint Anthony in the painting of the Louvre museum is a well-known shepherdess, through whom we recall the "Shepherdess, no temptation" of the first sentence.

The presence of Teniers in the message designates a path to follow from the church of Rennes-le-Château to the church of Saint-Luc (Saint Luke), a village further north. This is deduced from two anecdotes concerning the painter: the robe of his prosecutor and his professional affiliation. The last painting of Teniers represented a prosecutor in a black robe. When asked about his health, the very elderly painter replied that he had burnt his last tooth to obtain the black ivory colour of the robe. Very young, Teniers had been admitted as master of the Brotherhood of Saint Luke, which rallied all painters in Antwerp.

Certain details in the present church support this association:

At the foot of the lateral statue of Mary Magdalene, there is a death's head with a missing tooth with a little cross engraved on its crown.

The prosecutor of the church is Pontius Pilate, who is represented in the first station on the Way of the Cross. The one from Rennes-le-Château washes his hands in a white basin held by a small black boy.

The village and church of Saint Luke are at the foot of the Mont de la Mort (Mount of Death), like the cross on the skull at the foot of Mary Magdalene. When considering that the first station on the Way of the Cross leads to Golgotha, or to the Mount of Death, one obtains an itinerary from the church of Rennes-le-Château to the church of Saint Luke. One must object that this itinerary is contrary to Teniers's biography, which had to go from his youth, when he was accepted by the Brotherhood of Saint Luke, to his old age with the prosecutor. In fact, the path must be followed in reverse since Teniers was elected in Antwerp.

PAX DCLXXXI

In its most general meaning, PAX is a "mortépée" (dead sword), not so much in the sense of a "beatitude's nostalgia" that holds the world spellbound since the death of Abel, but rather as "war against war", the sense understood by the majority of the readers.

PAX has a more concrete meaning though, denoting the famous vision of Constantine in 312 CE in the shape of a radiating hexagon which the Greek construed as XPigtos and the Latins as PaX. The war cry In Hoc Signo Vinces accompanied the vision, a rather common motto in the Christian world. It appears in Latin in the church of Rennes-les-Bains, and in French Par ce signe tu le vaincras (By this sign you will conquer him) in the church of Rennes-le-Château. The translation is wrong as “le” (him) is superfluous, but is substantiated as it confirms the presence of the Devil Asmodeus in the slogan, as well as Father Saunière’s need to construct a twenty-two letter sentence.

The emblem PAX became known through its religious aspect when the papacy used it accompanied by A Ω, Alpha and Omega, producing APXΩ, or I rule. It seems that although the watchword of the Shepherds of Arcadia is in Latin, its Greek representation is justified, as shown on the tombstone where P ✠ X at the bottom of the left column invite A and Ω at the top and bottom of the right column, as follows:

A		Ω
	☧	
E		A
T		Δ ✠ I
I		A
N		E
A		Γ
P ✠ X		Ω

The claim the Church made over the emblem of the temporal prince is tied in with a long conflict between imperial Byzantium and pontifical Rome. There is a parallel to be established between the chasuble adorned with ☧ (Chi Rho, or Chrisma), and the red cloak of the emperors of Byzantium which displayed this symbol until 507 CE, when Anastasius appeared in a penitent’s white outfit. When the emperor of the Orient announced that he was going to sacrifice his own interests to those of the state, he received an ovation. However, the red cloak with the golden chrisma was not adopted immediately by the papacy. That same year, Saint Martin of Tours, ambassador of the Orient in Gaul, was commissioned to hand over the PAX to Clovis, the Merovingian King in whom the church saw the “Patrician” and “new Constantine”. A legendary tale relates this incident, describing Saint Martin cutting his cloak in two with his sword and giving one half to a "poor man", the latter being no other than the Roman emperor.

On reaching Gaul, the name PAX was replaced by that of "Labarum", or oriflamme because of its golden and red colours, and the war cry In Hoc Signo Vinces became Montjoie-Saint-Denis (Montjoy!)

PAX DCLXXXI signals the transfer of the monarchy to Rennes-le-Château in 681. The "Good King Dagobert", the one in the song and mentioned in Document I (The Small Parchment), died in Stenay on 23rd December 679; he was the only Merovingian King canonised by the Church in the hope that his male descent would be forgotten. From his marriage to the Visigothic princess Gisele du Razès, daughter of Bera II du Razès, Lord of Rennes-le-Château, the "Good King Dagobert" had two children, namely his son Sigebert IV, known as the Rejeton Ardent (Ardent Kid), and his daughter Rathilde whom Saint Wilfred rescued from the stranglehold of the Mayors of the Palace, future Carolingians. Sigebert and Rathilde sojourned one year in the Abbey of Oereen, where their half-sister Irmine, the progeny from Dagobert's first marriage in Ireland, resided. On 23rd December 680, one year to the day after the King's death, a commando of Knights led by Merovaeus Levi removed the Rejeton Ardent from the abbey and rode flat out to Languedoc to return him to his grandfather Bera II. As a reward for this exploit, the Visigoth gave Merovaeus Levi the seigniory of Mirepoix and the responsibility for raising Sigebert IV. From then on, the family of Merovaeus Levi embraced the watchword "Mira piscem e turribus" (Watch the fish from the top of the towers) [by "fish" they meant the dauphin, which in French means "dolphin", as well as "Dauphin" or heir apparent]. Here began the occult lineage of the Merovingian Kings, whose descendants have been waiting patiently for over thirteen Centuries for the end of the Carolingian or Capetian descent of the Mayors of the Palace.

Rathilde, the sister of Sigebert IV, lived in Oereen until 692, where she married Chilpéric II, by whom she had Chilpéric III, the last Merovingian in office. The descent of Merovaeus Levi, Lord of Mirepoix Levi, has nothing to do with the Levis-Mirepoix, but goes through the Lords of Bellissen, one of whom became famous as captain in charge of the fortress of Montségur when it was besieged.

The Key "With The Cross"

‡	✡	†	+
Cross of Lorraine	Seal of Solomon	Latin Cross	Greek Cross

Saint Peter intervenes here as dedicatee of the church in Rennes-le-Château, a title that goes to Saint Mary Magdalene after the Revolution. He was, indeed, the keeper of the keys to Heaven and the one who died crucified. Contrary to Jesus, who was exposed head up, Saint Peter was exhibited head down; the two crosses superimposed in a head to foot position create the image of the cross of Lorraine. If the Greek cross with branches of equal length was replaced by the Latin cross in a length 3 to width 2 ratio, it is precisely because the Latin cross implies the cross of Lorraine and the implication of a second width equal in size to the first one. The cross of Lorraine, the emblem of the Merovingian Kings of Austrasia, from whom Dagobert II descends, represents a Jesus-Peter or Judeo-Christian motion where the seal of Solomon is obtained by joining the six extremities of that cross. A constant hexagonal relationship is established between the Star of David ✡, the chrisma ☧, the fleur-de-lis, the French territory, and the cross of Lorraine ‡, which the Gaullist propaganda placed quite rightly in the centre of the country on its insignia. Besides, one knows that if the last Merovingian Kings were called Rois fainéants, it is because of the parable regarding the fleur-de-lis (lily flower), "Consider the lilies of the field, how they grow; they neither toil nor spin; yet I tell you, even Solomon in all his glory was not arrayed like one of these" [*Matthew 6, 28-29*]. Regarding the Lords of Rennes-le-Château, we note that the coats of arms of the Blancheforts include the seal of Solomon. The inversion of Saint Peter's cross against Jesus' cross is evoked on the tombstone by the initials P S, the purpose of which is to turn Saint Peter head to tail and to recall the words "Sabbath, Second First" mentioned on Document I (Small Parchment). The current church of Rennes-le-Château conjures up this inversion in another manner. At the bottom of the altar, there is the same citation as that found at the foot of Document II (Large Parchment), namely:

JESU.MEDÈLA.VULNÉRUM + SPES.UNA.POENITENTIUM.

PER.MAGDALENAE.LACRYMAS +
PECCATA.NOSTRA.DILUAS.

This invocation leads the priest towards the altar, but invites him to seek the tribunal at the other end of the church, under a large relief of Christ with arms spread out. Seated in the confessional, the priest sees Mary Magdalene at the bottom of the altar, which is an invitation for him to approach her. In other words, the church of Rennes-le-Château contains two churches top to bottom in the same building, inviting the priest to constantly pivot on himself solicited by both his Eucharistic and Penitential duties ("Solis Sacerdotibus"). The strange head to foot exercise carried out on Jesus and Peter, can equally be effected on Magdalene the Sinner, whom one evangelist depicts as pouring the very expensive perfume over Christ's head, whilst another says it was over Christ's feet so that she could wipe them with her own hair.

The Key "With This Horse Of God"

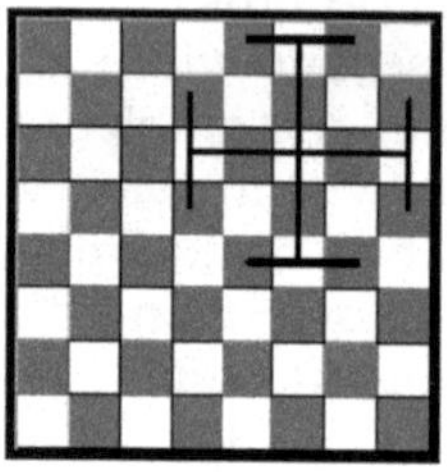

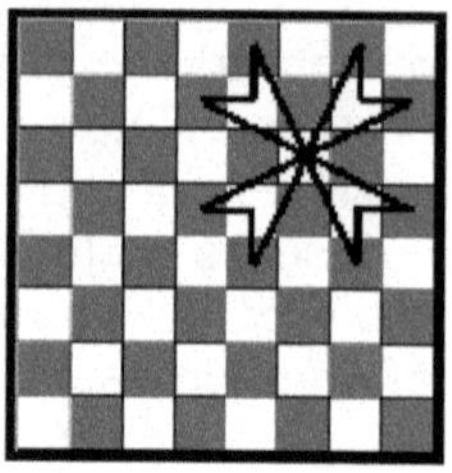

The horse of God is a sort of friendly salute to the individual who has decoded the message on a chessboard through the "Knight's Tour", as if to confirm to him that he made the right move. One must ensure that the rider is an incarnation of the eight-by-eight squared chessboard, having, from a given square, an option over eight leaps. In the same way, Godefroy de Bouillon constituted his society of chess players in the "stables of King Solomon" in Jerusalem and gave them a Potent cross ☩ for emblem, the meaning of which becomes apparent when placed on a chessboard; the horse is at the intersection and aims for the extremities of the cross. In 1118, when the Order of Sion founded by Godefroy de Bouillon concluded an alliance with that of the Templars, born from a pact between the Merovingian monarchy and the Capetians, the cross Pattée co-existed with the Potent cross, without changing the character of the chess game. The cross Pattée ✳ of the Knights Templar is, in fact, nothing more than a way of interpreting the knight's leap. Many other crosses were derived from the same model, including the Maltese cross, the Trinitarian cross, and others. But the Templars wanted to manifest their dependence on the chessboard by picturing a two-rider horse at the centre of their cross. Now, the emblem of the two-rider horse appeared in Rennes-le-Château three Centuries before the creation of the

Temple embellishing the tombstone of the male heirs of Blanchefort.

The two-rider horse in the church of Rennes-le-Château is derived from the classical mythology of Castor and Pollux, or the twin horsemen illustrating Gemini in the zodiac, and is an allusion to the rescue of Dagobert II's lineage; it portrays Merovaeus Levi bringing back young Sigebert IV on his horse from the Abbey of Oereen to the Razès where they arrived on 17th January 681 (PAX DCLXXXI).

This Horse of God is also Chiron, the good centaur, preceptor of the gods, and son of the lime tree nymph Philgia. If the two-rider horse designates Gemini, the good centaur remains the symbol of Sagittarius, in diametric opposition to it in the same manner that the fecundity of the genital glands (Gemini) opposes that of the phallic penetration (Sagittarius). Sagittarius (the Archer) contains, in fact, its own inversion when one realises that he shoots his arrows behind instead of in front of him; as the lower body of the horse is running faster than the torso of the man, a fortiori a legless cripple, it follows that the half man half horse overtakes himself and allows the man self to shoot himself in his lower part. This is why the Greek showed the good centaur Chiron injured at the knee. In the Christian world, the fête of Saint Genou (Knee) on 17th January, or Saint Genulfe's day, aims to preserve Chiron's role as "Horse of God". The poet Höderlin suggests another hypothesis, where the human upper part of the centaur shoots backwards in order to bring out the child in the man and to awaken the aggressiveness of that child.

"Prends un cheval maintenant, ceins ta cuirasse et prends ta lance légère mon enfant! La prophétie ne sera pas déchirée, ni vaine l'attente, jusqu'à le voir enfin ce retour d'Héraclès!" (Fetch a horse now, put on your breastplate and take your light lance my child! The prophecy will not be broken, nor will the wait be vain, until, at long last, we witness the return of Heracles!"

The first area of Rennes-le-Château where one can locate this "Horse of God" is at the top of Mount Serbairou. At the spot where the shepherdess noticed the reflection of a treasure, there are two beautiful white standing stones very similar to a large horse and a small one trotting side by side, their lower body sinking in the ground. The other area is more accessible; one is even forced to go through it on the road from Couiza to Rennes-le-Château, where it pierces the rock face via an aperture narrow enough to have hosted a guardroom in the past.

'You, on your way from Couiza to Rennes-le-Château, stop when you go through this aperture and look at the stony cluster on your left that represents a horse and his rider; then, in one sweep, muse over your birth, your love affairs, and how a womb becomes a vagina and prefigures your hole in the ground.'

This natural monument is situated on the Blanchefort-Espéraza line as the crow flies, where BLES or blés (wheat) is the slang word for wealth, or "dough". The war-horse is as much a plough-horse that will harrow and harvest. The key "With the Cross and this Horse of God" is conveyed in the rebus of the ninth station on the Way of the Cross in the church of Rennes-le-Château. Jesus, who fell on the ground under the weight of His cross, is dominated by a big horse which rears up, symbol of His own rebellion against rebellion.

I Conquer This Guardian Daemon In Middle Age

The visitors of Rennes-le-Château and the readers of Gérard de Sède know very well that the "guardian daemon" means the statue of the Devil that supports the stoup at the entrance of the church. His strange genuflexion has led to his identification, namely the limping devil, Asmodeus, "démon de midi", the daemon of lechery and middle age lust. Asmodeus is the adverse power that man discovers, half way through his life, when he reaches maturity. Between Asmodeus and the Pan god of the Arcadians, there is more than a lustful relationship, indeed the necessity to keep silent when reaching middle age for fear of being struck down. Only those who have conquered the guardian daemon in middle age and see themselves on the sloping side of their life are allowed to express themselves; the others, left with the "hippy" character of the horse, can only express themselves through a pathetic cry, the significance of which remains in their belly in the form of hope. To conquer this "guardian daemon in the prime of life", one must identify the right moment between youth that does not know yet, but can, and old age that cannot any more, but knows. Such watchfulness is only within the reach of poets.

The Bible and Jewish thinking have been more sensitive to the nature of Asmodeus as guardian of treasures than that of lustful demon. Asmodeus safeguarded the riches of King Solomon; he guarded them so well that, one day, he threw the King to the bottom of the stairs, pulling him by the hair, after the King presented himself at the treasure place without his seal-cum-pass. The suggested riddle is ingenious as it is about discovering that Solomon could only access the treasure when he was truly himself and punished himself when he was not. In other words, there is no demon outside the person, no Asmodeus outside Solomon, and vice and versa. Therefore, Solomon and Asmodeus share exactly the same seal, not in the manner that the key is identical to the lock, but that it is the inverse of the lock. The same rule that makes └ and ┐ symmetrical, and was used in the handling of the chessboard, applies here too, and provides with this anti-symmetry food for those who dream of going through the mirror.

Blue Apples

A poem from Paul Eluard makes an allusion to the "Earth blue like an orange". Two reveries overlap each other: one elementary, the other scholarly. An orange-coloured Earth travels through the firmament tinged with the complementary blue; this is the basic reverie. The learned reverie remembers oranges as "golden apples from the Garden of the Hesperides" in the legend of Hercules, and the great voyage of Jason and the Argonauts in their quest for the Golden Fleece. Both reveries come to the same conclusion about the treasure from the Eldorado, namely the Far West, where the Hesperides represent the West; or the Occident where the sun sheds all its impurities and treasures to rise again unsullied in the virginal Orient.

The theorem from Eluard, Orange-Bleue (blue orange) can develop into Pomme-Or-Bleue (blue gold apple), as a signal about the treasure of Rennes-le-Château through the insertion of the gold between the colour and the fruit. There is nothing to look for on that side other than an invitation to pursue the reverie on Orange-Bleue, which one will transcribe as Or-Ange-Bleu (gold blue angel). The simplest way, and the best, consists in viewing *"L'Ange Bleu"* (*The Blue Angel*), the famous film from Joseph Sternberg where we see Marlene Dietrich in the role of Lola-Lola, a singer who is the damnation of professor Rat-Unrat, academic turned clown. It is about discovering Mary Magdalene the Sinner behind Marlene-Lola-Lola, in order to find oneself in the church of Rennes-le-Château and realise that it is filled with angels. Regarding Sternberg (starry mountain), one can refer to his comment regarding mirrors, 'I do not like the stretches of water in my film Anatahan (Ana-ta-han), as water is the only real thing in the film', or even, 'I want to make the public aware that the errors it sees on screen are its own errors and to distinguish, therefore, two approaches, one through comprehension, the other through emotion'.

There are nineteen angels in Mary Magdalene's church, two for each statue on a pedestal, four above the stoup, four to hold Saint Anthony of Padua, and three to support the pilot light of the sanctuary... It is this last set that matters here: three little angels in gilded metal surround the red lamp which tells the congregation that the church is inhabited. In the presence of Mary Magdalene the Sinner, it would be false modesty to conceal that the red lamp is as much the mark of brothels as that of sanctuaries, and that places of pleasure and faith alike can only subsist through the offerings of their followers. Here, one can imagine the priest who operates the pulley to refill the lamp and, in so doing, produces a fall of gilded angels from the heights of a blue ceiling strewn with stars. When the three gilded angels, carriers of the red lamp, return to the blue firmament, thus creating the yellow, red and blue triad of fundamental colours, we obtain the complete unfolding of Eluard's theorem.

With This Horse Of God I Conquer This Guardian Daemon In Middle Age

This sentence is the signature of the artist who achieved the most beautiful play on words amidst all literary works worldwide and who has just, dear reader, started its interpretation in front of you, namely, me, Philippe de Cherisey, known as Amédée (Amadeus) at the theatre and under the pseudonym of Charlot in the fiction world.

The worst part of the job remains to be done now, as I have to convince you that I am indeed the author. Since dignity prevents me from treating the public like a tribunal, furthermore that not being accused I do not have to defend myself, and, finally, since my lineage has always considered that people place us in the spotlight in their desire to be enlightened when darkness descends, I only want to pursue the treasure trail of Rennes-le-Château that I have chosen.

To start with, I will explain how, with the means at my disposal, I managed to fabricate a trail which the cipher experts were able to work out, although without being able to discover the final text of the Bergère (Shepherdess). My first trick was the partial elimination of the letters K, W, Y and Z, which do not appear on Document II, Large Parchment, or in the funeral text, since they are both anagrams. Yet, during the exercises, we will see the letters K, Y and Z, crop up, which are, indeed, in the alphabetic decoding grid. There is a trap, in that my grid contains 25 letters while the French alphabet comprises 26; I have omitted the W. Did I cheat? No, not at all, since I wrote documents I and II using semi uncial characters to place them at a time when W was discarded by Westerners as it was divided between U and V. The falseness of documents I and II transpires as soon as one identifies U and V, S and Z, IJ and Y. Therefore, one should conclude that this is a hoax. Neither the historian nor the cipher expert can truly be interested in what is on offer, and this is what I depend upon; they will be even less interested when provided with photocopies of photocopies, or precisely what the readers have before their very eyes, and not the parchments carefully prepared by a clever forger. The best way to make a sale is to register it while persuading one's interlocutor that one is bluffing; an exercise that is truly quite scary as it places its adepts in a position where they can never say something again that will appear plausible, but an invigorating exercise in view of the superb results obtained. Imagine the uncontrollable laughter that seized me when Mr. Debant [See Appendix I], holder of a diploma from the Ecole des chartes (School of Palaeography and Librarianship in Paris), chief archivist for the Aude department, stated that the author is a scholar in mediaeval epigraphy and palaeography, who knows about semi-uncial writing, but is a hoaxer from after the Renaissance!; or, when Commandant Lerville and Colonel Arnaud declared about that same author that he is an Ecclesiastic nurtured on the Holy Writ, fond of mystery and imagination. Isn't this portrait of me admirable, knowing that I passed the French baccalauréat (G.C.E. A-levels, or high school diploma) several years ago and with great difficulties, that I dropped my university studies quite quickly to become an actor, that my knowledge of semi-uncial writing is from reading the "Grand Larousse", that my contacts with the Church are fewer and fewer since my first marriage in 1951, and that only one thing is of historical value, namely that I was born after the Renaissance?

Is this to say that "after umpteen tergiversations", I managed to forward to Gérard de Sède documents I and II without him knowing they were from me; and is this to say that, since that day and for seven years, I have not ceased to deride Mr. Debant, archivist, Commandant Lerville, president of the A.R.C. "Association des Réservistes du Chiffre" (Association of Cipher Reservists), and Colonel Arnaud, eminent cryptologist? No, it is not true. I have not made fun of any of these three gentlemen, whom I do not know any more than you do, dear reader, since they too, less credulous than yourself, refused to fall for it. If the portrait the three of them made of me amuses me, it is because of their ignorance of psychology which is today the common denominator among historians and mathematicians. My clever encoding has been determined by the importance of any consciousness; by the certainty that the world, although immense, is no bigger than my eyes to see it, my ears to hear it or my mouth to sing it; namely, by my very soul since it escapes all historical or mathematical investigation. This is how keywords are formed. Let us suppose, for instance, that I write each day "Mon poulet" (My chicken) to the one I love and that, one day, I write “Mon lapin” (My rabbit), she will be the only one able to guess that “lapin” is a signal and, possibly, a code. The only investigator capable of being more than just dazzled by it can be no other than someone who loves us. The advantage of those who understand us outstrips by far the knowledge of those who expound; and if I still love the theatre, it is precisely because of that quest for a code, not only between the comedians and the public, but within the world of theatre itself.

The relationship between the historian and the mathematician forms the second recipe for my encoding. This is why they could not decipher it. Take, for example, MORTEPEE, the keyword made of seven graphical mistakes TeMEEPO, and two historical ones, namely ER (NEGRE D’ARLES instead of NEGRI D’ABLES). If the logician is capable of identifying the seven graphical errors, the historian alone can see the other two. I then take as established that there is an impenetrable barrier between the logician and the historian. If indeed, having overcome the fear of ridicule, these two researchers are examining documents so notoriously apocryphal, it may be because they are both looking for the treasure of Rennes-le-Château. The historian with his two letters, against the sevens of the logician, will find himself in an inferior position; however, after understanding the mechanism, he will hold the secret over the letter R, since the E was spotted by the logician among the graphical mistakes. If we ask ourselves why the historian would keep quiet about the letters E and R, this is an astuteness with which I am not altogether dissatisfied. Around Rennes-le-Château, there is a Castle of Negre and a Darles Tower that the historian will save for himself. One can even intensify the phenomenon by publishing the text of the stele and its treasure, with the result that, for three years after the publication of Gérard de Sède’s book, readers will be seen from time to time scraping the ground or shifting stones at the castle and the tower. Even if the historian and the logician were united in a single mind, their association could only be on the basis of a reciprocal distrust. To heighten the debate, one could equally declare that the science ramifications, which isolate scientists in their own discipline, are the ruin of science, and summons the conscience to ponder over the utopia of “structures”, or mechanical cathedrals erected without our consent from data in the conscience, as if in that conscience one could reduce one’s actions to a “deal”.

A conversation I had with Mr. Dingon-Mozart from the Institute (Brotherhood) is worth reporting. My old master had been led to believe that the work of the anagram was extraordinary enough for its author to deserve the Légion d’honneur with decoration from the Ministry of Education. He was also convinced that documents I and II were a recent hoax, but could not accept that they were my compositions.

'It seems to me that you insist somewhat too heavily on the photocopy of a photocopy for Parchment II and maintain a questionable attitude concerning the stele and the tombstone, the very objects of the anagram. Now, the stele and the tombstone are from Father Bigou, who realised them between 1781, after the death of the late Marchioness, and 1792, when he left France with the nonjuring priests of Languedoc. Furthermore, the errors that enable the unfolding of the keyword MORTEPEE can be found in their entirety on the stele and the tombstone.

For your prank to be perfect, you would have to be able to claim the paternity of the two stone monuments which precede your birth by a century and a half at least. You may reply that these stones do not exist any more, having both been polished by Father Saunière in 1891, the virginal stele now in private hands in Paris and the tombstone, equally virginal, now a lid to the communal grave in the present cemetery of Rennes-le-Château.

So, nothing prevents you from stating that you are the author of both the stones and the papers. Nothing indeed, except they have been itemised three times before your birth. The first account by Mr. Stüblein was published before the smoothing of the stone and Gérard de Sède provided the reference for it at the National Library in Paris. The second account is, in fact, a reconstitution of a survey carried out amongst the inhabitants of Rennes-le-Château by Mr. Ernest Cros, interlocutor of Father Saunière at a time when you were not yet born. The third account was made by a local archaeologist, before the polishing, but was only published in the Bulletin de la Société d'Etudes Scientifiques du Département de l'Aude a few years later. So long as you cannot prove that these records anterior to your birth are your work, I will only consider you as a semi-hoaxer.

In my view, you started from the errors on the stele to identify the keyword MORTEPEE, which you used to fabricate the set of 128 parasitic letters + of Document II (Large Parchment). This is not detrimental to the achievement in the play on words, which is truly one of the finest to date, or to the ingenuity of your interpretation; however, it does not quite entitle you to be classified in the category of perfect hoaxes.'

'Thank you for your scepticism,' I replied to my old master. 'I did not expect any less of your clear-mindedness.'

So, let us take, one-by-one, the three accounts that place the stele and tombstone prior to my birth.

The account of Mr. Stüblein. The reference at the National Library provided by Gérard de Sède is indeed very impressive, but I would very much like to ascertain that this work is available on the shelves, that it has ever been taken out and in someone's hands, and what it contains. Apparently, it is a limited edition of an opuscule of engravings found on the "old stones of Languedoc". Mr. Descadeillas, librarian at the Library of Carcassonne, who is well placed to form an opinion, told me personally that this work never existed and that Mr. Stüblein, its alleged author, who was a meteorologist by profession, never showed, as far as anyone knows, any particular interest in old engraved stones.

The report from Mr. Ernest Cros is contestable, but in another manner. Nobody disputes that this individual was amongst Father Saunière's very good friends, that he was curious about the treasure affair, or that his family is in possession today of the polished stele of the late Marchioness. That Mr. Cros existed is one thing, that the small wad of typed pages were from a typewriter that he would have used himself, is another. As far as I know, as I held these pages in my hands, they could equally be my work, which I could have passed to Mr. Noël Corbu in Rennes-le-Château in exactly the same manner that I forwarded documents I and II to Gérard de Sède.

The article published in the *Bulletin de la Société d'Etudes Scientifiques du Département de l'Aude* is, in fact, the true stumbling block. One could have suspicions about a report concerning an inscription that vanished more than ten years before and not be very impressed that the monthly Bulletin had nothing better to publish. In fact, for as long as the interested parties will be able to obtain a copy of this old issue, I will only be a semi-hoaxer; that is, the heir of a pun that started some sixty years ago. But wait for the publication of this present book and I bet that, within six months, one will not find another copy of that issue of the Bulletin after it is swept by the interested parties. Then I will feel utterly comfortable to declare myself as the sole author of this prank. And, if today, I am only a semi-hoaxer, I will soon be a complete one. Following this trail, I will repeat what Father Saunière said regarding the treasure, 'Si me l'han donat, l'hay pant, l'hay panat e bé le teni', or 'Si on me l'a donné, je l'ai pris, je l'ai apprêté, et je le tiens bien' (As it was given to me, I took it, I adapted it, and I hold it tight).

Having established that, if there is a hoax, I cannot be excluded from it, let us establish now that the sentence Par ce cheval de Dieu, j'achève ce daemon de gardien à midi (With this horse of God, I conquer this guardian daemon in middle age) is my signature. My first name is Philippe and my surname is Cherisey, meaning respectively "lover of horses" and "friend of the gods". These two etymologies, both Greek, situate the trail under the invocation of the "Horse of God". When I decided to make a career as an actor, I took on the pseudonym of Amédée (Amadeus), its Latin etymology meaning "friend of the gods" like the Greek etymology of Cherisey. The play on words between AMEDEE (Amadeus) and A MIDI (meaning "midday" or "noon", as well as "middle age" or "prime of life") has been dictated by the transposition of the E by I, which led me to create a dame de Negre from a dame de Negri, and a Mortépée from a morte-pie (dead magpie). Besides, shall I mention that the passage from Amédée to A midi was done via "Aimedée", a rather mediocre poem from Barbey d'Aurevilly, where Aimedée "putana errante", wandering on the Norman beach of Carteret, finds herself caught between the poet Semigod (half god) and the sage Altai (mountain of gold), but finally flees, as elusive as the crossing of the mirror where both the sage and the poet would be reflection or reality.

Although I disapprove of the habit certain authors have taken to cite themselves as a reference, either through vanity or to encourage the sale of previous works, it would seem dishonest of me to keep silent about my novel *Le Méridien 0* (*Meridian Zero*), where "Amédée, ou comment s'en débarrasser" (Amadeus, or how to get rid of him) from Eugene Ionesco, prefigures "J'achève ce daemon de gardien" (I conquer this guardian daemon). To get rid of AMEDEE, one only has to pronounce it the English way, phonetically spelt A MIDI in French. So, in the first part of the novel, we saw how the operation carried out in reverse order enabled Meryon, the force-feeder, to slaughter Captain Marion during a cannibalistic meal. It is at the theatre of the Bouffes Parisiens (meaning Parisian "opéras bouffes" or comic operas, as well as Parisian "nosh"), the name of which has the same cannibalistic connotation as croque-monsieur ("man biter", as well as "toasted cheese sandwich with ham"), that the idea to substitute Asmodée (Asmodeus) with Amédée (Amadeus) was given to me by Albert Willemetz, 'Why not Asmodeus, which would be so much more striking?' I declined politely, not feeling sufficiently strong or wise to confront the devil in me. Today I am not yet Asmodeus, but the devil takes me if I do not succeed as I have hobbled so much on the paths of virtue.

Postscript

The insertion of a critical apparatus at the end of a book characterises reliable works. What follows is more like a postscript, somewhere to unload what could not be included in the blueprint of the story, and bury the residue of the mystery, like a conscientious rodent buries his roughage to leave the place tidy.

We will examine in turn:

- the nature of SION, to whom the treasure belongs together with King Dagobert II
- the work of Gérard de Sède
- the radical:

REDDIS	REGIS
CELLIS	ARCIS

- two forgotten mistakes, and
- the intrinsic value of the keyword MORTEPEE
- SION

In the year 1099, Godefroy de Bouillon, Merovingian prince, direct descendant through the male line of King Dagobert II, took Jerusalem, of which he was made King by his Lords. He challenged this title for two reasons, namely that it was that of Christ himself and that he was not the eldest son of the Merovingian lineage. A kingdom without a king established itself on the Mount of Sion, called "Moriah", or "Vainqueur – Mer" (Conqueror - Sea), equivalent to "Meer-weg", which we know through its distortion into Merovaeus. The Mount of Sion's architecture comprised three buildings which were linked to one another without outside communication, namely the cellars of the temple of Jerusalem spared from the blaze in 70 CE, the mosque erected under Omar's instructions in 637 CE, and a little sanctuary built on the orders of Godefroy de Bouillon called Abbaye de Notre Dame du Mont de Sion (Abbey of Our Lady on the Mount of Sion). Thus, it is an ecumenical ideal that brings together the knights of three religions: Jewish, Muslim and Christian. The Mosque of Cordoba provides an Arab replica of that architecture, in that it retains the synagogue and the cathedral. There is no equivalent amongst the Jews, as the Muslims and Christians barred their access to real estate, but it goes without saying that the Jewish Diaspora is essentially ecumenical.

The tri-partite society belonging to the architecture bore the name of the Christian building. Nineteen years later, on the death of Baudouin - brother of Godefroy - the Order of the Temple was established on a pact between both the Merovingian and the Capetian royalties. Among the nine Knights who instituted the new order, six were from the Order of Sion and three were from the invited party. We do not know the terms of the treaty but it was a blow to the religious equilibrium from the outset, following the suppression of the crescent at the top of the mosque and its replacement by a cross, an insult for which the Muslims will never forgive the Christians.

In 1148, King Louis VII brought ninety-five members of the Abbaye de Notre Dame du Mont de Sion back to France, seven of whom rejoined the Order of the Temple, whilst the remaining eighty-eight settled at the Prieuré Saint Samson d'Orléans and its branch of Saint Jean-le-Blanc. In return for his generosity, King Louis VII was allowed to bear the fleur-de-lis, the appanage of the Merovingians, on his coat of arms (although this favour was limited to a discrete semis of silver flowers and not the unique gold flower on a background of gules that no ruling king will ever have the right to assume).

The distribution of the eighty-eight members between sixty-two for Saint Samson and twenty-six for Saint Jean-le-Blanc was the object of a mathematical diversion on the mirror theme, in order to obtain the following:

$$62 \mid 26 \quad — \quad \frac{62 \mid 26}{2} \quad — \quad 31 \mid 13$$

A cleansing movement occurred within the P.S. (Priory of Sion) so as to secure a noble value or a quality inverse to the quantity. The little Prieuré de Saint Jean-le-Blanc, which was reduced to thirteen members, led the movement. This is how, to date, the farmers of the Orléanais are still giving the name of Jean-le-Blanc to a bird that gobbles up snakes without breaking them into pieces. The buildings of this little priory do not exist anymore, but the wanderer in Saint Jean-le-Blanc can look for its ruins in the locality called Mont de Sion which is mentioned on the Geological (Ordnance) Survey map.

The recapture of Jerusalem by the Muslims in 1187 provoked an insurgence against the Templars who were held responsible for its loss. The following year, a split happened between the huge Order of the Temple and the derisory little Priory of Sion in a field called "l'Ormeteau ferré", in Gisors. Rupture is not war; in this case, it was a kind of amicable divorce accompanied by a pact between the ex-partners. The unity of the Temple was ensured by the constitution of Master Roncelin de Fos, who was from the Priory of Sion and not a Knight Templar; on the other hand, the Priory of Sion had pledged a few objects to the Temple, notably the "Caput Sidon", a gold head. In 1307, as the future of the Templars seemed very gloomy, Guillaume de Gisors, representative of the Priory of Sion, received the gold head which Philippe le Bel sought so actively afterwards. This "Caput Sidon" is displayed as a rebus at the bottom of document II (Large Parchment). The graphic NOpIS is an invitation to reverse the rebus and read SIdON; I even went to the extent of inserting the character ∀ at the bottom of the picture, which one considers as a reversed A or Δ, namely a D. The alliance P∀ reminded me probably of the pédé (homosexual) jokes people made from my pseudonym Amédée.

This mirror technique has been used time and time again in imagery. The case of the painter Signol is a wonderful example. A great academician, Signol had the privilege to execute the portrait of Dagobert II which is exhibited in Versailles and the frescoes of the Eglise de la Madeleine (Saint Magdalene's church) in Paris. In his old age, he was commissioned to paint the four large frescoes of the Passion which decorate the wings of the Eglise Saint-Sulpice (Saint-Sulpice church). In fact, Signol, who had become unable to climb on the scaffoldings, handed over his sketches to the Art School students. Even Signol's signature, in capital letters on the frescoes, is not by him. Indeed, on Signol's instructions, the Art School students were given the task to transform his name into SIGИOL over two of the four frescoes. The inversion of N into И aimed at inversing the whole name to read LONGIS, and indicating the Meridian 0, which passes through the church in the form of a gilded line in the paving. Since there was a risk that this trick may go unnoticed, the sign of "Christ on the Cross" was reversed entirely to read MUROEDUJ XER IERAZAN SUSEJ instead of JESUS NAZAREI REX JUDEORUM.

The Meridian 0 of Saint Sulpice is a suggestion from the Church and does not coincide precisely with the meridian of the King based on the Observatory of Paris; it does, however, pass through the territory of Rennes-le-Château. This puerile game is another way of assigning South and North to S and N in the name SION and considering IO as a penetration into the hole. Is this to say that Signol acted purely like a joker? It depends how we interpret things. The painter's father had been the victim of a mirror phenomenon. Author of the vaudeville *The Duel* and an *Apology of the Duel*, he died in a duel in 1850. One should note that the painting with the inversed inscription above Christ's head is situated behind a painting of Saint Paul designating, with his sword, the path of the Meridian 0 in the paving. It is possible that the painter wanted to commemorate the memory of his father in his own way. Knowing that there is an inversion in Signol's signature on the Treason and Resurrection frescoes, and that the sign is inversed on the Crucifixion fresco, one should seek what should also be inversed in the Ascension fresco. There may be a clue in the posthumous novel of Signol's father *Le Commissionnaire* (*The Messenger*) written by George Sand and Jules Sandeau.

Gérard De Sède

What has just been said may seem like an attack against *Les Templiers sont parmi nous*, alias *L'énigme de Gisors*, which made Gérard de Sède's reputation with the general public. After the silence and contempt of the historians, and the mistrust with which the inhabitants of Gisors treat a man to whom they owe most of their city's profits from tourism, is there not some cowardice in minimising the role of the Templars in Gisors, a mere no-man's-land for the rupture in 1188?

Let us expand further. The well-known Saint-Catherine chapel, that was supposed to be under the donjon at the heart of the fortress, is, in fact, in the royal domain outside the ramparts. The access to the crypt is uphill on the rue de Vienne where, a few metres after the "Passage of the Monarch", one finds oneself in front of underground tunnels over several floors that are extremely well built. In 1306, the crypt of the Saint-Catherine's chapel became the domicile of the "Commandery of Saint-Gervais" under the supervision of the Priory of Sion which held its meetings there until the 18th Century. If there is a mystery in Gisors, it is not to be found in the discoveries made by Gérard de Sède, but in his silences, in the fit of laughter that seized us when we were perusing the tourist guide in use in Gisors prior to 1939. The chapel of Saint-Catherine was indeed mentioned in the royal domain but nobody protested, not so much through ignorance but through greed, each hoping to access the crypt and profit from the sales that the error generated. Gérard de Sède and I started the movement through the hire of a pneumatic drill. After boring through a wall, we reached a heap of secular poudrette (dried and powdered night-soil), the crystallised and well settled content of a latrine, where generations of inhabitants from Gisors, satisfying their needs, had left a trace of their passage in this world more durable and fecund than their bones. Why would I deride Gérard de Sède, after that poudrette baptism which we received together, and the certitude that came to us, as for the alchemists, that gold has a smell and is born of excrement? If the treasure of Gisors has something that repels, it is precisely the poudrette, namely the lack of sewers in the part of the city that accumulates the poudrette in the naves of a sunken cathedral.

The treasure of the Templars, contained in thirty chests, was stored in Gisors in 1526, two centuries after the disappearance of the Temple, in the crypt of the Saint-Catherine's chapel that was demolished above ground soon afterwards. A stone from the former cemetery, which was brought to the church Saint-Gervais, attests the event. After certain rumours that one was looking for a treasure consisting purely of archives, the Priory of Sion initiated a fictitious prank, which they dealt with rather briskly, to make historians shrug their shoulders and alert the soul of the nation. By spreading the rumour that there was a treasure in Gisors, one obtained the result that nobody dared using a rake, in the land of "Son et Lumière", without becoming suspect. Here the reader can draw two conclusions: either the thirty chests of the Saint-Catherine's chapel are still safeguarded by a rampart of poudrette, or, thanks to the fuss around these chests, the Priory of Sion managed to move them.

The affair of Gisors is somewhat outside our own, but if there was a need for just one example of the complicity between Gérard de Sède and me, I would produce document I (Small Parchment), about which the author of Le Trésor de Rennes stated expressly that "some letters are out of line". On a contiguous page to this statement, there is a photocopy of the precise document received by the author. Now, amongst a hundred thousand readers or so, not a single person worked out how this out of line business happened and that the phrase A DAGOBERT II ET A SION EST CE TRESOR ET IL EST LA MORT was obtained after identifying the out-of-line characters. No, not a single one! Oh, dear reader. Dear reader, to whom we tell everything, but who does not listen. In which esteem can we hold you, poor idiot, and how can we take your complaints of brainwashing seriously? Of course, Gérard de Sède and I brainwashed you. But did you not ask for this with your thirst for cheap fantastic literature that only increases our royalties?

So, you will probably think that we, the poets, take a sadistic pleasure in despising you. No, unfortunately! Hoax is a laborious ascesis, for which we are the first penitents until we obtain the lovely practical joke that will dupe us well before it does you. Before making fun of you, dear reader, we had to ridicule ourselves very dearly and ask ourselves, with Jesus, "What is truth?" We had to know that we must tell you all, without telling you everything, or you would not believe it. Remain, therefore, self-satisfied and dissatisfied, without pondering even how Gérard de Sède was able to present an ill-defined figure like that of King Dagobert II of Austrasia, in the vague hope that it would be refuted or confirmed by an historian as ignorant as you. And here we are, poor poets, hoping with the energy of despair that, since semi-uncial times, there are still readers who can read.

REDDIS	REGIS
CELLIS	ARCIS

The honour granted to me by Colonel Arnaud in placing me amongst ecclesiastics is not totally unjustified. During my career as Amédée, the actor, I played two roles as a priest. The first one was about a regular friar at the Bouffes Parisiens, and it was then that Albert Willemetz suggested I opted for Asmodée. The second role was as a Gascon parish priest in an American film shot in Saint-Tropez. I have a marvellous souvenir of wearing a sacerdotal outfit on a nocturnal tour of the brothels in Pigalle, where my face was unknown. One must not imagine that it was a bad taste joke from Pierre Fresnay celebrating Mass with champagne in an ice-bucket-cum-chalice. No. I did my best to understand what a priest in a soutane would do at two o'clock in the morning at "Jim's Joint", the "Bambolero", or the "Naturists". I did not drink any more gin-fizz than is appropriate for a priest prior to communion and kept a mind sufficiently clear to appreciate the diplomacy of the masculine staff that treated me just like any other client, and the charm of the girls who accepted a drink occasionally without any of them landing on my lap. Realising that my soutane could be equally visible and invisible, I found myself in the position of Narcissus succeeding in crossing the mirror.

It was a film where all that remains from my performance, which lasted a month and a half, is a lovely scene during which, at the top of a mountain and from a great height, I bless the grape harvest and Michèle Morgan in particular who, later on, disguised as Marie-Antoinette, is decapitated by me in the role of the executioner Samson. What a small world! During my extensive spare-time activities, I went to visit the astonishing relic of Saint Rosaline de Villeneuve, mummified since the 14th Century and blackened by the passage of time. I learnt that she was the abbess of the Celle aux Arcs and that her Provencal legend had been taken up literally to serve Saint Germaine Cousin of Languedoc, patron of the J.A.C. "Jeunesse Agricole Chrétienne" (Christian Agricultural Youth). Later, when I got involved in the affair of Rennes-le-Château, I spotted immediately the statue of Germaine Cousin amongst the saints in the church and the following inscription:

REDDIS	REGIS
CELLIS	ARCIS

Between Languedoc and Provence, an exchange took place; that of Germaine for Rosaline, of the shepherdess for the Celle aux Arcs. Then, I met my Rosaline who died on 6th August 1967, the feast day of the Transfiguration, whilst crossing the Meridian 0 by car. After that, I made the acquaintance of a German girl, who was a bit of a dyke and my "Germaine Cousin", as she was neither a cousine germaine (female first cousin) nor a cousin germain (male first cousin) ["Germaine Cousin" is a grammatical play on words with Germaine (feminine), followed by Cousin (masculine), which would be grammatically incorrect in French since both words should either be feminine or masculine]. Here, I feel compelled to refer the reader, once again, to the *Méridien 0*, the novel where I relate all this in great detail, and sometimes in tears. More specifically, with regard to Rennes-le-Château rather than my private life, the section CELLIS|ARCIS is an allusion to the destiny of the body of Mary Magdalene the Sinner, which was transferred from a tomb in alabaster to one in marble, at a time when the Infidels besieged the land. CELLIS corresponded to the white cell of the contemplative Christian and ARCIS to the fortress in black marble; if ARCIS belonged to the roi REGIS (king), then CELLIS had to go to the reine (queen) renamed Rennes, or REDDIS in Latin.

Father Saunière had respected the CELLIS ARCIS architecture inside his church, since it contains two buildings in a top to bottom position. The white alabaster CELLIS section of the contemplative queen corresponds to the chœur (chancel) and extends to the preacher's pulpit on one side and the statue of Saint Anthony of Padua on the other side. This is followed by the fortified marble ARCIS section of the black king which is delineated on the ceiling by a crenellated frieze. In other words, if, in a single building comprising two churches, one enters through a unique door located on the ARCIS side, this signifies that the same orifice gives access to two treasures; that of the king followed by that of the queen. The two treasures are like one in the eyes of the world, since the king and queen form a perfect couple living in joint estate and, therefore, there is no need to make a distinction between the gold of the King's Merovingians and that of the Queen's Visigoths. If, however, you penetrate the wonder, understand that, in their intimacy, the king is not alienated from the queen or the queen from the king. "Where your treasure is, your heart will be", such is the message of the red lamp supported by three gilded angels, "à la frontière du chœur qui est cœur" (on the borders of the chancel which is the heart). Therefore, ARCIS CELLIS simply represents the rainbow born from the three fundamental colours of yellow, red and blue. The treasure is not within the reach of the scientist who expounds, but within that of the poet who understands. Beware of liking me, dear reader; and as in the fable of *Le Singe et le Chat* [*The Monkey and the Cat* from La Fontaine], do not be Raton (the cat's-paw) which removes the chestnuts from the fire leaving me as Bertrand (the schemer).

The connection CELLIS white, ARCIS black, constitutes the nature of the chess game with its alternating squares. One will find in Rennes-le-Château, a great number of allusions to the alternance of these two colours. The most obvious one is the proximity of the black Rokko Negro and the white rock of Blanchefort. However, another allusion, more secret and striking, opposes the jet mines of Mount Serbairou in the South to the kaolin mines of Mount Cardou in the North. Two artificial constructions are also worth mentioning; namely, a chessboard in front of the confessional of Rennes-le-Château and an ingenious tombstone in Rennes-les-Bains, where the life of a former parish priest called Jean Vie was divided into thirty-two white years and thirty-two black years. Born in 1808, Jean Vie was appointed parish priest in 1840 and died in 1872.

If you are looking for the treasure of Rennes-le-Château, ponder over the chess rules; at the start of a game, the queen is on her colour, whilst the king is on the colour opposite to his own. The king and queen represent the germ of dissymmetry in symmetry.

Two Forgotten Mistakes

The strange written form of REQUIESCAT IN PACE or REQUIES CATIN PACE on the stele cannot have escaped the reader. The enjambment is sufficiently defective to question why the C is not part of the keyword in the same way as the M of the first line. In fact, there is a slight difference; whilst the enjambment of the M is clearly incorrect, the mistake associated with the letter C drags along all the letters of REQUIESCATIN, therefore, making it impossible to isolate it.

The written text on the stele of the poor Marchioness is not very kind to her. Even in the assurance that catins (trollops) reach beatitude (bliss) straightaway, how could a living soul have the heart to disclose the whore-like quality of a female member of the family on her headstone? To this, one would retort of course that, in 1891, the Hautpouls raised no objection to Father Saunière moving the bones of the female and male members of their family from the cemetery and the church to the communal grave covered by a smoothed stone. In fact, the word CATIN must be construed in its original meaning of trou de rocher (rock aperture), and the word putain (whore) in the sense of puits (well). What is meant is that a necropolis, where corpses are kept in peace (REQUIES), is found after passing (PACE) a rock aperture (CATIN).

Although the following is not about a treasure but simply an extraordinary massacre, the Germans and the Slavs agreed to bury the entire Polish chivalry in CATIN, namely in the grave of KATYN, as it is true that certain nations have an aggressive play on words and that the souvenir of the Teutonic Knights remains harsh.

Another mistake that was passed over in silence was HAUPOUL instead of HAUTPOUL. The missing T could not be inserted in the keyword any more than the U or P: two correct letters surrounded an absent one. This missing T evokes in fact the crossing of two imaginary lines, such as a longitude and a parallel of latitude which, although invisible in the landscape, do exist. This will remind us of course of Saint Anthony the Hermit, whose statue is in the church of Rennes-le-Château and whose emblem is a T. In fact, the saint one should consult is not Saint Anthony, but Saint Roch, who is also in the church. Saint Roch died alone and was identified by a red cross engraved on his chest, which was hidden by his coat. The invisible red cross of Saint Roch could only be revealed after his death and justifies the message derived from document I (Small Parchment), namely CE TRESOR EST LA MORT (THIS TREASURE IS DEATH). There is, therefore, no need to look for some unusual detail, or strange rock, as a would-be location for the treasure in the landscape of Rennes-le-Château. On the contrary, every precaution has been taken for thousands of years so that the treasure location is very obvious and very mundane at the same time, recognisable through a great number of landmarks, for which the reader will be thankful to us since we gave him the main ones.

Mortepee

During Jesus' arrest, Saint Peter is renowned for his aggression against an officer of whom he cut an ear with his sword. In response, Christ told him, 'Whoever strikes with the sword, will perish by the sword'. This anecdote is important in two differing ways; firstly, by the assignment of the church of Rennes-le-Château, now dedicated to Mary Magdalene, to Saint Peter, and, secondly, through the evangelical myth around an oracle that is clearly false, as Saint Peter was not beheaded with a sword, but died crucified, whilst the sword is the emblem of Saint Paul.

As we were keen on discovering anything reminiscent of a sword around Rennes-le-Château, our attention was drawn towards the village of Coustaussa, with its ruined fortress that is the focal point in the whole area. Coustaussa, in Languedocian, is the absolute equivalent of the French word custode, namely the sheath of a sword, and by extension, its custody. My friend Basil, Anne and I visited this village without encountering a living soul. This desert, the wind, and the ceiling of the church elated us in the certainty that living here and now "hic et nunc" was well worth our souls living elsewhere and forever "alibi et semper". Coustaussa does not have a treasure, and this is when it is appropriate to replace the sword in its sheath.

To be done with all this, here are a few insights into the nature of custodes, rather than the quality of swords.

Custode

A curtain drawn behind the altar of a church during baptism ceremonies. The catechumen entered the sanctuary, walked alongside the right wall and, passing behind the altar in the shelter of the curtain, found themselves in front of the central image of the old Way of the Cross, a picture of Jesus stripped of his clothes. Then, without distinction between the sexes, they took off their clothes and went down on the left hand side to be immersed entirely in the baptismal font. Their circuit was that of the sun – SOLIS SACERDOTIBUS – as grasped so well by Saint Ambrose when he relates that, facing the West, the baptized must immerse himself or herself completely, like a drowning man or woman, and then swivel round under water in order to emerge facing the East.

A purple and gold curtain, or transparent thin-veil curtain, drawn in front of the king and queen's bed on their wedding night. A torch above the bed lights up the square area like the stage of a theatre. Crouching in the darkness, the courtiers admire the elevation of the king and watch the blood shed by the queen on the sheets.

An eight-panel veil of ciborium resembling the eight tentacles of the octopus. The church uses it to cover the "Host", namely the ciborium, in the same manner that the Greeks portrayed an octopus on the doors of the bread ovens. Here, one must muse over the phenomenon of the octopus which, after the excretion of its ink, gains in transparency what it loses in tonicity; since this is my body and the beauty of all literature, sanctifying what I write as I shed my passion onto it, since this is my blood.

A gold-rimmed crystal monocle where, for the royal elevation, the Host of the Very Blessed Sacrament is in a monstrance; a representation of me in God or God in me, how would I know? An unsustainable stare passes through that monocle.

A special title born, since the poet Crescimbeni, by the president of the Arcadians Society, comprising fourteen shepherd members; as many as the verses in a sonnet, the statues in a Way of the Cross, and the letters in the motto ET IN ARCADIA EGO. But who can be ego? And could I presume that I am the man Diogenes was looking for, with a lantern, in broad daylight?

The End

MISCELLANEOUS

Clues In Stone And Paper Testimony

Stone is like Paper; it conveys meaning, it separates the wheat from the chaff, it grants the roses of the barn-owl to the companions of the "Shibboleth" (ear of grain in Hebrew) in a Sabbath where the first would be second and the second the first, without being able to really exist.

In the account of Philippe de Cherisey, the cubic stone has crumpled like an ear of grain and the paper has hardened infinitely.

The treasure thesis, an allusion to a former work of Alexander Dumas, comprises three elements, namely the hole, the sacristy and the mud wall "Introibit in Domum".

The Mountain Cavern is that of Plato, the gigantic necropolis of the God Sabbasius, who preceded Jesus in the revised gnosis.

The treasure, the death and its secret ET IN ARCADIO EGO represent the ancient myth of three alive and three dead (the tale of three young riders who come across three skeletons on three horses).

Dagobert the Second refers to Dagobert the First.

Sion or Moriah or Agartha, Earth-cum-cavern of initial sites.

The Dantean anagrams of 128 letters over two chessboards; the first anagram derived from the Large Parchment, the second from the stele and tombstone comprising 150 letters, including 22 superfluous characters from the false inscription REDDIS CELLIS REGIS ARCIS.

In fact, it was necessary to start at the end so that the reader could make sense of it all.

The keyword TEMEREPO is a trick worthy of the magic square, as the message in French reads MORTE EPEE (Dead Sword)

The knight does not perform the patience game over 64 squares, an allusion to 64 hiding places; in reality, and in accordance with the rules of chess, he does it over 63 "leaps"!

Shepherd Or Shepherdess?

The passage from one chessboard to the other generates three operations for the "Shepherdess".

The art of the anagram, ROMA-AMOR, proves that the latest one made of 128 letters is not from Bigou, as it has been realised recently and bears a signature.

Why shepherdess? Answer: because of the legend. It is the Shepherdess on the hill of Serbairou, which separates the valleys of la Blanque and la Sals, south of Rennes-les-Bains.

The jet mine, like the Magdalene's headspring, refers to the altar inscription.

The Shepherd, being first in history, has departed; the shepherdess dazzled by the reflection of the treasure is looking west.

The Mirror

An allusion to the legend of Labouisse-Rochefort in *Voyage à Rennes-les-Bains*, published in 1832. The Devil's gold is a musing over the mirror involving the stare and reflection; "I am looking for the Devil's gold treasure from the legend to which I refer, and I will leave it at that." Anticipating the quest is crossing the mirror. Hence, the importance of asymmetry.

Poulain - Poussin - Hautpoul

The Knights' tombstone is the tombstone of the Lords of Hautpoul.

The graffiti in the Prisoner's tower, in Gisors, are the work of Nicolas Poussin.

The surrealist game consists in combining the puns to precede the amalgam, so as to produce an unexpected result, namely Poussin ⇨ Hautpoul ⇨ Poulain ⇨ Poussin.

The two-rider horse, that follows the three cocks which are the emblem of the Templars, becomes Hautpoul-Blanchefort. This is how the Knights' tombstone becomes the Lords of Hautpoul's tombstone.

Et In Arcadio Ego

As a result of an acknowledged forgery of the Greek writing, Nicolas ("Stone" in Greek) Poussin (Chicken), le Poussin de Pierre (the Poussin of the tombstone), becomes, through this game, a parent of the Hautpoul-Blanchefort. This historical untruth accentuates the value of the stone (the Knights' tombstone) and the content of the parchments stemming from the stone.

The Temptation Of Saint Anthony

The Temptation of Saint Anthony, circa 1640-1650, but dated 1681, introduces the 17th January element and proves that the Hautpoul's tombstone is a fake.

Fabrication Of The Secret Merovingian Descent

Invention by deduction of the Greek writing ΑΡΧΩ, REDDIS in Latin.

Association of PAX with the war cry Montjoie-Saint-Denis (Montjoy!).

Additions justifying the transfer of the royalty.

Creation of Gisele of Razès.

Association of Mirepoix-Levi-Merovaeus with the Lords of Bellissen, or Lords of the Moon, oddly taken up by the author of the letter Les Ailes de la Jouannes (The Wings of the Jouannes). [See Appendix VI]

Association of the gold and silver keys of Saint Peter and of Saint Sulpice with Primo and Secundo, then with the Priory of Sion.

Associations and amalgams of the Cross of Lorraine, the Latin Cross, the Seal of Solomon, the chrisma and the fleurs-de-lis.

The Confession

The inscription Jésus Medèla was used to conclude the Large Parchment. Cherisey used the Vulgate for the latter and the Codex Bezae, from the dictionary of Fulcran Vigouroux, for the Small Parchment.

Roncelin De Fos = Priory Of Sion

This is the most important information. The enigma around Roncelin de Fos and his secret statutes, discovered in the Corsini Library, are at the very bottom of the creation of the Priory of Sion.

Recently, at the request of the Spanish neo-templar orders, the British Runciman found a letter from the Grand Master to the Supremus Magister. The nature of this letter proves beyond doubt that Roncelin de Fos has nothing to do with the invention of the Priory of Sion. But that the great secret is that of the "Resurrection" within the true gnosis of the Templars.

The Red Circle: Or Covert Aspects Of The Priory Of Sion Legacy

Professor Deuxaresvents removed his metal-rimmed glasses, stroked his old beard, enjoyed a honey cake, and put down the manuscript of the *Chèvre d'or* (the myth and allure of *La Cabra de Oro* or *Golden Goat*).

Quermancao, in Spain, is the Castle of the Grail of Salvador Dali. The golden goat had her odyssey there too; a little red circle followed her steadily, a shepherd was Knight of the Grail... and the gold of the Maures (Moors) was also that of the morts (dead). But let us follow the Ariadne's thread of this surrealist conspiracy.

1947 – Discovery by a shepherd of the *Dead Sea Scrolls.*

1956 – On its front page on 1st June, the newspaper Le Figaro breathes an idea to the reader which will mature slowly, "A treasure of 200 tons of gold and silver is buried near the current Israeli-Jordanian border." Followed by, "It is divided between 64 hiding places", another idea that will germinate and grow.

Let us compare this news with our story:

A legend claims that there is an immense treasure on a hill near Limoux. A monk from Rieux and his accomplices, who made "a wax effigy, and practised magic and alchemy" were the object of a sentence.

The hill of Limoux is a former district of Flacian, a town guarded and protected by an old castle called Reda. Notre-Dame de Marceille (Our Lady of Marceille) was built in the lower town. Nowadays, a villa on the hill bears the beautiful name of Eureka. Its landlords do not even know if they are sitting on a powder keg.

The legend of Labouisse-Rochefort borrows a few elements when transforming the shepherdess into the shepherd Pâris, evoking in this way the legend of Troy.

To master these legends, Plantard fits in with the story when creating imaginary exchanges with Corbu, but he makes a mistake regarding the location... Reda is indeed in Limoux.

With Corbu in the bag, Plantard schemes and receives the assistance of Philippe de Cherisey and Gérard de Sède.

Pierre de France remembers the Agartha, with one of its gates at Mont Saint-Michel, and another one since in Aereda. The Alpha-Galates, the Knights of the Light and the Latin Academy become the arches of the Priory of Sion, the Agartha, or the Moriah.

The imaginary torch, granted by the Law Professor Maurice Lecomte Moncharville when he was already dead, is of no use any more, like Genevieve Zaepffel's flag of the Southern Cross which Pierre Plantard appropriated in a shameless manner [1].

The discovery of the *Dead Sea Scrolls*, and the sixty-four hiding places of the treasure of Solomon inscribed on the copper roll of Qumran, are transferred, at first, to Gisors. Here lies the great skill of the three surrealists of the Red Circle.

A huge activity takes place, lures are on the increase, and fake documents and false genealogies multiply thanks to Anne Léa Hisler and the *Cahiers de l'Histoire* (*History Journals*) [2].

Gisors is to become the revelation of the Priory of Sion. The treasure will consist of the archives of the Society. The marketing is in place; André Malraux and the Military Engineers do the rest. De Sède finds a local artist in Roger Lhomoy. The key document from the shepherd Claude Rouët "concerning the missing sculptures", through which one discovers a retable of the chapel Saint Catherine, concludes the adventure.

The story of Qumran is transposed once more. We find it in Rennes-le-Château, with a Merovingian descent on a Merovingian tombstone (Knights' Tombstone) and a Carolingian pillar turned Visigothic.

In 1989, the search-warrant from the judge Thierry Jean-Pierre puts an end to the delirium of the saviour of the French.

The former sexton, son of a manservant, disintegrated in a fire [he was cremated], like the Cathars of Montségur, in the year 2000, the cycle end-date of the "Lupinian" Great Monarch.

A census reveals fourteen priories of Sion, with the last one established in Taiwan. One recognises Plantard's prose when typing "I am the Great Master of the Priory of Sion!" in a search engine.

The Anglo-American-Australian trio, who associated Jesus, Mary Magdalene and the last Merovingian, is, in turn, supplanted by an American author of esoteric-detective fiction in the name of Dan Brown.

The Da Vinci Code, which praises the esoteric sacred Feminine, is a disastrous movie grotesquely manipulated and of no real interest. It consists in releasing dangerous archetypes such as the Priory of Sion and the Sages of the Sion Protocols, and aims at politicising the masses against the televangelists in power with all available modern demagogies. After the *Satanic Verses*, a topsy-turvy Bible encourages us to reconsider the positive side of Mary Magdalene, first witness of the Resurrection, ahead of the disciples of Emmaus and the apostles.

The Phoenix Of The Red Circle

"When one inverts History too much, the cosmic clock pirouettes and the sixteen spectral lines of Lucifer's emerald carbuncle blind you. [*Citation of a Pilgrim*, friend of Saint Augustine] Then, History becomes human and simple again. The treasure linked to death concerns the tragedy that struck Philippe de Cherisey after he lost his girlfriend in a car accident; hence, the green-eyed Saint Rosaline, the Circuit to find the treasure, and the prayer to Mary Magdalene, witness to the Resurrection... Such are the covert aspects of the Priory of Sion Legacy.

Six Days Before Easter (Monday 10th April 2006).

30 - Plantard's flag of the Southern Cross copied from Genevieve Zaepffel

[1] Genevieve Zaepffel was a seeress in the noble sense of the term, an inspired woman capable of feeling and reading the most intimate thoughts of her interlocutors. She was able to make those who approached her accept the happy or tragic events she could foresee in their lives. She was very popular in the years preceding World War II, when her public appearances always attracted a large audience. In 1937, in the Pleyel conference room in Paris, she spoke in front of four thousand people! She was born in 1892, at the Manoir du Tertre, in the heart of the forest of Brocéliande. In 1946, during a visit of the General de Gaulle to the manor, she prophesised Europe and its unique currency for the year 2000! Nowadays, the Manoir du Tertre is a hotel restaurant where a full-length portrait of her dressed in a white cloak is hanging in the large sitting room. The present owners of the manor claim that, whilst Genevieve Zaepffel died in 1971, she is still keeping a watchful eye on the destinies of the place.

[2] In 1964, Mrs Anne Léa Hisler, Pierre Plantard's wife at the time, left at the National Library a copy of a work referenced B.N. 4°L37 96, entitled *Rois et Gouvernants de la France, les grandes dynasties depuis l'origine* (*Kings and Regents of France – Great Dynasties from the Beginning*). As the title implies, this work is a recital of all kings and heads of state who have governed France. A record was also made of their wives and children. However, it transpired that this excellent work was nothing less than a huge plagiary of the January 1960 thematic Issue No. 1 of the *Cahiers de l'Histoire entitled Les Rois et les Gouvernements de la France, des origines à nos jours* (*Kings and Governments of France from the beginning to the present day*) written by Louis Saurel. To crown it all, the long-term friend to whom I owe this prime information discovered also that Saurel himself had exploited a small book from Alfred Franklin, published fifty years earlier, entitled *Les Rois et les Gouvernements de la France, de Hugues Capet à l'année 1906* (*The Kings and Governments of France from Hugues Capet to 1906*). The difficulty for Louis Saurel was to fill in the previous years which Franklin had left fallow.

Magical Conclusions

About Theurgy

From time immemorial, mankind has felt a need to engage in a dialogue with the invisible in the knowledge that the visible is nothing. One contemplates, with stupefaction, Cro-Magnon men drawing animals in caverns, which, at a later date, become an integral part of their bodies. One perceives the beauty of prehistoric "cave painting hands" in Lascaux, Cosquer and Fieux, as an homage to the gods, and a way of thanking them for their sacred nourishment which, inevitably, came through terrestrial nutriments. Finally, one understands Abraham's terror in offering his son to the invisible God as proof of his love, and one guesses his joy when an angel's hand stopped the bloody deed. Through some operation, God revealed Himself as if concerned by this terrible act.

Theurgy has always been looked upon as a divine working which the officiant discovers, as Shakespeare said, at the right moment and time.

Even if they were inhaling the deleterious vapours of the volcanic underground, the Pythia of Delphi and the Virgins who accompanied her had to observe a certain ethic before soothsaying the diatribe, or Fate of the children and adults of this world, since, to tear the veil of Isis in order to read a few lines of God's plan presumes that God is in agreement with this and in tune with the supplicant of the sacred Astral.

This notion of incorporeal exchange took place with the conceivers of the Mysteries, whether those related to Isis or Osiris, Crete or Samothrace, the Cabiri or the disciples of Simon Magus, who shaped the corpus of the Great Gnosis. Proclus and Jamblique codified the Theurgy of the Greek and Egyptian mysteries.

The Cabbalists of the Safed region explained the import of the Word and unfolded the Number; the Old Man of the Mountain organised eschatological visions to reveal scraps of the Other World to the warriors; and the corpus of chess was taught to the Templars in the ancient stables of King Solomon. Although a game, it was a sacred game, comprising sixty four squares - thirty two black ones against thirty two white ones - which the knights had to master and experiment through duality, reduced accordingly to Oneness.

In those days, the theurgist was a chess player; a gambit of the stars, as recalled in a famous book, faced with the universal plan whose web was the appanage of the White Knight...

The Knights of the Round Table formed a circle, manoeuvring from their twelve seats – a lever that the followers of Joachim de Flore or Dante preserved in their divine comedy where hell and purgatory border a symbolic paradise identical to that of the Druses who fascinated Gérard de Nerval in his Voyage en Orient.

UNKNOWN PHILOSOPHER OR PHILOSOPHER OF THE UNKNOWN

According to Doctor Mallinger, Martines de Pasqually synthesised and organised this whole Tradition and made it operative. His doctrine about the Reintegration of the Soul is a jewel, an uncut diamond with multiple hidden facets, a fabulous opera with tortuous meanders which require parapets, guides and supervisors, attentive to the slightest drift, as there were some, notably that of Touzay Duchanteau.

A lawyer at the Court of Appeal in Brussels, Jean Mallinger, fervent admirer of Martines, studied "Martinism" (the Theurgy of Martines) very closely, and integrated the principal recommendations of the Great Teacher, whilst describing the obligations of the operator (theurgist), the nature of the operating area, the adjuvants and the formularies, in accordance with very precise instructions written between 1768 and 1770.

The operator must fast before each major operation, refrain from eating meat, and believe in the virtues of prayer. He must pray standing and on his knees, must not wear any metal, and must dress in a white gown with flame-coloured borders on their sleeves. Two scarves, one red and one sea-green, must cross each other on his chest.

The operating area must be a sacred place, thus devoted to the divinity. It is drawn with a chalk in the shape of a circle and, combined with a cosmic image surrounded by stars, it symbolises protection. It is, therefore, a privileged place as well as a circle of protection, oriented towards another living circle represented by the active power of the stars.

According to the instructions, the adjuvants consist of sacred lights, perfume, conditions regulated by Time, the position of the

Moon and the date in the seasons. In short, one must have Stars, incense, respect the time of day, operate during a waxing moon, and perform the important operations during the equinoxes. In one of his essays, Jerome Cardan explained that Time is alive and consists of Horai [Greek for the 24 rulers of the Sacred Time), angels, and hours; one thing leading to another.

The formularies are a collection of prayers and invocations very carefully selected by Martines.

Once these conditions are met, three types of operations can be envisaged:

Operations for the purification of the terrestrial aura. These purification operations must be carried out during the equinoxes. It should be noted that the exorcisms of the globe's aura may necessitate the presence of ninety-eight stars. These operations are for the general benefit of Humanity and, in many instances, belong to a deep thaumaturgy associated with the purification of our planet; in my humble opinion, modern ecology did not invent anything.

Operations Of Pagan Nature.

These involve remote actions enabling the curing of illnesses by means of prayer. Martines did this for his wife. Once again, this type of operation is aimed at "the other", which is significant, even essential, and reminds us of a given chapter in the Rule of Saint Bernard.

Operations Of Reconciliation And Reintegration.

These are aimed at the first-hand perception of one's Reconciliation. This is where the difficulties start, since Martines's followers will take time, not to grasp but to become really conscious of the process. His most loyal devotee, Louis Claude de Saint-Martin, will comprehend the true nature of this enlightenment at the dawn of his life.

Followers will talk about Flashes, glyphs [mystical signatures], and signs, also seen by the operators; some will specify their colours; others still will mention a sudden sensation of cold.

Thanks to precise symbols, the Passes [rites attached to the invocations], with 2,400 of them recorded in the cards of Touzay Duchanteau, trigger and create real manifestations. For example, on "24th December 1770, in a letter to Mr. de

Saint-Omer, the initiate Grainville wrote, 'It is the Thing itself that binds us to it, through the evidence, conviction and certitude that we have of it. If only we were able to convince of it too, brethren! We are unable to wish them the happiness we are enjoying'.
However, these operations of Reconciliation and Reintegration, or Astral Passes from Martines, much debated amongst the followers themselves, were looked upon as a coherent array of metaphysical happenings by practitioners. Louis Claude de Saint-Martin himself will recognise that the Master was right, whilst being fully aware that the occult character of the operation required an extreme vigilance and that he, himself, preferred a more contemplative and passive mysticism.

The history of Martinism proves that operative Theurgy continued to fascinate students, but that transmission was hard work and entirely singular. However, through another channel that was more mystical on the whole, Saint-Martin's disciples continued to hand on the torch, which consists of basic and reliable elements that theoreticians of pure Martinesism, like Jean Mallinger, refute.

MODERN THEURGISTS

Contrary to what we may believe, modern theurgists operate more often in laboratories than in oratories; rather special laboratories, I must admit, but, nevertheless, in well-identified workshops. Their common starting point is the reference to the ancient Gnosis.

Without going into detail about the works of Sprink, Keely, Wilhelm Reich, Dufourg, and especially Louis Boutard, it is worth mentioning that the ancients' notion of Aether, suppressed by the positivists of the 19th Century; received its deathblow with the first theories of Albert Einstein which drained about a hundred materialistic theories throughout the 20th Century. However, nobody noticed that, after failing to realize the unity of the Universe's fundamental forces, namely those represented by electromagnetism, gravitation, weak nuclear forces and strong nuclear forces, Albert Einstein went back on his theories in 1905 by reinstating the Aether, but it was already too late. History has proven this to us extensively. But what is Aether, or fifth force, or quintessence? In his works, Louis Boutard, who spoke fifty-two languages, tells us that it is an ocean of living particles, eternal, constituting Zoe or the Life, which the ancients venerated in their Mysteries, and which Mythology in its fables, fabliaux and allegories, relates in symbolic forms, or plain forms as soon as it transforms itself into an alchemical science. In short, it is about getting hold of this alchemical universal spirit and melting it, in order to reconstitute it in accordance with well-defined laws that are for the great benefit of all.

The problem for all of these scientists living in a materialistic world was that they remained completely misunderstood, since their systems went against experimental science. Their experiences were unique and, therefore, worthless in the well-known profitability area. Wilhelm Reich, with his orgone, was interned; Keely was involved in many lawsuits; Dufourg, with his real energy and opposite false energy, was condemned; and, despite having the highest connections, Louis Boutard was relegated to the oubliettes of History, even though a few tried to rescue him. Yet, Victor Meunier, the director of the Academy of Sciences, wrote to Louis Jobard, his counterpart in Brussels, 'I hold a discovery that frightens me; there are two types of electricity, one is alive and intelligent, the other is blind and earthy.'

Throughout History, we found the greatest theurgists amongst those who followed the first current, and the greatest scientists amongst those who organised electricity into a scientific corpus. Two currents based on one object and one study matter, with many levels, where heart and reason officiate in different ways.

I leave you to choose the place of Martines de Pasqually, who was truly one of the links of the Greek goddess Electra, and who resurrected the great Gnosis of the Ancients in associating Proclus, Jamblique, the *Torah* and the *Bible*.

The Mask And The Cloak

My impressions, as well as my sentiments regarding the initiation, are many, but impregnated, somehow, by a feeling of nothing new, which I explain.

Before the ceremony we talked about the mirror and its crossing, based on Jean Cocteau's magnificent film of the conscious and the unconscious and of the three worlds of Plato.

Then, the mirror was presented to me as an incorporeal connection integrating the reflection of my soul and that of my physical being, both linked to a chain of initiates going back to Saint-Martin and earlier. My first sensation was a feeling of vertigo since I was at the top of a Tower of Babel. To understand, I found myself travelling down and up whilst being sucked up, in an almost vampiric manner, by images in a very long chain, issued from the mists of time; from Louis Claude de

Saint-Martin to Martines de Pasqually; from my initiator whose gentleness lifted the veils with parsimony to show me an ordained light made of six cardinal points, namely three worlds and three directions, a trinity cocktail which organised the bounds of my singularity into a polyvalent unit. In short, the fixed symbols [glyphs] vibrated and created a series of movements very expertly activated by the Master.

So I felt appeased and trustful, forsaking my rebellious nature, leaving aside my pains and sorrows, my nightmares and tears; thus, letting go of my certainties full of illusions and losing, therefore, this "false ego" for a moment. In short, I recognized the necessity of the mask and I understood its depth as well its beauty. It was a second mirror that showed me the extent of the work to be done, like a consciousness of my obligations. In turn, I saw myself climbing Mount Tepozteco, in Mexico, to arrive at the ancient temple; then, counting the steps of the Tower Saint-Jacques, to reach the top of the church tower where the four statues of the Apocalypse rest and keep vigil in peace; and, finally, roaming the footpaths of an ancient hill with a Catharian fragrance in the Pyrenees, sanctified in the past by some Fellows with faces that were clean-shaven and toned up by the demands of their mutual passion.

In a word, these three ascensions made in the past forced me today to set out again for an Unknown Mountain, which the Ancients had already ascended and, as they held out their hand to me, I was surprised to see myself climbing on the first step.

On top of these four personal impressions of conscious happiness, came reality, like the heaviness of the Red Cloak awarded to me which, although filling me with pride at first, made me foresee, however, the extent of the task. My whole being shuddered, some doubt took hold of me; but, there again, my guide, like the brother who fitted the cloak on me, conscious of my hesitation and distress, did it so gently that, finally, I became their brother, naturally, with conviction and without ambiguity.

The Green Ray And Blue Apples

Saint Rosaline of Villeneuve's eyes were transparent when she was lying in her coffin, which did not please Louis XIV. He sent for one of his favourite doctors, just to see if there was a hidden secret in the coffin of one of the relatives of the alchemist Arnaud.

Under the ruffian's dagger, the crystalline lens popped out to become a dead star; thus, no secret in the eye, just a mirror of the light which she had absorbed a little too much and, therefore, retained.

In Rennes-le-Château, on Rosaline's saint's day, blue apples appear through a stained-glass window to hide and to form a pretty bouquet on the opposite wall; they are a reference to an anagram that a marquis invented in relation to the imaginary epitaph of a marchioness... That day, he was not praying; instead, he was observing the prisms of the mirrors from the beyond which reflected through a rainbow of supreme colours.

From the word Amor (Love) of the marchioness, he went readily to the word Mort (Death), then to Morte Epée (Dead Sword), the authentic sword of the last knights after they found Excalibur.

He stared wide-eyed at the tomb of Father Gélis, renovated on this 17th January 2006, proof that researchers have a heart and a certain talent in their quest for the Grail. He started to believe in humankind. A cold and dry wind titillated his cheeks as he dozed in front of the town hall of old Coustaussa, the guardian of the secrets of the Haut-Razès.

He was woken up by a quarrel between the watchmen of the Parchments; he smiled mischievously thinking that the past was indeed for tomorrow.

Advance, advance on the path of the Custode, master blackmailers, authors of hope sheets, intoxicated by the little tricks of the Devil and his laments of past times.

LINE OF THE PARIS MERIDIAN 0

Forty-four locations with a legend in France, namely:

1 location	Rennes-les-Bains (Aude).
3 locations	Dunkerque, Paris and Bourges.
9 locations	Eringhem, Saint-Pol sur Ternoise, Amiens, Saint-Denis, Arçay, Mauriac, Salsigne, Carcassonne, and le Pic de Costabonne.
27 locations	Bollezeele, Roquetoire, Doullens, Beauval, Fresnes, Yères-le-Chatel, Villemurlin, Bourgneuf, Culan, Saint-Sauvier, Treignat, Lussat, Le Chauchet, Arfeuille, Belvédère de Gratte Bruyère, Saint-Antoine, Belcastel, Colombiès, Naucelle, Saint-Martial, le Viaduc du Viaur, Serenac, Villefranche d'Albigeois, Teillet, Lafontasse, Terrolles, and La Villetelle.

The order of the locations with a legend on the red line (meridian line) are:

NORD

1	The zero of the Paris meridian line starts at a spot in Dunkerque called Saint-Pol-sur-Mer, next to Fort Mardyck, and goes through Petite Synthe.
2	Eringhem and its famous lime tree near a grave.
3	Bollezeele and its myth about the red line and golden belt from Spain.

PAS-DE-CALAIS

4	Roquetoire, with its myth around the sword of Saint-Michael and Notre-Dame d'Amour (Our Lady of Love).
5	Saint-Pol-sur-Ternoise, the city of the magical cloud and horse spreading on the ground.

SOMME

6	Doullens and a whole story based on the meridian.
7	Beauval.
8	Amiens and the sharing of Saint Martin's cloak by the red line, plus the sharing of the red cloak (given to Christ) played at dice (by a Roman soldier).

SEINE

9	Saint-Denis who walked headless from the cemetery of Montmartre whilst holding his head, which traced a red line as far as Saint-Denis; the martyr handed over his head to a woman called Catulla. (Thus, the saint went through Saint-Ouen).
10	Paris, with the cemetery of Montmartre and the line of Saint-Sulpice – P.S. / S.P.
11	Fresnes and its legend that concerns Morangis too.

LOIRET

12	Yères-le-Chatel.
13	Villemurlin.

CHER

14	Bourgneuf and its legend regarding the old priory and the famous oak.
15	Bourges; in reality, the legend goes back to a neighbourhood called "faubourg Saint-Sulpice".
16	Arçay.
17	Culan.

ALLIER

18	Saint-Sauveur.
19	Treignat.

CREUSE

20	Lussat and its cemetery.
21	Le Chauchet and its cemetery.
22	La Villetelle.
23	Arfeuille and its chapel, near Crocq.

CORREZE

24	The legend about the famous belvedere on the Dordogne river, called Belvédère de Gratte-Bruyère or Witch Pavilion.

CANTAL

25	Mauriac with its cemetery and famous tale regarding Théodechilde, daughter of Clovis, who, in 507, found the first statue of the Black Virgin, better known as Notre-Dame des Miracles (Our Lady of Miracles); a candle shone in front of the effigy until the French Revolution.
26	Saint-Antoine and its legend regarding Saint Anthony.

AVEYRON

27	Belcastel and its beautiful legend around the ruins of the castle, which at six hundred meters, overlooks the Aveyron on the meridian.
28	Colombiès and its legend regarding the passage of Saint Columba, who stayed there for over six days with an enormous she-bear from Spain, on her way to Sens (Yonne).
29	Naucelle.
30	Saint-Martial.
31	The Viaduc du Viaur which, at one hundred twenty meters, dominates the Viaur river; there is a very old and prophetic legend concerning the location of the viaduct and the meridian 0.

TARN

32	Serenac.
33	Villefranche d'Albigeois.
34	Teillet.
35	In the village of Lafontasse, on the meridian near Castres, there is a rock called Campsoleil; the legend is about the solar myth and granite plateau of Sidobre, where Saint Dominic went to take advice (from God).

AUDE

36	Salsigne.
37	Carcassonne.
38	Terrolles, which dominates Rennes-les-Bains.
39	Rennes-les-Bains.
40	The Pic de Costabonne, 2464 meters high, at the headstreams of the river Tech, which goes through Arles near Amélie-les-Bains. The Pic de Costabonne, however, is in the Pyrénées-Orientales.

One must go over forty legends to obtain the story of the red thread (Ariadne's thread) or red line in France.

SIONUS PRIORATUS

"IN HOC SIGNO VINCES"

Lectures In Rennes-Le-Château, Hôtel De La Tour Noël Corbu

Address of Pierre Plantard de Saint-Clair on 17th January 1964

Brethren!

Some years ago, an author wrote, "The root of humanity's misfortunes is a disregard for morality, sometimes even its total omission."

When one talks about "morality", one refers to a line of conduct governed by written laws, dogmatic tenets, and precepts which, from time immemorial, were imposed on individuals or inculcated in nations by means of persuasion that are more or less questionable.

What gives us the right to promulgate a law or moral standards? In the past, teachings that served the interests of society's mighty gave full powers to one or more divinities who, through some supernatural revelation, granted the ethical authority to intermediaries. Thus, accompanied by sanctions in the terrestrial existence and in a hypothetical future life, the law, or moral doctrine, was accepted unanimously, supremely and indisputably.

In this day and age, these outdated principles have hardly any hold on people and it is practically impossible to remind individuals, nations even less so, of the respect of moral standards based on religious belief. However, the laws of a country may, by force, reduce individuals to a temporary submission, simply because they cannot uphold insubordination to the State power.

As soon as the State must increase its police strength daily in order to maintain the law, the exercise of force to impose its moral code represents the failure of its system. One only has to look at the revolutions around the world to realise that this is the case in almost every State.

Nowadays, one does without the approval of the nation, and freedom of speech and action do not exist any more. In a State monopoly, one decrees automatically; one exercises the dictatorship of personal power to impose one's will.

Moreover, it is nearly impossible to apply the same methods at an international level. Security forces look more like the revival of an exploitation medium in the hands of trusts than a temple of universal consciousness.

Under the pretext of economic stabilisation, we are in the middle of a war on energy which will turn, before the end of this Century, into plain conflict.

One can even influence an entire population through diet, which conditions them physically; then, since the physical state affects the mental state, a newspaper, radio or State television will terminate the exploitation for the benefit of a cast that came into power.

There is no "Freedom" for human beings any more; records classify them; each individual is registered on the computer; one knows everything about them, namely their birth, family, health, studies, political and religious ideologies, activities; their whole private life is scrutinised...

In short, this is the end of an era; the agony of an epoch.

Law and Morality do not exist any more!

Law and Morality, "so-called immortal soul of humanity", the lifebelt that floated yesterday on the waters, explodes in the air like an over-inflated balloon.

Today, the compulsory respect of State laws, which would like to become the bounds of moral conscience, is a Utopia, since "Conscience rests with the human individual and not with the text of human laws."

In the future, individual conscience will replace the moral doctrine that was taught for fear of the Divine wrath. The regenerative fluid from its source will propagate from urn to urn to flood the community like the vase of Ganymede. The State that wants to usurp the moral authority of religion for its own benefit is mistaken; the disappearance of one will drag the other down.

A new cycle is beginning; even the Vatican, sensing that the structure of its vessel is cracking up on all sides, knows very well that the volte-face of their pontiffs will not prevent the boat from sinking in the tempest.

After the storm at the end of this Century, it is finally the voice of the people "Vox populi" that will dominate the world scene. True democracy will emerge victorious from the chaos.

Such is the symbol of the two gold and silver urns of Ganymede which will spread their regenerative fluids.

Parents who observe their children can also feel that an era is completed; they realise that the fragile barriers erected to contain the wave will be swept like a wisp of straw.

Young people are looking for a way. They will find it; but not in a doctrine, as they will overthrow taboos, moral standards and laws. Ganymede is the CHILD on the ROCK dominating BLACK and WHITE. The dualism of Beauseant [the battle-cry of the Knights Templar – old French name for a black and white horse], the Temple's standard, is still floating over the world.

Address Of Pierre Plantard De Saint-Clair On 6th June 1964

Brethren!

When entering the church of Rennes-le-Château, in the Aude valley, the visitor is welcomed by a "devil" whose stare points at the ground where sixty-four squares of alternating Black and White tiles form a chessboard. This game, which originated in the East and was introduced into Europe after the first Crusade, holds the legend of the grain of corn; one grain for the first square, two grains for the second, four for the third, eight for the fourth, and so on, until one reaches the sixty-fourth square, is nothing more that the symbol of mutation.

In the 12th Century, the word "eschequier" meant "royal treasure", because of the chequered cloth of sixty-four squares covering the table on which the Dukes of Normandy did their accounts; nowadays still, the cabinet minister responsible for finance in traditionalist Britain is called "Chancellor of the Exchequer".

A game of thirty-two pieces of differing value comprises, amongst others, two queens and two kings. If the king (Sun) is the master of the arena, the queen remains the mistress of the Game, particularly in the Mary-Magdalene's church at Rennes-le-Château.

Each square has a value in cuneiform characters.

The sixty-four characters are made up of mathematical layouts of six rows of even or uneven number of dots, known as geomancy figures.

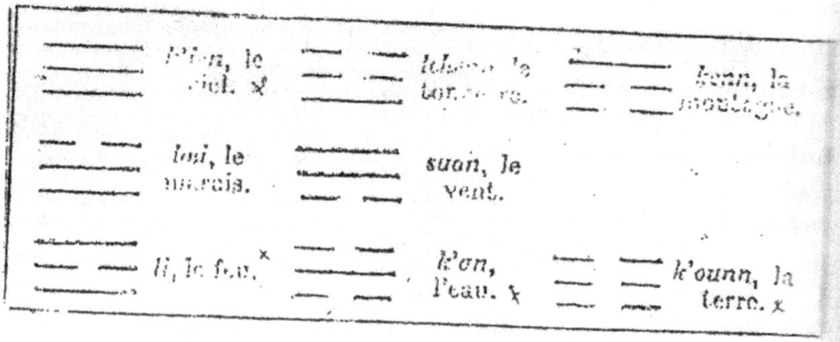

31 - Eight Trigrams

In combining the above eight trigrams, the Chinese Tchâng dé Tchéôu invented the 8 by 8 hexagrams, totalling 64, for which the descriptions and judgements (or commentaries) made by Tch'ang and Tan produced the famous *I Ching, The Book of Changes* or book of mutations.

The Sun, with its eight-beam rays adorning the speaker of the 18th Century Lodges, is nothing more than the symbol of the octopus; "The octopus is the most ancient symbol of all theogonies, the representation of the god Okeanos, father of all things.

There was an octopus above the Tripod at Delphi, also called the Delphic oracle, which prompted a modern author to question the relationship between Apollo and the octopod. Apollo represents the Sun god who, associated with the octopus, provides the initiate with the knowledge of mutations.

The image of the octopus is represented on several Greek urns in the Louvre Museum in Paris, and could be found also on ancient disk-shaped tombs in the Basque region and on Roman graves. In Rennes-le-Château, a few unscrupulous individuals did not hesitate to falsify a stone by scraping it in 1891 and adding their own octopus to it.

The antique symbol of the octopus was known in pre-Columbian America and all the way to the Mediterranean Sea; with its two eyes, it could turn anybody who looked at it into stone. Now, in alchemy, the Philosopher's stone could transmute metals into gold; thus, the above falsification would be justified in Rennes-le-Château where, according to legend, there should be a hidden "regal treasure".

In the past, Rennes-le-Château and Rennes-les-Bains were the Pagus Redensis, the old cities of Rheda, the big chariot and the small chariot, the celestial Bears; the Great Bear (Ursa Major) being Callisto and the Little Bear (Ursa Minor) being Arcas. Callisto, daughter of the Arcadian King Lycaon, and

Arcas, her son by Zeus, are the two polar constellations. The meridian that cuts across Rennes-les-Bains is pointing towards the Little Bear; the polished tombstone, which is now over the ossuary of Rennes-le-Château, was an enormous stone which bore the watchword ET IN ARCADIA EGO and an indication about its former location on the golden line between Peyrolles and Serres.

The falsification of the tombstone could have been aimed at representing Callisto and Arcas as the eyes of the octopus!

But, Mr. Chéza was far from reaching that conclusion, since he did not know that the octopus is a representation of the Chinese Hà-Dô and that, according to tradition, the emperor Fou-Hi discovered it whilst walking along the Yellow River.

The eyes of the octopus are the Yin and Yang.

In the Chinese Hà-Dô, there are two columns: Jos, red, on the right hand side of the octopus; Beth, green, on the left hand side. From its head, there are eight tentacles with the sucker combinations resulting in 8 signs. A primary mutation produces ten symbols, and each of these symbols receives one of the four elements since, according to Pythagoras, four creates ten, or 1 + 2 + 3 + 4 = 10; these principles were already followed by the Chaldeans who went from the concrete to the abstract, and vice and versa. Cuneiform characters form the only basis of their writing.

The first inscriptions were drawn in a magic square of 8 which, when multiplied, gives 64, that is 32 blacks and 32 whites. Each position could be occupied by a piece and the game of fate became infinite. It had its own importance and meaning, and on its invariable bases, one laid the sixty-four characters or geomancy dots.

52	61	4	13	20	29	36	45
14	3	62	51	46	35	30	19
53	60	5	12	21	28	37	44
11	6	59	54	43	38	27	22
42	39	26	23	10	7	58	55
24	25	40	41	56	57	8	9
47	34	31	18	15	2	63	50
17	32	33	48	49	64	1	16

32 - Number Square

Let's look at the above illustration where the numbers 1 to 64 in the squares have been arranged to obtain a basis of 260, that is the numerical value of the words "kobab kesef hayyim", or Etoile de vif-argent (Star of vivid silver).

Each horizontal line totals 260, each column totals 260, and each diagonal totals 260. The total of the eight horizontal lines or columns is 2080.

The octopus was simplified as an eight-point star, as shown on Babylonians cylinders. Without grasping its secret, tradition remains and the star of the Magi is found in numerous religious paintings dating from the Renaissance. To possess this star is to have knowledge; who better than an orator entrusted to transmit the teaching to bear this Sun with eight rays!

The majority of the Templars' buildings, together with their alphabet, were octagonal, as illustrated by the baptistery Saint-John in Poitiers. They took old boatmen constructions for a model. With the octagonal shape of its donjon, the castle of Gisors, in the department of the Eure, offers the best example of a hermetic fortress.

To be given the baptismal water with a scallop shell was nothing more than a reminder of the primitive teaching; this is why, in the past, Merovingian baptisteries displayed the symbolic octopus.

The Greek name for octopus, Sarros, meaning flesh, is found in the word pulpe in French and designates the pulp of fruits; to bite into the apple is to discover knowledge, to take in the pulp of the fruit. The apple divided by its equator, reveals in its core the hidden flamboyant Pythagorean five-point star (near the B (Boaz) column in a commandery (lodge)) from which the golden number is derived.

The devoted companion will have to go over the 64 squares before contemplating the three windows opening on the East (blue), South (golden yellow), and West (red), he; the first window dissipating the darkness as it lights up under the rays of the rising Sun, the second reducing to a minimum with day light, and the third letting the rays of the setting Sun outlive the past through a myriad of glitters.

In the temple, each square measures 34.5 cm; this number may be reduced by 10 or multiplied by 10 to infinity. A perfect chessboard measures 34.5 cm on each side.

The companion must make the Knight leap, like Perseus on the winged horse Pegasus born from the mutilated body of Medusa whom Perseus had beheaded; Perseus landed in Ethiopia, where the chessboard originated, and rescued Andromeda.

8	57	6	41	10	29	4	43
59	40	9	56	5	42	11	30
38	7	58	53	28	55	44	3
51	60	39	20	25	22	31	12
18	37	52	23	54	27	2	45
61	50	19	26	21	24	13	32
36	17	48	63	34	15	46	1
49	62	35	16	47	64	33	14

33 - Number Square

The symbolic walk (claudication in the past) respected by the initiate in the Priory of Sion, from number 1 to number 22 (from black to white), followed by number 22 to number 43 (from white to black), and finally number 43 to number 64 (from black to white), makes him an individual capable of covering the circuit of sixty-three leaps. This walk is done at right angles of three squares in every direction. There are three veils to lift, namely three passwords, to penetrate in the Arch.

When the knight carries the rose, he must conquer the esoteric chessboard through a last gesture, by accomplishing the last leap of the 3rd leg, namely by returning from 64 to 1, or get over the time-space. Only then will the initiate become the "checkmate", the "fool", the "bishop", whose hat is the mitre, "the cowl that covers the chimney".

The twenty-two leaps of the last leg are also the twenty-two cards (major arcana) of the Tarot from Marseille. Only one author, Oswald Wirth, who was in fact initiated, understood this matter very well in one of his works [*Le tarot des Imagiers du Moyen Age* (*The Tarot of Middle-Age Painters of Popular Pictures*) written in 1927.]

The 22nd leap does not have a number. “In Hoc Signo Vinces”

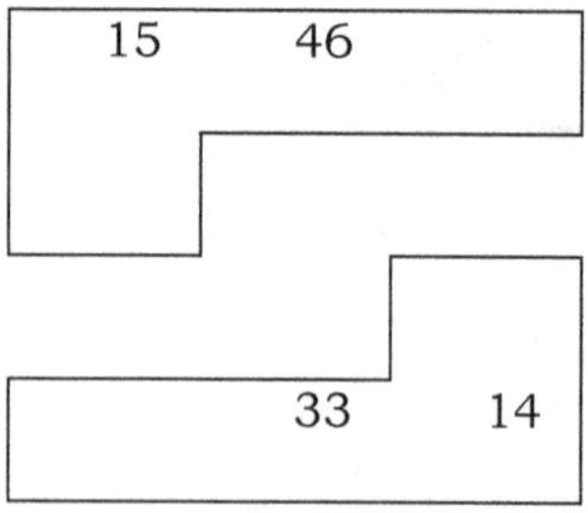

Address of Pierre Plantard de Saint-Clair on 17th January 1965

Brethren!

For a long time, no beacon enlightened our intelligence. The greatest ignorance enveloped our planet and its darkness encouraged the realisation of harmful schemes for the human race.

Where did we come from? After all the convulsions that transformed the globe, the mystery of our origin became lost in the memory of the human race as a whole. We did not know any more if we came from there or from somewhere else. Where were we going? For some it was to nothingness, for others to another world where life is eternal; a passage from present life to naught or to a future life; one feared death since the future life seemed even more frightening than nothingness.

The concept of providence spread in many ways that were impossible to coordinate. Humankind sought protection from the moment it faced adversity. Thousands of gods, good, nasty, rivalrous, jealous, vindictive, ridiculous, fearsome, ugly, powerful, mortal, immortal, visible or invisible, succeeded each other, since the notion of a creator God, illogical in itself, had to lead to chaos.

After the last big cataclysm, all civilisations relied on a blind faith fostered by the cleverest. Kings and emperors pretended to be descendants of gods. Depending on their shrewdness, those who discovered the trickery could, in turn, claim to be messengers or prophets of those very gods and rise to the highest posts.

The most reliable methods to encourage this climate presupposed a doctrine based 1) on high moral standards, where the chastity of the officiating priests in broad daylight was concealing a bestial sensuality; 2) on public virtues, very compatible with covert licentiousness; 3) on a social organisation of slavery, which lowered in status half of the human race to whom one preached total submission in the name of the divinity; and 4) on the public cult of bits of wood, stone or metal representing gods, demigods and saints.

Thus, from the outset, new religions sheltered a dragon with multiple heads, gorged with humanity's blood; a hideous monster in the name of which one only witnessed murders, rapes, deception and corruption.

How is it possible that, for centuries, the dragon managed to survive under the cloak of morality? The fertile imagination of the preachers and the credulity of the nations performed that miracle. It is that heritage that our ancestors handed down to us. The chimeras and wild imaginings of delirious minds into which simple people fell, followed by scholars, geniuses and great minds, and which aided kings and emperors in consolidating their thrones. The erection and restoration of the divinity's sumptuous buildings did not matter to them since the costs were invariably passed on to the oppressed masses.

It was not always like that. In six hundred thousand years of its existence [the oldest skull was found on 17th July 1958, in Kenya, by Professor Louis Leakey], the conscious human being has accumulated a great knowledge. As Plato wrote [*Timaeus*], "You have no memory of the centuries gone by and no knowledge of the beginnings. This ignorance is down to various multiple deaths and destructions".

Yet, in some corners of the planet, a few people preserved traces of the past in a legendary and symbolic form; this was used by all religions as the foundation of their doctrine and concealed under the veil of mystery.

On the threshold of each cycle, two great religions appeared; Buddhism [with five hundred million followers today] founded in the 5th Century B.C. by Prince Siddhartha (Gautama in Sanskrit) with its influence limited to the Far-East; and Christianity, founded in 3 CE by Jesus, with its prodigious expansion in the West. Islam, a third religious current founded by Mahomet around 630 CE, created the Muslim Nation.

Ah! Dear friend, we know you will protest and argue that "Christianity represents the worship of God made man; Jesus lived on our planet and preached neighbourly love to the Jews; his cult cannot be compared to that of other religions".

Don't you think, dear friend, that Christianity is also a vast enterprise, a faith business, totally contrary to the wishes of its founder? Its representatives live in luxury, whilst Jesus lived modestly. Everything can be bought in the Temple from which Jesus expelled the merchants.

This individual, like so many others, declared himself the Son of God. Unfortunately, the Jewish law had anticipated the eventuality of such an allegation, an example of which could be found amongst most nations. His declaration was considered a crime and the Jewish law was applied by the Romans against a man who had only done his people good. Most certainly he deserved the title of King of the Jews. But because of the colour of his skin, his claims to a divine origin, and his personal synthesis of various pre-existing mystical concepts, the teachings of Jesus remain those of a Galilean preaching for his race.

These acts and declarations are recorded in four Gospels, the exact content of which Catholicism found advisable to water down through the centuries, with the aid of translations, like the content of the Bible that is the very basis of its law.

In the Hebrew text of the Gospel according to Matthew, who wrote for the Jews and, therefore, could only give a law-abiding genealogy of Jesus, the latter has definitely existed and was recognised as a descendant of David through Joseph, the artisan.

Joseph, an eighty-three year old octogenarian, had children from two or three former marriages when he married Miriam (Mary), a thirteen year old girl who was fatherless since the age of ten.

Mary had been married for four months and had just reached fourteen when she found herself pregnant. Joseph, who was an honest and kind man, became suddenly aware of this and thought at once of repudiating her in silence. He did not want to put the child that he loved on trial; it would have meant lapidation for her and scandal for him.

Mary was black, as she was the daughter of Joachim "the black man converted to Judaism", and her mother was Anne, the prophetess. [Anne was seventy years old when she gave birth to Mary; at the death of her husband Joachim, she retired to the Temple of Jerusalem]. Anne was only recognised definitely as Mary's mother, out of political necessity, during the Middle Ages. Mary was heiress to her father's possessions. However, as she was underage, Joseph became her tutor and took charge of administering her inheritance, until such day when, out of interest as well as love, he married her secretly, whilst respecting her virtue. One can imagine his bitterness when he had to face the evidence regarding Mary's condition. One can also understand why Joseph, who knew the father, accepted the situation and the fury of King Herod the Great at the birth of Jesus.

Legally, Jesus was a descendant of David, son of Mary, and was recognised by Joseph. He could also aspire to the title of King of the Jews. This truth, revealed by Judas Iscariot to the Jewish priests during his betrayal, did not suit the Church at all, which opted for the subterfuge of a spontaneous generation.

Of course, Jesus preached a doctrine to the Jewish nation, but all great philosophers of the antiquity did the same for their nations; often, they even wrote admirable works which survived to our times, but they were not martyrs for this simple motive. The revelation of the secret around Jesus' birth was the cause of his martyrdom. The glory of his Crucifixion gave him a religion.

The expansion of Christianity can be justified by the decline of other religions, by the revival of the masses' need to believe in the possible sacrifice of an individual who claimed to push aside one's fear of nothingness and promised eternal felicity, and by the astonishing eloquence of the storytellers of the Orient who created a climate of collective hypnosis.

There was wonder, since Jesus was born at the dawn of a great cycle; one hundred fifty years after his birth, when Europe was desolate after the war with the occupying Roman armies, when no stone from the past was left standing by the invader on the Judean land, when Jerusalem was totally destroyed and its name changed into Aelia-Capitolina, the Rock of the Crucifixion suddenly appeared on the site of the Temple of Venus, the Sepulchre at the location of the statue of Jupiter, the entrance to the Via Dolorosa where there was formerly the image of a pig, and the Grotto of Bethlehem on the site of the Temple of Adonis.

Don't you believe me, Brethren? Then, search through history. The first person who brought the alleged location of the Grotto of Bethlehem to the attention of the world is Justin, martyr in 167 CE, who established it on the site of the Temple of Adonis, a version that was confirmed by Origen in 213 CE. Constantine started the shrine where the Temple of Venus once stood. The eighty year old Princess Helen, who arrived in Palestine in 326 CE, had greater difficulties in finding the site of the Sepulchre and chose the spot of the statue of Jupiter. Since crosses as torture implements were common in the Jewish community, excavations revealed quite a few. From that moment, one did not waste any time. In 333 CE, tourism was organised, that is an itinerary was defined for the pilgrims. In 379 CE, Saint Gregory of Nyssa blamed the abusive number of pilgrimages, but the Christian Church drowned his voice and consecrated openly all these events by attaching indulgences to them.

If miracle power exists, it is very much that one, namely that of humankind with its head under water for two thousand years, in the company of the "Fishes" (the era of Pisces), yet still able to surface in order to breathe and contemplate freely the sky into which it would like to ascend.

The prelude to this general impulse was given by France, on a day in 1789, when the call for the respect of Liberty, Equality and Fraternity amongst all beings remains the conscience symbol. Now, the revival of humankind's conscience will break the vessel of mysteries and will allow humans to taste the nectar from the fruits of the Tree of Knowledge.

So, let us remember Virgil's recommendation [*Georgics II-489*], "Felix qui potuit rerum cognosoere causas" or "Blessed is the one who penetrates the secret causes of things".

Forgive, Brethren, the frankness of a free man who remains devoted to you.

Loi du 1er Ju

S A T Z U N G E N
des
A L P H A - G A L A T E S

Grosser Ritterorden
27. Dezember 1937

(angemeldet bei der Polizeipräfektur)

Artikel 1.- Es wird von den, zu vorliegenden Satzungen beiretenden Personen ein "Grosser Ritterorden" unter dem Namen : ALPHA-GALATES gebildet.

Sein Gesellschaftssitz, Zentralarche genannt, befindet sich in PARIS (17°), rue Lebouteux N° 10. Er kann durch Entscheidungen des Generalgouverneurs überallhin übertragen werden.

Es könen Archen in der Provinz gegründet werden.

Seine Dauer ist unbegrenzt.

Artikel 2.- Der Orden hat den Zweck, seine Mitglieder in einem Werk von gegenseitiger und nationaler Nächstenhilfe zu vereinigen, ihre Kenntnisse zu erweitern, ihr Streben in einem ästhetischen Sinn zu leiten, ihnen ein ritterliches Ideal einzuprägen, das auf dem Willen beruht, in Ehre zu handeln und dem Vaterland zu dienen.

Infolgedessen wird der Orden folgendes begünstigen :

1.- Studien - und Vortragskreise ;
2.- Aufheiternde, kinematographische und musikalische Sitzungen ;
3.- Einrichtungen wie : das Camping, den Erholungsaufenthalt, das Ambulatorium, die sich mit der Gesundheit der Mitglieder beschäftigen ;
4.- Wohltätigkeitswerke wie der Besuch von Kranken, Beistand für Bedürftige, das Adoptieren verlassener oder Waisenkinder ;
5.- Die Schöpfung eines Volkssekretariats.

Artikel 3.- Um Mitglied des Ordens zu werden, muss man :

1.- Mehr als 18 Jahre alt sein ;
2.- Den vorliegenden Satzungen beitreten ;
3.- Von Zwei Mitgliedern des Ordens eingeführt werden ;
4.- Ein Beitrittsgesuch ausfüllen ;
5.- Eine Wohnnungsbescheinigung und 3 Identitätslichtbilder Beibringen ;
6.- Vom Generalgouverneur genehmigt werden ;
7.- Einen jährlichen Beitrag entrichten, der je nach der Grosszügigkeit eines jeden einzelnen verschieden ist, mit einem Mindestbetrag von fünfzig Francs ;

Die Mitglieder haben bei ihrem Ordenseintritt die Wahl zwischen zwei Kategorien :

A.- "Die Legion", damit betraut, über seine Sicherheit, seine Interessen zu wachen und sein Streben durchzuführen ;

B.- "Dir Phalanx", damit betraut, das Depot der erworbenen Wissenschaft zu bewahren, sich philosophischen Forschungen hinzugeben und die künftigen Ritter zu bilden.

34 - Statutes of Alpha-Galates in German dated 27th December 1937

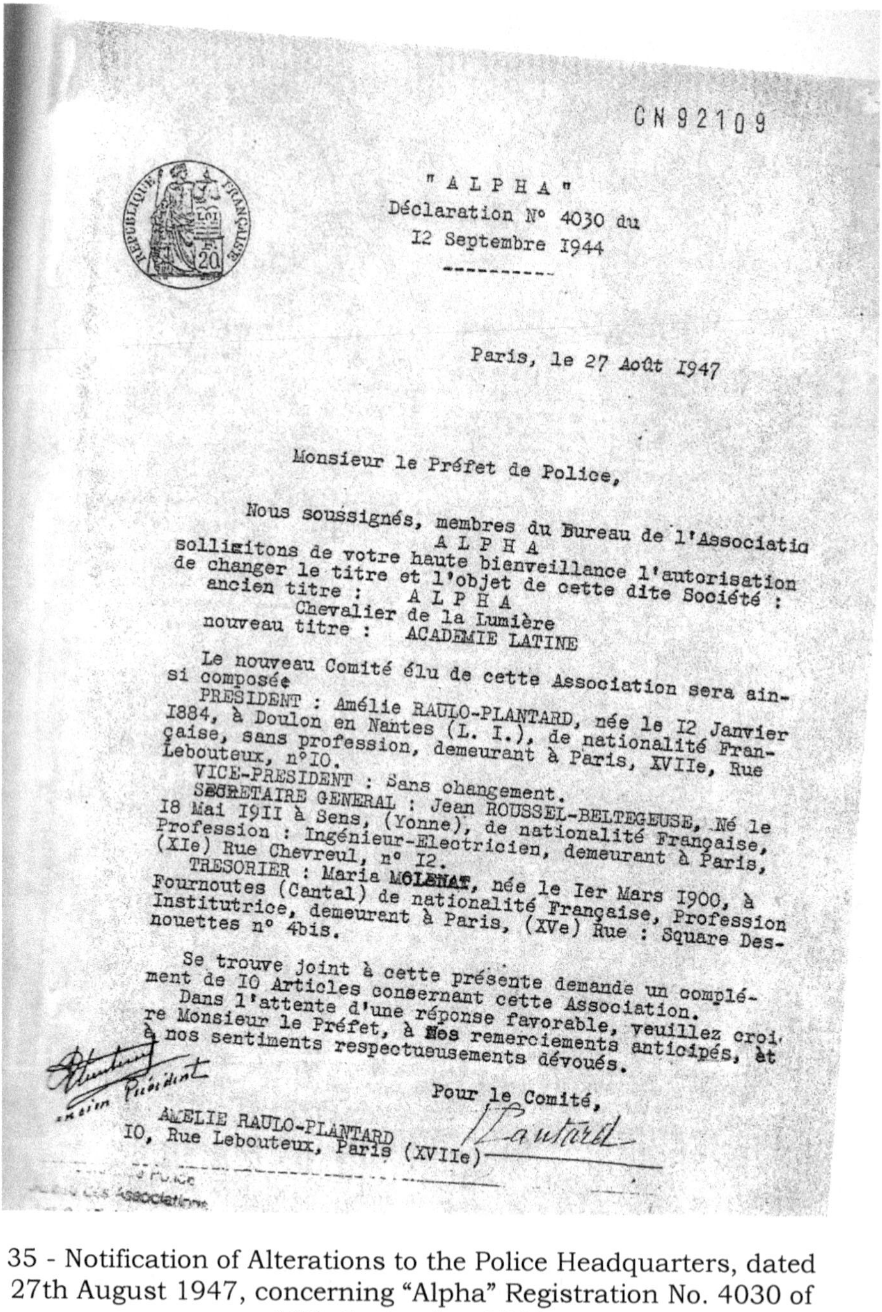

CN 92109

"A L P H A"
Déclaration N° 4030 du
I2 Septembre I944

Paris, le 27 Août I947

Monsieur le Préfet de Police,

Nous soussignés, membres du Bureau de l'Associatio
A L P H A
sollisitons de votre haute bienveillance l'autorisation de changer le titre et l'objet de cette dite Société :
ancien titre : A L P H A
Chevalier de la Lumière
nouveau titre : ACADEMIE LATINE

Le nouveau Comité élu de cette Association sera ainsi composée
PRESIDENT : Amélie RAULO-PLANTARD, née le I2 Janvier I884, à Doulon en Nantes (L. I.), de nationalité Française, sans profession, demeurant à Paris, XVIIe, Rue Lebouteux, n°IO.
VICE-PRESIDENT : Sans changement.
SECRETAIRE GENERAL : Jean ROUSSEL-BELTEGEUSE, Né le I8 Mai I9II à Sens, (Yonne), de nationalité Française, Profession : Ingénieur-Electricien, demeurant à Paris, (XIe) Rue Chevreul, n° I2.
TRESORIER : Maria MOLENAT, née le Ier Mars I900, à Fournoutes (Cantal) de nationalité Française, Profession Institutrice, demeurant à Paris, (XVe) Rue : Square Desnouettes n° 4bis.

Se trouve joint à cette présente demande un complément de IO Articles conсernant cette Association.
Dans l'attente d'une réponse favorable, veuillez croire Monsieur le Préfet, à nos remerciements anticipés, et à nos sentiments respectueusements dévoués.

Pour le Comité,

ancien Président

AMELIE RAULO-PLANTARD
IO, Rue Lebouteux, Paris (XVIIe)

35 - Notification of Alterations to the Police Headquarters, dated 27th August 1947, concerning "Alpha" Registration No. 4030 of 12th September 1944

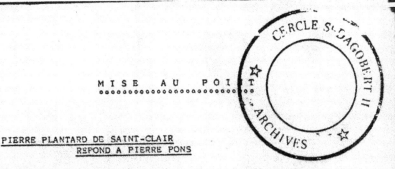

M I S E   A U   P O I N T
ooooooooooooooooooooooooooooooooo

PIERRE PLANTARD DE SAINT-CLAIR
REPOND A PIERRE PONS

Dans un article de la "DEPECHE" en date du Dimanche 4 Février 1979, Pierre PONS faisait citation de mon nom, ainsi que du livre "SIGNE: ROSE+CROIX" à propos de "...trois nouvelles victimes" du TRESOR MAUDIT DE RENNES-LE-CHATEAU.

C'est faire beaucoup d'honneur à ma personne en déclarant que cet ouvrage "...fait autorité en la matière...", car si tous les lecteurs savent que ce livre est la réédition de "L'OR DE RENNES" publié pour la première fois en Novembre 1967 aux Editions RENE JULLIARD, presque tous ignorent que l'écrivain GERARD de SEDE fut le prête nom de mes oeuvres.

Cette "Mise au Point", m'oblige à retracer en quelques lignes l'origine de la publication SIGNE: ROSE+CROIX et permettra aux lecteurs d'apprécier à sa juste valeur ma "Préface" du livre "LA VRAIE LANGUE CELTIQUE" de l'Abbé BOUDET, publié aux Editions PIERRE BELFONT en Décembre 1978.

Le 17 Juillet 1965, le manuscrit de L'OR DE RENNES étant achevé, suivant mon accord antérieur avec les Editions JULLIARD, j'en informais Mr. Pierre JAVET, Directeur d'éditions. C'est Melle Janine MUSY qui me fit réponse. Notre rencontre eut lieu le Lundi 26 Juillet 1965, et après lecture, la publication fut décidée.

Ne désirant pas voir "mon nom" figurer comme "auteur" de cet ouvrage, j'ai contacté Gérard de SEDE en Décembre 1965. Celui-ci ignorait totalement l'existence de RENNES-LE-CHATEAU, mais il était mon co-auteur du livre "LES TEMPLIERS SONT PARMI NOUS" et j'avais pour lui la sincère amitié du maître à son meilleur compagnon. Par acte du 31 Janvier 1966 enregistré n° H 27276, Gérard de SEDE, contre 35 % de mes droits d'auteur, cédait SON NOM pour "L'OR DE RENNES". Le contrat devait être signé chez l'éditeur le 1er Mars 1966...

Au moment de la signature, Gérard de Sède déclara qu'il était malade et téléphona par la suite pour me réclamer 50 % des droits d'auteurs afin de donner son nom. Ultérieurement il prétexta une demande de renseignements auprès de Mr. DEBANT, directeur des Archives de l'Aude et l'attente de la réponse du Colonel ARNAUD auxquels il avait demandé des précisions au sujet du codage de la pierre tombale de la Marquise de BLANCHEFORT! Ce marchandage dura jusqu'en Décembre 1966...

Devant ces faits, Mr. Christian BOURGOIS, directeur des Editions JULLIARD et moi-même, nous pensions publier L'OR DE RENNES sous le nom de Philippe de CHERISEY. C'est alors que Gérard de SEDE se décida à signer le contrat primitif, ceci le 13 Janvier 1967. Il fut alors convenu qu'il ferait la correction des épreuves de l'imprimeur. Moi-même, je m'engageais à le faire participer à une émission télévisée de Pierre LAFORET.

CERCLE S...

2

Lors de ma réception des volumes envoyés par les Editions JULLIARD le 10 Novembre 1967, grande fut ma stupéfaction de lire aux pages 132 à 137 un commentaire où il est question de Mr. DEBANT et du Colonel ARNAUD et agrémenté de la reproduction de "faux parchemins",(1) ainsi que du trucquage de certaines de mes photos. L'enquête révéla que Gérard de SEDE avait profité de son travail de correction des épreuves pour introduire dans l'ouvrage des éléments de sa pure fantaisie. Le livre se trouvait déjà dans le commerce, nous ne pouvions plus rien faire.

En Mars 1977, les Editions JULLIARD nous informèrent séparément, Gérard de SEDE et moi-même, qu'ils retiraient du circuit commercial L'OR DE RENNES qui avait 10 ans. Gérard de SEDE se présentant comme auteur aux Editions PLON, abusant de leur confiance, demanda la réédition de l'OR DE RENNES sous le titre de "SIGNE: ROSE+CROIX". C'est ainsi que le 20 Juin 1977 dans une librairie j'ai découvert le plagiat et la nouvelle forfaiture de celui qui "fait autorité en la matière", selon l'expression de Pierre PONS.

Depuis le 10 JUILLET 1977 j'ai fait interdire la vente du livre "SIGNE:ROSE+CROIX"qui fourmille d'erreurs, y compris la première page... (Gérard de SEDE dans son incompétence n'a même p... été fichu de s'apercevoir que la représentation du "diable" se trouvaitàl'envers). Le 24 Octobre 1977 j'ai refusé la publication dans les livres de poche "J'AI LU"... ce plagiat de l'OR DE RENN...

En Avril 1978, Mr. Pierre BELFONT prenait contact avec moi et m... demandait de bien vouloir écrire une préface au livre qu'il désirait rééditer: "LA VRAIE LANGUE CELTIQUE" de l'Abbé Henri BOUDET or avant de lui donner une réponse affirmative, j'ai consulté diverses personnes pour savoir l'opportunité de cette publication ... par une indiscrétion, Gérard de SEDE s'est trouvé au courant du projet. Utilisant alors des documentations que je lui avais confiées, ainsi que mes photocopies du livre de l'Abbé BOUDET, il s'est précipité de faire une réédition de la VRAIE LANGUE CELTIQUE

Je laisse aux lecteurs le soin d'apprécier les procédés de Gérard de SEDE, car ma présente réponse n'a d'autre objet qu'une "Mise au point" à un article de Pierre PONS.

Pierre PLANTARD de SAINT-CLAIR

(1) Mon Oncle a acheté à Mme JAMES en 1955, les trois parchemins découverts par l'Abbé SAUNIERE, curé de Rennes-le-Château, ces actes se trouvent depuis 24 ans dans le coffre d'une Banque Anglaise.

35 bis, Bd. de la République - 92250 LA GARENNE-COLOMBES
1er Mars 1979

36 - Clarification from Pierre Plantard de Saint Clair concerning an article written by Pierre Pons about his work “SIGNE: ROSE+CROIX”

P. de CHERISEY
10 rue des Celestines
4.000 LIEGE (Belgique)

29 janvier 1974

Monsieur

Suite à la visite que vous avez faite chez mes parents pour ajouter une correction à "Circuit" et à votre article publié dans "Pegase"

1) C'est moi qui ait traduit le code de la tombe de Rennes le Chateau et non pas le service du chiffre. Ne melangeons pas torchons et serviettes. Ou bien ne citez aucune reference, ou bien, à l'avenir citez moi.

2) Pas de "ET" explétif. Auriez vous lu le codage plus attentivement vous auriez vu qu'il faut compter sur le contenu de deux echiquiers (64 x 2) soit 128 lettres et non pas 130. La formule est bien "QUE POUSSIN TENIERS GARDENT LA CLEF

3) L'ecart de 225 metres qui vous surprend si fort chez G. de SEDE n'est pas depourvu de signification, c'est la distance qui separe deux meridiens O. de Paris, celui de l'eglise Saint-Sulpice et celui de l'Observatoire du Luxembourg. Le premier et le second sont definis par deux lignes d'or serties dans le dallage du gnomon pour l'eglise (transept) et par l'observatoire (au deuxieme étage)

4) Si l'on souhaite que POUSSIN-TENIERS gardent la clef c'est qu'elle ne tourne plus dans la serrure, et c'est bien pourquoi l'abbé Saunière a effacé l'inscription non sans en avoir lui meme donné le contenu dans le Bulletin Scientifique de l'Aude. Par ailleurs je vous signale le passage à Rennes le Chateau en date du 16 mai 1970 d'une equipe comprenant un archeologue, un photographe, un conservateur, un dessinateur. Le cliché aux infra-rouges a revelé le libellé effacé de la dalle horizontale

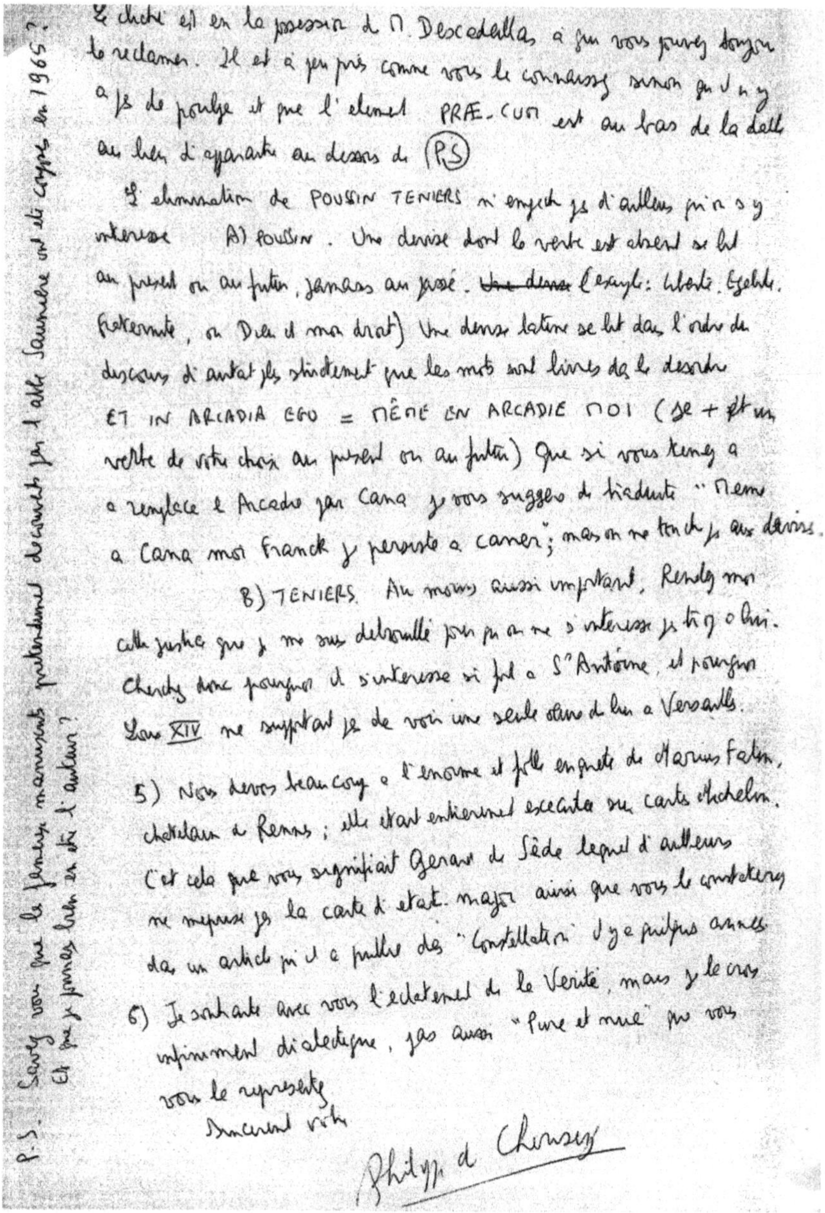
Le cliché est en la possession de M. Descadeillas à qui vous pouvez toujours le réclamer. Il est à peu près comme vous le connaissez sinon qu'il n'y a pas de poulpe et que l'élément PRÆ-CUM est au bas de la dalle au lieu d'apparaître au dessous de (P.S)

L'élimination de POUSSIN TENIERS n'empêche pas d'ailleurs qu'on s'y intéresse. A) POUSSIN. Une devise dont le verbe est absent se lit au présent ou au futur, jamais au passé. ~~Une devise~~ (exemple : Liberté, Egalité, Fraternité, ou Dieu et mon droit) Une devise latine se lit dans l'ordre du discours d'autant plus strictement que les mots sont livrés dans le désordre.

ET IN ARCADIA EGO = MÊME EN ARCADIE MOI (JE + Un verbe de votre choix au présent ou au futur) Que si vous tenez à remplacer l'Arcadie par Cana je vous suggère de traduire "Même à Cana moi Franck je persiste à caner" ; mais on ne touche pas aux devises.

B) TENIERS. Au moins aussi important. Rendez moi cette justice que je me suis débrouillé pour qu'on ne s'intéresse pas trop à lui. Cherchez donc pourquoi il s'intéresse si fort à St Antoine, et pourquoi Louis XIV ne supportait pas de voir une seule œuvre de lui à Versailles.

5) Nous devons beaucoup à l'énorme et folle enquête de Marius Fatin, châtelain de Rennes ; elle était entièrement exécutée sur cartes Michelin. C'est cela que vous signifiait Gérard de Sède lequel d'ailleurs ne méprise pas la carte d'état-major ainsi que vous le constaterez dans un article qu'il a publié dans "Constellation" il y a quelques années.

6) Je souhaite avec vous l'éclatement de la Vérité, mais je la crois infiniment dialectique, pas aussi "pure et nue" que vous vous la représentez.

Sincèrement vôtre

Philippe de Chérisey

P.S. Savez vous que les fameux manuscrits prétendument découverts par l'abbé Saunière ont été copiés en 1965 ? Et que je pourrais bien en être l'auteur ?

37 - Letter from Philippe de Cherisey to Franck Marie regarding the encoding of the stele and tombstone

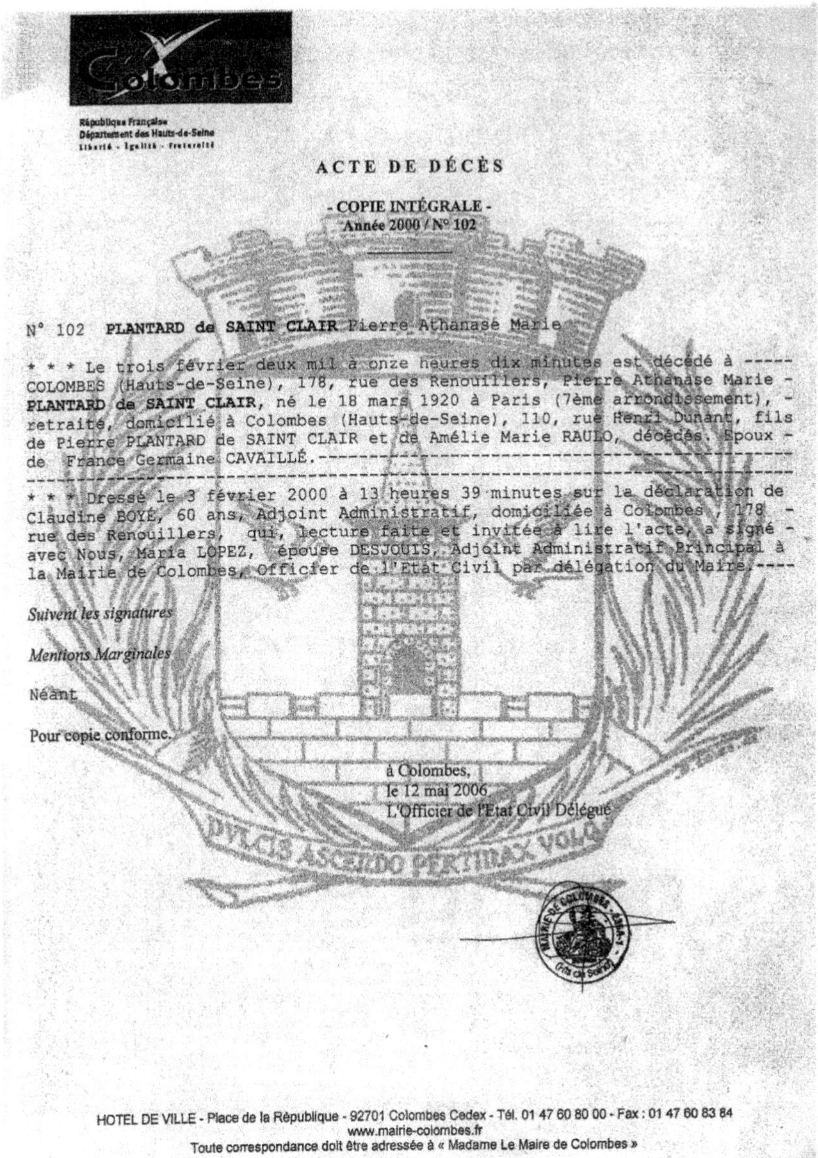
Colombes

République Française
Département des Hauts-de-Seine
Liberté - Egalité - Fraternité

ACTE DE DÉCÈS

- COPIE INTÉGRALE -
Année 2000 / N° 102

N° 102 **PLANTARD de SAINT CLAIR** Pierre Athanase Marie

* * * Le trois février deux mil à onze heures dix minutes est décédé à ----- COLOMBES (Hauts-de-Seine), 178, rue des Renouillers, Pierre Athanase Marie - **PLANTARD de SAINT CLAIR**, né le 18 mars 1920 à Paris (7ème arrondissement), - retraité, domicilié à Colombes (Hauts-de-Seine), 110, rue Henri Dunant, fils de Pierre PLANTARD de SAINT CLAIR et de Amélie Marie RAULO, décédés. Epoux - de France Germaine CAVAILLÉ.---

* * * Dressé le 3 février 2000 à 13 heures 39 minutes sur la déclaration de Claudine BOYÉ, 60 ans, Adjoint Administratif, domiciliée à Colombes, 178 - rue des Renouillers, qui, lecture faite et invitée à lire l'acte, a signé - avec Nous, Maria LOPEZ, épouse DESJOUIS, Adjoint Administratif Principal à la Mairie de Colombes, Officier de l'Etat Civil par délégation du Maire.----

Suivent les signatures

Mentions Marginales

Néant

Pour copie conforme.

à Colombes,
le 12 mai 2006
L'Officier de l'Etat Civil Délégué

HOTEL DE VILLE - Place de la République - 92701 Colombes Cedex - Tél. 01 47 60 80 00 - Fax : 01 47 60 83 84
www.mairie-colombes.fr
Toute correspondance doit être adressée à « Madame Le Maire de Colombes »

38 - Copy of Pierre Plantard's death certificate

minute

L'hebdo qui en sait trop • 13 octobre 1993 • N° 1643 • 15 F

UNE HISTOIRE DE FOUS !

Les mystères du Prieuré de Sion

UNE SOCIÉTÉ SECRÈTE DANS L'OMBRE DE MITTERRAND

Pelat en était-il le grand maître ?

39 - Cutting of the "Minute" newspaper of 13th October 1993

1681

SIONIS PRIORATUS
"PRIEURE DE SION"
In Hoc Signo Vinces
ooo

In Oriente Urbis Bletensis, ex tempore quintæ horæ Solis, 17mi Januarii I98I, per 92 adsistantes ex I2I partibus, Templo tecto, Conventus Priorati Sionis inceptus declaratus est.

Orator exponet:

PRIMO- Sub electione 22 Decembris 1963, Oriens Luteciæ, deminutio Conventus ad 72 adsistantes caruit effectu: 39 assensiones contra 35 non, erant inhabiles ad Dominen Priorati nominandum neque incaricandum.

SECUNDO- Iste creditus Dominus, via litteris suis publicis, ex tempore 23 Octobris I980 titulum suum muneraque sua ipse negavit; praeterea omisit præ scriptionem capitis XXII Constitutionis secundum qualem suum agendi modum probare debet.

TERTIO- Propter has causas, abbatus François DUCAUD - quoque DUCAUD-BOURGET, sacerdos ultra-catholicus, segregatus a Romæ Sancta Sede, materia vigilationis est.

QUARTO- Secundum vota Conventus, quatuor Fratres proponentur ad suffragium electionis Domini, quorum nomine sunt:

Tabella prima: Gaylord FREEMAN (U.S.A.)
Tabella secunda: Massimo SPADA (Italie)
Tabella tertia: Pierre PLANTARD de SAINT CLAIR (France)
Tabella quarta: Paul VAUCLAIR (Suisse)

Sub controversiam et emendationes usitatas, Conventus adoptat scripta quæ sequuntur.

DECRETUM I-

Suffragium 22 Decembris 1963, pro vitio Formæ, nullum est, Dominus sic electus de titulis et muneribus suis quæ sibi vindicat et negat amotus est. Radiatus est a Priorato Sionis.

(Suffragii:92 - Assensio per 91 contra 1 non)

DECRETUM II-

Jam nunc, Conventus ignorat et negat dispositiones jussaque quando hierint opera abbeti François DUCAUD, quoque DUCAUD-BOURGET, ultra-catholicus sacerdos.

(Suffragii:92 - Assensio per 87 contra 5 non)

DECRETUM III-

Sub Decreto I hodie adoptato, et sut Capitibus XV et XVI Constitutionis, Conventus Priorati Sionis pronuntiat effectus tabellerum electionis Domini:

Conversio Prima,

Tabella prima : Frater FREEMAN, assensio per 41 contra 51
Tabella secunda: Frater SPADA , assensio per 29 contra 63
Tabella tertia: Frater PLANTARD, assensio per 39 contra 53
Tabella quarta: Frater VAUCLAIR, assensio per 31 contra 61

Conversio Secunda,

Tabella prima : Frater FREEMAN , assensio per 44 contra 48
Tabella secunda: Frater PLANTARD, assensio per 47 contra 45

Conversio Tertia, Frater FREEMAN desistere,

Tabella prima : Frater PLANTARD, assensio per 83 contra 9

Ex tempore sextæ decimæ horæ Solis 17 Januarii I98I, in Oriente Urbis Bletensis, Frater Pierre PLANTARD de SAINT CLAIR electus est Dominus, et 27mus Nauta, sut nomine CHYREN.

Ex tempore septimæ decimæ horæ Solis Conventus sæptus dedaretus est.

Ego Secretarius generalis, in nomine Conventus testo de similitudine harum litterarum cum laboribus Concilii, et pono sigillum meum.

Pierre PLANTARD | Gaylord FREEMAN | John E. DRICK

EXEMPLAIRE A MONSIEUR CHAIMRII

1681

SIONIS PRIORATUS
"PRIEURE DE SION"
In Hoc Signo Vinces
ooo

Prieuré de Sion 1681

In Oriente Urbis Bletensis, ex tempore nonæ horæ Solis, 17mi Januarii 1981, per 92 adsistantes ex 121 partibus Conventus Priorati Sionis inceptus declaratus est.

Eligit coventus prœsidem concilii, secretarium, scribam et oratorem suos.

Sub controversiam et emendationem usitatas, abrogati sunt quatuor capiti antiquoe Constitutionis, secundum assensionem quorum jus suffragii habent, per 92 contra 0 non. Quibus capitis, secundum assensionem succedunt capiti sequentes.

CAPUT XIII- Conventus Sionis Priorati ipse per se judicabit de omni mùtatione constitutionis, ordinatonisque intériorœritus.
(Suffragii: 92 - Assensio per 91 contra 1 non)

CAPUT XIV- Omnis admissio decisa erit concilio tredecim Rosœ + Crucis.
Tituli muneraque à Domino Priorati tributi erunt.
Partes admissæ in Priorato retinent ejus optionem omne aetatis tempus.
Titulus cujusque partis revertitur pleno jure uno pruerorum ipsius quem nominaverit. Liber sic designatus suum jus abjicere potest; pro fratre, sorore, cognato neque quo circum eum sit non potest.
Abjiciens ullus nunquam in conventu restitutus erit.
(Suffragii: 92 - Assensio per 90 contra 2 non)

CAPUT XV- 27 diebus intermissis, duo Fratres, ut attingeant futurum impetratorem, percipeantque assensum suum, vel recusationem suam, mandati erunt.
Propter inopiam impetratoris hujus, recusatio cognita erit de jure post plenos 81 dies, sua sedes vacua judicata.
(Suffragii: 92 - Assensio per 86 contra 6 non)

CAPUT XVI- Ex jure hereditario titulus Monárchœ Priorati Sionis et munera pro ipsis juribus successori suo transmissibili erunt.
Cum Dominus de recto successore careret, debebit ad suam sedem providendam, electionem instaurare.
(Suffragii: 92 - Assensio per 83 contra 9 non)

Hora tertia decima Solis Concilium usque ad quintam decimam dismissum est.

Ego sectretarius generalis in nomine Conventus testo de similitudine harum litterarum cum laboribus concilii, et pono sigillum meum.

Gaylord Freeman　　A. Robert Abbou

Pierre Plantard　　John E. Drick

Prieuré de Sion - Secretariat -

EXEMPLAIRE A Mr. CHAUMEIL

40 - Minutes of the "Priory of Sion" in Latin
dated 17th January 1981

Prieuré de Sion

R C

N.

PARIS

Prieuré de Sion secrétariat général

A TOUS NOS Fr...,

Avec beaucoup de tristesse et d'émotion, nous avons reçu en cette soirée du 7 MARS 1989, l'annonce du décès de notre ancien Grand Maitre du PRIEURE de SION:

ROGER-PATRICE PELAT

à l'âge de soixante dix ans

démissionnaire de l'ORDRE depuis le 6 Février 1989. Il avait succédé à notre ancien Grand Maître , le Marquis Philippe de CHERISEY, lui aussi mort d'une embolie. Nous demandons à tous les initiés de l'ORDRE de bien vouloir observer une minute de silence à la mémoire de celui qui fut toujours un HOMME de l'ombre, parfaitement honnête et juste tombé sous les coups de certains "initiés" américains.

Après de nombreuses démarches et consultations, le PRIEURE de SION à demandé à notre ancien Grand Maître Pierre PLANTARD de SAINT CLAIR de reprendre la direction de l'ORDRE à dater du 9 MARS 1989, ceci dans les conditions suivantes

1- Les Frères de l'Ordre exclus par le Marquis de CHERISEY seront réintégrés.

2- L' article XIX et l'Article XXII des constitutions modifiés le 5 JUIN 1956 par le Grand Maître Jean COCTEAU seront annulés et l'ancien texte reprendra sa vigueur antérieure.

3- Les membres (de l'ORDRE) américains seront libres et indépendants, ils ne feront plus "intégration " dans le PRIEURE de SION qui restera exclusivement Europ...

Paris, 8 MARS 1989

Prieuré de Sion secrétariat général

41 - Circular from the Priory of Sion announcing the death of their Grand Master Roger-Patrice Pelat and reinstatement of Pierre Plantard de Saint Clair

Open Discussions With The Professionals

The Imposture Of The Priory Of Sion Related By Jean-Luc Chaumeil (JLC)

Interview carried out by Jean-Patrick Pourtal in the summer of 2001, published on the Internet at http://www.rennes-le-chateau.org in April 2002 under the title "Rennes-le-Château. Le Dossier!" (RLC-Le Dossier)

RLC-Le Dossier – 'Can you tell us how you became involved in the affair of Rennes-le-Château as a journalist and writer?'

JLC – 'Like a great many people at the time, I became interested in Rennes-le-Château after reading *L'Or de Rennes* (*The Gold of Rennes*) from Gérard de Sède, soon after its publication. Although I was prejudiced to start with, I knew that this story was not a joke. The story was mentioned to me again, later, when setting up the journal Europe. I have always been dubious about it and this suspicion has never left me. I had been given some hints about the discovery of a treasure in Rennes-le-Château and that the best pieces were kept in Geneva. Of course, with all the elements in my possession, the apocryphal documents in existence and the individuals around the story, I went to see Gérard de Sède. He was not the man portrayed to me; however, he was an excellent writer. During our encounter, he suggested that I meet the interested party number one. So, I was the first to interview Pierre Plantard. I refer to him this way as he was not using the epithet de Saint Clair yet. He was born on 18th March 1920, in Paris, and was the son of a manservant. For a while, I even thought of writing about *The Messiah and the Manservant's Son.*

RLC-Le Dossier – 'Astonishing lineage for the last Merovingian!"

JLC – 'Plantard had told me a few things. Amongst some of his tricks, I noticed that each time he came up with an essential piece of information there was no proof to corroborate it. Plantard emerged in this story as someone who had access to archives, since Gérard de Sède introduced him as a librarian, and also as a hermit who rented a room No. 35, avenue Victor Hugo, in Paris, although he maintained that it was a $60m^2$ apartment!'

RLC-Le Dossier – 'We noticed that he is mentioned as a librarian not only in *L'Or de Rennes* but also in another book of Gérard de Sède's entitled *Les Templiers sont parmi nous* (*The Templars are amongst us*), where he is also described as the well-known Hermetist.'

JLC – 'This is how Gérard de Sède introduces people. It is his storyteller side. He feels compelled to bring everything that will support his theory into the book; therefore, he will obviously exaggerate. When one reads *L'Or de Rennes*, one wonders why de Sède did not talk about the Priory of Sion. At the time, he did not believe in it at all. However, he thought it was good for the story and that is why he annexed some apocryphal documents. I immediately prepared a special issue of *Le Charivari* and had my first interview with Pierre Plantard, *Conversation with the Lost King*. My job as a journalist was to make him say as much as possible on the subject matter. Following that meeting, Claude Jacquemart and I had a few reservations about the individual's pretensions. We found his story attractive, nothing more. As far as the Priory of Sion is concerned, it goes without saying that it required a long investigation which meant going to Annemasse and acquiring the organisation's statutes, to realise at once, to be brief, that Plantard was not the president of the association, but that the post was held by a certain Mr. Bonhomme. I thought that "Bonhomme" was a pseudonym and meant "Cathar". Plantard was the treasurer of the Priory of Sion. It took me a while to locate this Pierre Bonhomme who explained to me that, in 1956, the association of the Priory of Sion, regulated by the law of 1901, was merely a non-profit-making organisation.'

RLC-Le Dossier – 'Which has nothing to do, in real terms, with what the Priory of Sion has become...?'

JLC – 'The Priory of Sion, in comparison with the statutes I published in *Le Charivari*, was an organisation responsible for the protection of the residents of council estates near Sion. That is all. It was an association of boy scouts; in fact, Plantard had been a Boy Scout leader, notably in Brittany. This is the association of the Priory of Sion as described by its President Pierre Bonhomme and Vice-President De Fagot. I thought that De Fagot was a pseudonym too. The association had some ecological functions other than the protection of residents of public sector housing. At a later date, I went to the Associations Office at the Police Headquarters. And there, surprise! I realised that the 1956 organisation was nothing but a third attempt to create the association. Before that, there was a cultural organisation which was called, if I remember correctly, La Rénovation Française (French Reform), whose president was Pierre Plantard's mother. There had also been an association called Alpha-Galates, with statutes written in German between 1942 and 1943.'

RLC-Le Dossier – 'You explain this also in your book *La Table d'Isis* (*The Table of Isis*).'

JLC – 'In that document there was a report from the security branch of the police force that was extremely clear, which stipulated that Plantard was just a visionary man who wanted to save France; who had declared some six thousand members whilst, in fact, they were only about ten, namely the committee members. The individuals who kept company with Plantard left him one after the other. As regards the Rénovation Française between 1940 and 1953, and other associations after 1956, we are dealing with small organisations only, very localised, and of no importance. Any pretension was purely in Plantard's head. I met with a third individual, the Marquis Philippe de Cherisey, whom I interviewed for *Le Charivari*. From real source material he had located, like Gérard de Sède, an abbey in Saint-Jean-le-Blanc, near Orleans, where monks had founded an entire chapter dedicated to Our Lady of Sion on their return from Jerusalem. Whilst it is true that there was once an organisation which had a rather similar trade description, it never had the importance of an occult society such as the "Hiéron du Val d'Or". One had tried to glue the pieces together in order to create a modern myth about a given work. Broadly speaking, the books of Gérard de Sède are just the text of Pierre Plantard's basic implement. If one examines Gérard de Sède's contracts with Julliard, publishers of *Les Templiers sont parmi nous* and *L'Or de Rennes*, one realises that the author has limited rights as a writer, and that Cherisey is more like the brain behind the document and the famous parchments from Father Saunière and Pierre Plantard is the ideas man, or the "Merlin" of the story. As these ideas had to be credible, there was a need for a specialist which he found in Gérard de Sède.'

RLC-Le Dossier – 'You've just said very hastily that Philippe de Cherisey was the creator and author of the documents and parchments, which caused so much ink to flow in the affair and which contemporary authors relied upon for their books...'

JLC – 'In order to settle this matter, I wrote about it in journals and talked about it in a programme on the BBC in 1997. It did not make any difference!'

RLC-Le Dossier – 'In fact, I think very few people know about this programme...'

JLC – 'It is true that few people know about it. There were protestations, but congratulations too. In the course of the programme, I showed the parchments...'

RLC-Le Dossier – 'So, you have the parchments?'

JLC – 'I have the parchments and I presented them, together with seven or eight fundamental key points proving that the facts concerning the treasure story of Father Saunière, the multimillionaire parish priest, were false. The parchments are forged and I showed them to the BBC. The way they have been construed and their encoding are explained in a document entitled *Pierre et Papier* (*Stone and Paper*). I described how Philippe de Cherisey encoded the text which he had copied in a religious section at the National Library in Paris, and I showed a page of his manuscript *Pierre et Papier*.'

RLC-Le Dossier – 'Was Philippe de Cherisey really versed in cryptography?'

JLC – 'For me, he is the brain behind the story; a brain, however, that cannot make use of history. Therefore, he is a librarian. He is an outstanding individual. I met him in Liège. In a very cautious way, he was part of the scheme, the literary side of it. I saw him make a scene of jealousy when Plantard announced loudly a session of the Priory of Sion, to which Philippe de Cherisey had not been invited!'

RLC-Le Dossier – 'One realises that this whole machination in the sixties was extremely well thought through and fabricated.'

JLC – 'Something both interested and fascinated me, namely, how an outstandingly erudite mind, with a phenomenal culture, was capable of doing genealogies of the Merovingian kings? It is hard enough to obtain documents about the Templars, let alone the Merovingians... One knows that eighty per cent of the charters are false. The forgery of official charters was a mania at the time. How can one perform such a colossal task under the label of the young Merovingian kings? That again required a lot of time; a lot of time to understand a simple thing, that this is the story of two friends. In my book *Le Trésor du Triangle d'Or* (*The Treasure of the Golden Triangle*), there is a photograph of Philippe de Cherisey, about thirty years old, with Plantard, a little older. They are at the entrance of a cave, and God knows how many there are in the region. It is the story of two friends. However, the problem is that one is a marquis, the Marquis Philippe de Cherisey, with umpteen degrees of noble lineage, when the other one is simply called Plantard and is the son of a manservant. Maybe, it is the jealousy of one against the fall of the other that led to what followed. Only one person benefited, namely the storyteller Gérard de Sède.'

RLC-Le Dossier – 'One notices that the story of Rennes-le-Château went through a "slack period"; but, in the 1980s, three new authors emerged. They were all anglophones, Michael Baigent, Richard Leigh and Henry Lincoln. In 1982, they co-authored *The Holy Blood and the Holy Grail* (*L'énigme sacrée* in

French) and revived the whole affair. I believe that, nowadays, everybody works on the basis of their information, which may not be the best at all. What do you think?'

JLC – 'I only have a bad opinion about it and may not be objective. For the French, it is evident that the essential points concerning the story of Rennes, as well as Gisors and Stenay, had been revealed at the end of the eighties. One day, I received the visit from Henry Lincoln, Michael Baigent and Richard Leigh. We had been introduced through a British lady called Jania Macgillivray, who wrote a ten-page document, published worldwide, about everything I had done. In fact, what the three Anglophones wanted was to get in touch with Pierre Plantard. Their objective was to develop a new ploy for the Anglo-Saxon and American public. They knew that I, as well as Gérard de Sède, had written quite a lot on the subject. We were contacted in turn. These people were brought together during the preparation of two documentaries, of poor quality it must be said. Their Ariadne's thread was the pentagram in Poussin's painting. We knew very well that the Bergers d'Arcadie (Shepherds of Arcadia) were not near Arques. Yet that was one of the points to be checked. We were aware that some treasure hunters had had the good taste to open the tomb, which displeased the owner of the land deeply and prompted him to erase the grave. If the tomb was so important, I would assume that Jack Lang's Ministry for the Preservation of Historic Monuments at the time would have vetoed that formally.

So, we all met in a very epic manner. There were quite a few of us. On the French side, there was Pierre Plantard, one of my readers in the name of Gino Sandri, and two editors from Belfond called Jean-Pierre Deloux and Jacques Brétigny. On the English side, there was the librarian Jania Macgillivray, Henry Lincoln, who worked for the BBC at the time, the American novelist Richard Leigh, and the Australian Michael Baigent, also a librarian. The film producer Roy David and the president of the Encres Européennes (European Inks) were there too. We found ourselves in a private film theatre on the Champs Elysées in Paris. Plantard believed in a very slow and progressive approach, so as to know exactly what they wanted. The theatre was fabulous; I had never seen anything like it! When the French group, to which I belonged, arrived, it was as if we were in the Mafia; everybody was suspicious, everybody checked their seats, everybody touched their jacket at the same place...

There was a memorable incident. Richard Leigh, who bore a blazon with the Hapsburg's medallion, came to Plantard and said "Good day, Majesty". At that moment, he slipped on a step and collapsed miserably. The atmosphere was a little more relaxed after that.

I read their books and I am mentioned in them one hundred and fifty three times. In the first book, *The Holy Blood and the Holy Grail*, I am described as a very kind person; in their second work, *The Messianic Legacy*, I am brandished as a bad person after having criticised them on several radio channels and in newspaper articles; and in the last book, *Key to the Sacred Pattern: The Untold Story of Rennes-le-Château*, by Henry Lincoln, I appeared even nastier. I am accused of being jealous for not participating in the programme in which Plantard was interviewed. And yet, I had lent my mother's art gallery for a shooting session with Plantard.'

RLC-Le Dossier – 'Is this the famous scene on the tape of *Le secret des Templiers* (*The Templars' Secret*) where we see Plantard answering a few questions from Henry Lincoln?'

JLC – 'Yes! It was worthy of a scene from "Tartuffe", when, at some point, Henry Lincoln got worked up and one sensed that he was after some key element. He asked Plantard, "But, why are the Merovingian kings important in the twentieth century?" He was trying to trap his interlocutor. At the time, Plantard was wearing a little grey suit of the 1930s; he spoke very slowly, as he had very bad diction and phrasing with a peasant accent. He paused... There was a lull and then he replied, "But, don't you know that the Merovingians created France?" Everything had been said! Of course, Lincoln, who for the last half hour had been struggling to make him say something else, was dumbfounded and did not dare ask any other questions. In the film, we see very little of the interview with Plantard. Each take was repeated at least thirty times and the shooting lasted some eighteen hours!

My mother's gallery is a surrealist one and the debate that took place in it was even more surreal. Perpignan's station was transformed into Rennes-le-Château station by Pierre Plantard.

Contrary to general belief, the anglophones did not invent anything in this affair. But they had the intelligence to say that Jesus had married Mary-Magdalene, that she had had children and that these were Merovingians! And that, so far as the Merovingian descendants were concerned, they had one in front of their eyes in the person of Pierre Plantard. Thus, it fitted exactly the Anglo-Saxon and American state of mind. Whilst, for about ninety percent of the population, the French have been atheists for a very long time and they couldn't care less about the story of Jesus...'

RLC-Le Dossier – 'Somehow, was there a notion of business in the Anglo-Saxon countries as they were not really affected by the problem of Rennes-le-Château?'

JLC – 'It is possible that Henry Lincoln was manipulated by the producer, who himself was the plaything of other people. If one could sense the best-seller at a financial level, others had different ambitions. A month before the publication of *The Holy Blood and the Holy Grail*, a great number of London buses displayed posters regarding Jesus true story! The manipulation was obvious! But, who was the manipulator? Who paid for these posters? It was not Henry Lincoln, nor Richard Leigh! At that time, there were not very well known. It was someone else...'

RLC-Le Dossier – 'Was this a real marketing operation?'

JLC – 'It was a marketing operation and an operation of religious propaganda! I have never seen posters for a French book on Parisian buses one month prior to its publication. No publisher would use this type of publicity. You should read the conclusion of *The Holy Blood and the Holy Grail*, which could be summarised as, "There was indeed the Ayatollah Khomeini; could Plantard be the French Ayatollah Khomeini?"

I think Plantard was manipulated. He even said so on the television channel France-Inter. Like all manipulated individuals, he felt flattered by this story and, of course, continued to play the game. In other words, the Anglophone story aside, being a recent affair, one witnessed the pure creation of a modern myth. In his 1982 book, *Rennes-le-Château, la colline envoûtée* (*Rennes-le-Château, the Haunted Hill*), Jean Robin described the affair of Rennes-le-Château as "mythological". René Descadeillas, the librarian in Carcassonne, expressed this view too in his 1974 book *Mythologie du Trésor de Rennes* (*Mythology of the Treasure of Rennes*). But his case is particular, as he carried out some excavations... Having performed the excavations himself, his writing of a mythological book about Rennes-le-Château was not credible any more.'

RLC-Le Dossier – 'Now we know for certain that Pierre Plantard is dead; it is official. We have proofs of it. Of course, the date was much debated. It is surprising to see that, since Plantard's death, a lot of things are stirring in Rennes-le-Château. For the moment, we are witnessing a huge media operation on various subjects. What do you think about all this?'

JLC – 'I believe that a similar media operation had already taken place around Mr. Léon Fontan, the engineer from Strasbourg, and another one at the time of Mr. Henri Buthion and his first team of researchers. Alain Châtillon wanted some reprieve in order to continue his excavations with Robert Charroux. There would be quite a lot to tell, notably about the former treasure hunters. However, that is another matter; but it is true that the modern affair, that is today's affair, is a repetition. The "Story of the Magdala tower", with its underground gallery and treasure hideout, is not new. You can find it in the newspaper *La Dépêche du Midi* from the 1960s, in 1970, in 1972, with engineers from Mossad wanting to recover the Ark of the Covenant, and in 1974. You will find it too in my quarterly journal *Le Charivari* and in all five editions of *Le Trésor des Templiers* (*The Templars' Treasure*). None of this is new. It has to be said too that, by a stroke of luck, all this is happening during the festive season... It is shady. "Nessie" (the monster of the Loch Ness) comes back, as well as the flying saucers and the Templars' treasure... It is true that, since the publication of the book by the anglophones, there have been some spectacular commercial operations; for instance, there was the "Rennes Tour" which brought hundreds of anglophones to France, not to see Paris, but to visit Rennes-le-Château and, at a pinch, Montségur. I say "at a pinch", since in fact the purpose of their visit was Rennes-le-Château. Why? This is somewhat linked to what was said previously as there were many books which went further than Lincoln's. Some said that it was the tomb of Christ, even the "Tomb of God". So, it is normal that a myth becomes a castle in the air and that, at that moment, there is extrapolation. Now, since the beginning of the century, everything that is spiritual is systematically crystallised and materialised... I am thinking about the black-cover collection of Robert Laffont and the J'ai Lu series that followed, where the same theme appears systematically. One materialises a spiritual idea. I think that by hitting at the top, namely at the Christ-God level, and talking more about materialist mystic hills, the anglophones have achieved an amazing commercial operation which corresponded to the spirit of the time, the spirit of a certain decadence; because from the moment one inverts ideas, there is decadence, real decadence.'

∴

Interview carried out by Johan Netchacovitch in December 2003, published on the Internet at http://www.portail-rennes-le-chateau.com in January 2004 on the web page Gazette et Portail de Rennes-le-Château. (GP-RLC)

GP-RLC – 'Jean-Luc Chaumeil, can you please introduce yourself to the readers of the *Gazette*.'

JLC – 'I was born on 20th October 1944, in Lille, at the end of a never-ending war. Ninety years earlier, the French poet Arthur Rimbaud, the god of my childhood, was getting ready to try a new style when he wrote on the walls of Charleville, "Merde à Dieu" (To hell with God). This did not prevent him, at the end of his life, from returning to the generous glimpse of Eternity, after discovering the queen of Ethiopia.

The philosopher Nietzsche, who was greatly misunderstood, added the notion of "the death of God" to Rimbaud's prophecies. The twentieth century was going to confirm these two prophecies by a third one, "the dead man" around Rennes-le-Château. In less than a century, we had all become orphans, real children of the widow or Reine du Midi (Freemasonry). The survivors, as well as the newcomers, were advised to take particular notice of these three notions.

It is within this context, or new delta of a "terra incognita", that several new religions attached themselves to the "Mythology of Rennes-le-Château"!'

GP-RLC – 'What do you retain from your youth in the castle of Taillefer in the Quercy region?'

JLC – 'I was just five years old when I experienced my first initiation with the elements; on a very thundery afternoon, I started to sweat and shiver in turn, and took refuge under a tree. From the second floor, my mother was watching my comings and goings whilst looking at the sky. A blinding flash of lightning opened the gates of the storm clouds and I received lightning like a gift from Heaven! One wanted to assassinate me already! Terrorised by the incident, and somewhat dazed, I took shelter under the roof of a barn. My mother came down the two floors in three seconds, and rushed to take me in her arms and verify that I was not a pile of ashes! After that, I saw the universe through a different angle; one had to be quick since the thread of life was fine, fragile, uncertain...

I started to read all the banned books in my father's library, when I became initiated to submarine war in twenty-four volumes.

Then adolescence came together with an extraordinary dialogue with the invisible at the castle of Taillefer and in Carennac, the village of my origins. An old sorcerer, teacher by trade, who had been living in Africa, practised the art of magic with bees. Worshipful Grand Master of an obedience, he taught me the subtle relation between the different worlds through the secret teaching of the analogical methods. From that time on, I had a manifold approach for each situation or given event, sometimes contradictory, but always enriching.

Aged eighteen, I started as a journalist and worked for various daily and weekly magazines. My first theatre play, *Béryl ou la Transparence* (*Beryl or Transparency*) was never performed, except in true life since my second daughter bears that name. A few of my poems from that period were published in 1981 in a book entitled *Apocalypse*, where I had predicted, amongst other things, the attack of 11th September 2001. Of course, nobody had noticed this prior to the event...'

GP-RLC – 'As a "reporter of the invisible", when and how did you discover the enigma of Rennes-le-Château?'

JLC – 'Painter or poet when the fancy takes me, journalist to earn a living, I very quickly made the acquaintance of Daniel Réju who asked me to write some articles for his journal *L'Ere d'Aquarius* (*The Era of Aquarius*). I worked also for the first European weekly journal Europe and was preparing a press review for the executives of a motorway company. Shortly before my divorce, as I married too young, a young writer called Claude Pimont, author of *Dieu n'existe pas, je l'ai rencontré* (*God does not exist, I met him*), in the company of Mr. Renard, a friend of Mr. Réju, spoke to me about *L'Or de Rennes* (*The Gold of Rennes*), a book about the story of a parish priest who, apparently, had discovered "billions" in the South of France! The book was from Gérard de Sède, author of another work entitled *Les Templiers sont parmi nous* (*The Templars are amongst us*), lent to my father by a police inspector and which I had read very attentively.

Knowing the story of Gisors, which I had previously come across, I was suspicious about *L'Or de Rennes*, and rightly so a priori... So, I preferred Arsène Lupin and the story of Etretat, especially after having read *Le Secret des Rois de France* from Valère Catogan and admired the painting L'Aiguille Creuse by Claude Monet. Let us not forget that I had carried out excavations in Taillefer after reading *Les Templiers sont parmi nous*. By way of a treasure, I had found a nest of vipers, very real, and quite clearly a world with a more interesting universe waiting to be discovered. I understood very early that it was always the same story and that the solution was not to discover such or such a treasure, but to see the man and the invisible, the "Other" of Rimbaud [poem where he says "I" is "another"], or the superman of Nietzsche. The hidden identity which makes fun of us and acts consciously to make us understand that through the game of discovery, there is another reality, very tangible, which concerns us personally. This is my definition of the "reporter of the invisible" and the process of a collective initiation, providing fixation on the gold is greatly dispelled.

In 1971, I read *Le Trésor Maudit de Rennes-le-Château* (*Accursed Treasure of Rennes-le-Château*), a hardly improved version of *L'Or de Rennes*. Claude Jacquemart, my chief editor, entrusted me with the writing of a thematic issue of *Le Charivari*, entitled *Les Archives du Prieuré de Sion* (*The Archives of the Priory of Sion*) republished by Pégase in 2006. Daniel Réju gave me Plantard's telephone number and I also met with Gérard de Sède, rue Damrémont. Also at that time, Mathieu Paoli, a friend of the Romanian writer Doru Todericiu, better known to the readers under the name Pierre Carnac, began a film for the television channel TSR about Arginy and Rennes-le-Château.

At the very beginning of 1972, I went on a mission to Rennes-le-Château with the photographer Bernard Roy.'

GP-RLC – 'What were your first impressions when you arrived in Rennes-le-Château?'

JLC – 'The trip took all night; the train arrived in Carcassonne and the railcar took us to Couiza. There were no taxis; and no cars, so hitch hiking was out of the question. We left on foot, gazing heavenwards in the direction of Rennes-le-Château. It was up there, in the early morning mist; I held my old Remco tape recorder very tightly against my chest, wiping it every now and then as the dew lingered on the leather.

After an intoxicating ascent, the photographer took shot after shot of the set and a picture of me in front of a sign reading "Fouilles interdites" (Excavations forbidden). Whilst passing in front of the castle belonging to a Mr. Henri Fatin, I thought about the maps of Marius, his father, who had devoted himself to the "hieroglyphics" of toponyms, souvenir of Piri Reis and Opicinus de Canistris! When we arrived at the foot of the Tower Magdala, its small size disappointed me and Bernard zoomed in on it to make it look bigger.'

GP-RLC – 'The previous owner of the parish priest's domain, Mr. Henri Buthion, was often described as an enigmatic person who liked to create a halo of mystery around him. How did he appear to you?'

JLC – 'Mr. Buthion stared down at us in a good-natured manner; he resembled Louis de Funès with his half smile and clasping his hands together endlessly. He lodged us on the top floor of the villa Bethania and offered us a coffee. I asked if I could take photographs in the church, but Mr. Buthion refused, saying that one needed an authorisation from the diocese. Our host was suspicious and pensive.

Then, we retreated to our bedroom, leaving a message on the tape recorder which related these two incidents, knowing very well that he would come to listen to them. Before leaving for Rennes-les-Bains, I opened a skylight to scrape a tile whilst remembering a text of the Marquis Philippe de Cherisey [see Appendix III], a friend of the Marquis de B..., the dentist Paul Rouelle [author of *Rennes-le-Château, an apocalypse story*, top secret in 2003, republished in 2006], and Mr. Nauvalerts; three princes of the Rosicrucian brotherhood in the pleasant city of Liège. Second disappointment, the roof tile was indeed from the neighbouring mine and nobody had painted it to hide its golden glint.

Using the long way round down to Rennes-les-Bains, we were seized with uncontrollable laughter when thinking about the divine marquis. We knew he was tenacious, stubborn, almost tender, and capable of sending us on trails at the end of which he himself had faced a closed door. We were warned and yet, since that was the direction of the quest, we had to continue. In Rennes-les-Bains, the painting of the Christ au Lièvre (Christ with the Hare) by Doctor Paul Rouelle, left us flabbergasted and a tiny bit derisive. On foot still, for the second time, we were following the way of the Golgotha, with the sensation of being somewhere else, in another place, tiredness contributing to this feeling at the end of a physically exhausting day.

There was a surprise for us at the top. Mr. Buthion had organised a feast and gave us the keys to the church for us to take our photographs, whilst following us, of course, on the pretext of his evening prayer. Under multiple flashlights, he unclasped his hands from time to time so as to grasp the meaning of our strategic photography. The third disappointment for us was that the photographs did not match Gérard de Sède's description. Invited to Mr. Buthion's table, we were taken for emissaries of the Priory of Sion and were introduced to the entire family, extremely welcoming, and a friend, Mr. André Varache, a highly skilled researcher.

The next day, our host took us in his car to the Bézu area to see the Visigothic herringbone stone vestiges, to the menhir of the three treasures called Pierre Droite de Peyrolles (The Standing Stone of Peyrolles) and to the tomb of Arques, commenting, without respite, on the various places we went through.'

GP-RLC – 'Then you followed in the footsteps of the inventors of history. How did you apprehend them?'

JLC – 'We visited the jet mines, which Pierre Plantard and Philippe de Cherisey had already searched, alone. The revelation occurred at the Pierre du Dé (Stone of the Dice); something fundamental gave us the impression once more that things were happening elsewhere, in another setting. Symbolically, the dice represents the seven gates, as well as the four minor holy orders and three major holy orders. It was no more a disappointment, but a strange certainty that reminded me of Gérard de Sède's warning, "Any similarity between the facts mentioned in this book and an hypothetical interpretation is pure coincidence. It is nonetheless strange, since the resemblance is striking." These first conclusions on the first page gave me the intimate conviction that Plantard, de Cherisey and Gérard de Sède were unusual but very genuine researchers. They were definitely trying to pretend that they knew the answer in order to attract real information to them, each in their own manner to become the lord of the place; but, as for Gisors, they had excavated almost everywhere before publishing, in the same way that I had scraped the tile at the villa Bethania. This is the first mistake that could bring many more with it! In other words, in an hypothetical interpretation, one should make a distinction between myth, symbol and reality, namely history. One must therefore make a choice after having examined the three facets of this conceptual dice in detail. This was our approach which we refined afterwards.'

GP-RLC – 'In your book, you mention several trios. Could you be more specific?'

JLC – 'Quite! The first threesome comprises Father Saunière, Marie Denarnaud, and Noël Corbu. The second includes Plantard, de Cherisey and de Sède.'

GP-RLC – 'Why do you present the second trio as the "Three Musketeers"?'

JLC – 'After many telephone conversations, I met Athos, namely Pierre Plantard. There were thousands of questions; however, the responses were allusive, and irritating on more than one account. He was a pleasant individual with a great sense of humour; however, he was a little bit of a crank. He resembled Joan of Arc in a 1930 suit, the Matrix "Hero in Black" originating from present times, his pockets full of documents, as if handy in advance. But I knew that he had been a sexton and clairvoyant when he officiated at Aulnay-sous-Bois under the name of "Chyren". Not only did he believe in his edicts, but he uttered prophecies by the dozen. I listened and wrote things down, aware sometimes of what was true and what was false. I did this for twelve years, amused but not duped. Plantard had the imagination that was missing in Gérard de Sède, whilst Philippe de Cherisey had fourteen degrees of noble lineage that Plantard was lacking. You know the rest; he became the "Lost King". My first interview with him was published in Issue No. 18 of *Le Charivari*, reiterated in *Le Triangle d'Or*, and confirmed in *Le Trésor des Templiers*. One day, Plantard, with a wink, offered me a basketful of bread; it came from a bakery in Colombes. Whilst giving me the large basket, he added seriously, "One day, you will be Prime Minister!" This is the kind of disconcerting remark he could fire! That day I did not dare ask him if he meant that of the "cult" since, having been with him in the church of Saint-Sulpice, I knew that his regrets as a former sexton were bordering exasperation. This is Plantard's secret and the only one...

He had become an atheist and regretted this. In Saint-Sulpice, for example, he spoke loudly and strongly when he saw a priest, which provoked an incident. He would add seriously, "Each time, it is the same..." This way, he transformed the Chapel of the Angels into a treasure map and Saint Peter, with his two keys, into a messenger pointing towards the crypt Notre Dame Sous Terre (Our Lady Underground) with its pagan Temple of Artemis. Plantard practised what we call today historic revisionism, centred round the Merovingian legitimacy.'

GP-RLC – 'What do you know about Gérard de Sède and how was he able to publish the famous parchments?'

JLC – 'Gérard de Sède, his real name being Géraud de Liéoux de Sède, was Pierre Plantard and Philippe de Cherisey's prime companion in the affair of Gisors. I went to see him in order to understand Plantard better as well as to show him a number of photographs of Visigothic jewels, which we will talk about within the context of the affair concerning Mathieu Paoli and Doru Todericiu.

His wife called him "Teddy Bear" and, despite his grumbling manner and imperturbable logic, he was like a child, fond of stories and fairy tales. First of all, I asked him when he had knowledge of the parchments. He told me that he had received them through the post! I did not insist, but saw in his side glance, that the question embarrassed him. Later, we shared information; then he mentioned he wanted to write a book with me [The book entitled *La clef des deux énigmes, Gisors et Rennes-le-Château* was never published].'

GP-RLC – 'Besides Rennes-le-Château, were you investigating Gisors as well?'

JLC – 'Correct. I had discovered two things. Firstly, that the chapel Saint-Catherine of Gisors had been built in 1530 by the

Lords of Flavacourt and that it was next to the Saint-Gervais church in Gisors. Secondly, in an old book of the late nineteeth century, I found an old legendary tale concerning François II, son of Catherine de Medici, who had been imprisoned in Gisors; all in all, a lost king.'

GP-RLC – 'It was at that time that an individual appeared whose role is still quite obscure today...'

JLC – 'You are referring to Mathieu Paoli, who appropriated a number of records from me concerning Madeleine Blancasall, Henri Lobineau and Serge Roux, in order to include them in his book published by Belfond, to finally land in Switzerland.

Mathieu Paoli, his real name being Ludwig Scheswig, was a strange person who was using people to achieve some hidden ends. Friend of Pierre Carnac, his real name being Doru Todericiu, he was trying to identify a large perforated plate, of Visigothic origin, that he had seen in the hands of an American archaeologist called Paterson, a great friend of the Countess de Goguë, in close contact with the Countess de Pierrefeu, a specialist concerning the Cathars.

After having interviewed Ferdinand Niel and met with Déodat Roché, who spoke about angels in an extraordinary manner, I left for Geneva in the hope of meeting the Countess de Pierrefeu and Professor Paterson. It is there that I was authorised to visit a magnificent crypt [mentioned in the first section of this book]. Back in Paris, I found some negatives that had been slid under the door at my domicile and which I had authenticated at the Museum of Saint-Germain en Laye. Apart from the perforated dish, the photographs slipped under my door by Paoli were all replicas of a treasure in Petroassa, according to Professor M. Duval. Later, thanks to Doru Todericiu, we found out that Mathieu Paoli had tried to play the role of a secret agent in Israel by playing a double game with the Egyptians. Supposedly, he was shot dead! Nevertheless, the enigma of the "perforated plate" remains as it not mentioned anywhere else!'

GP-RLC – 'Philippe de Cherisey occupied a special place in the trio. What role did he play?'

JLC – 'After Athos, we find ourselves with Aramis, namely the Marquis Philippe de Cherisey, gentleman and actor, inveterate drinker, knight of the Round Table and member of the Cincinnati, whose testimony can be found in the famous document *Pierre et Papier* (*Stone and Paper*) that he made me promise to publish twenty years after his death. I must admit that I shed more than one tear, in August 1985, for this man who had found the secret of death thanks to his sword Excalibur. In fact, it is to him that this book is dedicated, together with Daniel Réju and Moreau de Valdan, the great druid of the Ligurian brotherhood. Philippe was a very elegant man, careful about his appearance, a great erudite and an expert swordsman in a debate.

But he had a tendency to overdo it, swept by his passion and his gargantuan verve. This is how I learned, in one of his letters, that I had discovered the secret in the valley of the crosses, or Rennes-les-Bains. He nicknamed Plantard, Basil, after the Greek patriarch; with him, he carried out excavations in Gisors, in the cellars of Mrs. Breton where they had found tons of dung in place of the Templars' treasure, and in the region of Rennes-le-Château, notably near the Magdalene's headspring. At my mother's, he was meant to intervene within the context of the Priory of Sion but Plantard refused, sensing danger. What a shame! *The Holy Blood and the Holy Grail* might not have been published. In early January 1981, dumbfounded by the audacity of his master, Philippe de Cherisey expected to come to Blois, but in vain. Plantard had not invited him and for a very good reason... Plantard never left Colombes. I tailed him, and my hideaway, although uncomfortable, was very effective. For Cherisey, it was over, even if later he received a few symbolical crumbs for which he was never duped. As for Plantard, offended at Philippe's American friendships, he did not go to his burial. For a while, Plantard, who had been cheated and exploited by the anglophones and made to do a U-turn after the affair Pelat, gave up his pranks which some well-intentioned people took up later.'

GP-RLC – 'From the time of the aforementioned trio, only Gino Sandri is still alive. In which circumstances did you meet him and what was his role in the Priory of Sion?'

JLC – 'I have known Gino Sandri for a good quarter of a century. He has not changed and I consider him as the Poulidor [Poulidor was a racing cyclist that never won and always came second] of esotericism. I did say that I met him simply as a reader who wanted to meet Pierre Plantard at all costs. This was a done-deed during the filming of the BBC programme in my mother's gallery, 10, rue du Roi de Sicile. At that time, he introduced himself as "Secretary to Mr. Canseliet". He swore by "Fulcanelli", criticising Julien Champagne, whilst Robert Amadou and many others knew that this pseudonym was the work of a high-ranking college in Royal Art.'

GP-RLC – 'What would be your final recommendation in apprehending the story of Rennes-le-Château?'

JLC – 'As far as the place is concerned, one cannot understand the story of Rennes-le-Château without examining the hidden side of the affair of Gisors, such as the scheme involving the discovery of the *Dead Sea Scrolls* and, in particular, the famous copper roll of Qumran, restored recently by E.D.F. (the French Electricity Board), which indicates the hiding places of the treasure of Solomon.'

∴

Interview carried out by Louis Benedict and broadcasted by Sud Radio (SR) on Sunday 14th May 2006 upon the release of the film "The Da Vinci Code".

SR – 'Mr. Chaumeil, have you read *The Da Vinci Code*?'

JLC – 'Of course, I have. I even read it in English when a copy of the book was sent to me. I then read the French translation.'

SR – 'You knew Pierre Plantard. In 1983, he was subjected to a search of his home concerning a pamphlet in which he announced the death of Roger-Patrice Pelat, Grand Master of the Priory of Sion. Can one say that this move dealt a fatal blow to the whole story?'

JLC – 'Oh, it was already over before the search-warrant from Judge Jean-Pierre, who, at the time, was conducting the investigation in the Urba-Gracco affair, but it looks as though Plantard misjudged the consequences. Roger-Patrice Pelat was unable to protest about the imputations attributed to him. The report of Judge Jean-Pierre, with a passage [1] regarding the search at Plantard's, was published in *Le Point* (Issue No. 1112, 8-14 January 1994). At his home, police inspectors found a great number of stamps, some of them with the imprint of the Priory of Sion, and headed notepapers - in brief, a lot of material to produce the fakes that we know about.

Afterwards, Plantard enacted his resignation from the Priory of Sion. In fact, he resigned from an organisation that did not exist.'

SR – 'The web that you managed to untangle by means of patient investigations enabled you to uncover the personality of Pierre Plantard.'

JLC – 'To start with, he was a man who believed in God. Pierre Plantard wanted to be a priest; in fact, he was only sexton at the parish of Saint-Louis d'Antin in Paris. He had a strong taste for pseudonyms. Initially, he called himself Pierre de France, which speaks volumes about his megalomania. At the very beginning, he dispatched leaflets in Brittany under the assumed name Varran de Verestra.

He also had the bad habit of referring to individuals of a certain intellectual or political repute. But on simple verification, one realised that all these people were dead.

Between 1939 and 1945, he founded all sorts of associations, such as the Alpha-Galates, the Knights of the Light, and the Latin Academy, but none lasted more than a few months. Whilst France was occupied, he wrote to Marshal Pétain to denounce a Judeo-Masonic plot! This earned him a series of reports from the

General Inquiries office in which Pierre Plantard was considered a crank. In fact, the individual was not taken into consideration.'

SR – 'Is this how the Priory of Sion was created?'

JLC – 'This association was created in 1956 and its statutes registered at the sub-prefecture of Saint-Julien en Genevois. The term Sion relates to a mountain of that name between Annemasse and Geneva. This association, regulated by the law of 1901, was meant to protect the interests of the tenants of a council estate where Plantard lived. For instance, each member had the possibility to send their children on holiday in Plestin-les-Grèves, in Brittany. So, we are a long way from a secret organisation that goes back to Godefroy de Bouillon!

One can only understand Plantard in connection with two other individuals; between them they will form an explosive trio. One of them is Philippe de Cherisey. He has fourteen degrees of lineage and belongs to a surrealist movement called Oulipo. In front of him, Plantard feels at a loss; hence, the pseudonym Pierre de France. This is how he functions, "you are a marquis indeed, but I am king!"

In 1947, the press headlines are all about the discovery of the manuscripts of Qumran. Plantard follows this epic very attentively. In 1952, the information on the front page of the Figaro reads "the copper roll of Qumran reveals the presence of two hundred tons of gold buried in Palestine!" It is here that the affair of Gisors begins to take root, with its mysterious manuscripts and hidden gold.

In 1960, we have the encounter with Gérard de Sède. Thanks to the "fake" documents that Plantard gives him, our man writes Les Templiers sont parmi nous. We know the rest. Local archaeologists rebel and the 12th Military Engineers sent by Malraux start drillings all the way to the phreatic water. Result: nothing.

Soon, one discovers that the famous Saint-Catherine's chapel, so fiercely sought-after, was never under the mound supporting the donjon, but that it well and truly existed in the vicinity of the northern portal of the church of Gisors and was built in 1530 by the Lords of Fouilleuse de Flavacourt.

At the sight of the collapsing myth, Plantard delocalises this story and transfers it to Rennes-le-Château, which is becoming a topic of conversation. It is always the same scenario. One attracts people with the hypothesis and notion of a treasure; that of a whimsical parish priest turning everything into cash and whose superior is a bishop who experienced problems with the judiciary over the embezzlement of a heritage.

The game is surreal, as in Gisors. One knows that the surrealists had to perform a militant action. With this in mind, one can quote the UFO affair of 1965 regarding the planet Ummo. At that time, the writer Fernando Sesma frequented a smart café in Madrid called La Ballena Alegra. Straightaway, he put out the idea of extraterrestrial messages and letters sent by Ummites (the aliens from the planet Ummo). Antonio Ribeira took responsibility for this story and added a few developments. The French physician Jean-Pierre Petit, former director of CNRS (SRC) did the same and wrote a book on the subject matter, *Enquête sur les extraterrestres qui sont parmi nous* (*Investigation about the extraterrestrials amongst us*) published by Albin Michel in 1991, on the strength of Ummites' letters that Rafael Farriols entrusted to him, without realising that they contained Spanish-sounding spelling mistakes.

The affair that concerns us is a surrealist game which consists of transferring a true story in a different context. When it does not work anymore, it is transposed somewhere else. It is true that at that time one does not talk about Jesus or Mary Magdalene yet.

At the end of the seventies, I received the visit of a British freelance journalist in the name of Jania Macgillivray, who wished to work full time for the BBC. This was also when she made the acquaintance of Lincoln [2], a scriptwriter, film director and actor for the television. Thanks to her, he was able to meet Pierre Plantard through me. He had read Gérard de Sède's book and wished to shoot a film around the enigma of Rennes-le-Château. However, when Lincoln prepared his documentary, he knew very well that the whole affair was simply a series of fabrications, a transposed story. He was fully aware that the Priory of Sion was a hoax.

Yet, in 1982, he published *The Holy Blood and the Holy Grail* with Baigent and Leigh. And then, to one's stupefaction, the Merovingians became the descendants of Christ, simply because Sir Thomas Malory, a English author of the fifteenth century, committed an error of interpretation in his work *Le Morte d'Arthur* where he mixed up Saint-Graal (Holy Grail) with Sang Greal, or Sang Royal, (Holy Blood). As for the marriage story between Jesus and Mary Magdalene, this was an old idea introduced by an Austrian clergyman in 1850. The astuteness was to associate all this to the Merovingians.

Pierre Plantard was astounded. When interviewed by Jacques Pradel in February 1982, he protested by saying, "Yes, the Anglophone gentlemen have written a novel where they say I am a descendant of Jesus. It is a joke!"

But Lincoln and company repeated their offence in the *The Messianic Legacy* and the *The Holy Place*, where the scenario was taken up again and embellished.'

SR – 'Admittedly, this story has known various sudden developments.'

JLC – 'In fact, one could say that there were two "Priory of Sion". The first, with the trio Plantard, de Cherisey, de Sède, was a surrealist game, taken a bit far, it is true. The second, with the threesome Baigent, Leigh and Lincoln, distorted the spirit of the first one entirely with a descendant story from Mary Magdalene. Yet, everyone knows that Mary Magdalene is the symbol of the phoenix and of the Resurrection. With her, Christianity is triumphant. But, she must be understood as a symbol and not as a historic character. The process is reversed with Dan Brown. And there, we see another side of things, a sort of manipulation where the Anglo-Saxon authors associate the Priory of Sion to the Sages of the Protocols of Sion. This can be found in *The Holy Blood and the Holy Grail*, *The Messianic Legacy*, as well as in *The Da Vinci Code*. From that moment, there is a geopolitical aspect which is definitely more dangerous, since there is an amalgamation with the anti-Semite mystification elaborated from start to finish by the Tsarist police in 1905, and taken up again, less than forty years later, by the man with the moustache and cowlick, to justify the pogroms. Yet, nowadays, the Protocols of the Sages of Sion are presented as pedagogic principles to children in Syria, Lebanon and Iran. This confusion in lifestyles is very detestable. One is trying to lend some credence to something that does not exist!'

SR – 'What you are talking about is worrying...'

JLC – 'It is the archetype of the plot theory, the Judeo-Masonic plot.'

SR – 'So, what about Dan Brown who took this up without shocking his readership?'

JLC – 'Behind Dan Brown, there was quite a crowd, if I may put it like that. To start with, there was the trio Baigent, Leigh and Lincoln, who carried out Pierre Plantard's first interview in 1981. There was also an individual called Colin Bloy, who was the President of the Encres Européennes, a company with their head office in Barcelona. This company supplies ink to most of the large printing houses in Europe. But he was also an ex-serviceman in Her Gracious Majesty's secret service and prided himself on a number of anti-cultural propaganda operations.

Around three o'clock in the morning, in an aside at a reception in Paris, he said, "Jean-Luc, what shall one do with this Priory of Sion's story?" In other words, what does one do to make it a disinformation tool!

That was in 1981. At the time, Lincoln was simply a freelance journalist for the BBC, Michael Baigent was an assistant librarian, whilst Richard Leigh wrote science-fiction novels. Yet, one month prior to the release of *The Holy Blood and the Holy Grail,* there were advertisements for their book on many of the London buses. Who paid for this? Not the authors or the publisher. However, in 1982, Colin Bloy was also production director at the BBC. I let you conclude...

In France, we witnessed the same manipulation at the release of *The Da Vinci Code.* In Paris, for instance, the "Concorde" metro station became a virtual shop window for Dan Brown's book.

But why bother denouncing all this. I exposed all these facts, and many others, to journalists and foreign televisions – Australian, English, and American – including the CBS... Yet, each time, my explanations are cut during the editing.'

SR – 'In your opinion, the Dan Brown wave, with the reestablishment of the Priory of Sion, is everything but commendable...'

JLC – 'Quite! We are witnessing a process of systematic reversal of values. The novel is thus consistent in its reasoning. You must have noticed that the book is divided into one hundred and eight chapters, a real synopsis for a film. Yet, Dan Brown's previous books, such as *Deception Point* and *Angels and Demons* were not really successful. One cannot predict if such or such title will win public favour. Though, *The Da Vinci Code* benefited from an exceptional launch.

Of course, it is a very powerful thriller that follows strict rules, according to the American school. But the fact that the book is presented in the form of a scenario made me foresee that it would have another impact. I was not mistaken!

In fact, Dan Brown's book falls within the present American political context, where one attacks religion and the Opus Dei. They are attacked because, to some extent, one tries to discredit President Bush and his Christian faith. But, there is worse. The success of the book rests on the public's lack of education. One inverts concepts in materialising spiritual ideas. In the past, one would have talked about satanic notions! When everything is based on lack of education, suppression of philosophy and rejection of religion, one can see very well where this is leading. It is as if one was burning all the books. In front of our very eyes, we are witnessing a real worldwide auto-da-fé!

Of course, one touches the right chords! One glorifies the woman goddess, who, in this instance, is none other than the voting American woman, knowing very well that more women than men express their opinion. No, really, all this is too well done to be honest.'

[1] "On 28th September 1993, Mr. René-Roger Dagobert left a number of documents at the Tribunal; amongst them a letter on the "Priory of Sion" headed notepaper dated 8th March 1989, reporting the death of "our former Grand Master... a self-effacing man, quite honest and fair, who had fallen under the blows of certain American initiates, namely Roger-Patrice Pelat. In a book on the subject matter, it was mentioned that, between 1963 and 1981, one of the leaders of the organisation was Pierre Plantard. Heard on 19th October 1993, Pierre Plantard, known as Pierre Plantard de Saint-Clair, declared that the Priory of Sion was an initiatory order with a pyramidal structure, comprising a Nautonier, three Supervisors, nine other members forming the High Committee, and groups of three people each recruiting three more individuals, in order to attain the total number of 121. Furthermore, Mr. Plantard maintained that, since 1984, he did not know anything about the Order.

On 15th November 1993, an article in *France-Soir* made out a list of the alleged Grand Masters of the Priory of Sion, among them Thomas Plantard since 1989. After localisation, the latter was immediately heard and subjected to a search at his home. He declared that a great number of the "Order's brothers were businessmen", that he had been Grand Master of the Order for thirty-six days, that he never attended any meeting and that he did not know any of the members. A magazine entitled Le Cercle, artistically assembled with articles from other esoteric journals, press reviews and photomontages, was seized at his home. Reheard on 23rd November 1993, Mr. Pierre Plantard finally admitted that he was absolutely certain that Roger-Patrice Pelat had never been Grand Master or indeed a member of the Priory of Sion. He simply stated "that he had been in touch with Roger-Patrice Pelat in 1970 regarding the financing of a film entitled *L'Or du diable* (*The Devil's Gold*)". This plan never saw the light of day. Mr. Pelat had suggested Roger Hanin for the role of Father Saunière. There was, therefore, every good reason for thinking that Mr. Dagobert's letter, on the Priory of Sion headed notepaper, concerning the death of Roger-Patrice Pelat, was a fake document."

[2] Henry Lincoln, his real name being Henry Soskin, made films essentially for British television, in series such as *The Avengers* between 1961 and 1963, *Public Eye* in 1965, *The Saint* in 1967, and *The Champions* in 1969. He appeared also in the *The Secret of the Nubian Tomb* in 1961, and co-wrote in 1968, the script for *The Curse of the Crimson Altar*, starring the actors Boris Karloff and Christopher Lee.

APPENDIX I

CLOSE EXAMINATION OF FATHER SAUNIÈRE'S ALLEGED "PARCHMENTS"

BY ROBERT DEBANT

Les deux textes appelés "parchemins de Rennes" offrent un mélange de caractères qui appartiennent à des types d'écritures très différents et d'époques fort diverses:

1) Certaines lettres (G, T) semblent évoquer la capitale romaine qui fut en honneur aux II° et III° s.

2) D'autres, plus nombreuses, l'"onciale", écriture de livres qui fleurit du IV° au VIII° s. (ϵ, ꟿ, qui revêt la forme d'un omméga retourné; L)

3) D'autres encore, très abondantes elles aussi, s'apparentent à la minuscule "caroline" des IX° et X° s. Il s'agit notamment de ꝛ a, d, b . La boucle de cette dernière est souvent terminée vers la gauche par un léger épaississement du trait (cf. lignes 5, 8, 11 du texte "Jesus ergo...")

4) Quelques lettres appartiennent à l'alphabet grec. Ainsi le θ (figure 31, lignes 2 et 13).

Les dimensions des lettres elles-mêmes sont très inégales. Les lignes 16, 18 et 19 de "Jesus ergo..."renferment des caractères (ꟿ, v, N, T) de trois à quatre fois plus petits que ceux entre lesquels ils sont insérés.

On relève enfin des signes de ponctuation et d'accentuation insolites. Un point surmonté d'une virgule retournée est utilisé comme point d'interrogation ("Jesus ergo...", ligne 10) alors que ce genre de caractère ne prend guère cette signification qu'avec l'apparition de l'imprimerie. Plusieurs ϵ sont surmontés d'accents, aigus ou graves (" Jesus ergo..", ligne 10), signes qui ne seront en honneur qu'au temps de la Renaissance.

On peut ainsi conclure de ces observations que les "parchemins de Rennes" sont des essais d'imitation très frustes de certains manuscrits littéraires du haut Moyen Age. L'emploi de plusieurs des signes que nous venons de noter, en particulier celui des lettres qui évoquent les écritures onciales et carolines, revèle sans doute chez leur auteur une relative connaissance de la paléographie ou, tout au moins, de l'épigraphie médiévale. La diversité des écritures que renferment ces textes et les anachronismes qui s'y glissent sont toutefois si frappants que celui-ci paraît avoir voulu se livrer à une facétie, beaucoup plus qu'à une contrefaçon.

x

x x

Le premier document contient le texte intégral du passage de l'évangile selon saint Jean (chap. XII, versets 1 à 11) qui relate la visite du Christ à Béthanie chez Lazare, Marthe et Marie, six jours avant la Pâque et débute par ces mots: "Jesus ergo ante sex dies Paschae venit Bethaniam..."

L'auteur s'y livre à quelques fantaisies de graphie dont les plus caractéristiques sont les suivantes:

1) Il ajoute à l'intérieur ou à la fin de la plupart des mots des lettres superflues:

a) à l'intérieur des mots:

Ex: JESVS EVRGO ANTCE SEX DTPES
<u>pour Jesus ergo ante sex dies</u> (ligne 1)

FVERAOT LAZARVVS MORTYVVS
<u>pour fuerat Lazarus mortuus</u> (ligne 2)

Le même mot, cependant, peut être ou non pourvu d'une lettre supplémentaire dans le cours du texte:

Ex: EVRGO pour ergo (ligne 1)

ERGO " (ligne 4)

On peut noter qu'un u vient fréquemment s'accoler à l'o, et inversement:

Ex: EX DTSCOUMBENTITBVS pour <u>ex discumbentibus</u> (ligne 4)

PRETTOUST pour <u>pretiosi</u> (ligne 5)

b) à la fin des mots.

On relève à cet égard une tendance de l'auteur à redoubler le T final:

Ex: VNXVS ERATT   pour unus erat (ligne 4)

2) Il modifie parfois l'ordre des lettres à l'intérieur d'un mot:

Ex: PROTEPR   pour propter (ligne 16)

3) Il intercale de temps en temps une lettre entre deux mots:

Ex: MARTA L ERGO   pour Maria ergo (ligne 4)

4) Il supprime parfois certaines lettres, en les remplaçant:

a) soit par d'autres lettres, ~~de même nombre que les premières~~, choisies de façon tout à fait arbitraire:

Ex: TERVA   pour Jesus

b) soit par des abréviations:

Ex: CVS M   pour cum eo (ligne 4)

5) Il utilise, à peu près constamment, pour représenter l'I, un signe qui est semblable au T:

Ex: EVENSTT BETAQANTAM pour evenit Bethaniam (ligne 1)

Au texte de l'évangile fait suite une formule de piété, écrite sur deux lignes, qui débute par les mots: "Jesu. Medela vulnerum...". Si la forme des lettres et l'accentuation offrent les mêmes particularités que dans le reste du document, l'auteur a évité d'étendre à ce passage les procédés graphiques que nous avons mentionnés.

x

x x

Le second "parchemin de Rennes" est un curieux amalgame des versions que donnent les évangiles synoptiques, d'un épisode de la vie du Christ. Comme Jésus et ses disciples traversaient un champ cultivé le jour du sabbat, ceux-ci se prirent à froisser quelques épis entre leurs mains pour apaiser leur faim. Les Pharisiens se scandalisèrent de leur peu de respect pour le repos que la loi mosaïque prescrit d'observer le jour du seigneur. Le Christ leur rétorqua qu'il convenait de s'élever au-dessus de l'ancienne loi lorsque des exigences supérieures se présentaient. (Mathieu, chap. XII, versets 1 à 12; Marc, chap. II, versets 23 à 27; Luc, chap. VI, versets 1 à 10).

L'auteur du document, familier du Nouveau Testament, a composé une nouvelle leçon du récit évangélique en puisant à son gré dans les trois premières.

Ex:

St Mathieu: "Discipuli autem ejus esurientes coeperunt vellere spicas et manducare"

St Marc: "Discipuli ejus coeperunt pregredi et vellere spicas"

St Luc: "Vellebant discipuli ejus spicas et manducabant confricantes manibus"

Document "Discipuli autem illius coeperunt vellere spicas et, fricantes manibus, manducabant" (lignes 3 et 4)

L'auteur, qui semble avoir quelque connaissance de la langue latine, remplace cependant, à l'occasion, certains termes évangéliques par leurs synonymes. Les "Synoptiques", écrivant que le Seigneur passait à travers les moissons, donnent:

St Mathieu: "Abiit .. per sata"

St Marc: "Cum Dominus ambularet per sata"

St Luc: "Cum transiret per sata"

Le document: "Cum abire (+) per segetes".

-5-

Les fantaisies graphiques qui caractérisaient le premier "parchemin" se retrouvent dans le second, mais à un moindre degré.

Les deux textes ont de toute évidence le même auteur.

R. Debant

APPENDIX II

PIERRE ET PAPIER BY PHILIPPE DE CHERISEY

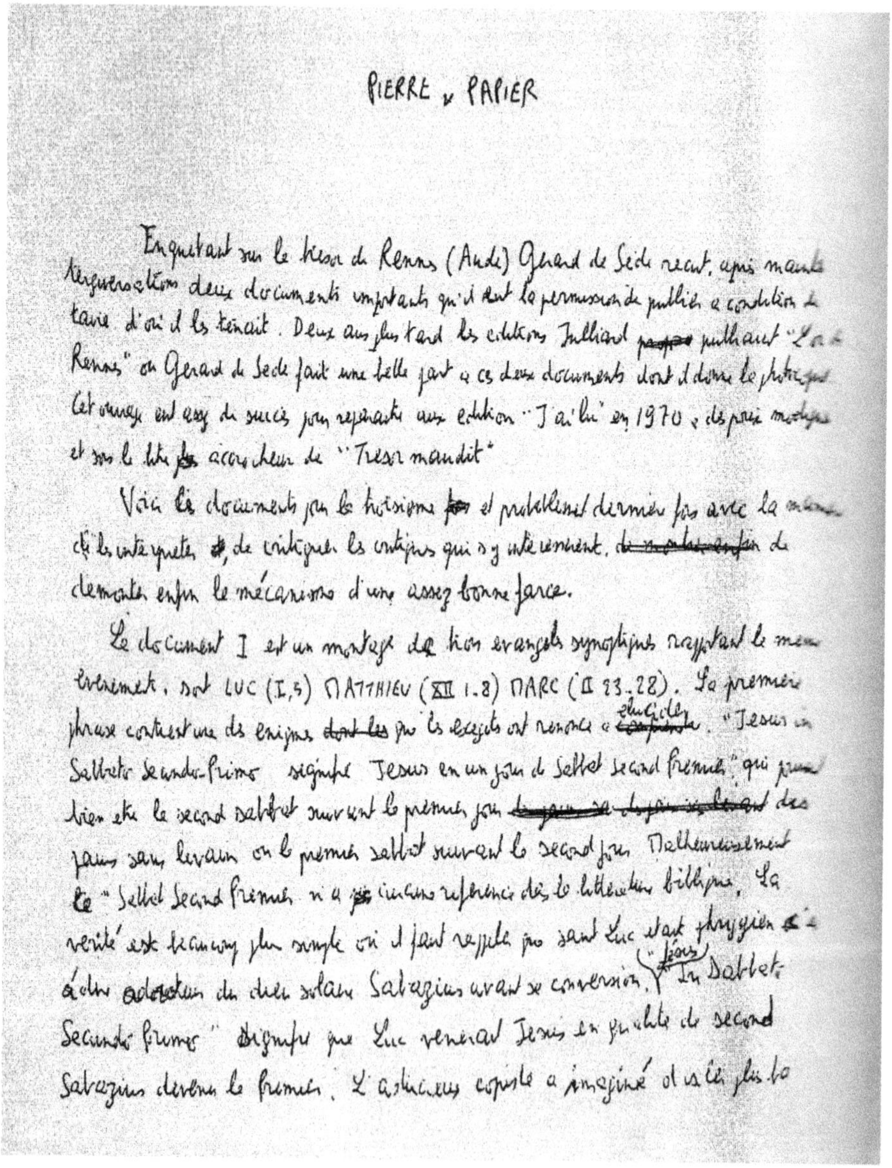

PIERRE ET PAPIER

Enquêtant sur le trésor de Rennes (Aude) Gérard de Sède reçut, après maintes tergiversations deux documents importants qu'il eut la permission de publier à condition de taire d'où il les tenait. Deux ans plus tard les éditions Julliard [illegible] publiaient "L'or de Rennes" où Gérard de Sède fait une belle part à ces deux documents dont il donne la photo. Cet ouvrage eut assez de succès pour reparaître aux éditions "J'ai lu" en 1970 à des prix modiques et sous le titre [illegible] accrocheur de "Trésor maudit"

Voici les documents pour la troisième [illegible] et probablement dernière fois avec la manière d'les interpréter [illegible], de critiquer les critiques qui s'y intéressent. [illegible] de démonter enfin le mécanisme d'une assez bonne farce.

Le document I est un montage de trois évangiles synoptiques rapportant le même événement, soit LUC (I,5) MATTHIEU (XII 1.8) MARC (II 23.28). La première phrase contient une des énigmes [illegible] que les exégètes ont renoncé à élucider. "Jesus in Sabbato Secundo-Primo" signifie Jésus en un jour de Sabbat second premier" qui peut bien être le second sabbat suivant le premier jour [illegible] des pains sans levain ou le premier sabbat suivant le second jour. Malheureusement le "Sabbat Second Premier" n'a [illegible] aucune référence dans la littérature biblique. La vérité est beaucoup plus simple où il faut rappeler que saint Luc était phrygien et adorateur du dieu solaire Sabazius avant sa conversion. "Jésus In Sabbato Secundo Primo" signifie que Luc vénérait Jésus en qualité de second Sabazius devenu le premier. L'astucieux copiste a imaginé de ici plus ta la mention SOLIS SACERDOTIBUS signifiant ainsi "aux seuls prêtres" mais aussi bien "aux prêtres du soleil". Il va sans dire que le même Luc n'a jamais entendu déclarer de la sorte du texte mon figuré ici que "le fils de l'homme est maître du sabbat", car cela ne veut rien dire, mais bien qu'il était "maître de Sabazius". De même dira-t-on que le sabbat des sorciers n'a guère de rapport avec un jour particulier de la semaine mais avec les Sabazies, fêtes dédiées au dieu déchu qui avait pris des allures de coboljes.

Le document II retrace un texte évangélique de JEAN (XII, 1-12). Il s'agit ici de la fameuse histoire de Madeleine la pécheresse renversant un vase de parfum très [illegible] sur Jésus une semaine avant la Passion. Ce geste généreux indigna les apôtres estimant que le parfum valant 300 deniers eut pu être vendu et le produit de sa vente distribué aux pauvres. En sa qualité de trésorier percevant 10% des recettes Judas se sentit particulièrement frustré mais récupéra son manque à gagner en vendant le Christ pour 30 deniers. Par cette jolie parabole l'évangéliste Jean a lancé un avertissement que les historiens de l'Église ne semblent pas avoir très bien entendu : son histoire dans la chair du Christ est à son parfum dans la proportion de 10%. son histoire est à sa légende comme de 30 à 300.

En ce qui concerne l'affaire du trésor ce texte dans autres sens. Il s'agit d'avertir l'inventeur éventuel que, se trouvant dans la situation de Judas il n'aura pas le droit d'en sortir plus que la dixième part. L'abbé Saunière ayant appris à ses dépens ce qu'il en coûte de dépasser les honoraires du mauvais apôtre étant décédé le 22 janvier 1917 quelques jours après une ponction trop abondante. Il s'agit encore d'accoutumer l'inventeur à la perspective de fouiller une nécropole où les morts depuis tant de siècles dansaient naturellement momifiés et en assez bel état de conservation. Sous cet angle on est prié de considérer

Madeleine la pécheresse en qualité de patronne des embaumeuses, ce que dit fort bien le Christ en déclarant qu'elle avait versé le parfum pour sa sépulture.

La disposition des caractères sur le document I représente la coupe d'une montagne où la caverne du trésor est représentée par un trou presque inaccessible ~~à moins de demander les~~ ~~[illegible]~~. Pourtant l'auvent qui surplombe la caverne d'entrée donne INTROIBIT IN DOMUM = « il entrera dans la maison ». Le trésor est donc à la fois accessible et inaccessible et c'est bien aussi ce que signifie l'abbé Saunière par sa sacristie à double fond, trucage très bien agencé et très évident qui permet toujours d'entrer dans l'armoire sacristie comme dans un moulin. Cela veut dire simplement que la caverne est assez humide pour qu'un mur de boue se reforme sans cesse dès qu'on l'a percé. Celui qui entre dans la caverne sans être prévenu ~~croit~~ se croit dans un ~~[illegible]~~ cul de sac et ne s'imagine pas qu'il suffit de dégager la boue ~~[illegible]~~.

~~[illegible]~~

Ce scénario a été exploité ~~par Alexandre Dumas~~ dans le comte Monte-Cristo où le héros entrant dans la caverne où il pensait trouver le trésor est désappointé de la trouver vide mais découvre que une des parois est en carton-pierre et se défait sans difficulté. Le fameux roman d'Alexandre Dumas est une des meilleures pistes du trésor de Rennes. On lira avec profit la Postface où l'auteur se défend d'avoir plagié une œuvre préexistante, et y cite le dernier paragraphe avec très beau clin au lecteur.

~~A ceux qui s'effrayeraient de~~

Le texte évangélique latin dissimule un message en français dont, je ne sais trop pour quelle raison, aucun critique ni même aucun lecteur ne semble aussi découverte bien que ce soit extrêmement facile. On doit s'aviser que les caractères ne sont pas très bien alignés. Alors en appliquant une feuille de papier au ras supérieur de chaque ligne on relèvera les quarante cinq lettres qui dépassent.

	ADA
sur 2ème ligne	G-C
3ème	B
4e ligne	ERT
5e ligne	II
6e ligne	ROI
7e ligne	ETA
8e ligne	SION
9e ligne	ESTCETR
10e ligne	ESOR
11e ligne	ETILES
12e ligne	T
13e ligne.	LAMORT

Autrement dit : A DAGOBERT II (ROI) ET A SION EST CE TRESOR ET IL EST LA MORT

On l'on remarquera que le nom de SION est donné par les ~~[illegible]~~ lettres qui forment le mur du fond de la caverne.

Le commandant Lerville, président de l'ARC (Association des Réservistes du Chiffre) eminent cryptologue ayant examiné les deux documents de colonel Arnaud ~~[illegible]~~ ont déclaré à Gérard de Sède qu'ils étaient "comment codés par une substitution à double clef puis par une transposition effectuée au moyen d'un échiquier", mais qu'ils erreurs avaient été introduites à dessein pour dérouter les tentatives de déchiffrement en lançant les chercheurs sur des fausses pistes.

La première conclusion est presque entièrement exacte et c'est la méthode que nous emploierons ayant comme matériel le texte du document I, celui de la sépulture des femmes de Hautpoul-Blanchefort, une grille de transposition et d'un échiquier. Le document II n'intervient pas. Ce travail ~~est~~ un peu long mais très simple mettre le lecteur moyen comme nous même en état de supériorité sur les ordinateurs les plus perfectionnés. La deuxième conclusion ~~est entièrement fausse~~ du commandant Lerville et du colonel Arnaud est entièrement fausse puisque les erreurs, loin d'avoir été introduites pour dérouter le chercheur, ont au contraire pour fonction de fournir la piste. Utilisons donc le système préconisé par ces militaires, de la substitution à double clef et de la transposition au jeu d'échec.

Le premier exercice consiste à éliminer du document II les lettres parasitaires qui a introduites le rédacteur dans le texte évangélique de Jean ~~[illegible]~~ rendant aussi la lecture difficile. L'ensemble de ces lettres donne, dans l'ordre

\+

V C P S J φ R O V Y Π Y Y D L T P O H R B O X T O D J ∠ B K N J
F φ U E P A J Y N P P B F E I E L R G H I I R Y B T T C V X G D
L U C C V Π T E J H P N P G S V φ J H G Π L F T S V J L Z φ Π T
O X A N P E Π U P H K O R P K H V J C Π C A T L V φ X G G N D T

Soit 128 lettres qui donne au cryptologue l'idée que l'on utilisera deux échiquiers nombreux de 64 cases chacun.

Le texte de la Vulgate donne en effet JESUS ERGO ANTE SEX DIES PASCHAE VENIT...

et non pas comme ici JESUSE(V)RGOANT(E)ESEXDI(P)ESPASC(S)HAEVEN(J)IT.....

Le deuxième exercice consiste à rechercher sur les pierres tombales, la stèle et la dalle un ensemble de 128 lettres qui puisse permettre une substitution, c'est à dire le codage d'un texte par l'autre. En éliminant les quatorze lettres grecques on a 150 lettres dont 22 sont en trop. Les [illegible] qui existent verticalement la dalle ...

vingt deux supplémentaires sont évidemment celles de la mention

REDDIS | REGIS
CELLIS | ARCIS

Reste un ensemble 128 lettres constitué par l'intégralité de la stèle et la mention PS PRAECUM sur la dalle. Pour corser la difficulté l'on a imaginé de lire le texte funéraire en commençant par la fin soit:

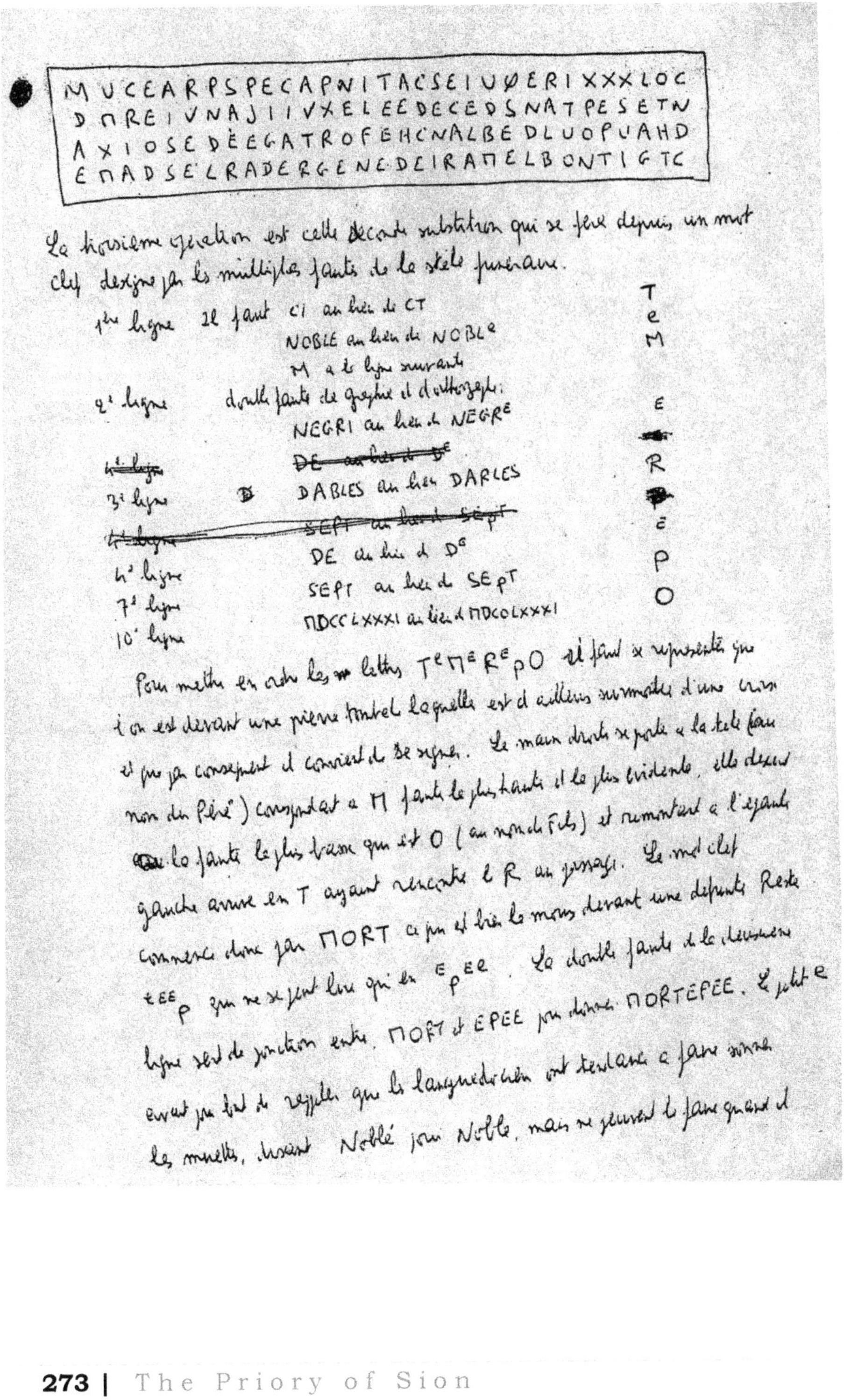

MUCEARPSPECAPNITACSEIUØERIXXXLOC
DΠREIVNAJIIVXELEEDECEDSNATPESETN
AXIOSEDÈEGATROFEHCNALBEDLUOPUAHD
EΠADSELRADERGENEDEIRAΠELBONTIGTC

La troisième opération est celle de cette substitution qui se fera depuis un mot clef désigné par les multiples fautes de la stèle funéraire.

1ère ligne Il faut CI au lieu de CT
NOBLE au lieu de NOBLe
M à la ligne suivante
2e ligne double faute de graphie et d'orthographe:
NEGRI au lieu de NEGRE
~~4e ligne~~ ~~DE au lieu de De~~
3e ligne DABLES au lieu DARLES
~~4e ligne~~ ~~SEPT au lieu de SEpT~~
4e ligne DE au lieu de De
7e ligne SEPT au lieu de SEpT
10e ligne MDCCLXXXI au lieu de MDCOLXXXI

T
e
M
E
R
E
P
O

Pour mettre en ordre les lettres TeMeReEpO il faut se représenter que l'on est devant une pierre tombale laquelle est d'ailleurs surmontée d'une croix et que par conséquent il convient de se signer. La main droite se porte à la tête (au nom du Père) correspondant à M faute la plus haute et la plus évidente, elle descend à la faute la plus basse qui est O (au nom du Fils) et remontant à l'épaule gauche arrive en T ayant rencontré l'R au passage. Le mot clef commence donc par MORT ce qui est bien le moins devant une défunte. Reste la double faute de la deuxième ligne $e^{EE}p$ qui ne se peut lire qu'en $E^{ee}P$. La double faute de la deuxième ligne ^{EE}p qui ne se peut lire qu'en $_{p}^{EE}$. MORT et EPEE qui donne MORTEPEE. Le petit e sert de jonction entre MORT et EPEE pour donner MORTEPEE. Le petit e de la ligne sert de jonction entre. ... avant pour but de rappeler que les languedociens ont tendance à faire sonner les muettes, disant Noblé pour Noble, mais ne peuvent le faire quand il ...

Il s'agit d'une épée

Δ ΠORTEPEE

La quatrième opération consiste à appliquer le mot clef Δ sur la série + à l'aide de la grille la plus simple de toutes qui met l'alphabet en ~~abcisse~~ ordonnées et en abcisses. Quand les huit lettres de ΠORTEPEE sont épuisées elles reprennent indéfiniment jusqu'à épuisement du texte. ~~Pour~~ V passant à la clef Π devrait donner I mais pour cause on peut les difficultés on prend la lettre J voisine de droite ou du dessous. Ça la clef O donne R, P à la clef R donne I, S à la clef T donne N etc.. D'où j'obtiens l'ensemble ⊞ qui est la première substitution soit

⊞
```
JRINOHXTJNFSDTφZDEAΠGFCZCSCGGBSO
SGNZUφODBFIVKUNJZHZCNZXDOJΠXBNLI
ZKUXBDZJXXIIUXYBEZABRCKZGLCGEHRZ
CΠSIUURADDDJXGPΠJZUHHφZφJGPBLEIZ
```

La cinquième opération applique l'ensemble ● comme clef sur l'ensemble ⊞ en utilisant encore une fois la même grille. J passant à la clef Π donne X, R passant à la clef U donne N, I passant à la clef C donne L, N passant à la clef E donne S. ~~La deuxième~~ ~~Cet~~ deuxième substitution donne ainsi l'ensemble

✳
```
XNLSPANNASITTIATEXRRPBTEUCAEENIR
XTGEENDELORSIAAOELEFSDφRPEDCUPGX
AIEΠUIDOCESPNΠEGΠCOCEEPDSHRXAIAD
HATΠOAESEBICELERNEEAIEEDLVEVULDC
```

Avant de passer au dernier travail et pour réveiller un peu le lecteur qui comme moi même se sentirait gagné par la nausée je voudrais lui faire remarquer un phénomène prodigieux et dont aucun logicien n'a pu expliquer comment il s'obtenait : ayant confronté un texte + avec un texte Δ pour obtenir un texte ⊞ lequel par confrontation avec un texte ●

donne un texte * il arrive que ce texte * est exactement l'anagramme du texte ● étant composé des mêmes lettres que lui c'est à dire

A	12
B	2
C	7
D	9
E	24
F	1
G	3
H	2
I	9
J	1
L	6
M	4
N	7
O	5
P	5
Q	1
R	7
S	6
T	6
U	4
V	2
X	4
	128

Or sachant que le jeu des substitutions est terminé et qu'il s'agit maintenant d'utiliser un échiquier pour mettre ces 128 lettres en ordre ce serait déjà prodigieux si, au terme de ce travail nous arrivions seulement à reconstituer le texte funéraire. Prodigieux et parfaitement exact. Mais que notre lecteur se réserve et va découvrir un autre texte, anagramme de la pierre tombale : [illegible] l'espace du miracle qui va se produire [illegible] [illegible] de l'anagramme

La dernière opération effectuée par l'échiquier est bien connue des cryptographes sous le nom de "clef Vigenère" comme la plus ancienne forme d'alphabet secret. On en trouvera l'exposé dans "La cryptographie" de René Cellier aux éditions "Que sais-je" Elle a vu le jour à Jérusalem dans les "Écuries du roi Salomon" du temps que ces fameuses caves du Temple abritaient une société de chevaliers joueurs d'échecs mais ne fut publiée que sous la Renaissance par Blaise de Vigenère secrétaire du duc de Nevers. Il s'agit d'une réussite avec le Cavalier qui doit parcourir les soixante quatre cases du jeu sans passer deux fois par la même case. Cette réussite a laissé une trace merveilleuse dans les romans ~~de chevalerie où~~ médiévaux où l'on voit un chevalier jouer dans un château désert pour affronter ~~un autre~~ aux échecs un adversaire invisible et, le plupart du temps se fâcher d'être battu ; où il fait entendre le mécontentement particulier qu'éprouvent les adeptes des réussites quand ils échouent et se trouvent ainsi vaincus par eux-mêmes

Le passage d'un echiquier à l'autre se fera, comme on a dit, sans interruption. c'est à dire comme si l'on n'avait pas quitté le premier echiquier ~~mais seulement~~ que l'on aurait seulement regarni avec le deuxieme contingent de soixante-quatre lettres. Le deuxieme circuit ~~sera~~ se fera bien sûr selon le meme circuit mais deux fois symetrique, mettant à droite ce qui etait à gauche et en haut ce qui etait en bas de la meme maniere que L et 7 sont symetriques dans une croix gammee qui se resout en †. En d'autres termes le passage d'un echiquier à l'autre ~~est~~ sera analogue à la traversee d'un miroir expliquant ainsi ~~[illegible]~~ à quel mecontentement est sujet celui qui ~~rate~~ ratent une reussite ~~et~~ n'a pu ni vaincre ni etre vaincu faute de se rencontrer lui meme.

~~Ajou~~ Garnissons donc les deux echiquiers par les 128 lettres de l'ensemble * relevees dans l'ordre normal d'une lecture et decoupons les deux circuits symetriques en trois etapes chacun ~~[illegible]~~ afin que le lecteur ~~[illegible]~~ goûte mieux le charme de cette operation. En fin d'etape nous mettrons en pointillé l'indication du debut de la suivante

Le resultat obtenu est

BERGEREPASDETENTATIONQUEPOUSSINT
ENIERSGARDENTLACLEFPAXDCLXXXIPAR
LACROIXETCECHEVALDEDIEUJACHEVECE
DAEMONDEGARDIENAMIDIPOMMESBLEUES

Qu'on lira ainsi :

BERGERE, PAS DE TENTATION !
QUE POUSSIN, TENIERS GARDENT LA CLEF !
– PAX DCLXXXI
PAR LA CROIX ET CE CHEVAL DE DIEU
J'ACHEVE CE DAEMON DE GARDIEN
A MIDI
POMMES BLEUES

L'art de l'anagramme tient des mathématiques où la perfection d'un anagramme donné est proportionnelle au nombre des lettres qui y entrent en composition. Faire TUB avec BUT est aisé, LEGER avec GRELE plus difficile, SABRES avec BRASSE encore plus difficile et...

L'anagramme de Gisors proposé par Gerard de Sède portant sur dix-neuf lettres est un joli tour de force en décomposant AMO DEMETER ET TIMEO sous O MATER DEI MEMENTO MEI, bien des critiques qui se sont élevés contre une telle interprétation eussent été bien en peine d'en donner une autre

Deux anagrammes jugés exceptionnels figurent dans les dictionnaires. Le premier porte sur les vingt huit lettres qui débutent ~~l'Ave~~ l'"Ave Maria"

AVE MARIA GRATIA PLENA DOMINUS TECUM.

donne VIRGO SERENA PIA MUNDA ET IMMACULATA.

Le second sur trente huit lettres est un hommage italien au bel canto

RIME DI AMORE CHE TENNE LA LUCIA DI LAMMERMOOR.

donne UDRAI NEL MAR CHE MORMORA L'ECO DEI MIEI LAMENTI.

Le championnat des anagrammes semble détenu par un ballet de treize danseurs mobilisés en l'honneur de Stanislas Leczinski. Chacun des danseurs portait une lettre de la désignation DOMUS LESCINIA dont on dériva cinq figures

1re figure ADES INCOLUMIS

2e figure OMNIS ES LUCIDA

3e figure MANE SIDUS LOCI

4e figure SIS COLUMNA DEI

5e figure I SCANDE SOLIUM

A côté de ces anagrammes celui que nous avons exposé, portant sur cent vingt huit lettres dépasse de très loin tout ce qui s'est fait dans le genre, non seulement en Français mais dans tous les langages phonétiques du monde. L'auteur entre d'emblée dans la catégorie des génies, et il y entre surtout par ce fait qu'a la ~~[illegible]~~

de tous ses congénères notre anagramme se ~~[illegible]~~ déchiffre par ses propres moyens. Une
opinion reçue veut que l'abbé Bigou ~~[illegible]~~ curé de Rennes le Château (en 1781) et rédacteur
de la stèle funéraire soit l'auteur de ce divertissement. Telle n'est pas notre opinion, l'
anagramme a été réalisé de nos jours et porte même une signature que nous découvrirons
par l'analyse du texte décodé.

BERGERE PAS DE TENTATION

Les curieux du trésor de Rennes savent bien de quelle anecdote il s'agit. Gérard
de Sède la rapporte dans son ouvrage. Une bergère de Rennes se lève tôt matin et voit
le diable étaler ses trésors au soleil. "Toute la bonne colline en était illuminée"
L'endroit est connu par la littérature locale et par une tradition populaire encore
vivace par par "Bonne Colline" entend le mont Serbaïrou situé au sud de Rennes
les Bains séparant les vallées de la Blanque et de la Sals qui convergent à son pied.
Il y a là un labyrinthe artificiel formé par les couloirs d'une ancienne mine de
jais fermée un peu le Révolution Française avant c'est à dire au plus au temps
où mourait la dernière marquise d'Hautpoul-Blanchefort. L'endroit apparaît
d'autant plus séduisant qu'on y voit suinter certaine "source de la Madeleine"
~~[illegible]~~ renvoyant au texte évangélique du document II et à la
dédicataire de l'église de Rennes le Château.
Que de vrais n'avons nous pas faits l'ami Basile et moi-même dans ces
couloirs nauséabonds jusqu'au jour où méditant mieux sur BERGERE PAS
DE TENTATION la recherche nous semble ~~[illegible]~~ aussi stérile que (voulois) saisir le
reflet ~~d'~~ d'un trésor et confondre l'ombre avec la proie. Une tentation excitant

à laquelle il ne fallait pas succomber. Si, au lever du jour la bergère est éblouie
non par l'or du trésor mais par son reflet, c'est qu'elle a le soleil derrière elle et que par
conséquent elle regarde vers ~~[illegible]~~ l'occident. Il importait donc bien plus de savoir
où se trouvait la bergère que de savoir où elle regardait. Asmodée le diable qui
garde l'église de Rennes le Château nous en donnait la confirmation ; "quiconque
prétend avoir vu un trésor d'Asmodée n'y accèdera jamais car il l'a sous les pieds"
Ceci est une des raisons pour lesquelles, désireux comme vous même d'accéder au trésor
vous jugerez raisonnable que je m'en tienne là. N'ayant pas l'outrecuidance de me
croire plus intelligent que l'ami lecteur je le prierai de poursuivre la méditation du
miroir et de rêver avec moi de quelle manière le regard et le reflet ont
moins d'importance que la traversée du miroir, et le phénomène antisymétrique qui
oppose L et 7. Tant qu'on n'est pas rodé à cette gymnastique il n'est pas ~~[illegible]~~
utile d'aller à Rennes ni même de regarder la carte ; mieux vaut se regarder
soi même [dans une glace] [avec courage]

QUE POUSSIN, TENIERS GARDENT LA CLEF

Poussin et Teniers n'ont d'autre rapport que d'avoir illustré l'art de la
peinture au XVII' siècle. Ils entrent ~~[illegible]~~ la piste du trésor par deux voies
différentes

Nicolas Poussin est né entre Les Andelys et Gisors dans un petit village
que l'on n'a pas pu identifier. Si l'on excepte un passage orageux à Paris où
Richelieu lui avait passé une commande toute la carrière du peintre s'est
déroulée en Italie. On croit que ses parents appartenaient à une petite noblesse
des environs de Soissons mais ~~[illegible]~~ lui même refusa toujours l'anoblissement qu'on

effet Bien des artistes ont été considérés. Poussin ne laissait dans l'ombre que les "poulains" une société
de libertins français vivant en Italie et si amoureux de leur pays d'origine qu'ils s'étaient juré de n'y plus
revenir tant qu'il ne se rapprochait de l'image idéale qu'ils s'en faisaient. Poussin fréquentait les "poulains"
même avant son départ en Italie. Il y a de fortes chances pour que les fameux graffiti ~~de~~ signés "Nicolas
~~Poussin~~ Poullain" dans le donjon de la prisonnière de Gisors soit le fait de Nicolas Poussin et non pas d'un
mystérieux captif du ~~[illegible]~~ XIVe ou du XVe siècle

L'apparition du nom de Poussin sur la tombe de la comtesse de Rennes porte à demander s'il n'y a
pas un calembour avec les "hautes portes" qui sont l'emblème de la famille d'Hautpoul, facilitant
ainsi le passage de poulain à poussin. On remarquera d'ailleurs que si trois coqs ornent l'emblème
des Hautpoul, la pierre tombale (~~de~~ d'Hautpoul-Blanchefort des morts) qui était dans l'église sous l'autel
représentait un cheval deux fois monté permettant de situer le calembour "poulain-poussin" antérieurement
au XVIIe siècle.

~~L~~Une relation encore plus évidente entre Poussin et Rennes le Château apparaît ~~[illegible]~~ enfin
par la devise ET IN ARCADIA EGO des Bergers d'Arcadie qui illustra Nicolas Poussin et qui apparaît
sur la dalle en graphie grecque ET IN APXADIA ETΩ renvoyant ainsi à ~~la [illegible]~~
~~la~~ l'injonction de la bergère sans tentation. Ce petit ensemble est assez séduisant pour suggérer
une appartenance légitime ou bâtarde de Nicolas Poussin à la famille d'Hautpoul-Blanchefort.

Si Poussin renvoie à la bergère, Teniers renvoie à la tentation. Peintre profane
Teniers n'a exploité qu'un sujet religieux mais à maintes reprises : la tentation de Saint Antoine.
La mort de la dernière marquise d'Hautpoul-Blanchefort ~~[illegible]~~ survenue le 17
janvier MDCCLXXXI peut être signée par Teniers a) le 17 janvier est la fête de Saint
Antoine l'ermite aux fameuses tentations b) MDCOLXXXI est une graphie
fautive dès lors que le O ne figure pas parmi les chiffres romains. En lisant 16081 au
lieu de 1781, date réelle de la mort on se réfère à la plus fameuse des "Tentations de saint Antoine":
celle du Louvre, exécutée en 1681 c) le principal tentateur de saint Antoine
sur la toile du Louvre est une bergère comme on pu l'on reconnaîtra la ~~bergère~~
"bergère pas de tentation" de la première ligne

La présence de Teniers sur le message indique un chemin à parcourir depuis ~~[illegible]~~ l'église de Rennes le Chateau jusqu'à celle de Saint Luc, village situé plus au nord. Ceci se déduit de deux anecdotes concernant le peintre, la robe de son procureur, son affiliation professionnelle. ~~Car~~ Le dernier portrait de Teniers représentait un procureur en robe noire. Comme on demandait au peintre très âgé des nouvelles de sa santé il répondait qu'il avait brûlé sa dernière dent pour obtenir le noir d'ivoire de la robe. Etant très jeune Téniers avait été reçu à Anvers, maître de la confrérie de Saint Luc groupant tous les peintres

Certains détails de l'église actuelle jouent sur ~~[illegible]~~ cet ensemble a) Au pied de la statue de Madeleine il y a une tête de mort à laquelle manque une dent et au sommet de laquelle on a gravé une petite croix b) La présence dans une église de Ponce-Pilate qui figure à la première station du chemin de croix. Celui de Rennes se lave les mains dans la cuvette blanche que lui présente un petit noir

Le village de Saint Luc et sa église sont au pied du mont de la Mort, comme la croix sur le même au pied de Madeleine. Considérant que la première station du chemin de croix doit mener au Golgotha c'est à dire au mont de la Mort, on obtient un itinéraire de l'église de Rennes le Chateau à celle de Saint-Luc. On objectera que cet itinéraire est contraire à la biographie de Teniers qui devait aller de sa ~~[illegible]~~ jeunesse où il est reçu par la confrérie de Saint Luc jusqu'à sa ~~[illegible]~~ vieillesse avec le procureur. En fait le chemin doit être pris à l'envers, puisque Teniers est élu à Anvers.

PAX DCLXXXI

En son sens le plus régardé PAX est une "mortepée" non tant la nostalgie de béatitude qui tient le monde en haleine depuis la mort d'Abel mais plutôt la "guerre à la guerre" dans le sens où l'entend la majorité de nos lecteurs

PAX a un sens plus concret, désignant la fameuse vision de Constantin en 312, un ~~[illegible]~~ hexagone

rayonnant que les grecs lisaient XPICTOC et les latins PAX. Un cri de guerre "In Hoc Signo Vinces" accompagnait la vision, devise assez commune dans le monde chrétien ; ~~et qui~~ il figure en latin dans l'église de Rennes les Bains, et en français "Par ce signe tu le vaincras" dans celle de Rennes le Château, traduction fautive – "Le" est de trop – mais qui se justifie par la présence du diable Asmodée sous la devise, comme par la nécessité qu'éprouve l'abbé Saunière de former une phrase de vingt deux lettres

L'emblème PAX ~~est~~ est commune par sa dérivation religieuse quand la papauté s'en sert par ~~[illegible]~~

l'exaltation de AΩ, alpha et oméga, l'ensemble se lisant APXΩ, je commande. Il semble bien que la devise des Bergers d'Arcadie ~~[illegible]~~ bien qu'elle soit latine ~~se~~ soit justifiée par une graphie grecque, ainsi qu'il apparaît sur la dalle où P+X au bas de la colonne de gauche appelle A et Ω qui débutent et achèvent la colonne de droite.

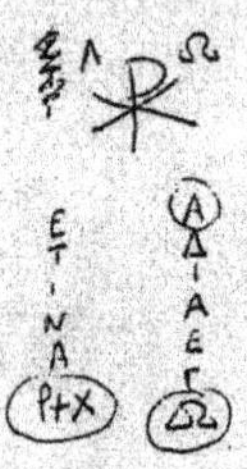

~~En~~ Le privilège qu'a pris l'Église sur l'emblème du prince temporel ~~est~~ a suscité dès un long conflit entre Byzance impériale et Rome pontificale. Il y a un parallèle à établir entre la chasuble ornée du ☧ et le manteau rouge des empereurs de Byzance qui portèrent l'emblème jusqu'en l'an 507 quand ~~l'empereur~~ Anastase l'empereur d'Orient annonce parut au concile en tenue blanche de pénitent. On lui fit une qu'il allait sacrifier ses intérêts particuliers à l'intérêt public. On lui fit une ovation. Il ne s'agissait pas que le manteau rouge au ☧ brodé d'or passe directement à la papauté. En cette même année saint Martin de Tours ambassadeur d'Orient en Gaule était chargé de remettre le PAX à Clovis le roi mérovingien – en qui l'Église se plaisait à reconnaître le "Patrice" et le "nouveau Constantin". Une image légendaire nous fait part de cet événement, celle de saint Martin coupant son manteau en deux avec l'épée pour en donner la moitié à un "pauvre" où il faut reconnaître l'empereur romain

Parvenu en Gaule ~~le croix~~ le nom de PAX fut remplacé par celui de "Labarum" ou d'oriflamme par allusion à ses couleurs d'or et de rouge tandis que le cri de guerre "In Hoc Signo Vinces" devenait Montjoie - Saint-Denis

PAX DCLXXXI est le signal du transfert de la royauté à Rennes le Chateau en 681. Le "bon roi Dagobert" celui ~~[illegible]~~ de la chanson et qui figure au document I était mort à Stenay le 23 decembre 679, seul merovingien que l'eglise ait canonisé dans le but de faire oublier qu'il avait laissé une descendance mâle. ~~[illegible]~~ De son mariage avec Giselle de Razès princesse wisigothe et fille de Bera II de Razès seigneur de Rennes, le "bon roi Dagobert" avait deux enfants, un garçon Sigebert IV dit "le rejeton ardent" et une fille Rathilde que saint Wilfrid avait reussi à tirer de la mainmise des maires du palais, futurs carolingiens. Sigebert et Rathilde recevait ~~[illegible]~~ sejour pendant un an ~~[illegible]~~ à l'abbaye d'Oereen que s'y tenait Irmine leur demi-soeur, était née d'un premier mariage de Dagobert en Irlande. Le 23 decembre 680, un an jour pour jour après la mort du roi un commando de chevaliers mené par Merovée Levi enlevait ~~Sigebert~~ le rejeton ardent de l'abbaye et le rapportait à bride abattue vers ~~Rennes le Chateau~~ le Languedoc où était Bera II son grand père. En recompense de cet exploit la wisigoth donna la seigneurie de Mirepoix et la charge d'élever Sigebert IV à Merovée Levi. La famille de Merovée Levi prit alors la devise "Mirepoix ... e tenebris" : merveille le ~~dauph~~ poisson (le dauphin du haut des tours) Ici commence la descendance occulte des rois merovingiens dont la descendance attend patiemment depuis treize siecle que ~~[illegible]~~ cesse de se produire la descendance carolingienne ou capetienne des maires du palais

Rathilde soeur de Sigebert IV resta à Oereen jusqu'en 692 où elle epouse Chilperic II dont elle eut Chilperic III le dernier merovingien en exercice. La descendance de Merovée Levi seigneurs de Mirepoix. Levi n'a aucun rapport avec les Levis Mirepoix mais ~~[illegible]~~ pris par les seigneurs de Bellissen dont un s'illustra en qualité de capitaine commandant la forteresse de Montségur quand elle fut assiegée.

LA CLEF PAR LA CROIX

Saint Pierre, ~~[illegible]~~ invoqué ici en sa qualité de
dédicataire de l'église de Rennes le Château qui revint à sainte Madeleine après la Révolution
Il fut en effet le détenteur des clefs du paradis et celui qui mourut crucifié, ~~[illegible]~~
A la différence de Jésus exposé tête en haut, saint Pierre fut exposé la tête en bas, les
deux croix étant tête bêche et donnant, par application de l'une sur l'autre, l'image de la
croix de Lorraine. Si la croix grecque aux branches égales fut remplacée par la croix latine
de longueur 3 pour une largeur 2 c'est bien précisément par la croix latine sous entend la
croix de Lorraine et l'intervention d'une seconde largeur égale à la première. La croix de
Lorraine emblème des rois ~~[illegible]~~ mérovingiens d'Austrasie dont procède
Dagobert II représente un mouvement Jésus-Pierre ou judéo-chrétien. Un
le sceau de Salomon s'obtient en joignant les six extrémités de cette croix. Un
rapport hexagonal constant s'établit entre ~~[illegible]~~ l'étoile
juive, le [symbol], la fleur de lis, ~~[illegible]~~ le territoire français et la croix
de Lorraine que la propagande gaulliste a fort justement utilisé dans sa
établis au centre du pays. L'on sait bien par ailleurs que si les rois
mérovingiens furent appelés "fainéants" c'est à cause de la parabole
sur la fleur de lis "qui ne moissonne ni ne file mais le roi Salomon
"dans toute sa gloire n'a pas été vêtu comme l'une d'elles. En ce qui
concerne les seigneurs de Rennes ~~[illegible]~~ on remarquera que les armoiries

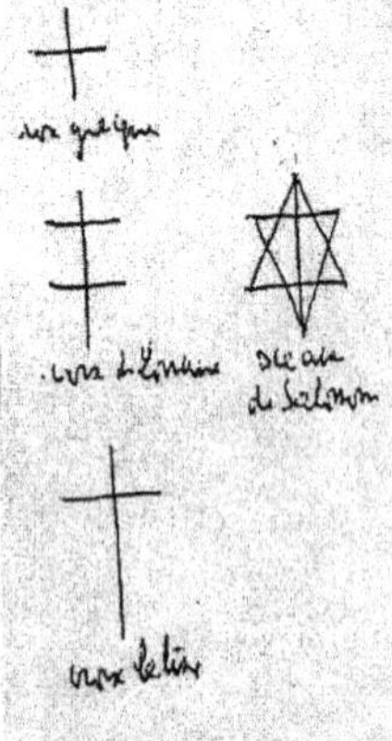

des Blanchefort figurent le sceau de Salomon.

~~[illegible]~~ L'inversion de la croix de saint Pierre par rapport à celle de Jésus est
évoquée sur la dalle funéraire par le sigle (SP) qui a pour but à la fois
~~[illegible]~~ de la basilique St Pierre et de rappeler le sottise Secret Premier qui figure au
document I. L'actuelle église de Rennes le Château évoque ce renversement

dans un autre style. Au pied de l'autel se trouve la même indication qu'au pied du

document II : JESU MEDELA VULNERUM + SPES UNA POENITENTIUM
PER MAGDALENAE LACRYMAS + PECCATA NOSTRA DILUAS.

Cette invocation amène le ~~[illegible]~~ prêtre vers l'autel mais l'invite à rechercher le tribunal qui est à l'ombre, à l'opposé de l'église, sous un grand relief du Christ aux bras étendus ~~[illegible]~~ Assis dans le confessionnal le prêtre revoit devant lui Madeleine sous l'autel par le pied de verre à elle ~~[illegible]~~. En d'autres termes l'église ~~[illegible]~~ de Rennes le château contient deux églises tête bêche dans un même bâtiment invitant le prêtre à tourner sans arrêt sur lui même sollicité par ses deux fonctions d'Eucharistie et de Pénitence. (SOLIS SACERDOTIBUS)

L'étrange exercice qui s'est fait sur Jésus et Pierre tête bêche se fait aussi bien sur Madeleine la pécheresse chez un évangéliste disant qu'elle verse le parfum d'un grand prix sur la tête du Christ et un autre qu'elle lui versa sur les pieds puis les essuya de ses propres cheveux.

LA CLEF PAR CE CHEVAL DE DIEU

Le cheval de Dieu est d'abord une sorte de salut amical à celui qui a décodé le message par le "saut du cavalier" sur un jeu d'échecs, comme pour lui confirmer qu'il avait eu raison d'en agir ainsi. L'on doit s'aviser que le cavalier est à lui seul une incarnation ~~[illegible]~~ de l'échiquier de huit cases sur huit ~~[illegible]~~ ayant depuis une case donnée une option sur huit emplacements. Aussi est-ce que Godefroy de Bouillon ~~[illegible]~~ instituant sa société de joueurs d'échecs dans les "écuries du roi Salomon" à Jérusalem leur donna pour emblème la croix potencée dont le sens apparaît si on la place sur un échiquier : le cheval est à la barre et ses aboutissements à chaque extrémité de la croix.

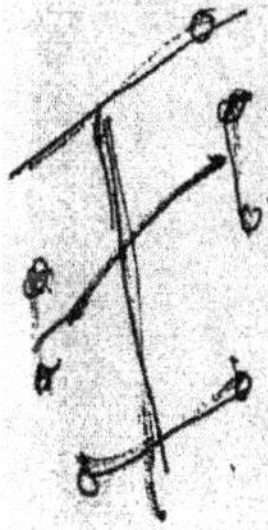

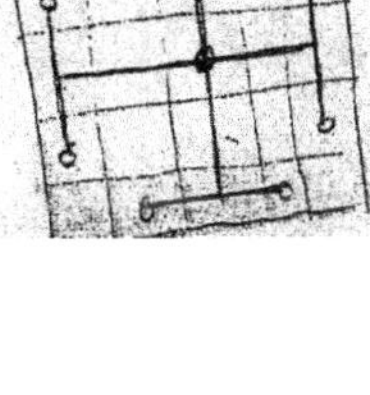

En 1118 quand la société fondée par Godefroy de Bouillon fit une alliance avec celle des Templiers ~~[illegible]~~ née d'un pacte entre les croyants ~~[illegible]~~ et les capétiens - la croix patte coexiste avec la croix potencée mais sans changer la qualité du jeu d'échecs. La croix

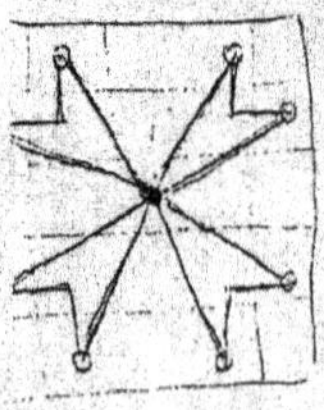

pattée des Templiers n'est en effet pas autre chose qu'une manière d'interpréter le jeu du cavalier. Quand d'autres croix se firent sur le même modèle, celle de Malte, des Trinitaires etc... ~~[illegible]~~ mais les Templiers tinrent à manifester leur dépendance de l'échiquier en représentant au centre de la croix l'image du cheval deux fois monté ~~[illegible]~~. Or l'emblème du cheval deux fois monté apparaît à Rennes-le-Château très tôt avant la fondation du Temple, ~~[illegible]~~ ornait la dalle funéraire des marquis de Blanchefort.

Le cheval deux fois monté de l'église de Rennes-le-Château se rattache à la vieille mythologie de Castor et Pollux, jumeaux cavaliers désignant les Gémeaux dans le zodiaque, mais il est allusion au sauvetage de la lignée de Dagobert II représentant Mérovée Lévi emmenant le petit Sigebert IV sur son cheval depuis l'abbaye de Ocrées jusqu'à celle de Razès où ils arrivèrent le 17 janvier 681 (PAX DCLXXXI).

Le "cheval de Dieu" est encore Chiron le bon centaure, précepteur des dieux, fils de Philyre la nymphe du tilleul. Si le cheval deux fois monté désigne les Gémeaux, le bon centaure devient l'emblème du Sagittaire qui lui est diamétralement opposé à peu près de la même manière que la fécondité des glandes génitales (Gémeaux) s'oppose à celle de la génération phallique (Sagittaire). Le Sagittaire ~~[illegible]~~ contient d'ailleurs sa propre inversion quand on voit qu'il tire derrière et non pas devant lui : le corps du cheval courant plus vite que le buste d'homme, a fortiori que la flèche, il s'ensuit que l'homme cheval se dépasse lui-même et permet à l'homme de tirer sur l'homme en sa part inférieure. D'où vient que les Grecs ont voulu que Chiron le bon centaure soit blessé au genou.. En système chrétien la fête de Saint Genou, fixée au 17 janvier n'a pour but de préserver à Chiron son rôle de "cheval de Dieu".

du centaure quant elle tire es arrivee atteint l'enfant pur et dans l'homme et reveille l'esperance

du cet enfant — Prends un cheval maintenant, ceins ta cuirasse et prends

– Ta lance legere mon enfant ! Le prophete

– Ne serez pas dechiree ni vaine l'attente

– Jusqu'a le voir enfin. Le retour d'Heracles.

Le sommet du mont Serbairou est le premier endroit de Rennes où situer « ce cheval de Dieu ». A l'endroit où le berger aperçut le reflet du trésor il y a deux belles pierres blanches ~~qui~~ très semblables à un grand cheval et un petit marchant l'un à côté de l'autre, le bas du poitrail s'enfonçant dans la terre. L'autre endroit est plus accessible, on est même obligé d'y passer par la route de Couiza à Rennes le Château quand elle perce le pavé rocheux par un ~~[illegible]~~ orifice assez étroit pour qu'on y ait jadis installé un poste de garde. Toi qui viens de Couiza à Rennes arrête-toi au moment de traverser ~~cette [illegible] naturelle~~ cette coupure, ~~et~~ regarde sur ta gauche cet amas de roches qui représente un cheval et son cavalier, et songe d'un seul coup à ta naissance ! à tes amours à celle qui fait qu'une matrice devient vagin et préfigure le trou de ta mort. Ce monument naturel est situé sur la ligne Blanchefort. Espérage à vol d'oiseau ou BLES ~~et l'ange~~ appartient à l'argot qui désigne les richesses ; le cheval de guerre est aussi bien cheval de passion pour le héros ou massonne.

La « CLEF PAR LA CROIX ET CE CHEVAL DE DIEU » est ~~de~~ traduite dans l'église de Rennes le Château par un rébus sur la IXe station du chemin de croix. Jésus tombe à terre avec sa croix et domine par un grand cheval qui se cabre. Image de sa propre révolte contre la révolte.

S'ACHEVE CE DAEMON DE GARDIEN A MIDI

~~Le daemon de gardien~~

Les visiteurs de Rennes le Château ~~connaissent bien ce daemon de gardien~~ et les lecteurs de Gérard de Sède connaissent bien ce « daemon de gardien » qu'est la statue du diable de bénitier qui se trouve à l'entrée de l'église. La génuflexion bizarre qu'il fait a permis qu'on l'identifie : ~~Asmodée~~ le diable boiteux c'est à dire Asmodée, daemon de la luxure, démon de midi. Asmodée est cette puissance adverse que l'homme trouve quand il arrive à se manifeste, au milieu du chemin de sa vie. Entre Asmodée et le dieu Pan des Arcadiens il y a plus qu'un rapport de lubricité mais la nécessité de garder le silence quand vient midi sous peine d'être foudroyé. Seuls ont le droit de s'exprimer ceux qui ont achevé le démon de gardien à midi et se voient sur le déversant de leur âge, les autres n'ayant des cheveux qu'un caractère "hippie" peuvent s'exprimer seulement par un pathétique dont la signification demeure à l'intérieur de leur ventre en germe d'espérance. Pour achever ce "daemon de gardien à midi" il faut trouver le bon moment entre la jeunesse qui ne sait pas encore mais qui peut et la vieillesse qui ne peut plus mais qui sait. Une telle vigilance n'est qu'à la portée des poètes

La Bible et la pensée juive ont été plus sensibles à la qualité d'Asmodée gardien de trésors qu'à celle de démon lubrique. Asmodée gardait les trésors du roi Salomon et les gardait si bien qu'un jour il précipita le roi ~~hors~~ au fin des mondes en le tirant par les cheveux parce que Salomon s'était présenté au trésor ~~sans~~ ~~démuni~~ démuni de son sceau qui ~~...~~ formait laissez-passer. L'emprise ~~...~~ et ingénieuse où il s'agit de découvrir que Salomon ne put entrer dans le trésor que quand il était absolument lui-même et se châtiait lui-même quand il n'y arrivait pas. En d'autres termes il n'y a pas de démon extérieur à l'être, pas d'Asmodée hors de Salomon et vice-versa. Salomon et Asmodée ont donc exactement le même sceau ~~mais dans le même~~ ... de la manière que la clef est soumise à la serrure mais à l'envers de la serrure ~~...~~ la même règle qui

fait L et 7 symétriques et ~~...~~ servit dans le maniement de l'échiquier s'applique encore en faisant de cette antisymétrie ... l'aliment de ces qui revient à la hiérarchie du miroir

L 7

POMMES BLEUES

Un poème d'Éluard fait état de « la terre bleue comme une orange ». Deux rêveries se chevauchent, l'une élémentaire, l'autre savante. Une terre orangée passe à travers le firmament ~~qui~~ teinté de bleu complémentaire, voici la rêverie élémentaire. La rêverie savante se souvient des oranges en leur qualité de « pommes d'or du jardin des Hespérides » dans la légende d'Hercule mais aussi du grand voyage de Jason et des Argonautes en quête de la Toison d'or. L'une et l'autre rêverie concordent sur la conclusion du trésor de l'Eldorado, c'est-à-dire du Far West, où les Hespérides sont le pays du couchant, de l'Occident où le soleil s'épure de toutes ses immondices et de toutes ses heures pour renaître à l'Orient vierge.

La théorie d'Éluard ORANGE - BLEU peut se développer en POMME-OR-BLEU comme signal du trésor de Rennes par insertion de l'or entre le fruit et la couleur. Il n'y a rien à chercher de ce côté ~~mais~~ sinon un encouragement à poursuivre la rêverie sur ORANGE-BLEU que l'on écrira OR-ANGE-BLEU. La ~~méth~~ plus simple méthode est la meilleure pour connaître : voir « L'Ange bleu » de Joseph Sternberg, célèbre film ~~[illegible]~~ où l'on voit Marlène Dietrich dans le rôle de Lola-Lola chanteuse ~~qui~~ qui est la damnation du professeur Rat-Unrat universitaire devenu clown. Il s'agit derrière Marlène-Lola Lola de découvrir Madeleine la pécheresse qui se retrouve dans l'église de Rennes et si ainsi qu'elle est remplie d'anges. Quant au réalisateur Sternberg (montagne étoilée) on ~~se confessa~~ peut se référer à ce qu'il dit des miroirs : « Je n'aime pas les plans d'eau de mon film Ana-ta-han parce que l'eau est la seule chose réelle de mon film » ou encore : « Je veux rendre le public conscient que les erreurs qu'il voit sur l'écran sont ses propres erreurs » et distingue ainsi deux approches l'une par la compréhension, l'autre par l'émotion.

Les anges de l'église Sainte-Madeleine sont au nombre de dix neuf soit deux par socle de statue, quatre ~~pour~~ au-dessus du bénitier, quatre pour soutenir saint Antoine de Padoue et trois qui soutien les veilleuses du sanctuaire. C'est ce dernier ensemble qui importe ici : trois petits anges en métal doré encadrent la lampe rouge qui signale aux fidèles par l'église et tabernacle. En présence de Madeleine le pécheur ou aurait quelque pudeur à se discommuniquer par la lampe rouge et signal des bordels autant que de sanctuaire et que les lieux du plaisir comme de la foi ne peuvent subsister que par les offrandes de leurs fidèles. Ici l'on se mettra dans la situation du curé qui ~~rejoint la lampe~~ pour rejoindre la lampe, monsieur le prêtre opérant ainsi une chute des anges dorés depuis les hauteurs d'un plafond peint en bleu et semé d'étoiles. Quand les trois anges dorés pleurant de la lampe rouge remontent vers le firmament bleu reculant aussi le trio JAUNE-ROUGE-BLEU des couleurs fondamentales on obtient le développement complet du théorème d'Eluard.

PAR CE CHEVAL DE DIEU J'ACHEVE CE DAEMON DE GARDIEN A MIDI

Cette proposition est la signature de l'artiste qui réalisa le plus beau jeu de mots de toutes les littératures mondiales et qui vient aux lecteurs d'en amorcer l'interprétation devant vous. C'est à dire moi, Philippe de Chérisey faisant Amédée par pseudonyme au théâtre et se faisant représenter sous le nom de Charlot dans l'univers romanesque. La plus difficile partie du travail me reste à faire maintenant, celle de vous convaincre que c'est bien moi l'auteur. Comme ma dignité m'interdit de considérer le public comme un tribunal, que n'étant pas accusé je n'ai pas à me défendre, et que enfin mon ascendance a toujours considéré que le peuple nous mettait à la lanterne dans le désir qu'il a d'être éclairé quand vient la nuit. Je ne veux que poursuivre la piste du trésor de Rennes que j'ai moi-même tracée

Je dirai d'abord comment je m'y suis pris pour fabriquer, avec les moyens du bord une piste dont les techniciens du chiffre ont bien vu comment elle fonctionnait sans pouvoir découvrir le texte final de la bergère

Mon premier truc est l'élimination partielle des lettres K W Y Z qui ne figurent ni sur le document II ni sur le texte français l'un et l'autre étant anagrammes. L'on verra pourtant au cours des opérations surgir ~~[illegible]~~ les lettres K, Y, et Z qui se trouvent en effet sur la grille de décodage. Il y a un piège en ceci que ma grille a 25 lettres quand l'alphabet français en compte 26. J'ai omis le W. Ai-je triché ? non pas du tout puisque j'ai rédigé les documents I et II en écriture semi-onciale pour les situer en un temps où le W était ignoré des occidentaux, car il se partageait entre U et V. La fausseté des documents I et II apparaît dès l'instant où l'on distingue U et V, S et Z, I, J et Y. D'où l'on doit conclure que ceci est une mystification. Ni l'historien ni le technicien ~~[illegible]~~ du chiffre ne peuvent véritablement s'intéresser à ce qui ~~[illegible]~~ leur est offert et c'est bien le dessein que je compte ils s'y intéresseront d'autant moins qu'ils disposent non pas de ~~[illegible]~~ parchemins mensongers par un savant faussaire mais de photocopies de photocopies, soit exactement ce que le lecteur a eu sous les yeux. ~~[illegible]~~ La meilleure manière de faire une vente consiste à la déclarer en persuadant son interlocuteur que l'on bluffe ; exercice à vrai dire pas mal effrayant car elle met ~~[illegible]~~ ses adeptes en état qu'ils ne puissent plus jamais rien dire qui paraît vraisemblable, mais exercice réjouissant par les surprenants effets que l'on y obtient. Songez à la crise de fou rire que me prends quand Monsieur Debant, diplômé de l'école des Chartes, archiviste en chef du département de l'Aude déclare que le rédacteur est "un homme instruit en épigraphie et paléographie médiévale, connaissant l'usage de l'écriture semi-onciale" ~~on prend le commandant Lerville et le colonel Arnaud des services du chiffre déclarant que le rédacteur~~ mais un mystificateur postérieur à la Renaissance" — on prend le commandant Lerville et le colonel Arnaud déclarant ce même rédacteur "~~[illegible]~~" "un ecclésiastique nourri d'Écriture Sainte"

aimant le mystère et la fantaisie". Le portrait de ma personne n'est-il pas admirable, songeant
que j'ai passé mon baccalauréat il y a longtemps et avec difficultés, que j'ai lâché assez vite les études
universitaires pour le métier d'acteur, que l'usage de la semi-onciale m'a été enseigné par la
lecture du grand Larousse, et que mes rapports avec l'Église sont de plus en plus rares depuis
mon premier mariage survenu en 1951 et qu'une seule note a valeur historique : je suis

né après la Renaissance.

Est-ce à dire que depuis le jour où "après mainte tergiversation" j'ai fini par avouer à
Gérard de Sède les documents I et II sans qu'il sache qu'ils venaient de moi, est-ce à dire que
depuis ce jour et pendant près de sept années je n'ai cessé de me gausser de ~~[illegible]~~,
~~[illegible]~~ M. Debant archiviste ~~[illegible]~~, du commandant Lerville président de l'ARC (Association
des Réservistes du Chiffre) et du colonel Armand, éminent cryptologue ? Non cela n'est pas
vrai, je ne me suis payé la tête d'aucun de ces très messieurs ~~[illegible]~~ que je ne connais pas plus
que toi, l'ami lecteur, ~~[illegible]~~ puisqu'aussi bien eux-mêmes, moins crédules que toi devraient
refuser de tomber dans un panneau. Si le portrait qu'ils ont à eux trois dressé de ma
personne a le don de me divertir c'est par une méconnaissance de la psychologie qui
est aujourd'hui le dénominateur commun des historiens et des mathématiciens. Mon
devant collège a été déterminé par l'importance de toute conscience, par cette certitude que
le monde malgré son immensité ~~[illegible]~~ n'est pas plus grand que mes yeux pour le voir, mes
oreilles pour l'entendre ou ma bouche pour le chanter, c'est à dire mon âme elle-même en la
qu'elle échappe à toute investigation historique ou mathématique. Ainsi se forment les mots-clefs.
Supposons en effet que j'écrive chaque jour "Mon poulet" à celle que j'aime et qu'un jour
je lui écrive "Mon lapin", elle est la seule à pouvoir deviner que "lapin" ~~[illegible]~~ désigne un
état d'alerte et, éventuellement, une clef. Le seul policier capable d'y voir autre chose que
des fleurs ~~[illegible]~~ ne peut avoir d'autre représentant que ceux qui nous aiment. La force de
ceux qui nous comprennent dépasse infiniment le silence de ceux qui nous expliquent ; et

si j'aime encore le theatre c'est bien pour cette recherche du code non seulement entre comediens et public mais dans l'interieur meme du milieu theatreux.

Les rapports de l'historien et du mathematicien posent la deuxieme realite de mon codage, cela pourquoi il n'y avait pas moyen precis le dechiffrent. Prenez le cas de MORTEPEE, le mot clef dont nous avons vu qu'il contenait sept fautes de graphie T^e Π^ee pO et deux fautes historiques IR (Negri d'Ables et non pas Negre d'Arles). Si le logicien est a meme de discerner les sept fautes, l'historien seul peut discerner les deux autres. Je peux alors pas acquerir une cloison etanche entre le logicien et l'historien

Si, en effet ces deux chercheurs, ayant franchi la crainte du ridicule en se penchant sur des documents si notoirement apocryphes ce n'est peut etre pas dans le but d'une recherche commune du tresor de Rennes. L'historien par ses deux lettres contre sept au logicien ne se trouve en situation inferieure mais apprenant comment la mecanique fonctionne ne garde le secret sur une lettre le R puisqu'aussi bien le E a ete vu par le logicien de les erreurs de graphie. Si l'on demande pourquoi l'historien se taisait sur E

voici une astuce dont je ne suis pas mecontent il y a dans les environs de Rennes le Chateau un chateau de NEGRE et une tour DARLES que l'historien ne se reserve. L'on peut meme causer le phenomene en publiant le texte de la stele au tresor et l'historien est effet que depuis trois ans qu'a paru l'ouvrage de Gerard de Sede il y a des lecteurs qui viennent de tous cotes le sol ou remuer des pierres au chateau et a la tour. L'association de l'historien et du logicien quand bien meme les deux personnages seraient reunis dans le meme cerveau doit necessairement se produire par mefiance reciproque. Pour eviter le delit l'on devait tout aussi bien que la ramification des sciences isolant les savants chacun dans sa discipline a pour effet de ruiner la science et met la conscience en demeure de rever sur l'utopie des "structures" cathedrales mecaniques edifiees sans notre participation. a partir des donnees de la conscience excédant comme si dans cette conscience l'on pouvait ramener ce que nous faisons d'un "donné".

Une conversation ~~dialogue~~ que j'eus avec ~~mon vieux maître~~, Monsieur Dingeon-Mozart de l'Institut demeurant près de la ... . Mon vieux maître s'était laissé convaincre que le travail de l'ingénieur était assez extraordinaire pour ~~...~~ valoir la Légion d'Honneur avec palmes académiques à son auteur. Il était également persuadé que les documents I et II étaient une mystification toute récente ; mais ne pouvait croire qu'ils fussent mon œuvre.

— Vous insistez, me dit-il, un peu trop lourdement sur ~~...~~ la photocopie d'une photocopie des parchemins I/II mais observez une attitude très douteuse concernant la stèle et la dalle objets de l'abbé Bigou pour les mots de l'anagramme. Or la stèle et la dalle sont ~~...~~ de l'abbé Bigou réalisées entre 1781, mort de la dernière marquise et 1792 date ~~...~~ où il sortit de France avec ~~...~~ les prêtres réfractaires du Languedoc. Par ailleurs les erreurs qui permettent de déchiffrer MORTEPEE se trouvent intégralement sur la stèle et la dalle. Pour que votre fable soit parfaite il faudrait que vous puissiez revendiquer la paternité de deux monuments en pierre qui sont antérieurs à votre naissance d'au moins un siècle et demi.

À quoi vous me répondrez peut-être que ces deux pierres n'existent plus, ayant été brisées l'une et l'autre par l'abbé Saunière vers 1891, la stèle se trouvant vierge à Paris chez un particulier et la dalle également vierge dans l'actuel cimetière de Rennes-le-Château formant couvercle à la fosse commune. Rien ne vous empêchait donc de ~~...~~ vous déclarer l'auteur aussi bien des pierres que des papiers, rien en effet sinon qu'elles ont été répertoriées à trois reprises avant votre naissance ~~...~~

Le premier relevé a paru avant ~~...~~ Le premier relevé ... et Gérard de Sède en donne la référence à la ... Le deuxième relevé est en fait une reconstitution ... Bibliothèque Nationale de Paris.

opérée sur enquête opérée auprès des habitants de Rennes par M. Ernest Cros, collaborateur de l'abbé Saunière, en un temps où vous n'étiez pas né. Le deuxième relevé a été opéré par un archéologue local avant le bissage mais n'a paru que quelques années plus tard dans le Bulletin des Études Scientifiques du département de l'Aude. Tant donc que vous n'aurez pas pu établir que ces ~~deux~~ relevés antérieurs à votre naissance sont votre œuvre je ne vous considérerai seulement comme un semi-faussaire.

A mon avis vous êtes parti des fautes de la pierre pour dégager le mot MORTEPEE dont vous vous êtes servi pour fabriquer ~~l~~ l'ensemble + des 128 ~~lettres~~ parasites du document II. Ceci n'ôte rien à la performance du Calendrier qui est en effet le plus beau connu jusqu'à ce jour ni à l'ingéniosité de votre interprétation, mais ne permet pas de vous classer tout à fait dans la catégorie des mystifications parfaites.

~~A~~ – Merci bien de votre scepticisme, ai-je repris mon vieux maître; je n'en attendais pas moins de votre lucidité. Reprenons donc un par un les trois ~~docum~~ ouvrages qui citent les pierres tombales avant ma naissance

a) L'œuvre de M. Stüblein. La référence que Gérard de Sède donne à la Bibliothèque Nationale est en effet très impressionnante mais j'aimerais bien savoir que cet ouvrage figure sur les rayons, ~~et~~ qu'il en soit jamais sorti. Il [illegible] que quelqu'un l'ait entre les mains, et ce qu'il contient. On dit qu'il s'agit d'un opuscule de gravures sur les vieilles pierres du Languedoc à tirage très limité. M. Descadeillas, conservateur de la Bibliothèque de Carcassonne et bien placé pour en juger m'a personnellement déclaré que cet ouvrage n'a jamais existé; et que d'ailleurs M. Stüblein son prétendu auteur, [illegible] météorologiste de profession n'a jamais éprouvé, que l'on sache, aucun intérêt particulier pour les vieilles pierres gravées

b) Le rapport de monsieur Ernest Cros est contestable mais d'une autre manière. Nul ne met en doute que ce personnage ait compté parmi les familiers de l'abbé Saunière et qu'il ait éprouvé des curiosités sur l'affaire du trésor, ni même que sa famille détienne aujourd'hui les stèles laissées de la dernière marquise. Une chose pourtant est que M. Cros ait existé, une autre que les petites liasses de feuillets dactylographiés sortis d'une machine à écrire où il aurait tapé de ses propres doigts. Pour autant que je sache et pour je les ai eus entre les mains ces feuillets pourraient bien être mes œuvres que j'aurais fait ~~transmettre~~ passer à monsieur Noël Corbu de Rennes le Château exactement de la même manière que j'ai fait passer les documents I et II à Gérard de Sède.

c) L'article publié dans le "Bulletin des Études Scientifiques du département de l'Aude" est en ~~effet~~ fait la véritable pierre d'achoppement. On pourrait peut être trouver suspecte le compte rendu sur une inscription disparue depuis ~~dix~~ plus de dix ans et mal se satisfaire que ce mois de la ~~pub~~ publication le Bulletin n'ayant rien autre à se mettre sous la presse. En fait, tant que les curieux pourront se procurer cet ancien numéro je ne serai qu'un demi-farceur, c'est à dire l'héritier d'une farce ~~en~~ lancée voici une soixantaine d'années. Mais attends un peu que paraisse le présent ouvrage et je ne donne pas six mois pour que, raflé par les curieux, l'on ne trouve plus aucun exemplaire de cet exemplaire du Bulletin. Alors je me sentirai tout à fait à l'aise pour ~~dire~~ me déclarer l'unique auteur de cette plaisanterie. Que si aujourd'hui je ne suis qu'un demi farceur, ~~demain~~ j'en serai bientôt un complet. Parlant de cette porte je dirai ce que l'abbé Saunière disait à propos du trésor "Si me l'han donat, l'hay,

Ayant ainsi établi que, si fraude il y a, je ne saurais en être exclu, j'affirme maintenant que la mention "PAR CE CHEVAL DE DIEU J'ACHEVE CE ~~GARD~~ DAEMON DE GARDIEN A MIDI" est ma signature.

Mon ~~nom est~~ prénom est Philippe et mon nom Chérisey signifient respectivement ami des chevaux et ami des dieux. ~~dont~~ Ces deux étymologies, l'une et l'autre grecques, expliquent le poste sous l'invocation du cheval de Dieu. Quand il fallut que je m'engage dans la carrière de comédien je me suis fait le pseudonyme d'Amédée dont ~~l'~~ l'étymologie latine "ami des dieux" ~~comme~~ équivalait à l'étymologie grecque de Chérisey. Le jeu qui se fait depuis AMEDEE jusqu'à A MIDI a été dicté par la transformation de l'E en I qui fait d'une dame de Nègre, j'ai fait une dame de Nègre, ou d'une morte-pie une Matégée. Devrai-je par ailleurs [illegible] que le passage d'Amédée à Amidi se fit par l'intermédiaire d'"Aimedée" [illegible] "putana errante", roman médiéval prose de Barbey d'Aurevilly ou Aimedée sur la plage normande de Carteret se trouve prise entre le poète Serringaud (demi-dieu) et le sage Altaï (montagne d'or) et peut par suite, aussi, [illegible] par la traversée du miroir où le sage et poète seraient l'un à l'autre reflet et réalité.

Encore que je réprouve l'habitude qu'ont prise les auteurs de se citer eux-mêmes en référence soit par vanité, soit pour encourager la vente de leurs ouvrages antérieurs, il me ~~semblerait~~ semblerait malhonnête de passer sous silence "Le Mendiant O", roman [illegible] de "Amédée ou comment s'en débarrasser" d'Eugène Ionesco [illegible]. Pour se débarrasser d'Amédée il suffit de "j'achève ce daemon de gardien".

~~En 1950 Albert Willemetz ~~[illegible]~~ m'engagea pour jouer le Amédée au théâtre des Bouffes Parisiens dont le nom [illegible] un relent de cannibalisme [illegible] le monde des croque-monsieur. Ce directeur s'étonna que je n'aie pas choisi plutôt le pseudonyme d'Asmodée qui lui semblait plus éclatant; ~~[illegible]~~ je [illegible] La tentation [illegible] pour n'avoir pas [illegible] la valeur d'être mon propre diable.~~

de l'énoncé à l'anglaise AMIDI. Aussi a-t-on vu en première partie comment l'opération poétique en sens inverse permettait au garçon MERYON de messacrer le capitaine MARION dans un repas de cannibales.

C'est au théâtre des "Bouffes-Parisiens" dont le nom a le même sens caractéristique que les rogne-monsieur, c'est là que l'idée de substituer Asmodée à Amédée me fut donnée par Albert Willemetz. "Pourquoi pas Asmodée qui serait tellement plus éclatant?" Je refusai poliment ne me jugeant pas encore assez puissant ni assez sage pour affronter le diable qui était en moi. Aujourd'hui je ne suis pas encore Asmodée mais du diable si je n'y arriverai pas. Tellement, j'aurai boité sur les sentiers de la vertu

POST-SCRIPTUM:

L'usage de placer un appareil critique à la fin d'un livre qualifie les ouvrages sérieux. Ce qui va suivre est plutôt un post-scriptum, un endroit où verser ~~[illegible]~~ ce qui ne pouvait entrer dans le plan de l'exposé, où enterrer les reliquats de mystère comme un campeur honnête enterre ses détritus pour laisser la place nette. Dans l'ordre ~~[illegible]~~ de lecture on passera en revue la nature de SION auquel revient le trésor conjointement avec le roi Dagobert II

l'œuvre de Gérard de Sède.
le radical RESPIS CELLIS | REGIS ARCIS
deux parts
la valeur intrinsèque

du mot clef MORTEPEE

SION

En l'an 1.099 Godefroi de Bouillon prince mérovingien descendant ~~[illegible]~~ direct par les mâles du roi Dagobert II prit Jérusalem et où il fut nommé roi par 33 barons. Il refusa ce titre pour deux raisons, parce c'était celui du Christ lui-même, et parce il n'était pas le fils aîné de la lignée mérovingienne. Une royauté sans roi s'installa sur la montagne de Sion qui s'appelait alors Moria, c'est à dire "vainqueur-mer", nom égal à Meer-wig que nous connaissons par sa déformation en Mérovée. L'architecture du mont de Sion comprenait trois édifices communiquant entre eux sans passer par l'extérieur ; les caves du temple de Jérusalem épargnées ~~Titus ayant brûlé en l'an 70~~ par l'incendie de l'an 70, la mosquée édifiée sur l'ordre d'Omar en 637, une petite sanctuaire église sur ordre de Bouillon et appelé « Abbaye de Notre-Dame du mont de Sion ». Aussi est-ce par un idéal œcuménique groupant (les chercheurs des) les trois religions : le juive, la musulmane et la chrétienne. La mosquée de Cordoue donne une réplique arabe à cette architecture en ce qu'elle conserve la synagogue et la cathédrale. On ne trouvera pas d'équivalent chez les juifs parce que [illegible] les musulmans et les chrétiens leur aient interdit d'accéder à la propriété foncière mais il va de soi que la Diaspora juive est essentiellement œcuménique.

Une société très fermée correspondait à l'architecture portant le nom du bâtiment chrétien. Deux neuf ans plus tard à la mort de Baudouin, frère de Godefroi, la fondation de l'Ordre du Temple s'établit sur un pacte entre la royauté mérovingienne et la capétienne. Sur les neuf chevaliers qui inaugurèrent le nouvel ordre six représentaient l'ordre de Sion et trois la part [illegible]. Les termes du traité ne nous sont pas connus mais le départ fut une atteinte à l'équilibre religieux par la suppression du croissant qui coiffait la mosquée et son remplacement par une croix, insulte que jamais les musulmans ne pardonnèrent aux chrétiens.

~~Les musulmans ayant repris Jérusalem en 1187 une orage éclata contre les Templiers que les Templiers furent tenus pour responsables tous jugés responsables de la perte de la Ville Sainte. La rupture entre le Temple et Sion se produisant l'année suivante à Gisors dans le champ dit de l'orme ferré ; et la date de 1188 a paru si importante qu'elle figure encore au dessus des armoiries de la ville. Cette rupture [illegible] fut une prise d'indépendance, un divorce à l'amiable et non pas une déclaration de guerre. L'ordre de Sion devenu Prieuré de Sion réduisit ses effectifs à treize membres pour un nouveau départ. L'unité de l'Ordre du Temple étant assurée par la constitution de Mantes Roselin de Fos lequel n'était pas [illegible] templier mais membre du P.S.~~

En 1148 le roi Louis VII ramena en France ramena en France quatre-vingt-quinze membres du « Prieuré de l'Abbaye de Notre Dame du mont de Sion » dont sept [illegible] le Temple tandis que les quatre-vingt-huit autres s'installaient au prieuré Saint Samson d'Orléans et à sa succursale de Saint Jean le Blanc. Pour se libérer le roi Louis VII reçut la permission d'arborer dans ses armoiries la fleur de lis qui était l'apanage des ~~[illegible]~~ mérovingiens encore cette faveur se limitait à un dessin semé de fleurs d'argent mais non pas à la fleur d'or unique sur fond de gueules que aucun roi en exercice n'avait jamais le droit d'~~[illegible]~~ assumer.

La répartition des quatre-vingt-huit membres entre 62 (Saint Samson) et 26 (Jean le Blanc) était l'objet d'un divertissement mathématique sur le thème du miroir de manière à obtenir

62 | 26 — 62 | 26 / 2 — 31 | 13

Un mouvement d'épuration se produisit à l'intérieur du P.S afin d'obtenir une valeur noble c'est-à-dire une qualité inverse de la quantité. Le Petit Prieuré de Saint Jean le Blanc réduit à treize membres fut la tête du mouvement. L'on vient que aujourd'hui encore les paysans de l'orléanais appellent "Jean-le-Blanc" un oiseau qui a la réputation de manger les serpents d'une seule bouchée sans les couper en morceaux. Les bâtiments de ce petit prieuré n'existent plus mais le flâneur de Saint Jean le Blanc ~~[illegible]~~ peut en chercher les ruines sur le lieu-dit "mont de Sion" qui figure sur la carte d'état-major.

La reprise de Jérusalem par les musulmans en 1187 provoque un mouvement d'opinion contre les Templiers ~~qui étaient~~ dont on les tint responsables. L'année suivante à Gisors, dans le champ dit "de l'ormeteau ferré" eut lieu la rupture entre l'immense Ordre du Temple et le dérisoire "Petit Prieuré de Sion", et la date de 1188 parut si importante qu'elle figure au dessus des armoiries de Gisors. Rupture n'est pas juste mais en l'occurrence une acte ~~de divorce à l'amiable agrémenté d'un~~ pacte entre les ex-conjoints. L'unité du Temple était assurée par la constitution de Maître Rosselin de Fos lequel était du PS et non pas templier; en revanche le P.S avait laissé en gage au Temple certains objets dont la "Caput SIDON" ~~ou~~ une tête d'or. En 1307 comme l'avenir des Templiers [illegible] Guillaume de Gisors, représentant le P.S. reçut la tête d'or que Philippe le Bel devait un jour rechercher si activement. Cette caput Sidon figure en rébus à la base du document II. Le graphie NOPIS invite à retourner l'image pour y lire SION ; j'ai même poussé le scrupule jusqu'à figurer en bas de l'image un ∀ que l'on considérera comme un A ou un Δ renversé, c'est-à-dire un D. L'alliance P∀ me rappelait sans doute les plaisanteries sur "pédé" que l'on faisait depuis mon pseudonyme Amédée.

Ce jeu de miroir a été utilisé maintes et maintes fois dans l'imagerie. Le cas du peintre ~~[illegible]~~ Signol en donne un exemple flagrant. Auteur très académique Signol eut le privilège d'exécuter le portrait de Dagobert II qui figure à Versailles et les fresques de l'église de la Madeleine à Paris. Étant très âgé on le chargea d'exécuter les quatre grandes fresques de la Passion qui ornent les autels de l'église Saint Sulpice. En fait Signol étant devenu incapable de grimper sur les échafaudages donna les cartons dont l'exécution fut remise aux élèves des Beaux-Arts. La signature de Signol sur les fresques, réalisée en lettres capitales n'est pas même de sa main, mais sur son ordre les élèves des Beaux Arts eurent pour tâche de transformer en SIGИOL le nom de leur patron en deux fresques sur quatre. L'inversion du N en И avait pour but de renverser le nom tout entier pour donner LONGIS et l'indication du méridien O qui passe dans l'église sous forme d'une ligne ~~[illegible]~~ de métal doré serti dans le dallage. Puis comme ce jeu risquait de passer inaperçu la pancarte du Christ en croix fut elle aussi entièrement inversée donnant MUROEDUJXERIERAN SUSEJ au lieu de JESUS NAZAREI REX JUDEORUM.

Le méridien O de Saint Sulpice ~~[illegible]~~ est une proportion de l'Église et ne coïncide pas tout à fait avec celui du Roi basé sur l'Observatoire mais n'en passe pas moins sur le territoire de Rennes. Ce jeu puéril n'est qu'une manière de placer S et N en qualité de Sud et Nord dans le nom de SION et de considérer IO comme une pénétration dans le [illegible].

(Duch page 36 bis)

GERARD DE SEDE

Ce qui vient d'être dit ~~[illegible]~~ semblera sans doute une attaque contre "Les Templiers sont parmi nous", ~~[illegible]~~ "L'énigme de Gisors" qui a fait la réputation de Gérard de Sède. Après ~~[illegible]~~ le silence et le mépris des historiens, après la vogue du grand public.

Est-ce à dire que Signol ait agi tout à fait en plaisantin ? Cela dépend comment on l'entend. Le père de ce peintre ~~était~~ avait été victime d'un phénomène de miroir : Auteur d'un vaudeville "Le duel" et d'une "Apologie du duel", il était mort en ~~duel~~ 1850 au cours d'un duel. Et l'on remarquera que les toiles qui ornent la pancarte sur la tête du Christ est située derrière une image de Saint Paul désignant avec son épée le passage du méridien 0 à travers le dallage. Il se peut fort bien que le peintre ait entendu célébrer à sa manière la mémoire de son père. ~~tra~~ Sachant que la signature est inversée sur les pages de la Trahison et de la Résurrection, que la pancarte est inversée sur les pages de la Crucifixion l'on devrait ~~sur~~ rechercher ce qui devrait également s'inverser sur les ~~peintures~~ pages de l'Ascension. Peut-être que tout un poste des "L'[illegible] commémoration [illegible] posthume du père de Signol qui fut rédigé par George Sand et Jules Sandeau.

retour page 36

méfiance dont les gisorsiens entourent un homme auquel ils doivent le plus clair des bénéfices touristiques de leur ville, n'y a-t-il pas quelque lâcheté à minimiser le rôle des Templiers à Gisors simple no man's land pour la rupture d'1188?

Allons plus loin encore, cette fameuse chapelle Saint Catherine qui devait se trouver sous le donjon, au cœur de la citadelle, est en réalité au dehors des remparts, dans le domaine royal. L'accès à la crypte se fait dans la montée de la rue de Vienne, quelques mètres après le "passage du Monarque" d'où l'on se trouve devant un réseau souterrain de plusieurs étages et fort bien construit. La crypte de la chapelle Sainte Catherine devint en 1306 le domicile de la "commanderie Saint Gervais" relevant du Prieuré de Sion qui y tint ses assises jusqu'au milieu du XVIIIe siècle. S'il y a un mystère à Gisors il n'est pas dans les découvertes de Gérard de Sède mais dans ses silences, dans la crise de fou rire qui nous prit en consultant le guide touristique de consommation courante à Gisors avant 1939. La chapelle Sainte Catherine y était bel et bien mentionnée dans le domaine royal, mais nul ne [illegible] non tant par ignorance que par cupidité, chacun espérant accéder à la crypte et profiter des ventes par débusquant l'erreur. Gérard de Sède et moi même avons lancé le mouvement [illegible] nous glosions sur une [illegible] par la location d'un manteau populeux, perçant une muraille le contenu confit et bien tassé d'une cargaison de "poudrette" séculaire, le contenu [illegible] satisfaisant leurs besoins avaient laissé de leur latrine ou des générations de gisorsiens, satisfaisant leurs besoins avaient laissé de leur passage en ce monde une trace plus durable et plus féconde que leurs os. Et moi [illegible], après ce baptême de poudrette que nous reçûmes ~~Gérard de Sède~~, après cette certitude qui nous venait comme aux alchimistes : que l'or a ensemble, cette certitude qui nous venait comme aux alchimistes : que l'or a une odeur et naît de l'excrément, j'avais moqué Gérard de Sède? Si le trésor de Gisors a quelque chose qui rebute, c'est précisément la poudrette, c'est-à-dire l'absence d'égouts en cette partie de la ville qui accumule la poudrette dans les nefs ~~de [illegible]~~ d'une cathédrale engloutie.

Le "trésor des Templiers" de ~~Gisors~~ ~~[illegible]~~ contenu en trente coffres fut entreposé à Gisors en 1526 deux siècles après la disparition du Temple, dans la crypte de la chapelle Saint Catherine qui ne tarderait pas à être démolie en surface. Une pierre de ~~tombe~~ l'ancien cimetière ramenée à ~~la cathédrale~~ l'église Saint Gervais fait foi de l'événement. Certaines rumeurs ayant couru que l'on cherchait ce trésor uniquement ~~[illegible]~~ constitué d'archives, le P.S prit l'initiative d'une fausse rumeur assez vivement menée pour faire fausser les égouts aux historiens et mettre en alerte l'âme populaire : en faisant courir le bruit qu'il y avait un trésor à Gisors on obtenait ce résultat que ~~plus~~ dès le jour arrosé ~~[illegible]~~ "Son et Lumière" plus personne n'osait toucher un râteau sans se rendre suspecte. Ici le lecteur peut imaginer deux conclusions, ou bien les trente coffres de la chapelle Sainte Catherine continuent d'être gardés par un [illegible] de [illegible] ~~[illegible]~~ et jamais à la [illegible] poudrette, ou bien, à la faveur du tam-tam le PS [illegible]

Suite p. 38 bis

~~Pour en finir sur cette affaire un peu extérieure à la [illegible] je voudrais dire que [illegible] mystification qui n'est [illegible] de naissance, [illegible] plus de [illegible] est une ascèse qui se perfectionne [illegible] de telle manière [illegible] jouer la tête des gens [illegible] leur offrir la [illegible]~~

REPPIS REGIS
CELLIS ARCIS

L'honneur que me fait le colonel ~~[illegible]~~ Armand en me confiant pour le [illegible] ecclésiastique n'est pas entièrement injustifié. Dans ma carrière d'Amédée acteur j'ai tenu deux rôles de prêtre. Le premier, un moine régulier, fut aux Bouffes Parisiens et c'est à son sujet que Albert Willemetz me suggéra d'opter pour Asmodée. Le second était un curé ~~[illegible]~~ gascon pour un film américain tourné ~~[illegible]~~ à Saint Tropez. J'ai un souvenir émerveillé d'une veillée nocturne en termes [illegible] dès les

Cette affaire de Gisors est, je doute un peu extérieure à la notre mais s'il ne fallait qu'un ~~Si l'on fallait qu'un~~ exemple de notre complicité entre Gérard de Sède et moi-même, je n'en voudrais pour exemple que le document n°I dont l'auteur dans "Rennes" déclare expressément qu'il y a "des lettres décalées". Sur la page contiguë apparaît la photocopie du document susdit à ce que l'auteur a écrit. Or sur une centaine de milliers de lecteurs pas un ne s'est demandé par quelle manière ce décalage s'était opéré ~~et pourquoi~~ ni que relevant ces décalages on obtient la mention "A DAGOBERT II ROI ET A SION EST CE TRESOR ET IL EST LA MORT": non pas un jeu. Ô ami lecteur, ami lecteur qui nous disons tout et n'entendez rien de quelle astuce joueuse accidentelle, permettez-nous vous honorer, et comment ~~[illegible]~~ prendriez-vous au sérieux vos jugements que l'on vous fasse le crâne. ~~[illegible]~~ [illegible] que Gérard de Sède et moi vous tenions [illegible] le cas [illegible] de fantastique à bon marché ~~[illegible]~~ qui ne [illegible] l'ayant demandé, [illegible] que nos droits d'auteur.

Alors je doute [illegible] vous croire que nous autres potes, éprouvons un plaisir sadique à vous mépriser. Non lecteur. La mystification est une œuvre laborieuse, [illegible] comme les premiers pratiquants jusqu'à [illegible] la telle plaisanterie ~~qui~~ qui nous [illegible] avant vous. Avant de nous/~~me~~ payer votre tête, ami lecteur, il aura fallu que nous nous payions ~~[illegible]~~ la notre ~~[illegible]~~ la plus chère et que nous nous demandions ~~[illegible]~~ avec Jésus: "Qu'est-ce que la vérité?", et il fallait que nous sachions qu'il fallait tout vous dire mais qu'en vous disant tout vous ne le croiriez pas. [illegible] [illegible] récits et [illegible] [illegible] [illegible]

ce qui permettait à Gérard de Sède de [illegible]

présenter une semblable information comme le texte du roi Dagobert II et [illegible], [illegible] [illegible] qu'un historien [illegible] [illegible] démentir ou confirmer. Et nous sommes là. [illegible] [illegible] que vous [illegible] l'énergie du [illegible] que, depuis le temps de la semi-[illegible] poètes [illegible] avec l'énergie du [illegible] il y aura encore des lecteurs, sachant lire

RETOUR page 38

bords de Pigalle où ma figure était inconnue. On n'allait pas croire à une blague de mauvais goût de Pierre Fresnay célébrant la messe au champagne dans un seau à glace formant calice. Non, je fis de mon mieux pour comprendre ce qu'un prêtre ferait en soutane à deux heures du matin au "Jim's Joint", au "Bambolero" ou aux "Naturistes". Je ne bus pas plus de gin-fizz qu'il ne convient à un prêtre avant la communion et gardai les coudes assez dans pour apprécier la diplomatie du personnel masculin qui me servait comme tout autre client, et le charme des filles qui se faisaient parfois offrir un verre sans qu'aucune ne se soit aventurée sur mes genoux. Constatant que ma soutane pouvait être à la fois tout à fait invisible et tout à fait voyante je me trouvai dans cette situation du Narcisse universel à travers le miroir.

C'était un film où de ma prédiction qui dura un mois et demi ne subsiste qu'un beau passage où du sommet d'une colline et de très haut je bénis les vendanges en général et Michèle Morgan en particulier, elle qui déguisée plus tard en Marie Antoinette serait décapitée par moi déguisé en bourreau Samson, que le monde est petit. Au cours de mes copieux loisirs je m'en fus visiter l'étonnante relique de sainte Roseline de Villeneuve momifiée depuis le XIVe siècle et noircie par le temps. J'appris qu'elle était abbesse de la Celle aux Arcs et que sa légende provençale avait été reprise littéralement pour sainte Germaine Cousin, languedocienne et patronne de la S.A.C. Plus tard quand j'entrai dans l'affaire de Rennes je vis d'un seul coup la statue de Germaine Cousin parmi les saints de l'église et cette inscription REDDIS / CELLIS | REGIS / ARCIS

Entre Languedoc et Provence il y avait un échange, celui de Germaine contre Roseline, celui de la Bergère contre la Celle aux Arcs. Puis je connus une Roseline qui mourut le 6 août 1967 fête de la Transfiguration en franchissant le méridien 0 en voiture. Puis je connus aussi une allemande un peu gourmande, qui me fit Germaine Cousin pour ni être ni cousin germain ni cousin germain. Force m'est ici de renvoyer encore une fois le lecteur à mon "Le Serpent Rouge" où j'ai dit tout ça en long, en large et quelquefois en pleurs. En ce qui concerne plus proprement Rennes que ma vie parmi la section CELLIS / ARCIS est une allusion à la détresse du corps de Madeleine la pécheresse qui fut transféré de son tombeau d'albâtre à celui de marbre en un temps où les infidèles assiégeaient le pays. "Cellis" correspondait à la cellule blanche du chrétien contemplatif et "Arcis" à la forteresse de marbre noir ; si ARCIS revenait au roi REGIS, alors CELLIS devait revenir à la reine rebaptisée Rennes pour donner REDDIS en latin.

L'abbé Saunière a respecté l'architecture Cellis-Arcis à l'intérieur de son église dont à maints qu'elle contenait deux bâtiments tête-bêche. La part blanche CELLIS ~~celle~~ de l'albâtre, de la reine contemplative correspond au choeur et se prolonge ~~~~ jusqu'à la chaire du prédicateur d'une côté ~~part~~ et la statue de St Antoine de Padoue de l'autre côté ~~~~. ~~Alors commence le côté ARCIS de~~ Alors commence la part fortifiée ARCIS, ~~l'église~~ celle du marbre, du roi noir, était indiquée au plafond par une frise crénelée. En d'autres termes, si dans le bâtiment unique d'une église double ~~~~ on ne pénètre que par une seule porte ~~~~ ~~du côté ARCIS cela voudrait dire~~ située du côté ARCIS cela signifie qu'un même orifice donne accès à deux trésors celui du roi, puis celui de la reine. ~~Ces~~ Deux trésors n'en font qu'un aux yeux du monde car le roi et la reine sont un couple parfait qui vit en communauté de biens, et il n'y a pas lieu de distinguer entre l'or des ~~~~ mérovingiens ~~et celui~~ du roi et des vestiges de la reine. Si pourtant tu pénètres dans la merveille apprends que dès liens intimes le roi n'est pas enchaîné à la reine ni la reine au roi.

"La où est ton trésor là sera ton coeur" tel est le message de l'ampoule en ~~~~ soutenue par les trois anges en métal doré à la frontière du choeur qui est celui ARCIS. CELLIS ne désigne alors que l'arc en ciel né des trois couleurs fondamentales jaune, rouge, bleu. Le trésor ~~est~~ n'est pas à la portée du savant qui explique mais

~~de l'amateur~~ du poète / qui comprend. Méfiez vous de ni aimer, ami lecteur et dans le symbole du singe et du chat, ne soyez pas ~~[illegible]~~ Raton qui tire les marrons du feu ~~[illegible]~~ me laissant Bertrand qui les mange.

~~Echec / Le rapport Rennes Echec~~

Le rapport CELLIS blanc ARCIS noir fonde la nature du jeu d'échec aux cases alternées. On trouve dans Rennes un grand nombre d'allusion à l'alternance des deux couleurs. La plus évidente est le voisinage du Rokko Negro noir et du rocher de Blanchefort blanc, mais une autre allusion plus secrète et plus savoureuse oppose les mines de jais du mont Serbairou au sud et les mines de kaolin du mont Cardou au nord. Deux constructions artificielles valent d'être citées, ~~[illegible]~~ un échiquier situé devant le confessionnal de Rennes le Château et à Rennes les bains une ingénieuse pierre tombale où la vie d'un ancien curé, Jean Vié est partagée en 32 années blanches et 32 noires : Né en 1808 - ~~Nommé~~ curé en 1840 - Mort en 1872. Si tu cherches le trésor de Rennes songe à la loi des échecs : la reine est sur sa couleur et le roi sur la couleur opposée à la sienne. Le roi et la reine sont le germe de la dissymétrie dans la symétrie

DEUX FAUTES OUBLIEES

L'étrange graphie REQUIES CATIN PACE pour REQUIESCAT IN PACE ~~[illegible]~~ sur la stèle funéraire n'a certainement pas échappé au lecteur. L'enjambement est encore défectueux par demander pourquoi le C ~~[illegible]~~ ne figure pas dans le mot clef au même titre que le Π de la première ligne. En fait il y a une sensible différence : si le Π en rejet est [illegible] partie le C ~~[illegible]~~ entraîne dans sa faute toutes les lettres de REQUIESCATIN et, à ce titre il n'y a pas moyen de l'isoler.

Telle qu'elle est rédigée la stèle ~~[illegible]~~ de cette pieuse marquise n'est pas très aimable à son égard. Même dans l'assurance que les catins accèdent directement à la béatitude [illegible] avant le ciel de faire état d'une qualité putassière sur le tombeau d'une femme de sa famille ? ~~[illegible]~~ A quoi l'on dira bien sûr que les Hautpoul ne virent aucun inconvénient quand l'abbé Saunière en 1891 déménagea les ossements des femmes et des hommes de leur famille ~~[illegible]~~ depuis le cimetière et depuis l'église pour les transférer dans la fosse commune sous la pierre lissée. En fait le mot CATIN doit se prendre au sens original de "trou de rocher" comme celui de "putain" au sens de puits. L'on a voulu dire par là qu'une nécropole où la mort a conservé les corps en repos (REQUIES) se découvre quand on a passé (PACE) un trou de rocher (CATIN)

Encore qu'il ne s'agisse pas là d'un trésor mais seulement d'un fabuleux massacre les germains et les slaves se sont entendus pour inhumer en CATIN c'est à dire dans la fosse de KATYN toute la chevalerie polonaise tant il est vrai que certains peuples ont le calembour agressif et tant est demeurée violente le souvenir des ordres teutoniques

Une autre faute fut également passée sous silence : HAUPOUL pour HAUTPOUL. Le T absent ne pouvant pas plus figurer dans le mot clef que le U et le P. : deux lettres connexes encadrant une absence ~~[illegible]~~ Cette carence du T évoque en fait le croisement de deux lignes imaginaires comme on dirait par exemple, d'une longitude et d'un parallèle que leur invisibilité dans le paysage n'empêche pas d'exister. ~~[illegible]~~ L'on penserait bien entendu à saint Antoine l'Ermite dont la statue figure dans l'église de Rennes le Château et pour qui le T pour emblème. En fait le saint à consulter n'est pas Antoine mais bien Roch qui figure également dans l'église. Il faut savoir que ce saint Roch mourut dans la solitude et fut identifié par une croix rouge gravée sur sa poitrine mais dissimulée par son manteau. L'invisible croix rouge de saint Roch, ne pouvait se manifester qu'après son décès justifie le message extrait du document I selon lequel "CE TRESOR EST LA MORT"

Il n'y a donc pas lieu de rechercher dans le paysage de Rennes quelque détail insolite, quelque rocher bizarre comme devant être l'emplacement du trésor. Toutes précautions ont été prises depuis des millénaires pour que au contraire l'emplacement du trésor soit à la fois très évident et très banal, ~~et dont le lecteur nous saura gré de lui avoir désigné les plus~~ remarquables à un grand nombre de points de repère dont le lecteur nous saura gré de lui avoir donné les principales

MORTEPÉE

Saint Pierre s'illustra lors de l'arrestation du Christ par son agression sur un gendarme qui fut il coupa l'oreille avec son épée. ~~Lui~~ Alors le Christ lui déclara "Quiconque frappe avec l'épée périra par l'épée". Cette anecdote est importante à deux titres divers, l'affectation à saint Pierre de l'église de Rennes le Château aujourd'hui dédiée à Madeleine, mais aussi la mystification évangélique d'un oracle délibérément faux : Pierre ne sera pas décapité à l'épée mais meurt crucifié tandis que l'épée sera l'emblème de saint Paul

Soucieux de découvrir ce qui, dans les alentours de Rennes, évoquait une épée notre attention fut attirée par le village de Coustaussa dont la forteresse ruinée est le point de mire de tous les environs. Coustaussa est en languedocien l'équivalent de l'ancien français Custode, fourreau de l'épée et par extension, se garde. L'ami Baudi Anne et moi visitons ce village sans y rencontrer âme qui vive. Ce désert, le vent le plafond de l'église nous excitèrent par cette certitude que vivre ici et maintenant "hic et nunc" valait bien que nos amis lesquels vivent ailleurs et toujours "alibi et semper". Coustaussa n'a pas de trésor mais c'est le point

connet de remettre l'épée au fourreau

Pour en finir avec tout cela voici quelques opérations sur la notion non des épées mais des custodes

CUSTODE a) Rideau tiré derrière l'autel d'une église lors de cérémonies du baptême. Les catéchumènes ~~les~~ entraient dans le sanctuaire

longeaient le mur de droite, et, passant derrière l'autel, à l'abri de la cathédrale, se
trouvaient devant une image de Jésus dépouillé de ses vêtements, image centrale de l'ancien
chemin de croix. Alors sans distinction de sexe ils se mettaient eux-mêmes entièrement nus
et redescendaient par le gauche vers les fonts baptismaux pour une immersion totale. Leur
croyant avait été celui du Soleil – SOLIS SACERDOTIBUS – comme le voit fort bien saint
Ambroise quand il dit que la baptisé faisant face à l'Occident dont s'immerge complètement
comme un noyé et pourtant sous l'eau du monde a émerger face à l'Orient
b) Rideau de pourpre et d'or, mais aussi bien rideau de gaze transparents
tiré devant le lit du roi et de la reine pendant la nuit de noces. Dès la hauteur
du lit un flambeau éclaire ~~le carré du lit comme~~ le lit carré comme l'estrade d'un
théâtre. Tapis dans l'ombre les courtisans admirent l'élévation du roi et regardent sur
les draps le sang qu'a versé la reine
c) Pavillon à huit pans imitant les huit tentacules du poulpe. L'église s'en
sert pour recouvrir le "saint-chrême" c'est-à-dire le ciboire de la même manière que
les grecs représentaient un poulpe sur le pot des fours à pain. Il faut songer ici
à ce phénomène du poulpe qui en expulsant son encre gagne en transparence la
qualité perd en tonicité car ceci est mon corps et la beauté de toute littérature,
sanctifiait ce que j'écris à mesure que j'y verse ma passion car ceci est mon
sang.
d) Monocle de cristal cerclé d'or ou, pour l'élévation royale dès un soleil
et incluse l'hostie du Très Saint Sacrement, image de mon œil Dieu ou de Dieu
en moi, comment saurais-je. Par ce monocle passe un regard ostensiblement.
e) Titre particulier porté, depuis le poète Crescimbeni, par le président de la "société
des Arcadiens comptant quatorze membres bergers, autant qu'il y a de vers dans
un sonnet et, des stations au chemin de croix, de lettres dans la devise ET
IN ARCADIA EGO". Mais qui sait être ego, et pourquoi je crois que
je suis l'homme que cherchait Diogène en plein jour avec sa lanterne.
FIN

APPENDIX III

FROM THE CROSS TO THE TREASURE OF THE GREAT ROMAN

Circuit, by Philippe de Cherisey, is the story of a honeymoon in the Canaries. However, this trip finishes as a treasure hunt in Rennes-le-Château. Eventually, the author brings two young people, Marie-Madeleine (Mary Magdalene) and Charlot, face to face. He meets her in the Chapel of the Angels, in the church of Saint Sulpice in Paris, whilst she is taking a photograph of Eugène Delacroix's fresco Héliodore chassé du Temple (Heliodorus thrown out of the Temple). They get on so well that, at some point, he lets out that he must be in Marseille the next day. As for Marie-Madeleine, she must go to Our Lady of Marceille, near Limoux. At their mutual stupefaction, they show each other half a banknote. In fact, they both had to meet up at our Lady of Marceille, in the Aude, to carry out a mission entrusted to them individually. Charlot had confused Marseille with Marceille.

On their trip in the High Valley of the Aude, they can finally compare the documents in their possession.

Charlot produces his document on horror-film background music.
[See illustration of Large Parchment before chapter entitled *Stone and Paper*]

Marie-Madeleine produces her document on Mozartean harpsichord music, in a pop style, stopped by a clap of thunder and stormy weather.

[See illustrations of the stele and tombstone of the Marchioness of Blanchefort before chapter entitled *Stone and Paper*]

Room 22 at the Hôtel des Thermes Romains in Rennes-les-Bains. Charlot is lying down and playing chess on a mini-chessboard in an air of profound disgust. He does checkmate; but having won with the whites and lost with the blacks, he is equally placed with himself which disgusts him even more. Marie-Madeleine is naked by the window.

Charlot – 'Why send me to Marseille, when it is you who had the rest of the Victor Hugo?'

Marie-Madeleine – 'The truth is that I also had to go to Marseille. It is after our meeting yesterday that I was told of the change and instructed to involve you today. But, admittedly, it is rather stupid to have given us documents that everybody knows about, in view of the fact that the *Le Trésor Maudit de Rennes-le-Château* was released by Julliard Publishers last year and recently in paperback format by "J'ai Lu" Publishers. Unless...'

Charlot – 'Unless?'

Marie-Madeleine – 'The important thing is not that these documents are public, but that we have been brought together to look at them here. In my view, we should acquire Gérard de Sède's book, which must be selling around here like hot cakes, and follow the clues that it provides.'

Inside "Flamand", the newsagent-hairdresser of Rennes-les-Bains, during daytime. The rain has stopped. Flamand is cutting Charlot's hair and giving Marie-Madeleine a shampoo, going from one to the other.

Marie-Madeleine – 'I am at page 110, which reads "The texts have indeed been encoded through a double-key substitution, followed by a transposition on a chessboard." A very technical paper by Commandant Lerville, president of the "Association des Réservistes du Chiffre" (Association of Cipher Reservists).'

Charlot – 'Let's start with the chessboard. On my document, there are 128 letters, namely the contents of two chessboards.'

Marie-Madeleine – 'On mine, there are 128 letters too many, which prevent its understanding.'

They take down the letters from their documents, in sequence, which Marie-Madeleine transcribes with red lipstick on the hairdresser's mirror.

Namely,

(1) Charlot	(2) Marie-Madeleine
CTGITNOB	VCPSJQRO
LEMARIED	VYMYYDLT
ENEGREDA	POHRBOXT
RLESDAME	ODJLBKNJ

DHAUPOUL	FQUEPAJY
DEBLANCH	NPPBFEIE
EFORTAGE	LRGHIIRY
EDESOIXA	BTTCVXGD

NTESEPTA	LUCCVMTE
NSDECEDE	JHPNPGSV
ELEXVIIJ	QJHGMLFT
ANVIERMD	SVJLZQMT
COLXXXIR	OXANPEMU
EQUIESCA	PHKORPKH
TINPACEP	VJCMCQTL
SPRAECUM	VQXGGNDT

Marie-Madeleine – 'Commandant Lerville mentions further that errors have been introduced on purpose in order to send the reader on the wrong track.'

Charlot – 'This serviceman is a joker as, on the contrary, the errors help discover the eight-letter keyword, namely MORTEPEE, from the eight spelling mistakes in my document.

Marie-Madeleine is surprised as she can only identify six mistakes. In fact, she does not know that the lady in question was called Negri d'Ables and not Negre Darles. They both rejoice for scoring two extra points over the computers of the Association of Cipher Reservists of Commandant Lerville. One only has to apply MORTEPEE over one of the two texts, either of them. We select the text from Marie-Madeleine which from (2) becomes (3), as follows:

JRINOHXT	ZKUXBDZJ
JNFSDTQZ	XXIIUXYB
DEAMGFCZ	EZABRCKZ
CSCGGBSO	GLCGEHRZ
SGNZVQOD	CMSIUURA
BFIVKUNJ	DDDJXGPM
ZHZCNZXD	JZUHHQZQ
OJMXBNLI	JGPBLEIZ

What Commandant Lerville calls a "second key" (double-key substitution) is also the "second keyhole", which consists in applying to character set (3) the key formed by character set (1) which is likewise similar. Namely:

CDLUVEVL	XGPUCDEP
DEEIAEEN	RQDSFELE
RELECIBE	OAAISROL
SEAOMTAH	EDNEEGTX
DAIAXRHS	RINEEACU
DPEECOCM	ETBPRRXE
GEMNDJEC	TAITTISA
ODIUMEIA	NNAPSLNX

Marie-Madeleine – 'There is the double chessboard of Commandant Lerville which Gérard de Sède was not capable of explaining. So what?'

Charlot – 'So what, Eleanor?'

Marie-Madeleine – 'So what, Heliodorus?'

They are standing under the white horse of Saint Sulpice church.

Charlot – 'You are a genius Marie. It is the most famous key of the secret alphabets, the one about the "Knight's Tour" over a chessboard. It is a patience game that consists in making a lone knight leap over all the squares of a chessboard without passing once over the same square. Unfortunately, neither you nor I know this patience game, and even if we did, there are about one hundred solutions with which we would have to scrabble, which could take days, possibly months!'

Marie-Madeleine could weep over this.

Marie-Madeleine – 'My kingdom for a horse.'

Charlot – 'Fortune hard to find.'

Marie-Madeleine and Charlot are morose over lunch in the dining room of the Hôtel des Thermes Romains. It's hopeless. The door slams three times with the wind. Irritated, Charlot gets up to shut it and comes to a standstill in front of the door; an Empire-style cabinet depicts an angel standing on a ball and brandishing a crown, accompanied by four bees.

Charlot – 'The angel! The bees that form a cross! The Chapel of the Angels! Where is the church of Rennes-les-Bains? Where is the cemetery?'

Marie-Madeleine – 'Over there, I think.'

Charlot – 'Come!'

They arrive at the church and go through the cemetery where there is a superb lime tree.

Charlot – 'The lime tree; we are getting hot. Between the lime tree and the church, there is a tomb for us.'

They discover the grave of Jean Vie mentioned page 125 of their paperback, which reads "Here rests Jean Vie, born in 1808, made parish priest in 1840, deceased on 1st September 1872. Pray for him."

Charlot – 'There it is, the chess game; 1808 to 1840 and 1840 to 1872, or 32 white years and 32 black years. Wait, wait; the cemetery, the passage with the crosses, the Way of the Cross in the Chapel of the Angels in the church of Saint Sulpice in Paris...What was written on the 7th Station? Was it "Jésus épuisé retombe"(Exhausted, Jesus falls down again)?

Marie-Madeleine – 'I remember. It read "Retire-moi de la boue que je n'y reste pas enfoncé" (Pull me out of the mud so that I don't remain stuck in it).'

Charlot – 'That's it; he is in the mud and we must get him out of it. '

He digs the ground to the left of the grave, near the old stone decked with flowers, and discovers a strange copper plate, covered in verdigris, with a deeply engraved grid. It gives the circuit of the "saut du cavalier" (knight's leap). After a rigorous cleaning in the river Sals nearby, Charlot applies the circuit to the text of the double chessboard previously mentioned, through which one can read:

BERGERE PAS DE TENTATION

QUE POUSSIN, TENIERS GARDENT LA CLEF

PAX DCLXXXI

J'ACHEVE CE DAEMON DE GARDIEN

A MIDI

POMMES BLEUES

Faced with that new problem, Marie-Madeleine becomes discouraged. Will the search never end? But now nothing can stop Charlot who cannot get his words out quickly enough. Poussin and Teniers are two painters who won fame with the "Shepherds of Arcadia" and "The Temptation of Saint Anthony" respectively. The shepherdess belongs to Poussin, in the same way that the temptation belongs to Teniers. If they can hold the key, it is because there is no longer a keyhole for that object, and that the parchments were not anterior to the Revolution and did not come from Antoine Bigou, but were from 1861, the era of the third painter.

Marie-Madeleine – 'What third painter?'

Charlot – 'The one with the horse of God that rears up over Heliodorus.'

Marie-Madeleine – 'Delacroix?'

Charlot – 'The citizen Delacroix, formerly Mr. de Lacroix.'

Marie-Madeleine – 'But what about the pommes bleues (blue apples)?'

Charlot – 'Think about another cavalier (knight, also gentleman), more recent, and his connection with apples.'

Marie-Madeleine – 'Ma pomme (my face or head), c'est moi (it's me!)!

Charlot – 'You've got it; it is Maurice Chevalier.'

Marie-Madeleine – 'But how can ma pomme be blue at noon?'

Charlot – 'If it is lit up at noon by the light through a blue stained-glass window representing apples. It would not be any midday, of course, but that of January 17th in the Chapel of the Angels of the Saint Sulpice church in Paris; a midday that will give you an astronomical head.'

Marie-Madeleine – 'Funny, except that there are no pommes bleues (blue apples) on the stained-glass window of the Chapel of the Angels.'

Charlot – 'Are you sure? Shit, it's too bad.'

Marie-Madeleine – 'Wait! Yes, there were some when Delacroix came to inaugurate the chapel; the stained-glass window represented Adam and Eve expelled from Paradise because of a blue apple that the angel had thrown on the ground. This stained-glass window had been mysteriously broken in 1900 and replaced the following year.'

Charlot – 'Perfect.'

Marie-Madeleine – 'What do you mean, perfect? If the blue apple is broken, what can we do?'

Charlot – 'That the apple is blue or that the blue is an apple is irrelevant, since all that matters is for you to position ta pomme (your head) at the right place within the allocated time, and then look.'

Marie-Madeleine – 'Look at what?'

Charlot – 'The horse of God, namely that of Heliodorus thrown out of the Temple. From where you are, there is a detail that cannot be seen from anywhere else.'

Marie-Madeleine – 'So, will we have to return to Paris?'

Charlot – 'Something tells me that Heaven is on our side. Do you want a bet that your bad photograph was taken from the right place? In fact, the horse profile provides a geographic region, the map of Rennes-les-Bains and the itinerary for the treasure.'

Charlot and Marie-Madeleine are going through a rugged area. The landscape is marked by the contrast between the black rock and the white rock.

Marie-Madeleine – 'And PAX DCLXXXI, what does that mean?'

Charlot – 'If you translate this into Arab numerals, you obtain 681; a play between the golden number 1.681 and 1861, the date of the painting by Delacroix. Historically, 17th January 681 commemorates the arrival in Rennes-le-Château of the Rejeton Ardent (Ardent Kid), son of King Dagobert II, Lorraine's survivor on the white horse of Merovaeus Levi. As for PAX, it is the inscription on the Labarum, "oriflamme" preserved in Saint-Denis, the scarlet flag that leads to victory.'

Marie-Madeleine – 'Well, what shall I do?'

Charlot – 'Wait here, or over there, at the place I marked with a cross on the map. In any event, I will find you.'

The landscape is rocky and thorny. Charlot strips to his underpants and, with just two watertight electric torches, climbs a rough slope on all fours.

Charlot – 'Hello, explorers of Montferrand and of Cardou, diggers of tunnels in churches and cemeteries!'

After a last glance at the countryside, he crawls through a rocky crack called 'catin', which one could pass a thousand times without noticing, advancing through a narrow bottleneck. At the end of a rather short leg that seemed interminable, he reaches a junction in a cesspit. 'Cellis or arcis?' 'Right or left?' 'Let's go left, and long live the King'. Face down, he crawls through a whitish gunk with emanations that bring tears to his eyes and make him cough. After about thirty metres, the narrow passageway meets a smooth vertical wall where the previous dragoons carved a few notches in the rock. A little rivulet oozes from the sixth notch. Charlot nearly loses his balance, his knee hitting the stone harshly. Painfully, he reaches a solid platform at the top where, coated in white and with blood running down his leg, he advances looking like a limping ghost.

At an elevated vaulted crossroads in the middle of the platform, there is the tomb of the Great Roman. Two inscriptions on the plinth celebrate the one whose hermetically sealed lead coffin does not bear a single scratch. Charlot kisses the tomb. There is no sign of a treasure, other than some copper veins on the inner walls of the vault. Several caves plunge into depths that the ray of the torch cannot reach. There is a deadly passage under a collapsing vault; this is the right passageway that Charlot thanks Heaven for disregarding earlier.

The caves are flooded at knee level; however one can walk on all fours on a low narrow side wall made of tiles piled up on one another without cement. The ceiling is whitish and made of somewhat friable stone. Progress is slow. Charlot stops to get his breath back, switches on his second torch, and, to kill time, lifts a tile to see how tileries worked in the past. The tile is very heavy as it is made of gold, which transpires after scratching it with a nail. With such a tile, one can live comfortably for two years, and there are kilometres of the same, that is to say millennia of going on a spree. But to carry that tile on all fours when one is naked in the cold and one sees behind oneself the trail of blood that marks out the travelled route, is not fun; life is not fun anymore, bloody hell!

Charlot – 'Bloody hell!'

The Echo – 'Hell!'

He replaces the slab on the low wall, where he found it, and covers it up with dust, as he found it, then continues on his return journey through the cave until he finds himself back behind the tomb of the great Roman. The smooth vertical wall that was so difficult to climb seems vertiginous on the way down. Somewhat haphazardly, Charlot follows another passage and is rather satisfied by his choice on seeing daylight in the distance. However, to his horror, the cave that opens to daylight is the residence of the Great Roman's sentries. These are corpses buried half way in a hole, brandishing their curved tile, like a cripple would brandish a leg-iron. These are people of different ages in death, as there are perfect skeletons amongst them, together with figures so well preserved by the atmospheric conditions that they resemble stars from the Grévin Museum.

Charlot – "Terribilis est locus iste'

He infiltrates the dead, slips on a shinbone and falls, his head hitting a skull which separates from its trunk with a sharp snap. His hand looks for support and rests on a round object, a coin. The sun light falls in the cave which is dazzling under piles of diverse silver and gold plates. Here is the store of the multimillionaire little priest.

A torch is still lit. Charlot leans forward above the drop. Here death; in the distance, the beautiful ruin guardian of the sword; over there, down below, it must be the light-coloured dress of Marie-Madeleine, but she cannot see the ray of the torch in her back. One can shout, she cannot hear.

Retracing his steps inside the cave, Charlot notices a gallery which descends slowly. He crawls more than he walks. His eyes are burning and his breathing is more and more laboured. But then, he reaches a dead end. He screams, falls to the ground, screams again and faints. Marie-Madeleine heard the voice that seemed to originate from under a large stone. She clears some shrubs, small stones, and soil, and, with great difficulty, extricates this poor young Lazarus risen from the dead. She washes off the white coating, tends to his wounds, wraps him in the sleeping bag and gives him a tipple of rum. Thank you.

Marie-Madeleine – 'The most beautiful girl in the world can only give what she has.'

Charlot – 'Not true. She doesn't give it, she lends it; I have lived, I know what I am talking about.'

Marie-Madeleine – 'How much do you want to bet?'

Charlot – 'Nothing, I am poor.'

Marie-Madeleine – 'Wasn't there a treasure?'

Charlot replies in the affirmative; he says that there was a dreadful one and a fabulous one, enough to sustain various empires, but, in truth, he'd rather die than touch it.

Charlot – 'We will wait until someone from the rond de lis (fleur-de-lis circle) claims it or an honest Head of State turns up, which can happen sometimes.'

Marie-Madeleine – 'But what about you?'

Charlot – 'Free, loved by the most beautiful girl in the world. What else can one ask for?'

Marie-Madeleine – 'I've already loved a lot.'

Charlot – 'Then, a lot will be forgiven to you.'

Marie-Madeleine – 'It's a rumour that's going round.'

Charlot – 'Let's run as fast as the rumour, my angel.'

APPENDIX IV

ALCHEMIST MONKS AT THE ABBEY OF BOULBONNE (1339)

By J.M. Vidal, Chaplain At The Caousou, Toulouse Excerpt (Tome IX, 1903) From The *Bulletin Périodique De La Société Ariégeoise Des Sciences, Lettres Et Arts*

This is not a tale, although there is enough material to make one; it is a "trivial event", a feature of the monastic practices, a curious aspect of the religious beliefs of past times. [1]

Four monks of Boulbonne [2], Raymond Fenouil, Arnaud Gifre, Bernard Aynier and Bertrand de Cahuzac [3] are bored in their cloister. The world they left is more appealing. They are naïve, curious, greedy and hungry for wealth. They are superstitious and believe in alchemy, bewitchment and sorcery. They are dreaming of hidden gold ingots and enchanted caves sheltering enormous riches. Their accomplice, a cleric from Rieux called Guillaume de Mosset, an illegitimate child, tells them that, near Limoux, there is a mysterious mountain which conceals an "infinite" treasure guarded by a fairy. During a clandestine meeting at the gate of the monastery, they consult each other, staking their lives on never breathing a word about it. They decide to acquire a wax effigy of the fairy, to christen her, and to force her to talk by stabbing her in the heart. She will reveal the secret of the grotto.

The plot is going well. The bastard de Mosset acquires the doll and Pierre Garaud, a bourgeois from Pamiers, hides it for a while at his home. Raymond Fenouil collects it and brings it to the monastery; he places it on the altar of Saint-Catherine where several masses are celebrated daily. Oddly, nobody notices it or suspects the sacrilegious purpose in store for it.

Raymond Fenouil tries to christen it. A friend of Bernard Aynier, cleric at the church of Montaut [4], lends him the christening rite but refuses categorically to anoint the consecrated oil. This is an unexpected, and seemingly, insurmountable obstacle. Discouraged, monk Raymond brings the "wax effigy" back to Pierre Garaud, from Pamiers. Foolishly, in front of the latter, Guillaume de Mosset asks his accomplice if the rite is accomplished.

Everything is lost. Garaud uncovers the plot and hands over the small box, containing the wax effigy and nine stabbing needles, to Durand, Senior Abbot of Boulbonne.

Durand carries out an investigation, interrogates the guilty parties and witnesses. Benoît XII is told. Since Boulbonne accommodated him in his early years, he took the good reputation of the monastery and eradication of such abuse to heart. On 2nd December 1339, he instructs Abbot Durand to complete his inquiry, to seize all books, documents and personal belongings from the conspirators and to keep the latter under guard.

The abbot hastens to put them in prison and conducts the investigation for the case. On 23rd December 1340, in full knowledge of the facts, the pope appoints the investigating abbot and his colleague Raymond de Tousins of Berdoues, to close the trial and punish the sacrilegious individuals. I did not find a reference to the sentence, but it is likely that it decreed no less than degradation and life imprisonment on bread and water for the main culprits.

[1] I examined the two bulls of Pope Benoît XII and wish to highlight to the readers that the narrative part of these documents simply reproduces Father Boulbonne's report to the pope. He had carried out an investigation. The guilty parties owned up. Did they confess of their own free will or by force? Nobody can tell.

[2] Boulbonne, commune of Cintegabelle, district of Muret (Haute-Garonne).

[3] Cahuzac, district of Belpech (Aude).

[4] Montaut, district of Saverdun (Ariège).

[5] Pope Benoît XII, Jacques Fournier, was born in Saverdun, in the county of Foix. First, he was a monk at the Abbey of Boulbonne, then Abbot of Fontfroide, near Narbonne. He became Bishop of Pamiers in 1317 and was transferred to Mirepoix in 1326. He left that Episcopal See in 1328 following his promotion to cardinalship the previous year. On 20th December 1334, he was made pope under the name Benoît XII. He died on 25th April 1342.

APPENDIX V

ET IN ARCADIA EGO - ODE TO SAINT SPÉRIE

In the middle of the 8th Century, Saint Céré, in the Quercy region, was just a large castle, fief of Sérénus, duke of Aquitaine. His daughter Spérie intended to go to the convent, whilst her brother Clarus wanted to see the young princess marry Elidius, Lord of Castelnau. As she could not escape the guardianship of her elder brother, she chose to flee on her wedding day. Tired, the boor caught up with her in a place called Le Ruisseau des Barbares (The Brook of the Barbarians) and, furious about her rebelliousness, cut off her head with his sword! But, to everybody's surprise, the young woman got up, took her head and went down to the nearby stream to wash it. At this sight, Clarus repented and promised to devote his life to God.

The present church of Saint-Céré was built on the very spot of this wonder. The grave is still visible in a $6m^2$ crypt in front of the chancel.

A sculpted tombstone next to it, probably of Carolingian origin, illustrates a biblical scene with a much damaged inscription above it. Six letters in uncial writing reveal the famous phrase taken up nine hundred years later by Nicolas Poussin. Yet, it appears already in the homily of Saint Caesarius and in the texts of Charlemagne's *Book of Prayer.*

APPENDIX VI

LES AILES DE LA JOUANNES

(The Wings Of The Jouannes)

Dear Mr. Chaumeil,

It is with caution and a definite detachment that I read *Les Secrets du Code Da Vinci* (*The Secrets of the Code*) by Dan Burstein, released by City publishers in 2004. This work was concocted by eminent specialists in the history of religions, rigorous journalists and a few academics in order to be done with what could be referred to as "The Story of Rennes-le-Château".

It is regrettable that Plantard mixed up history with his dreams, as this has not helped towards objective analysis of this affair. Contrary to what certain actors of this critique are maintaining loudly and strongly, something big happened in the region of Rennes-le-Château and Rennes-les-Bains.

So much has been written on the Merovingians of this region, that I find it surprising that not a single academic joined the debate.

No descendants of Clovis in Romania? What is that about?

I take the liberty to quote Mrs. Renée Mussot-Goulard, an academic, Senior Lecturer in Paris IV, PhD (Doctor of Philosophy), "We do not know yet the connexions between Duke Loup II, contemporary of Charlemagne, and his homonym of the previous century, Loup I, as the Charter of Alaon from 845 CE, which evokes the links, does not receive the unanimous approval of historians. There seemed to be some connexions nevertheless."

The charter, disputed by certain academics, was authenticated by Dom Vic and Dom Vaissette, who borrowed it from Cardinal d'Aguirre. It had been mapped out in the presence of the most important lords of the region. So, why deny it? Because, it highlights that the families of Saint Bertrand of Comminges, Foix and Carcassonne, decimated during the Albigensian wars, were amongst them.

An old legend, and it is not just a legend, relates that all these families bore moons identical to those of Clovis on their coats of arms. Furthermore, the Catharist actors, who defended with desperate energy the originality of the Romanic metaphysics until Montségur, were called sons of the Moon. Is this a purely theoretical view? No, since as soon as Montségur is destroyed, Rome removes the moons from the coats of arms of the Mirepoix family to replace them with the shells of Compostela and the staff of the pilgrim.

The Hautpoul belonged to the "Bellissen", like the Toulouse family whose origins go back to the Gothic Marquis in the name of Ursio!

The Occitan people who want to defend these theses are ridiculed. The only one who listens to them is Otto Rahn, a German journalist who publishes a book in Germany in 1933. In 1964, the book is republished by Hans E. Gunther. René Nelli, the man from Montségur, signs the preface of the translated work published in France by Stock. Reading this work means approaching the Iberian civilisation and entering a "fabulous" story which took place in the land of the Sordes, indeed in Auch.

Rahn takes up the work of Wolfram d'Eschenbach and understands very quickly that the Occitan troubadours dissimulated moments in their history in poems where real-life characters were disguised under fictitious names.

The key to these written works is la langue des oiseaux (the language of the birds), a practice already used by the Celts in the 5th century CE, as mentioned by Ernest Renan, author of *The Life of Jesus*.

One should note that the Media kingdom, under the Persian thrust, is moving towards the Occident and that Romania, as well as Ireland, are involved in that migration. Ancient kingdoms remain until the arrival of the Romans. Even when these old kingdoms disappear, the druids preserve their tradition both in Ireland and Romania.

This is so true that Rome will not rest in its pursuit of these sages until their extinction. The latter could have happened were it not for the pugnacity of Columba, the Irish man of Iona. It is he who transmits the Celtic tradition to the order of Saint Benoît. It is in Iona that we find the greatest grammarians, and where the Greek books and works rescued from the fire at the Alexandrian Library are translated.

If, in Europe, it is difficult to form an opinion on the Jesus affair, it does not present a problem for those who are studying in Alexandria. Important elements in this affair go back to Ireland via Galicia and Santa-Maria de Bretonna. One must remember that in the 4th Century CE, Priscillian is burnt alive with all his followers in Trier. He is an ascetic, like the anchorites, eremites and coenobites.

The Benedictines are confronted with a multitude of problems. Convents of Benedictines replace the druidic colleges. In 601 CE, one thousand two hundred monks from Canterbury are slaughtered at the request of Rome. It is Benedictine Pope Gregory I who retrieves the situation by declaring that Benedictines will not come under the bishops, cardinals and various lords any more.

Monasteries are erected in the South of Gaul under the supervision of the Benedictine "mastermind" at the Abbey of Fleury-sur-Loire.

Around 585 CE, convents of a similar type exist already in Alet and in Jaffus, on the plateau between Rennes-le-Château and Rennes-les-Bains. It is certain that the monks feel secure in the kingdom of the Goths since, as soon as the Franks arrive in Aquitaine, the Benedictines move the archives from Fleury-sur-Loire. Saint Guillaume, the first troubadour, is excommunicated even though he protects the Benedictines! In 1004, Abbon, an abbot of Fleury, is assassinated by henchmen from Rome.

There is something odd about all this since the Goths are Arians. They study the Bible translated by Ulfila and their metaphysical philosophy strangely resembles that of the prophet Mani who taught in Alexandria; yet, they get on well with the Benedictines.

The big cleanup is carried out by Bernard the Cistercian; whole monasteries are emptied of their monks, especially those who had contacts with the "Scotist" Irish monks.

The novel *The Name of the Rose* describes monastic life in those days, as well as how certain monks preserved banned works, very well.

The Catharist movement develops, backed up by the monks who consider them full Christians. This does not take account of the spiritual and temporal power of Rome who cannot stand that "Idea". So, whilst the monks and "good people" assist the poor, Rome declares that idea heretical.

On one side, there is the Languedoc with the monks, troubadours, families of Saint Bertrand of Comminges, Foix, Carcassonne and Mirepoix; on the other, there is Rome and the crusaders from the North. But let us go back to the Goths.

When Alaric "the winged king" goes through Rome, he strips the eternal city of the jewels that are stored in the Temple of Peace. These do not only include the objects from the Temple of Jerusalem, but also archives and genealogies which the "Scotists" transport to the Abbey of Iona. When the Roman clergy arrive in Scotland, the Ionian archives are moved to Bangor in Ireland.

With regard to the objects of the temple, these are kept for a while in Toulouse, then in Carcassonne (Procopius).

Under the thrust of the Moorish General Tarik, at the beginning of the 8th Century, the Goths are driven back to the North. The Arabs do not respect the abbeys; it is a disaster. The Benedictines decide to dissimulate the treasure of Carcassonne in a hypogeum where kings are buried, those of the "lignée des Epis" (the sacred lineage of the Merovingian monarchy).

Of course, it is this lineage of Merovingian monarchs that is upsetting. I do not want to interpret what Bigou encrypted, but the one who usually bears the "Epis" ("ears" of grain, as well as "Spicas" of Virgo) is the Virgin! Is she Mary-Magdalene? Is she the lunar Lady, the goddess, the one who leaves her name to the Bellissen? I do not know. What I am sure of is that this moon crescent is a nightmare for Rome.

This secret belongs to a Gothic family, that of the Count "Bel-on" of Carcassonne in 812 CE. How does he manage to reach the lady of Blancafort? He does it through the marriage of Arnaud I, son of Clovis with Clotaire, to Arsinde, the Gothic infanta and heiress of the "Bel-on" lineage.

Now, we get to the heart of the matter.

Let us suppose that Father Bigou receives the confession of the Hautpoul lady, who tells him that, in the vicinity of Rennes-les-Bains, there is a grave of a lady and various kings of Merovingian descent, as well as the treasure of Jerusalem. The parish priest is Occitan and may wish to leave a message out of respect for all those massacred during the Albigensian wars. He decides to produce two parchments which he hides in the chapel. These will facilitate the reading of the epitaph on the stele of the Hautpoul lady's tomb.

What has always intrigued me is that certain terms, very legible on the epitaph, remained in the background. One can clearly read the words "Ide", from the Greek, and "lune" (moon) placed side by side [vertically on the stele starting from the "I" in the word GIT and the "L" in DARLES], or "héritiers de la lune" (heirs to the moon); similarly, one can find the words "Col" [horizontally in MDCOLXXXI] and "Axe" (Axis) vertically starting with the "A" in JANVIER]. The erroneous date of 1681 instead of 1781 written in Roman numerals and containing an O arouses our curiosity. It is in 1681 that Cassini the Elder, the geographer of Louis XIV, comes to the Col de la Sals, near Rennes-les-Bains, to calculate the meridian zero, today at 2 degrees 15 minutes 20 seconds. Curiously, this imaginary line goes through the hypogeum, as well as the Observatory of Paris established by Cassini on a 21st June. Who decides on the trajectory? Did King Louis XIV give that instruction? If this is the case, it means that the monarch also knows about the royal tomb. One must not overlook the fact that the preceptor of Louis XV is a de Fleury... What annoys me are the searches carried out at Colbert's request in the old mines of the Razès, and those effected by Le Doat, adviser of King Louis XIV, in the archives of the prestigious Houses of Languedoc. Colbert, in fact, is working in the background for Rome. Is he the one who organises all this?

Nevertheless, the confiscation of the painting by Poussin and the imprisonment of Fouquet are undoubtedly linked to this affair. You should see the precision with which Poussin marked out the principal landmarks seen from the mountain of Rhodes; to the east, Bugarach; to the south-south-east, the Canigou; to the south-south-west, the Tipliès; and to the west, the rock of L'Homme Mort (the Dead Man) and the upper part of Montségur.

The stele of the Hautpoul lady's tombstone has been encrypted by a genius who utilises the language of the birds. When, with the large parchment, one derives "Que Poussin et Teniers gardent la clef Pax DCLXXXI", one should construe Pax as peace, which in the Celtic language means Sidh, namely tomb. DCL must be read as "déceler", to discover, that is to reveal three crosses and a bar, namely the axis. It is for this very reason that Philippe de Cherisey's claim to the authorship of the two parchments does not make sense. De Cherisey is incapable of imagining such a fabrication. Here is a little demonstration.

With a ruler, link the M, outside the text top right, to the O of the date. This seems logical since MO stands for Meridian 0. In the inferior part [in an inversed "V" shape from the O], one can read A.Q.O.I., which in the language of the birds means AQUA, or water in Latin. Can this be exploited? Of course! On your way to the Col de la Sals, you will pass a cavity on your right, called "Catin" in Latin as mentioned on the stele; then you will arrive at the Col where the axis (red line or meridian line) passes; further along, you will reach a little river down below which flows from the mountain of Rhodes, that of the roses, and you will then understand that this stele is a real geographical map. The hypogeum is five hundred meters away as the crow flies. To find it, you need other elements that are also on the stele of the Hautpoul lady's tombstone. These elements, which nobody has noticed so far, match those found on an old map.

When I arrived in front of the stele, everything became clear, whether the chapel of Rennes-le-Château or the book of Henri Boudet. This hypogeum was definitely sealed by the Goths since their signature, known to the troubadours of Languedoc, is found in the toponym itself, namely the Ailes de Jean (The

Wings of John), mentioned on the map of Cassini as "A la Jouannes", "Jouannes" hypocoristic of "Jean". The mount was called "Hill" on the same map.

I have spent more than twenty years on this affair. I have protected my discovery and registered it officially. I am looking for a journalist capable of following this affair and thought of you since you were already interested in it in the past. You see, Mr. Chaumeil, fiction is closely akin to reality. You will soon understand the reasons why nobody before me reached the hypogeum. It goes without saying that if we work together, I will let you have all the elements of the dossier, and they are many. I am looking forward to seeing you in Paris.

Yours sincerely,

LIST OF FIGURES

INDEX